S0-ADZ-537

Providing all students with a fair opportunity to learn (OTL) is perhaps the most pressing issue facing the U.S. education system. Moving beyond conventional notions of OTL – as access to content, often content tested; access to resources; or access to instructional processes – the authors reconceptualize OTL in terms of interaction among learners and elements of their learning environments. Drawing on socio-cultural, sociological, psychometric, and legal perspectives, this book provides historical critique, theory and principles, and concrete examples of practice through which learning, teaching, and assessment can be re-envisioned to support fair OTL for all students.

This book offers educators, researchers, and policy analysts new to sociocultural perspectives a readable and engaging introduction to fresh ideas for conceptualizing, enhancing, and assessing OTL; encourages those who already draw on sociocultural resources to focus attention on OTL and assessment; and nurtures collaboration among members of discourse communities who have rarely engaged one another's work.

Pamela A. Moss is a professor of education at the University of Michigan School of Education. She is co-founder and co-editor of the journal *Measurement: Interdisciplinary Research and Perspectives* and editor of *Evidence and Decision Making*, the 2007 yearbook of the National Society for the Study of Education.

Diana C. Pullin is a professor in the Lynch School of Education and an affiliate professor of law at Boston College. She serves as an expert advisor to the National Research Council of the National Academy of Sciences on panels advising the U.S. Congress and federal government on testing and assessment in education and employment and is associate editor of *Education Policy*.

James Paul Gee received his PhD in linguistics from Stanford University in 1975 and is a member of the National Academy of Education. His most recent publications include *What Video Games Have to Teach Us About Learning and Literacy* (2003) and *Good Video Games and Good Learning* (2007).

Edward H. Haertel is the Jacks Family Professor of Education at Stanford University. His recent publications include articles in *Educational Measurement: Issues and Practice* and *Measurement: Interdisciplinary Research and Perspectives*, a co-edited yearbook for the National Society for the Study of Education, and a chapter in the most recent edition of *Educational Measurement*.

Lauren Jones Young is Director for the Spencer Foundation Teaching, Learning, and Instructional Resources Program. In addition to two edited books and a number of monographs, she has published in several journals, including *Educational Researcher, Anthropology and Education Quarterly, Harvard Educational Review, Women and Health, The National Law Review, Phi Delta Kappan, Theory into Practice,* and *Journal of Teacher Education*.

CAMBRIDGE UNIVERSITY PRESS
Cambridge, New York, Melbourne, Madrid, Cape Town, Singapore, São Paulo, Delhi

Cambridge University Press
32 Avenue of the Americas, New York, NY 10013-2473, USA

www.cambridge.org
Information on this title: www.cambridge.org/9780521706599

First published 2008

Printed in the United States of America

A catalog record for this publication is available from the British Library.

Library of Congress Cataloging in Publication Data

Assessment, equity, and opportunity to learn / [edited by] Pamela Moss . . .
[et al.].
    p.   cm.
Includes bibliographical references and index.
ISBN 978-0-521-88045-9 (hardback) – ISBN 978-0-521-70659-9 (pbk.)
1. Educational sociology – United States.   2. Educational equalization – United States.
3. Educational tests and measurements – Social aspects – United States   I. Moss, Pamela, 1952–
LC191.4.A77   2008
379.2′6 – dc22   2007036964

ISBN   978-0-521-88045-9 hardback
ISBN   978-0-521-70659-9 paperback

Contents

Preface

Since its beginnings, the Spencer Foundation[1] has sought to advance knowledge about education with the aim of educational improvement. Although its core mission remains steadfast, in recent years the foundation has initiated proactive practices to identify research and other compelling projects that show promise for the improvement of teaching and learning and the realization of the potential for education to promote more equalizing opportunities. In its pursuit of research agendas in these areas of inquiry, Spencer has been been able to organize the convening of scholars and practitioners who may not otherwise have had occasion to do so regarding important problems of education. It was such a project that led to the publication of *Assessment, Equity, and Opportunity to Learn.*

During its 100-year history, testing likely has not had the powerful influence it has in today's "culture of evidence" climate. Assessments of student learning have taken on major importance in the current educational policy context, with significant consequences for individual children and their teachers and their schools. It was in this high-stakes climate in late 2001 that Pamela A. Moss, Diana C. Pullin, James Paul Gee, and Edward H. Haertel approached Spencer to support an interdisciplinary initiative focused on expanding the foundations of educational assessment. Their intention was to enhance the dialogue concerning the theories and methods through which assessment is conceptualized, practiced, and evaluated by bringing together scholars from several disciplines to study its practice. They had observed that educational assessment is largely informed by the field of psychometrics and the disciplines of psychology and mathematics on which it draws. They wondered what assessment might look like were it informed by additional research traditions. By casting a wider disciplinary net that included sociocultural and situated perspectives from within anthropology, linguistics, sociology, and psychology, they hoped to explore a range of assumptions about assessment and imagine an array of alternative practices. With Spencer's support, this small core group of scholars was expanded to include King Beach, James G. Greeno, Carol D. Lee, Hugh Mehan, Robert J. Mislevy, Fritz Mosher, and Lauren Jones Young, with staff assistance provided by Doris Fischer and Andrew Ho.

The goal for the first few meetings was to look broadly at testing practices and outline a research and development agenda to conceptualize and study various means of assessment – alternative strategies for gathering, warranting, and using trustworthy evidence about individuals and institutions – that might complement and/or challenge practices based in psychometrics. A second aim was to situate psychometric and alternative assessment practices in their sociocultural contexts in order to illuminate their limitations and effects. Such discussions were intended to surface tacit assumptions, identify the unintended consequences of current practices in educational assessment, and specify the kinds of new knowledge that might be needed to inform more constructive and equitable practices in the future.

Early in the discussions, the group learned that the participants could talk to each other in spite of occasional translation difficulties and that there were good reasons to try to overcome these difficulties. Modern psychometricians have tools that can be used to model or measure almost anything about which one can be really clear, including the kinds of capabilities that can be considered to exist in a community of practice and the social artifacts that support it in its area of activity. This is no longer your daddy's psychometrics, but you do have to be clear about what you want to model. All, or most, of the group would probably accept that it would be possible to think of such group products as having reflections of some sort inside individuals' "heads," but it became clear that the "psych" part of psychometrics is not essential and that our colleagues could simply be called metricians or be prefixed however seemed most appropriate to the task at hand.

Second, it did not take long to realize that everyone agreed the real issue is not testing per se so much as learning and teaching – what should students learn, and what is the school's responsibility for whether they learn it? Tests or assessments come into the picture because of school systems' reliance on them as evidence of what individual students or groups have learned and as evidence of whether schools are meeting their responsibility in enabling students to learn what they should, or at least in providing them a fair opportunity to learn.

Our discussions focused on the issues of whether currently widely used assessments represent a valid report of whether students are able to meet the publicly asserted state standards for "proficiency" in core subjects and skills and whether those standards themselves adequately reflect what would be required to meet the more general rhetorical requirement that students be able to function adequately in further education or in the modern economy and polity.

A thoroughgoing critique from the perspectives of both cognitive science and the situative, sociological, sociocultural, and sociolinguistic viewpoints of the sort to be found in this volume suggests that they have not been validated for either. Current assessments seem to focus primarily on coverage of subject matter content and basic skills. It may be that successful performance on these assessments also requires other aptitudes or capabilities, but if teachers and other educators who are held accountable for students' success on these assessments think that their main focus is on discrete facts and skills, the tests may "drive" instruction to concentrate on just those things. However, if real proficiency requires students to have additional skills, dispositions, and aptitudes, tests of this sort can deprive them – particularly those at highest risk of performing badly – of the opportunity to gain this necessary knowledge by narrowing instruction only to what the tests are perceived to emphasize.

Our discussions, in fact, focused in some detail on the other kinds of experiences and chances to participate in and acquire the practices that characterize effective functioning in disciplinary or occupational groups, which might also be called habits of discourse or subject- or activity-specific aptitudes or dispositions. These experiences and opportunities are hardly evenly distributed among students from different social groups in this country, and although the resulting practices seem to play a strong role in how easily students learn more traditional content in school, they do not tend to be taught explicitly in school, nor are students given exposure to them. If assessments were developed that were designed to measure and report specifically on such practices, their results could make it clear that some children have not had the opportunity to learn or be exposed to them. On the other hand, they would probably be even "harder" than conventional tests for students from disadvantaged groups, so if they were used for purposes that were consequential for those students, they would seem to be even more unfair. However, if they were treated as measures of opportunity to learn that were consequential to schools, they might raise the question of whether the schools should be held responsible for providing experiences they had never tried to provide before.

This is only a taste of the complexity of the group's deliberations, but we would suggest that our answer comes down on the side of yes – the schools should be responsible for learning what kinds of experiences are required for students to be able to participate effectively in the practices that will give them reasonable access to the benefits of modern society; for trying to provide all of those experiences that are reasonably within their power; and for advocating for more of the needed resources if they are falling short. Given that there is only limited knowledge available on how to do this – in the schools or anywhere else – it would not be reasonable to frame accountability in any punitive way for not succeeding in fulfilling this responsibility. Rather, the requirement should be to attend to each student's and all students' progress through assessment and observational processes appropriate to that task and to make best-effort attempts to respond to their stages of progress. The goal should be to move the students ahead while taking steps to keep track of the results of those efforts in order to contribute to the store of knowledge about what it takes to provide real opportunities to learn what really is required for opportunity in this society. Clearly, it should be the responsibility of the research community to work with the schools to help them in fulfilling these obligations.

We suggest that this book is advocating not just an *equal* opportunity to learn as a criterion for judging our schools, but rather an "*equalizing* opportunity to learn." Students differ in ways that require differential experiences if they are all to reach or exceed some real standard for what is required for adequate functioning in modern society. Within the limits of their capabilities, schools should adapt to those needs. It will be clear to readers of this book that we all have a great deal to learn in order to know how to do this, but we hope that following the paths suggested will considerably increase the chances of finding the answers.

Fritz Mosher
Lauren Jones Young

Note

1. The opinions expressed in this publication are those of the authors alone and do not necessarily reflect the views of the Spencer Foundation.

List of Contributors

James Paul Gee is the Mary Lou Fulton Presidential Professor of Literacy Studies at Arizona State University. He is a member of the National Academy of Education. His book *Sociolinguistics and Literacies* (1990) was one of the founding documents in the formation of the New Literacy Studies, an interdisciplinary field devoted to studying language, learning, and literacy in an integrated way, in the full range of their cognitive, social, and cultural contexts. His book *An Introduction to Discourse Analysis* (1999) brings together his work on a methodology for studying communication in its cultural settings, an approach that has been widely influential over the last two decades. His most recent books both deal with video games, language, and learning. *What Video Games Have to Teach Us About Learning and Literacy* (2003) argues that good video games are designed to enhance learning through effective learning principles supported by research in the learning sciences. *Situated Language and Learning* (2004) places video games within an overall theory of learning and literacy and shows how they can help us in thinking about the reform of schools. Professor Gee has published widely in journals in linguistics, psychology, the social sciences, and education.

Brian J. Girard is a doctoral student in educational foundations and policy at the University of Michigan and a former junior high school English and history teacher in Philadelphia. His research interests include multicultural education, sociocultural theory, and disciplinary knowledge in teaching history and social studies.

James G. Greeno is a cognitive scientist who has studied understanding and learning of concepts throughout the nearly five decades of his career. Currently, his research focuses on conceptual understanding and learning in discourse, especially in middle school mathematics classrooms. He also has written general articles and review chapters contributing to the development of a situative view of cognition and learning, aimed toward integrating concepts and methods of the individual cognitive-science and sociocultural approaches to cognition and learning. Greeno's PhD, in experimental psychology, was granted by the University of Minnesota, Minneapolis. He taught in departments of psychology at Indiana University, Bloomington; the University of Michigan, Ann Arbor; and the University of Pittsburgh, and in schools of education at the University of California, Berkeley, and Stanford University. He is a Margaret Jacks Professor of Education Emeritus, Stanford University and a Visiting Professor of Education, University of Pittsburgh. He is a member of the National Academy of Education, the Society of Experimental Psychologists, the American Psychological Association, the Cognitive Science Society, the American Educational Research Association, the Society of the Learning Sciences, and the National Council of Teachers of Mathematics.

Melissa S. Gresalfi is assistant Professor in the learning sciences at Indiana University. Her work examines how opportunities to learn get constructed in mathematics classrooms and how, when, and why different students take up those opportunities. This focus enables exploration of the extent to which classroom practices are equitable and examination of categories such as race, gender, and previous mathematical experience as they arise in interaction.

Edward H. Haertel is the Jacks Family Professor of Education and Associate Dean for Faculty Affairs at Stanford University, where he has served on the faculty since 1980. Haertel is an expert in educational testing and assessment, working at the intersection of technical and policy issues that arise in the uses of achievement testing for accountability. He has been closely involved in the creation and maintenance of California's school accountability system and has advised other states and testing companies. Haertel is also concerned with the construction of validity arguments for high-stakes testing, the logic and implementation of standard-setting methods, and comparisons of trends on different tests and in different reporting metrics. Haertel has served as president of the National Council on Measurement in Education (1998–99), as a member of the National Assessment Governing Board (1997–2003), and as a member of the joint committee responsible for the 1999 edition of the *Standards for Educational and Psychological Testing* (1994–99). He was a Fellow at the Center for Advanced Study in the Behavioral Sciences (1994–95), is a Fellow of the American Psychological Association, and is a member of the National Academy of Education.

Carol D. Lee is Professor of Education and Social Policy in the Learning Sciences Program, School of Education and Social Policy, at Northwestern University. She is a member of the National Academy of Education, Vice President of Division G of the American Educational Research Association, past President of the National Conference of Research on Language and Literacy, and former Fellow at the Center for Advanced Study in the Behavioral Sciences. Her research focuses on scaffolding the everyday knowledge and practices of students to support disciplinary reasoning and literacy practices, with particular attention to African American students and the uses of African American English Vernacular in classroom discourse. Her research is based on an eco-cultural framework that examines the coordination of culturally situated cognitive and psycho-social resources entailed in learning within and across settings. Her books include *Culture, Literacy and Learning: Taking Bloom in the Midst of the Whirlwind* (2007) and *Signifying as a Scaffold for Literary Interpretation* (1993) and a co-edited volume, *Vygotskian Perspectives on Literacy Research* (1999). She is a founder of four African-centered schools in Chicago over a span of 36 years, three of which are charter schools, all currently in operation.

Hugh ("Bud") Mehan is Professor of Sociology and Director of the Center for Research on Educational Equity, Access, and Teaching Excellence (CREATE) at the University of California, San Diego (UCSD), appointments that link his commitments to research and practice. CREATE coordinates efforts at UCSD to improve the academic preparation of underrepresented students in the community through partnerships with K-12 schools and districts and the Preuss School, UCSD on-campus model charter school. Mehan has studied the social organization of schooling and the construction of academic identities. He has authored five books: *The Reality of Ethnomethodology*, *Learning Lessons*, *Handicapping the Handicapped*, *Constructing School Success*, and *Extending School Reform: From One School to Many*. His most recent book, *Extending School Reform: From One School to Many* (with Amanda Datnow and Lea Hubbard), discusses the processes, challenges, and consequences of "scaling up" educational reforms. A member of the National Academy of Education, he is the recipient of multiple teaching awards at UCSD.

Robert J. Mislevy is Professor of Measurement and Statistics at the University of Maryland, College Park, and was previously a Distinguished Research Scientist at ETS. He earned his PhD in methodology of behavioral research at the University of Chicago in 1981 and has a background in statistics and cognitive psychology. His research centers on applying developments in technology, statistical methodology, and cognitive psychology to practical problems in educational measurement. His recent work includes simulation-based assessment of networking with Cisco Systems, Inc. He has received awards for career contributions to educational assessment from the National Council on Measurement in Education and the American Educational Research Association, and he is a member of the National Academy of Education.

Frederic A. (Fritz) Mosher is a retired foundation officer (36 years at Carnegie Corporation of New York) and currently a senior consultant to the Consortium for Policy Research in Education (CPRE), based at Teachers College, Columbia University, in New York. He is a social/cognitive psychologist by training and by choice an advocate for sensible approaches to helping schools learn how to enable their students to succeed.

Pamela A. Moss is Professor of Education at the University of Michigan School of Education. Her research agenda focuses on validity theory in educational assessment, assessment as a social practice, and the assessment of teaching. Her approach to the study of assessment engages the critical potential of dialogue across research discourses–educational measurement, hermeneutics and critical theory, and sociocultural studies sometimes to complement, sometimes to challenge, established theory and practice in assessment. She was a member of the joint committee revising the 1999 AERA, APA, NCME *Standards for Educational and Psychological Testing*, a member of the National Research Council's Committee on Assessment and Teacher Quality, and chair of AERA's Task Force on *Standards for Reporting on Empirical Social Science Research in AERA Publications*. She is co-founder and co-editor of the journal *Measurement: Interdisciplinary Research and Perspectives* and editor of the 2007 yearbook for the National Society for the Study of Education on *Evidence and Decision Making*.

Diana C. Pullin is Professor in the Lynch School of Education and Affiliate Professor of Law at Boston College. Her research agenda focuses on issues of education law and public policy, with an emphasis on the provision of educational opportunity for at-risk students, particularly minority students and students with disabilities. She has served as legal counsel for students, teachers, and school systems in education law and testing disputes. She has published numerous books, chapters, and articles on education law and public policy, the use of social science evidence in education law, educational and employment testing, and individuals with disabilities. She was a member of the joint committee revising the 1999 AERA, APA, NCME *Standards for Educational and Psychological Testing*. She has served on several expert panels at the National Research Council and is a member of the Board on Testing and Assessment of the National Research Council of the National Academy of Sciences. She is Associate Editor of the interdisciplinary journal *Educational Policy*.

Lauren Jones Young is Director of the Spencer Foundation's Teaching, Learning, and Instructional Resources Program. Prior to her appointment at Spencer, Young was Associate Professor of Teacher Education and Educational Administration at Michigan State University. She was the recipient of the university's Teacher-Scholar and Crystal Apple awards for her teaching and research focused on issues of race, gender, class, and social justice in teacher preparation and teaching practices. In addition to two edited books and a number of monographs, she has published several articles in leading education journals. A graduate of the Harvard University program in social policy and education, Dr. Young's life's work, both in and outside the academy, has centered on expanding learning and life opportunities for children.

1   Introduction

Edward H. Haertel, Pamela A. Moss, Diana C. Pullin, and James Paul Gee[1]

The most pressing issue facing U.S. education may be providing all students with a fair opportunity to learn (OTL). Although most would embrace the goal of enhancing OTL, there are fundamental disagreements about how best to accomplish this and different understandings of the meaning of "opportunity to learn." Historically, conceptions of OTL have been closely tied to the practice of testing. OTL has been conceptualized as opportunity to learn what is tested, and test-based accountability has been widely implemented as a means of enhancing OTL. In the United States, policy makers have embraced test-based accountability as a means of somehow forcing schools to bring "all children" to a "proficient" level of achievement. By law, tests must be "aligned" to rigorous "academic achievement standards." Thus, standardized tests are relied upon to provide both the definition of successful learning and the means to assure that OTL is extended to all learners. Against this vision, many have criticized the conception of learning underlying large-scale testing programs and have argued that test-based accountability has, in fact, undermined many students' opportunities to learn.

It is rare to find any productive dialogue between the critics and the proponents of test-based accountability systems. By and large, testing advocates embrace a straightforward account of educational improvement. It is taken as a given that schools are doing a poor job – the goal of schooling is to impart skills to students, and it is common knowledge that many students graduate without having acquired the skills they need. Moreover, learning opportunities are unequally distributed, as attested by large differences in test score distributions (read uncritically as indicators of skill distributions) for groups defined by race and ethnicity, poverty or parent education, language background, or disability status. Tests indicate which students, individually and collectively, have or have not acquired the skills expected, and thus provide a quantitative index of school performance. If "teaching to the test" turns out to mean cheating – teaching children the answers to actual test questions, for example – then that is clearly a problem. However, if "teaching to the test" means instruction aimed broadly at the skills tested, then that is precisely what schooling ought to be about. Therefore, testing guides educators' efforts, providing both the means and the measure of schooling success.

The various critics of test-based accountability offer no such single, tidy account. Many are concerned that the accountability testing reform model is *incomplete*, that "reform" turns out to mean accountability testing and little else. If educators are to be held accountable for bringing "all children" to "proficient," then teachers must have more and better preservice preparation and inservice professional development; school facilities must be upgraded; more and better instructional materials must be provided. In short, capacity building and accountability must go hand in hand if educational reforms are to succeed.

Others are concerned that the accountability testing reform model has been *poorly implemented*. Definitions of "proficient" vary wildly from place to place; achievement targets and timelines are often grossly unrealistic; the special needs of particular groups of learners are ignored. Alternately, requirements are implemented in such a way that successful schools are penalized and failing schools escape sanctions, or regulations have weakened the legislation to the extent that there is no longer any real accountability at all.

Others contend that the accountability testing reform model must employ *better or different tests*. The multiple-choice tests used from one year to the next resemble each other too closely, permitting teachers to ignore material not on the examination. Another argument holds that to assess the "thinking curriculum" (Resnick and Resnick 1992), one must set aside multiple-choice tests in favor of high-quality performance assessments, so that "teaching to the test" means providing meaningful, engaging instruction. A closely related critique, grounded in modern cognitive psychology, found its fullest expression in the National Research Council's recent publication, *Knowing What Students Know* (National Research Council 2001). This report makes the case that testing practice is largely out of touch with contemporary psychology, particularly cognitive science. It calls for enhanced collaboration between psychometrics and cognitive science and offers a carefully theorized vision of how collaboration "among researchers and assessment developers working at the intersection of cognitive theory and educational measurement" (p. 13) might enhance learning and assessment. Existing tests offer snapshots of isolated elements of factual and procedural knowledge. A new and better generation of tests could provide rich diagnostic information about students' complex, evolving knowledge structures.

Our book could be read as a critique of the logic and the effects of high-stakes testing, but that is not its primary goal. By and large, the authors represented are skeptical about the benefits of contemporary accountability testing, but we offer no simple list of recommendations for improvements. We share deep concerns about the direction and effects of contemporary accountability testing and would probably agree with many of the criticisms just cited: Accountability and capacity building must go hand in hand; state and federal laws and regulations are technically flawed; the tests used are of insufficient scope and quality, are disproportionately multiple-choice, and are based on outmoded theories of cognition and learning. That said, most of the authors represented here view these concerns and criticisms as almost beside the point. These sorts of problems are serious but in principle remediable. Our book interrogates instead the fundamental premise that schooling is about imparting skills and that OTL is simply a matter of ensuring universal skills acquisition. In various ways, different chapters call into question the meaningfulness and the trustworthiness of test scores as evidence about learning that matters. If rising test scores cannot be taken as evidence of better student learning, then test-based reforms cannot be relied upon to extend OTL to all learners.

PSYCHOMETRIC AND SOCIOCULTURAL/SITUATIVE PERSPECTIVES

One could, somewhat unfairly, characterize prevailing conceptions of learning and OTL as locating knowledge inside the heads of individual learners, privileging symbolic representation over embodied experience, and relegating the social dimensions of learning, however important, to the role of background or context in the business of measuring learning outcomes. These views comport with a psychometric perspective, with its roots in mathematics and psychology, and with the conceptual and statistical tools of educational testing as currently practiced. To be sure, not all psychometricians would agree with this caricature (e.g., Brennan 2005). As Mislevy's chapter in this volume explains, the conceptual and statistical tools of psychometrics may also be quite compatible with very different conceptions of knowledge and learning.

Although a version of the psychometric perspective is represented in this volume, most of the chapters represent one or another variant of either sociocultural theory or situated cognition – collectively the *SC perspectives*. (This *SC* label glosses over important, some would say fundamental, theoretical differences. It is used here in contrast to the similarly simplified *psychometric* label.) SC perspectives locate knowledge not primarily inside the head, but rather in the relationship between a person and an environment in which that person thinks and feels, acts and interacts. The SC approaches represented here are variously rooted in the learning sciences, sociolinguistics, sociology, and cognitive anthropology. They differ in focus but are generally compatible. Some highlight social interaction and participation, characterizing learning by individuals and groups through interactions within an *activity system* and conceiving learning and knowing from the perspective of distributed cognition. Others focus more sharply on notions of *embodied cognition*, attending to the ways in which perception and cognition are connected with human bodies embedded in a material and social world, including the social and cultural contexts of students' lives outside school. These chapters raise questions as to what OTL means, how it might be productively conceptualized at different levels of the educational system, what constrains and enables it, and how it can be assessed in a way that supports rather than undermines learning. Subsequent chapters pursue these questions, offering accounts of classroom and large-scale assessment and their functions in different activity systems for different purposes, informed by the SC perspectives developed in earlier chapters.

ORIGINS OF THE COLLABORATION

The idea for what was originally called "The Idea of Testing Project" first arose in a conversation between Pullin and Moss in a coffee shop in Montreal at the annual conference of the American Educational Research Association (AERA) in April 1999. With the year 2000 looming, a conference session on "Testing in the 21st Century" had set forth an optimistic vision, comfortably focused on the intersection between psychometrics and cognitive psychology. That prompted Moss and Pullin to wonder what "testing" might look like, and what its impact on schooling might be, if it were informed by conversations with scholars from other fields as well. They invited Haertel and Gee to join them in exploring that question. Following several desultory conversations during the ensuing months, the group of four "organizers" met for half a day the following year in Chicago at AERA 2000. At that point, the organizers developed a list of colleagues to invite to join in their exploration – all of whom said yes – and decided to seek funding. Young, from the Spencer Foundation, was enthusiastic and supportive, so the Spencer Foundation came to support the work of the group, which now grew to include Beach, Greeno, Lee, Mehan, and Mislevy. The four organizers met for the first time with Young at Stanford in early 2002. She became the fifth organizer;

and Mosher (consultant to the Spencer Foundation) also joined the project. A description of the project as it was originally conceptualized appears on the Spencer Web site; the manuscript that informed our original proposal to Spencer, "The Idea of Testing: Psychometric and Sociocultural Perspectives" is published in *Measurement: Interdisciplinary Research and Perspectives* (Moss et al. 2005). Then, like all truly collaborative efforts, the project evolved as our new collaborators joined the conversation.

The full group met for the first time in San Diego in April 2002. In addition to outstanding support from the staff of the Spencer Foundation, Andrew Ho, at that time a graduate student at Stanford University, offered his assistance as note taker and synthesizer. Given the group's multidisciplinary membership, a primary goal for the first meeting was to learn about each other's work. To that end, all participants were asked to share an example of their work that would introduce to a multidisciplinary audience the perspectives and practices of their field. The organizers also requested that everyone read and prepare to comment on a common text, *Knowing What Students Know* (National Research Council 2001). Participants were also asked to consider the following questions: How do you see your work or that of others in your field illuminating the conceptualization, practice, and use of assessment? What alternatives or analogues to assessments based in psychometrics/cognitive science do you imagine might be developed? How might your work or that of others in your field critically examine the way assessments shape and are shaped by the social contexts in which they are produced and received?

As a result of that three-day discussion, it became clear that OTL was at the heart of all of our interests. Thus, the group decided that exploring the concept of OTL and its relationship to teaching and assessment would provide an important and productive focus for our joint work. We wanted to develop a manuscript that would illustrate, for a broad educational audience, how the concept of OTL could be productively conceptualized, studied, and enacted from the intersections of our fields of work. Thus, although rethinking assessment has remained one important goal of our work, our interest in assessment has come to be framed in terms of the intersection between assessment and OTL.

The group met seven times between 2002 and 2005. Four of the meetings, like the first, were three-day meetings in settings where both formal and informal conversations could occur. Agendas for these meetings are posted on the Spencer Web site (www.spencer.org/publications). We also met just before each annual AERA meeting from 2003 to 2005 and presented our work at two of those meetings. The organizers relied on e-mail, conference calls, and additional meetings to plan experiences for the group that would foster the collaboration. We became friends as well as colleagues and began to develop a language for talking across our different research perspectives that has served us well as we have worked to make our ideas available to a broader audience.

The early meetings followed the pattern of the first meeting, where participants shared their own work, read common "texts," and used those texts as springboards for sharing their perspectives on OTL. At the second and third meetings, we focused on a case prepared by Pullin about the Massachusetts student-testing program, on videotapes and other artifacts from classrooms studied by Lee and Greeno and on complex context-sensitive performance assessments studied by Mislevy. Conversations about these common texts were crucial to our developing a common language for talking about OTL. As the meetings progressed, we began to develop drafts of chapters for this volume. As these initial chapters evolved, the need for new chapters arose, and the manuscript came to take the form in which it now appears.

OUR ARGUMENT IN A NUTSHELL

How might our collaboration across sociocultural and psychometric perspectives extend conventional discourse in the educational research and policy communities about learning, OTL, assessment, and the relationships among them? Like all concepts, the meanings of learning, OTL, and assessment are deeply situated in people's experiences of them in educational practice. In chapter 2, Pullin and Haertel set the stage for our argument by situating conventional conceptions of OTL and its relationship with testing, historically, in terms of access to content, resources, and instructional processes, typically assessed via standardized tests and related indicators that students have been exposed to the content tested. We contend that these understandings and indicators of OTL are at best inadequate. Opportunities to learn do not exist for learners who cannot take advantage of them. Questions of OTL cannot be equitably addressed by looking simply at content, resources, or processes of instruction, or even by looking at all three. Although these are surely important, one must look further at the relationships among particular learners and these elements of their learning environments. Furthermore, neither tests in common use (as noted above) nor any particular assessments (including the more powerful ones described in subsequent chapters) should or could embody a vision of learning sufficient to orient educational practice. Much more is needed.

Our argument begins with a theory of learning informed by sociocultural, situative, and sociological perspectives alongside more familiar cognitivist ones. What is it (we hope) students are learning, how, and why (Engeström

2001)? Using the work of many contemporary educational theorists, we endorse a theory of learning that moves beyond an emphasis on acquiring information and skills to an emphasis on rich conceptual understanding, reasoning, and problem solving in a domain. However, sociocultural perspectives push us still further by emphasizing the deeply situated nature of learning in the social contexts and experiences in which it is put to work. This has multiple implications for conceptualizing and supporting learning. *First*, as Gee argues (this volume, chapter 8), "Any actual domain of knowledge, academic or not, is first and foremost a set of activities (special ways of acting and interacting so as to produce and use knowledge) and experiences (special ways of seeing, valuing, and being in the world). Physicists *do* physics. They *talk* physics. And when they are being physicists, they *see* and *value* the world in a different way than do non-physicists" (p. 200). The same goes for any other domain of knowledge. Of course, students "learn" to *do* school – to act, talk, perceive, and value in the ways they experience there – but unless these experiences are preparing them to act, and to learn, in ways that are valued outside school, schools are not serving them well.

Second, this emphasis on activities and experiences reminds us that learning entails *interaction* between learners and the other people and tools in their environment. By tools, we mean both physical tools (such as calculators and dictionaries, pens and paper, computers, and so on) and conceptual tools (like domain-specific language and representations), all of which mediate learning. Learning can only be developed, enacted, supported, or observed in interaction between learners and these elements of their environment. Sociocultural perspectives provide multiple lenses through which we can understand learning as the interaction, or relationship, between learners and their environments. In addition to asking questions about (changes in) what they know and can do or how they engage in reasoning and problem solving, we can also ask questions about (changes in) what they mean when they act and interact (Gee, this volume, chapter 4); about how they are using domain-specific language, representations, and culture (Gee, this volume, chapter 4; Lee, this volume); about how they are participating in the activities of their local (school and other) communities; about the positions they are enacting with respect to one another and the subject matter (e.g., raising questions or simply answering them? challenging interpretations or simply reproducing them?) (Greeno and Gresalfi, this volume); about the resultant identities they are developing; about the social networks in which they participate (Mehan, this volume); and so on. Of course, sociocultural theorists also privilege a particular set of answers to these questions. These answers involve knowledge useful in the world; complex, authentic, and domain-specific forms for reasoning and problem solving; identities and positions that enact conceptual agency (choices in formulating questions, choosing methods, explaining solutions); critical reflection on multiple values and worldviews; a view of learning as important to one's growth; and so on (see, Moss, this volume, Figure 9.2, for one summary of the criteria valued by the authors).

Third, sociocultural studies draw our attention, explicitly, to what learners – with minds and bodies, home and peer cultures and languages, previous learning experiences, interests and values – bring to their learning environments and how that shapes their interactions with those learning environments. Thus, all of the questions about meaning, experience, language, culture, positioning, identities, and so on need to be asked about the interactions between particular learners and their learning environments as they evolve over time (their "learning trajectories").

Fourth, providing adequate OTL means scaffolding the dynamic interaction between students' "forms of knowledge and ways of using language [from their] everyday experiences in families and communities" (Lee, this volume, p. 136) and the resources of their learning environments. Furthermore, as Gee (this volume, chapter 8) notes, this can't be accomplished by simply "telling" students what to do or by "turning them loose" in the domain's activities; rather, what is needed is a combination of "immersion and guidance." Thus, a socioculturally informed theory of learning entails a well-designed curriculum with a coherent learning trajectory, connections that build on students' prior knowledge and experiences, explicit instruction that involves connections between academic and everyday language, just-in-time feedback as experience is unfolding (Gee, this volume, chapter 8), meta-conversations about how you know what you know (Lee, this volume), activities that permit meaningful participation in the group's work (Greeno and Gresalfi, this volume), and so on. It also entails social scaffolds beyond the classroom that support academically oriented friendships; productive connections among home, school, college, and business; explicit socialization in how to participate in these social networks; and so on (Mehan, this volume).

The chapters that follow are rich with extended concrete examples of practice consistent with this theory of learning – in classrooms, schools, and districts or other external organizations that support multiple schools – along with the theoretical tools for analyzing these examples of practice to support the design of learning environments.

How can we conceptualize assessment in light of the complex demands of a socioculturally informed learning theory? We consider classroom assessment as well as assessment that crosses boundaries from the classroom to the school, district, and beyond to inform professional learning, evaluation, and accountability. This portion of our argument entails three underlying premises about assessment: assessment should support teachers and other educational professionals in learning how better to support students' and one another's learning; professionals working in different contexts (classrooms, faculty study groups, district offices, etc.) have different information needs; and assessment and the routines that surround it do far more than provide information – they shape people's understanding about what is important to learn, what learning is, and who learners are.

Our reconceptualization of assessment is deeply informed by "reading" accounts of educational practice, consistent with our learning theory, for how evidence is used to monitor and support learning. Such readings suggest that assessment can be most productively conceptualized around the particular questions or problems that evidence is needed to address rather than around a particular instrument or activity ("a test") and the circumscribed evidence it provides (Moss, Girard, and Haniford 2006). The types of questions addressed include classroom teachers' moment-to-moment questions about "what to do next"; their questions about how to plan and enact lessons, revise curricular routines, solve particular pedagogical problems, or inform parents and guardians about students' learning; and the questions school, district and other educational leaders face about allocating resources, planning professional development, selecting and refining curricula, developing policies, and evaluating the impact of these choices. Answering any particular question entails multiple sorts of evidence about the evolving interaction between learners and their learning environments (their learning trajectories). Thus, our conception of assessment includes formal assessments that we recognize as "*an* assessment," as well as informal evaluations and judgments, both tacit and explicit, that routinely occur in classroom interactions and in other educational settings (Jordan and Putz 2004).

This conception of assessment certainly recognizes the need for large-scale standardized[2] assessments to assist in addressing many questions that educators face. Mislevy (this volume) offers theory and examples of how large-scale standardized assessments, far more consistent with socioculturally informed theories of learning, might be developed, implemented, and evaluated. Other chapters provide examples of professional environments where large-scale assessments may be useful alongside other evidence and practices of interpretation, decision making, and learning (Lee; Mehan; Moss, Girard, and Greeno, all this volume). It is important to note, however, that standardized assessments, like other activities, entail social situations, including routines, roles, and responsibilities for different people, and conceptions of what counts as progress. Questions about the generalizability of knowledge from students' participation in the social situation of the standardized test to their participation in the many other social situations where knowledge is used cannot be answered satisfactorily from within the framework of standardized testing alone (Gee, this volume, chapter 4).

Furthermore, it is important to note that when standardized assessments are intended to inform particular decisions in local contexts, they can be meaningfully interpreted only in light of locally relevant evidence. The results from a standardized assessment form, at best, a good hypothesis about a particular case (student, school) that must then be evaluated from the ground up by local interpreters who are using it in their own contexts of work. This means that *any* practice of assessment depends, in large part, on the capacity of local interpreters (e.g., teachers making instructional decisions; school and district leaders making decisions about allocating resources; students whose understandings of themselves may well be shaped by the assessment) to interpret it in light of other relevant evidence and in light of the questions or problems they are using it to address. The essential role of local interpreters illuminates the need for professional development and for a professional environment that supports this sort of inquiry into students' learning. Furthermore, it calls into serious question prominent practices of large-scale assessment that enforce particular decisions or actions based solely on the scores a particular individual or organization has received (Mislevy, Gee, and Moss, in press).

Our socioculturally informed learning theory reminds us that assessment practices are inevitably elements of learning environments that shape (enable and constrain) learning and opportunities to learn. Any robust practice of assessment, consistent with high-quality learning and OTL, must turn the lens of inquiry back on itself. All of this suggests that developing useful assessment practices – practices that function productively at different levels of the educational system – will depend on richly contextualized understandings of what information is needed, how it is used, and the effects of this use.

We hope that we have succeeded in providing readers with a new set of theoretical resources for conceptualizing, enhancing, and evaluating OTL and for rethinking the theory and practice of assessment through new disciplinary lenses. We hope to introduce educators, researchers, school leaders, and policy analysts who are new to sociocultural perspectives to the power of these theoretical resources for conceptualizing, enhancing, and assessing OTL; to encourage those who already draw on sociocultural resources to focus attention on OTL and assessment in ways that will impact educational policy and practice; and, more generally, to nurture dialogue and collaboration among members of discourse communities who have rarely engaged one another's work.

OVERVIEW OF THE VOLUME

Following this introduction, the next three chapters provide an historical overview of OTL (chapter 2) and broad examinations of OTL as conceptualized through the lenses of sociological (chapter 3) and SC (chapter 4) perspectives. The subsequent four chapters further develop and illustrate specific themes, viewing learning and OTL from the perspectives of education for students with disabilities (chapter 5), education incorporating cultural practices in the classroom (chapter 6), an analysis of education that foregrounds community participation (chapter 7), and game-like learning practices and principles, including video games (chapter 8). Chapters 9, 10, and 11 return to a focus on assessment, drawing upon the earlier chapters to once again highlight SC perspectives on classroom assessment (chapter 9), an integration of SC and psychometric perspectives for large-scale assessment (chapter 10), and applications of SC principles to a consideration of professional learning, evaluation, and accountability (chapter 11). The final chapter briefly recapitulates the themes of the preceding chapters and concludes with a set of principles underlying fair OTL. To assist the reader, the remainder of this introduction describes what is to follow in slightly more detail.

Chapter 2 (Pullin and Haertel) provides a historical perspective to set the context for the rest of the volume. After describing the interplay of assessment with conceptions of OTL in terms of (1) content taught; (2) adequacy and allocation of educational resources; and (3) teaching processes, this chapter turns to five cases that illustrate some of these intersections. Four of the cases are historical: the intelligence-testing movement of the early twentieth century, Ralph W. Tyler's Eight-Year Study in the 1930s, the beginnings of the minimum competency testing movement in the late 1970s and early 1980s, and the performance assessment movement of the 1990s. The last case discussed concerns current standards-based reforms. Pullin and Haertel highlight the tension between the fundamentally egalitarian rhetoric of OTL and the origins and uses of testing for ranking, classifying, sorting, selecting, and excluding. They develop the idea that any conception of OTL embodies a conception of learning and a set of judgments about what is worth measuring. They close by foreshadowing the profound contrast between conventional understanding of OTL and the sociological and sociocultural understandings developed in subsequent chapters.

Chapter 3 (Mehan) reviews major conceptions of OTL and assessment within the discipline of sociology. He contrasts the traditional view of schooling as a meritocratic sorting device with (1) a view that asserts schools (either wittingly or unwittingly) serve to reproduce the existing hierarchies of privilege; (2) a view that asserts that schools, peers, and families mediate the relations between structural constraints and human action; and (3) a resurgent democratic conception of schooling. The traditional, meritocratic conception of OTL and assessment holds that schools provide students with avenues to compete as individuals for valued resources. The reproduction and production conceptions of OTL question whether students have equal access to valued educational and cultural resources. The resurgent democratic conception of schooling defines OTL in terms of conditions within schools for the open flow of ideas and consideration of problems connected to the "real world." Within this democratic conception, multiple measures, especially portfolios and demonstrations that assess learning in authentic contexts, are preferred to standardized tests as assessment tools (cf. Gee, this volume, chapter 4; Mislevy, this volume). Two extended cases of democratic schooling are provided: the "Advancement Via Individual Determination" (AVID) program, designed to help low-achieving students with high academic potential prepare for entrance to colleges and universities; and the Preuss School, which offers only a college preparatory curriculum in grades six through twelve to its 700-plus students, all of whom are selected by lottery from low-income backgrounds.

Chapter 4 (Gee) provides a theoretical overview of SC perspectives through which OTL might be conceptualized. Gee begins with a consideration of the traditional perspective in psychology that views knowledge and learning through the lens of mental representations in individuals' heads. He points out that even in this traditional view, many of the issues that SC perspectives foreground also arise, though in a more backgrounded way. These include the role of prior knowledge, access to more and less powerful representational resources, and affective filters that shape "intake" of knowledge to which individuals have been exposed. He then takes up variations of an SC perspective, starting with the relationship between learners and their learning environments. In subsequent sections, this relationship is spelled out in terms of the connections between learning and learners' experiences in the world; how knowledge is distributed across people and their tools; the central importance of people's participation in shared talk and social practices; and the special varieties of language used in talk and participation when learning in the content areas in school – areas like math, science, social studies, and literature. In conclusion, Gee takes up the relationship between culture and participation in school practices.

Chapter 5 (Pullin) views assessment and OTL from the perspective of students with disabilities, contrasting general and special education. Pullin proposes that this special case provides insight into new ways of understanding and reconceptualizing OTL and assessment. She argues that the perspectives offered in this volume imply the necessity of new approaches for the education and assessment of students with disabilities as well as for students in the general population. Drawing from sociological, sociocultural, and situative perspectives, Pullin discusses the procedures and practices for defining OTL for students with disabilities and the uses of assessment for placement, programming, and accountability for these students. She also considers the roles of parents and educators in using assessment and promoting OTL and highlights the ambiguities associated with bureaucratized responses to externally imposed individual rights and the possibilities arising from a system calling for a more individualized, learner-centered, collaborative model for teaching and learning.

Chapter 6 (Lee) illustrates and further develops the sociocultural perspectives introduced by Mehan and Gee with rich examples of classroom practice. Lee examines how opportunities to learn are structured in classrooms serving culturally diverse students in ways that (1) build on fundamental propositions in cognition; (2) focus on generative topics, concepts, and forms of problem solving within subject matters; and (3) scaffold forms of knowledge and ways of using language emerging from students' everyday experiences in families and communities. Her basic argument is that reconceptualizing forms of assessment in the absence of reconceptualizing instruction will yield few results. The chapter is influenced by conceptions of human learning from three perspectives – schema theory, distributed cognition, and situated cognition – each with implications for the design of instruction that is culturally responsive to students as learners and true to the disciplinary foundations of the subject matters. Three extended cases illustrate these instructional practices: the Cultural Modeling Project, the Algebra Project, and Chèche Konen.

Chapter 7 (Greeno and Gresalfi) also complements and illustrates the theoretical resources introduced by Gee and Mehan. In their "situative" view, learning by an individual in a community is conceptualized as a trajectory of that student's participation in the community – a path with a past and present, shaping possibilities for future participation. Learning by a group or community is also conceptualized as a trajectory – a path that corresponds to change in the community's practices. Thus, rather than considering learning as a process of acquiring cognitive structures, Greeno and Gresalfi conceptualize it as a process in which individuals participate more proficiently in structured practices. This shift changes the ways we think about learning and identify or account for problems with learning, in particular the persistent achievement gap between students of different races, ethnicities, and social classes, and the solutions we seek to those problems. The chapter focuses on two aspects of student learning: informational, involving students' interactions with information, concepts, and principles of subject-matter domains; and interpersonal, involving students' interactions with each other, a teacher, and other people. The authors conceive of OTL in terms of affordances for participation by students that support trajectories toward stronger valued capabilities and dispositions, including learning tasks with high levels of cognitive demand, involving meaningful social interaction and significant contact with concepts and principles of subject-matter domains; participation structures with significant scope for conceptual agency; and adequate skills and knowledge for routine procedures and information. They illustrate the analytic potential of their model with examples of practice from mathematics classrooms.

Chapter 8 (Gee) draws on examples of game-like learning to illuminate ways in which the principles developed in chapter 4 can be instantiated in practice. The perspective Gee further develops here, which stresses knowledge as activity and experience before knowledge as facts and information and also stresses embodied understandings as precedent to verbal understandings, has powerful implications for both the nature and the assessment of learning and teaching. Recently, researchers in several different areas have raised the possibility that what we might call "game like" learning through digital technologies can facilitate situated understandings in the context of activity and experience grounded in perception. Gee illustrates these ideas, first, with an application of what he considers game-like learning that uses no real game; next, with a game made explicitly to enhance school-based learning; then with a commercial game that enhances deep learning in a crucially important way; and finally, with a game-like simulation built into an overall learning system using many of the same learning principles as the commercial game. He concludes with a consideration of the implications of game-like learning, especially for issues of assessment and OTL.

Chapter 9 (Moss) introduces additional theoretical tools useful in applying the SC perspectives of the preceding chapters to conceptualize assessment, and its relation to OTL, at the level of individual classrooms, and it illustrates them with an extended example of assessment practice. First, Moss suggests that assessment be conceptualized around particular questions or problems and the evidence needed to address them. She then elaborates on a set of theoretical tools, presented in earlier chapters, for analyzing a dynamic learning environment, to illuminate (1) the kinds of evidence that one might want to consider in addressing a question about learning or OTL; (2) perspectives from which one can analyze how assessment functions within a learning environment to monitor and support learning; and (3) criteria for evaluating the quality of learning and OTL in a learning environment. The extended example draws on Lampert's (2001) yearlong analysis of teaching and learning in her fifth-grade mathematics classroom to illustrate assessment practices that are consistent with these perspectives and to show the value of understanding assessment as part of an evolving activity system.

Chapter 10 (Mislevy) turns to the implications of SC perspectives for large-scale assessment. An SC view of assessment "emphasizes questions about the quality of student participation in activities of inquiry and sense making, and considers assessment practices as integral components of the general systems of activity in which they occur" (Greeno, Collins, and Resnick 1997, 37). This chapter addresses two issues. The first is understanding the SC view of assessment through the lens of an "evidence centered" design framework that has proven useful for assessments cast in trait, behavioral, and information-processing perspectives. The second is addressing issues that arise when one attempts to design assessments that are at once compatible with SC principles and also suitable for large-scale use. Illustrations are drawn from the Advanced Placement Studio Art portfolio assessment and the Hydrive intelligent tutoring system.

Chapter 11 (Moss, Girard, and Greeno) further develops the implications of SC perspectives for assessment, focusing on assessment that crosses the boundaries – from the classroom to the school and from the school to the district, external organization or beyond – to serve purposes of professional learning, evaluation, and accountability. The authors analyze four examples of assessment systems that range along a continuum from one where the information by which a school or classroom is evaluated is primarily externally defined to those that make increasingly more room for evidence that represents local practice in its own terms. Extending the framework developed in chapter 9, they raise questions intended to illuminate the affordances and constraints of these different types of assessment systems in terms of both documenting and enhancing OTL as conceptualized by the authors of this volume.

Chapter 12 (Pullin) provides a review of key ideas from the previous chapters, leading to a set of principles underlying fair OTL.

forms of assessment, which for Tyler had been a necessary concomitant of educational reform, became the principal driver of reform. Finally, current, standards-based reforms are considered. Under the 1994 and 2001 reauthorizations of the Elementary and Secondary Education Act of 1965, states were required to adopt rigorous academic content standards and to hold schools accountable using achievement tests aligned with those standards. Testing requirements under standards-based reforms could affect curriculum content, instructional resource allocations, and instructional practices in complex ways, both intended and unintended. Recent efforts to influence OTL using high-stakes assessments have demonstrated that test scores for some students can be raised, but if test scores are the measure of OTL, then it is clear that test-based reforms have not yet succeeded in extending OTL to *all* students. More importantly, there are serious questions as to the *kinds* of educational opportunities attested by rising test scores alone. Thus, the imperfect relationship between testing and OTL continues, even as we expand our understanding of teaching and learning, as discussed throughout this volume.

CONCEPTIONS OF OTL

Issues concerning the relationship between testing and OTL have arisen with increasing frequency over the past several decades. As the broader discourse about educational goals and aspirations has shifted over time, attention has focused less on issues of learning opportunity and more on the significance of assessment. This reflects a growing use of testing as a policy tool (McDonnell 2004). The interplay of assessment and OTL is increasingly governed by the manner in which testing is used as a mechanism to address our public policy choices concerning the provision and outcomes of education, coupled with evolving notions about the provision of learning opportunities. Over time, educators and social scientists have greatly expanded their understanding of the conditions for effective education, even as they have continued to struggle with the appropriate role for assessment in achieving educational goals.

A history of considerations of OTL by researchers and policy makers illuminates at least three broad mechanisms whereby testing may influence students' learning outcomes. These three paths of influence correspond with three broad definitions of OTL in terms of instructional content, resources, and processes. All are found in policy arguments about test-driven educational reform (e.g., Linn 1993, 2000; Porter 1995).

OTL and the Content of Curriculum and Instruction

Whatever else OTL may entail, it must surely encompass a consideration of the content taught. Students can scarcely be said to have had an opportunity to learn content they have never encountered. Likewise, it is axiomatic that achievement tests must reflect the contents of instruction (Messick 1984). The relationship between test content and instructional content has been of concern to educational researchers for decades (Haertel 1989, 1999b; Haertel and Calfee 1983; Haertel and Herman 2005; Heubert and Hauser 1999; Madaus 1983, 1988; McDonnell 1995; Messick 1984; Porter 2002; Tyler 1949; Wang 1998). Although not all methods used for assessing the nature and consequences of this relationship have been well developed, it is clear that tests may influence what is taught, how it is learned, and what counts as mastery by encouraging teachers to focus on the knowledge and skills tested (and therefore, presumably, valued) and by signaling students about intended learning outcomes. Indeed, the most recent standards-based education reforms rest directly on the presumption that external test mandates will enhance OTL through "hortatory" policies importuning local schools to improve their curricula and instruction to respond to test-based accountability requirements (McDonnell 2004). It is no surprise, then, that definitions of OTL in terms of content taught are closely bound up with testing practices. As Porter (2002, 3) points out, although "the content of instruction plays a primary role in determining gains in student achievement ... the content of instruction has largely been taken for granted – in educational research and often in educational practice." The "gains in student achievement" that Porter refers to are, of course, gains in test scores.

McDonnell (1995) asserts that the discussion of OTL began originally as a research question arising from efforts to conduct international testing for comparative studies of educational achievement – in particular, the Second International Mathematics Study (SIMS) conducted by the International Association for the Evaluation of Educational Achievement (IEA) in the late 1970s and early 1980s. The problem was that no test could be equally aligned with different nations' curricula, but methods were nonetheless required to enable fair cross-national comparisons. The creation of fair comparisons of scores on a common test in nations with differing curricula required, first, cross-national collaboration in the definition of the content to be tested. Then, when tests were administered in various nations, teacher judgments of OTL were collected concurrently with test data. Finally, a differential weighting of items was made to reflect the educational priorities of each nation for purposes of comparing its own achievement with those of other nations. As described later in this chapter, in a similar manner, broad queries to teachers about whether they taught the content assessed by tests were later used in meeting legal requirements to establish that students had had an opportunity to learn the material covered on high school graduation tests.

As international comparative studies heightened the nation's awareness of the outcomes of education, politicians and policy makers began efforts to enhance educational achievement through the adoption of public standards for educational outcomes. Following the issuance of *A Nation at Risk* by the National Commission on Excellence in Education (1983), improving educational achievement became a national imperative. *A Nation at Risk* recommended that "standardized tests of achievement (not to be confused with aptitude tests) should be administered at major transition points from one level of schooling to another and particularly from high school to college or work... [in order to]: (1) certify the student's credentials, (2) identify the need for remedial intervention, and (3) identify the opportunity for advanced or accelerated work" (NCEE 1983 28).

The influence of tests on curriculum content is salient in the cases of Tyler's Eight-Year Study, performance assessment, and current standards-based reforms. Other illustrations beyond the scope of this chapter might include curricula for Advanced Placement or International Baccalaureate courses; for preservice teacher education programs (Melnick and Pullin 2000; Pullin 2004); and, historically, measurement-driven instructional management systems, including programmed instruction (Lange 1967), Mastery Learning (Bloom 1971) and the Criterion-Referenced Testing movement (Glaser 1963, 1994; Popham 1994). More recently, the National Council on Education Standards and Testing (NCEST) (1992) called for a system of national Content Standards together with Performance Standards keyed to "world-class" performance levels along with a system of assessments keyed to those standards (Vinovskis 1999).

The relationship between assessment and curriculum has become a critical focus of concern in the implementation of the No Child Left Behind Act of 2001 (NCLB) by states and local schools (Carnoy, Elmore and Siskin 2003; Elmore 2004; McDonnell 2004).

OTL and Resources for Educating

OTL can also be defined in terms of *resources* to support teaching and learning, including teacher qualifications, technology, supportive services, expenditures, and the like. The matter of resources and their role in determining educational opportunity has been a source of considerable debate in the past forty years among both policy makers and social scientists (Cohen, Raudenbush, and Ball 2003). Yet whatever the perspective on which resources – family background, funding for schools, teacher quality, or student capability – "count" or count the most, testing plays an increasingly important role in the determination of resource allocation to support the opportunity to learn for all students.

Testing can affect overall *levels* of educational resources when test scores become part of a rhetoric of educational crisis that leads to increased expenditures or other external interventions. More commonly, testing affects the *allocation* of educational resources. For individual students, definitions of disability or language-minority status, based in part on test scores, may significantly affect the educational resources made available to them and, consequently, their OTL (Pullin, this volume). More generally, all students' learning opportunities throughout their formal schooling may be shaped by placement and selection decisions informed by test scores. In addition, financial rewards and sanctions may be attached to school-level performance as indexed by test score summaries; accountability formulas may be crafted to encourage allocation of more instructional time and resources to lower-performing student groups or to foster parental choice to access supplemental services or different schools for their children.

Although the primary focus of *A Nation at Risk* and the later NCEST report was achievement, in the 1980s and 1990s, a resource-based conception of OTL also emerged in discussions of federal education policy (Vinovskis 1999). It was debated at the time whether it was fair or appropriate to hold students accountable for test results if they had not been afforded adequate opportunity to learn the material on which they were to be tested. Some advocates and researchers argued that enhanced curriculum alone would be insufficient to significantly improve educational outcomes without systemic reform of schools, the availability of competent educators, and the provision of sufficient resources to support the implementation of state curriculum frameworks closely aligned with student assessments (Smith and O'Day 1993). In the NCEST (1992) report, the need for OTL Standards was added to calls for Content Standards and Performance Standards. These OTL Standards were to define the resources required to enable students and schools to meet expectations laid out in the content and performance standards.

Enthusiasm for this aspect of OTL – the establishment of OTL Standards as a policy tool – quickly faded after it was proposed as an element of federal education law in the deliberations over the Goals 2000: Educate America Act. That Act called for the creation of a "National Education Standards and

Improvement Council" to approve *voluntary* national OTL standards. These standards called on states to address the quality and availability of curricula, instructional materials, libraries, and technologies; teacher quality; access to professional development; alignment of curricula, instruction, and assessment with voluntary national content standards; and safe schools.

The notion of imposing mandatory OTL standards (or "Educational Delivery" standards) on states and local schools had been quickly dropped for political reasons, as federal officials and policy makers grew skittish about federal intrusion into state and local curricula (McGuinn 2006; Vinovskis 1999) and the dollar costs of equalizing instructional resources were more clearly seen. The "voluntary" standards were a compromise on the OTL issue following a debate in which OTL standards were seen by critics as an intrusion on states' rights and local flexibility; costly; a potential cause for unleashing a torrent of lawsuits; and (perhaps most interestingly) too difficult to define and hard to measure. The National Education Standards and Improvement Council was never implemented, and the 1996 budget authorization eliminated OTL standards and OTL strategy requirements within the state plans mandated by the Goals 2000 Act (McGuinn 2006).

These policy debates about learning represented not only disputes over the governance of education but also a shift in perspective about the social policy goals for schools. As considerations of the provision of education proceeded, attention shifted away from considerations of equity for particular groups to accountability for all students. At the same time, the national discourse also began to shift from consideration of the resources, or inputs, for education to outputs, or achievement performance, of students (McGuinn 2006).

At about the same time, more attention began to be paid to teacher tests. It is clear that, to the extent that teacher certification tests influence teacher quality, these tests are also influencing a critical educational resource (National Research Council 2001). Testing of teachers helps define teacher qualifications and affects salaries and allocations of budget and materials to schools. Indeed, the National Board for Professional Teaching Standards was created with the goal of developing a system of advanced certification tests that could both improve teaching practices and enhance the status of teaching as a profession (Carnegie Forum on Education and the Economy 1986). Today, National Board–certified teachers receive higher salaries in many states.

The rhetoric of high-stakes testing sometimes reinforces the mantra that "money doesn't matter." By proposing high-stakes tests as a solution to the perceived failings of public education, elected officials and other policy makers create an impression that improvement will occur simply by holding students, teachers, and administrators accountable. By implying that accountability per se is the means to foster achievement, such testing policies send a message that teachers and students just need to work harder; thus, reliance on testing per se as an instrument for educational reform also affects OTL by shifting the policy discussion away from resource considerations that may be out of teachers' or schools' control – from capacity building to accountability (Elmore 2002; McDonnell 2004; Pullin 2007; Spillane 2004).

The influence of testing on allocation of instructional resources is clear in the case of intelligence testing. With MCT, some additional remediation was provided to students who failed, but this was often limited and was rarely supported by any supplemental appropriation of funds to support remedial programs. The efficacy of these efforts in enhancing OTL is called into question, however, by continuing failure rates on the tests and in particular by the persistent achievement gaps between advantaged and disadvantaged students. Some standards-based reforms have linked school or district resource allocations with test performance, but, as discussed below, a more significant effect of these reforms may have been to reinforce the notion that money doesn't matter.

OTL and the Process and Practices of Education

Finally, OTL can be defined in terms of classroom *processes and practices* enabling learning for individual students or groups of students. Although this third conception of OTL has been less well developed in the educational literature, again, testing shapes ideas of what counts as learning. The ready availability of a quantitative index of schools' "output" may support a simplistic view of the goals of schooling, the nature of school learning, and the relative merit of alternative pedagogical approaches. Yet a growing number of authors assert that meaningful OTL must be based on a theory of learning and models of teaching and schooling, including instructional leadership and professional development, that take into account a full and rich understanding of the process and practices of education to attain meaningful results, as discussed later in this volume. In short, the key focus for improving schools is situated in instruction (Cohen, Raudenbush, and Ball 2003; Pullin 2007).

Shepard (2000) has argued that test-driven reform, and current testing practice more generally, may be grounded in outmoded views of the teaching and learning processes. In so doing, she joins a sociocultural critique to Mislevy's (1996) cognitivist critique of contemporary measurement practices (cf. also Resnick and Resnick 1992). In her case study of high-stakes testing effects, McNeil (2000) also documents influences of testing on the teaching and learning process, as have other authors now reporting on the implementation of recent standards-based, test-driven education reforms (Carnoy, Elmore, and Siskin 2003; McDonnell 2004; Spillane 2004; Wilson

children of immigrants and children of color. If these children lacked native ability, they could not be expected to perform as well as others. Thus, IQ testing reinforced and legitimated societal beliefs and schooling practices, and tracking based on IQ testing was widely adopted (Chapman 1988).

Increased "educational efficiency" was expected to result from homogeneous grouping. Although the term OTL was not in use at the time, the argument was that testing would lead to more efficient use of instructional resources, especially teacher time, thereby increasing OTL, on average, for all students. The argument for efficiency through homogeneous grouping fits well into a teacher-centered, direct instruction model of schooling. It is noteworthy that explicit consideration of curriculum content was almost completely absent from this discussion, although Terman wrote elsewhere about the differentiation of the curriculum and instruction according to the presumed future vocations of pupils in different IQ strata (Terman 1919). IQ testing did influence OTL – not as intended, but instead via the differentiated content and pacing of instruction it supported. It is now understood that IQ scores are strongly influenced by out-of-school learning opportunities, not just by innate ability. When low-scoring children are tracked to receive a limited or slower-paced curriculum, the result is a self-fulfilling prophecy of lower achievement, irrespective of innate potential.

CREATING OTL THROUGH ALIGNMENT OF ASSESSMENT
WITH NEW CONCEPTIONS OF CURRICULUM AND INSTRUCTION:
THE EIGHT-YEAR STUDY

The Eight-Year Study, begun in 1933 by the Progressive Education Association, was a major initiative among educators and social scientists to establish and evaluate a progressive program of curriculum and instruction in thirty high schools nationwide. The study was centered at the University of Chicago under the leadership of Research Director Ralph Tyler. Associate directors and associates included Oscar Buros, Bruno Bettelheim, and Hilda Taba, among others. The study was intended as a demonstration project, implementing a bold new vision of secondary school education. Wilford M. Aikin, overall study director and chairman of the Progressive Education Association's Commission on the Relation of School and College, criticized prevailing secondary student evaluation practices as follows:

[High schools] seldom attempt seriously to find out what changes schooling brings about in students.... There are doubtless many causes [for this lack of knowledge], but one of the most obvious is the universal emphasis upon the accumulation of credits for promotion, graduation, and admission to college. To secure a credit or unit the student must "pass" a course. To pass a course he must remember certain facts and show proficiency in certain skills. Therefore, remembering knowledge and practicing techniques for examinations become the purposes of education for pupils and teachers alike. What goes on the school record becomes the real objective of the student, no matter what the school *says* its purposes are.... Concentration on these worthy but limited goals seems to make teachers and students forget the larger, long-range purposes of education. (Smith, Tyler, and the Evaluation Staff 1942, xvii)

Aikin was concerned with the influence of what is now called "high-stakes testing" on curriculum and instruction. Many critics of high-stakes testing have echoed his concerns (Black and Wiliam 1998; Madaus 1988; Resnick and Resnick 1992). In the terminology of this chapter, consequential examinations limited OTL through their influence on both curriculum content and instructional processes.

The staff of the Eight-Year Study recognized that radical changes could not be made to curriculum and instruction unless influential student evaluation methods were changed at the same time. Thus, students from the thirty schools were evaluated using specially designed "comprehensive evaluations," and agreement was obtained from over 300 colleges to accept the evidence of these evaluations in lieu of more conventional transcripts and examination results (Madaus, Stufflebeam, and Scriven 1983; Smith et al. 1942). The "comprehensive evaluations" included not only such traditional academic concerns as the application of general science principles but also scales of beliefs, interest indices, and responses to social problems. Information from assessments was combined with teachers' observations and judgments to develop comprehensive records of student performance that were to be used by colleges. It is of interest to note that the records used narrative descriptions, not numerical scores, to characterize student accomplishment.

High school teachers were centrally involved in creating the Eight-Year Study's comprehensive evaluations, and from the account given by Smith, Tyler, and their collaborators (1942), another mechanism may be identified through which new forms of testing reinforced new opportunities to learn:

As the evaluation committees carried out their work, it became clear that an evaluation program is also a potent method of continued teacher education. The recurring demand for the formulation and clarification of objectives, the continuing study of the reactions of students in terms of these objectives, and the persistent attempt to relate the results obtained from various sorts of measurement are all means for focusing the interests and efforts of teachers upon the most vital parts of the educational process. (Smith et al. 1942, 30)

Just as conventional tests limited OTL, new forms of assessment could expand OTL by focusing teachers' efforts and making them aware of new possibilities. The Eight-Year Study was remarkably successful. There was broad satisfaction with the educational changes effected in the thirty schools, and graduates performed well in college. Unfortunately, as the study drew to a close, the nation's attention was focused elsewhere. In the midst of the mobilization for impending war, there was little enthusiasm for progressive educational reform, and the Eight-Year Study was largely forgotten.

THE FORMULATION OF OTL AS A LEGAL RIGHT: SCHOOL DESEGREGATION, MINIMUM COMPETENCY TESTING, AND *DEBRA P. V. TURLINGTON*

Education policy in the 1970s, as today, was characterized by a sense of crisis. Continuing achievement gaps and a perceived "test score decline" beginning in the late 1960s and continuing into the 1970s, high levels of youth unemployment, and alarmist reports from blue-ribbon panels all fueled a popular perception that high school graduation standards had plummeted. From these concerns, the MCT movement was born. Legislators and other public policy makers, rather than educators or social scientists, played the predominant initiating role. The MCT requirements did not seek to define the content or processes for educating or provide new resources for schooling. Instead, the explicit public policy goal of MCT was to restore the credibility of the high school diploma. MCT, typically consisting of basic-skills tests in reading and mathematics, was used in a few school districts as early as 1962. By 1980, statewide MCT requirements had been implemented in 29 states, most having been initiated in 1975 or later. Typically, a fixed passing score on each portion of the MCT was required in order for a student to receive a regular high school diploma (Haertel and Herman 2005).

It was in this context, long before discussions in the nation's capitol about addressing OTL in the Goals 2000 Act, that OTL first became an issue in court cases concerning achievement tests as high school graduation requirements. This litigation from the late 1970s and 1980s becomes particularly relevant in the contemporary context as more states begin to implement high school graduation testing requirements and as every state implements the comprehensive testing and accountability requirements imposed by NCLB as a condition for receiving federal financial assistance. A landmark federal appellate court case, *Debra P. v. Turlington* (1981), challenging a Florida high school graduation test established that, as a matter of federal constitutional due process and equal protection rights, students must have had a fair opportunity to learn what is covered on a high school graduation test. This judicial decision established not only a legal requirement concerning the relationship between public schools and their students in a high-stakes testing context but also highlighted the difficulties associated with defining, and appropriately assaying, OTL.

As framed in this chapter, the *Debra P.* litigation addressed only the "content" aspect of OTL. The OTL requirement (described by the Florida courts as "curricular validity" and "instructional validity") set out by the federal appellate court in *Debra P.* was successfully met by the State of Florida on the basis of evidence from expert witnesses. A key part of this evidence was a two-question survey of the state's teachers asking them whether they had provided instruction in the skills covered on the test, and if so, whether that instruction was sufficient. There is little likelihood that any teacher would feel comfortable answering "no" to those questions.

Subsequent to *Debra P.*, the OTL issue arose in other reported state and federal court cases concerning K–12 high-stakes educational testing. In each instance, fairly instrumental approaches to judging OTL were taken, and courts were persuaded of the legal acceptability of the programs based on such factors as elapse of time between announcement of the program and test administration; multiple retake opportunities; remedial classes; coverage of test content in the individual education programs (IEPs) of students with disabilities; and educator assurance of content coverage. None of these, of course, really addresses the complexity of the OTL-assessment relationship.

However, the shortcomings of judicial scrutiny of OTL issues in the MCT context should not be surprising. The first and most famous education law case, *Brown v. Board of Education* (1954), also addressed what we now have come to call OTL when the U.S. Supreme Court determined that racially segregated schools denied the constitutional rights of black children to equal protection of the law. The Court, after describing education as the most important function of state and local government, required the dismantlement of segregated schools on grounds that black children were denied educational opportunity. This legal determination rested on the use of evidence from social psychology and developmental psychology that separate schools caused such severe emotional harm in damaging black children's self-perceptions as learners that they were presumed to have been denied learning opportunities. The use of social science evidence was revolutionary for the Court, and the social and political consequences of the Court's decision were profound. Although the definition of OTL was simplistic, with little attention to the content or processes for educating children, it was also prophetic:

Learning opportunities rest upon cultural constructs (see Lee, this volume; Mehan, this volume).

The post-*Debra P.* quest to address OTL as defined by content alignment has remained a focus of discussion among psychometricians and other education researchers (e.g., Porter and Smithson 2001), although there has been neither widespread methodological agreement nor broad implementation of this type of research. Although alignment studies have varied across curriculum mapping, analysis of instructional materials, teacher surveys, and matrix matching of content and performance standards, these approaches have generally sought to assess opportunity to learn what is tested rather than applying any broader set of criteria for what constitutes valuable learning. Thus, conceptions of OTL as content alignment have failed even to account for recent developments in the cognitive sciences, let alone for the broader methodological contributions of sociocultural approaches to educational research (see Gee, this volume, chapter 4; Moss et al. 2005).

IMPROVING OTL THROUGH THE POWER OF MEASUREMENT-DRIVEN INSTRUCTION: THE PERFORMANCE ASSESSMENT MOVEMENT OF THE 1990S

Over time, the perennial concern with low achievement has prompted different explanations, each tied with some favored remedy. In the early 1990s, one popular explanation had to do with multiple-choice testing. Prior to that time, multiple-choice tests were already regarded with some suspicion. Persistent score gaps fueled the belief that multiple-choice tests were biased, perhaps because they were suffused with the dominant middle-class white culture, perhaps because minority test takers were underrepresented in norming samples, or perhaps simply because they were designed to place everyone on a "bell curve." After all, norm-referenced interpretations doomed roughly half of the student population to the "below average" label. In addition, many teachers and researchers believe strongly that multiple-choice tests fail to measure some of the most important outcomes of schooling. Frederiksen (1984) viewed "the real test bias" as arising from the use of item formats best suited to posing well-structured problems – those with a single best answer, clear criteria for determining that answer, and often with routine solution procedures guaranteed to reach that answer. More interesting, real-world "ill-structured" problems were generally approached by "satisficing" along multiple dimensions. They had no guaranteed route to a solution. Indeed, there was no single best solution, and alternative possibilities might be evaluated according to multiple criteria.

These abiding concerns set the stage for a sophisticated psychological critique, which was combined with a persuasive policy argument. In their influential chapter "Assessing the Thinking Curriculum," Lauren and Daniel Resnick (1992) argued that although multiple-choice testing comported well with the behaviorist psychology of earlier decades, advances in the cognitive psychology of school subjects had revealed its profound limitations. They argued that behaviorism embraced assumptions of decomposability and decontextualization – complex performances were to be broken into small units, to be practiced and mastered individually, stripped of any meaningful context. Multiple-choice testing likewise focused on mastery of small, isolated bits of knowledge or skill, attested by darkened circles on a multiple-choice answer sheet. Echoing Aikin's critique from fifty years earlier, Resnick and Resnick (1992) saw multiple-choice testing driving curriculum and instruction toward dull, meaningless learning activities. Worse, the pedagogy these tests encouraged was leaving students ill prepared for "adaptive functioning in a technically complex environment" (Resnick and Resnick 1992, 38).

Their proposed policy response was compelling. The demands of the twenty-first century workplace made it imperative that schooling move toward teaching "the thinking curriculum," so new kinds of tests were required for "assessing the thinking curriculum." These new tests – performance assessments – must be created to harness the power of measurement-driven instruction for good rather than for ill. These tests would be engaging. They would be of intrinsic instructional value. They would let students show what they really could do and thus, perhaps, reduce the persistent achievement gaps seen with multiple-choice tests. Echoing another idea from the Eight-Year Study, the Resnicks viewed teacher involvement in the creation, administration, and scoring of performance assessments as a powerful form of in-service training, educating teachers about new kinds of instructional activities, opening their eyes to their students' unrecognized capabilities, and thereby raising their expectations for student performance.

Another proponent, Grant Wiggins (1992), challenged educators to create and use "tests worth taking." Assessment tasks should be authentic and meaningful. Scoring should be standards-based, anchored to "genuine benchmarks, not arbitrary cutscores or provincial schools norms" (Wiggins 1992, 27). Such tasks would measure "higher order thinking." They would be complex, nonalgorithmic, often yielding multiple solutions to be evaluated with respect to multiple, sometimes conflicting criteria, calling for nuanced judgment and interpretation. Wiggins (1992, 33) echoed the message that "good teaching is inseparable from good assessing" and nicely recapitulated Resnick and Resnick's (1992) policy proposal with his observation that "assessment reform is the Trojan horse of real school reform."

The performance assessment movement quickly faded when "political rhetoric" met "measurement reality" (Shavelson, Baxter, and Pine 1992). The kinds of tasks Resnick and Resnick (1992) or Wiggins (1992) envisioned were simply incompatible with the constraints inherent in large-scale, high-stakes testing programs (Haertel 1999a). The lack of standardization that was part of the appeal of performance assessments meant that these tasks provided much less reliable information per unit of testing time. They were expensive to build and score. Hastily constructed tests were often of poor quality (Baxter and Glaser 1998), so disillusionment set in. Like the Progressive Education Association in the 1930s, the advocates of performance assessment in the 1990s failed to launch a revolution.

OTL AND STANDARDS-BASED REFORM: THE NO CHILD LEFT BEHIND ACT OF 2001

Since the mid-1970s, public policy makers have placed increasing reliance on tests as public policy tools to promote education reform. Under NCLB, rigorous academic content standards are coupled with increased use of tests for enhanced educational accountability. Indeed, unlike the use of MCT, in which high-stakes testing came to be seen as *requiring* OTL, the framers of NCLB embrace a conception in which accountability testing *creates* OTL (McDonnell 2004). NCLB requires states and local schools to increase substantially their use of tests as part of an initiative to improve student achievement and educator accountability and to increase reliance upon "scientifically based evidence." The law also advances market-based parental choice approaches, which generally rely on standardized test scores to provide a common metric by which consumers can compare the "success" of schools. In addition to those concerns, the new law requires inclusion in testing programs of students with disabilities and children with limited English proficiency – students who present a unique set of educational and public policy issues.

The state of research evidence concerning OTL and the content of curriculum and instruction are particularly significant, given new federal requirements about the evidentiary grounding required for federally sponsored education programs. Federal policy makers have articulated some relevant, and controversial, requirements – without resolving OTL issues – about how disputes over education programs should be resolved. In addition to its other mandates, NCLB requires scientifically based evidence to substantiate education programs and privileges experimental methodologies in the generation of that evidence. It also requires adherence in federally funded programs to relevant professional and technical standards. Prior to the passage of NCLB, for testing and assessment programs, courts widely recognized that the relevant technical standards are the *Standards for Educational and Psychological Testing* (AERA, APA, NCME 1999). These *Standards* require that in high-stakes educational achievement testing, there must be an assurance that a test covers only content and skills students have had an opportunity to learn (AERA, APA, NCME 1999, 146). The 1999 *Standards* reflect the federal constitutional standard articulated in *Debra P*. Standard 13.5 requires:

When test results substantially contribute to making decisions about student promotion or graduation, there should be evidence that the test adequately covers only the specific or generalized content and skills that students have had an opportunity to learn.

The "Comment" to that Standard further explains that:

Students, parents, and educational staff should be informed of the domains on which the students will be tested, the nature of the item types, and the standards for mastery. Reasonable efforts should be made to document the provision of instruction on tested content and skills, even though it may not be possible or feasible to determine the specific content of instruction for every student.

Proponents of test-driven education reform assert that testing clarifies intended learning outcomes and expected performance levels, focuses instructional resources on valued content and learning outcomes, and encourages and rewards greater effort on the part of educators and students. It is argued that test-driven reform will improve student motivation by setting clear expectations and reduce inequities by indicating how to target resources more effectively. There is also the hope that test-driven reform will encourage the use of proven instructional strategies to increase achievement. Thus, this current model for measurement-driven reform touches upon OTL in each of its three broad aspects: instructional content, resources, and processes. All three are controversial.

Critics of test-driven education reform are concerned that not all students will have access to the educational opportunities needed to succeed in these systems or that instruction may be narrowed to the form and content of the test itself, so that rising scores offer an illusion of improvement even as achievement across a broader domain of intended learning outcomes remains flat or declines (Koretz 2005). It is argued that test-driven reform will narrow instruction to only what is directly tested and drive instruction toward the use of worksheets and scripted curricula, discouraging exploration, discussion, creativity, and critical thinking. Critics fear that the reform will undermine motivation by making high test scores the de facto goal of education. There is a concern that test-driven reform will perpetuate inequities by substituting symbolic action for increased resources.

Recent research on the implementation of the new reforms (Carnoy, Elmore, and Siskin 2003; Cohen and Hill 2001; Elmore 2004) and comments from policy makers indicate growing recognition that lack of capacity on the part of educators is the Achilles' heel (Elmore 2004, 118) of test-driven, standards-based accountability and that OTL for educators themselves will be a critical variable in the provision of enhanced educational opportunity for students. According to this interpretation, capacity is the result of a complex relationship between teacher knowledge of content, teacher pedagogic knowledge, internal shared norms and values to educate all students to ambitious goals of attainment, distributed leadership through the school system, and sufficient resources in the form of time, money, information, materials, and external support (Carnoy, Elmore, and Siskin 2003).

Even where there is agreement among proponents and opponents as to some particular effect of high-stakes testing, for example, a reallocation of time away from discussion of mathematical ideas toward practice solving algebra problems, there may be disagreement as to whether that effect is good or bad. For both proponents and critics of test-driven education reform, there are some fundamental assumptions about the relationship between tests and instruction and about the nature of intended learning outcomes of formal schooling. These contrasting assumptions and presumptive outcomes of measurement-driven reform can be framed in terms of high-stakes tests' influences on students' OTL.

THE FUTURE OF TESTING AND OTL

Schools exist to offer opportunities to learn; the study of OTL is the study of schooling. In turn, OTL is linked to every form of assessment in education, and especially so when high-stakes consequences for individuals, institutions, or educational systems are tied to test performance. The federal No Child Left Behind Act of 2001 mandates accountability testing to promote educational reform in each state receiving federal financial aid for elementary and secondary education. Many state laws also require student testing to determine promotion and high school graduation. Curriculum-embedded and classroom assessments of students are still used in schools. Individual testing also continues as a means to assist determinations of special educational placements, eligibility for special programs, and English language proficiency. Most states require teacher licensure and certification testing either for all candidates for a credential or for those seeking a credential through some alternate route, either as a result of state initiatives or because NCLB requires it in order for teachers to be deemed "highly qualified." In each area of assessment practice, the linking of assessment and OTL goes both ways – each form of testing can influence OTL. Conversely, the valid interpretation of test data of any kind is conditioned by the relevant antecedent experiences of the examinees.

The definition of OTL in the *Debra P.* decision and subsequent school testing lawsuits represents a very limited, traditional view of teaching and learning and vastly shortchanges even that traditional view. This traditional view calls for exposure to particular content knowledge to allow a student to fulfill a responsibility to identify important content knowledge, store it, and retrieve it when tested (see Gee, this volume, chapter 4). Yet even traditional perspectives on learning recognized that OTL required more than exposure to content. Also, while learning opportunities for some high-risk students never well served by our schools were no doubt enhanced by the articulation of an obligation to provide OTL so conceived, the "teach to the test" response represented a much narrower view of teaching and learning than the nation's schoolchildren deserved.

As our understanding of the conditions for effective teaching and learning have evolved, so too has the opportunity for the legal system to apply a richer and broader set of requirements for acceptable approaches to the provision of educational services. When the federal constitution left to the states the power to define and govern access to elementary and secondary education, much latitude for local variation was created. At various points in our nation's history, those local options were sometimes exercised in astonishing ways, such as when some Southern states or school districts chose to eliminate entirely access for all to an opportunity to learn by closing down their systems of public education in the face of federal requirements to desegregate schools (Kirp et al. 2001). Now, however, all states have adopted state constitutional provisions requiring public education and, in many of the states, requiring that education meet particular standards of quality. As a result, many states have a state constitutional requirement to afford students an "adequate education." Court disputes over the definition of adequate education and the mechanisms for ensuring it is provided involve politically heated, scientifically difficult, and long-running quests to ascertain, first, how to define an adequate education and second, how and whether to ensure that there are the financing and the means to afford an adequate education. In some instances, courts became involved in defining the necessary conditions for schools, ordering that legislatures take action to meet the constitutional mandates to educate. In these circumstances, courts have begun to define a new legal approach to OTL in which there is recognition of a broad set of conditions and environmental factors essential for learning, including teacher and administrator quality, access to high-quality early childhood education, and so forth, reaching beyond a content-based conception of OTL to embrace resources and perhaps even classroom process.

This recent generation of court cases takes the definition of OTL well beyond the rudimentary and insufficient standards articulated in the *Debra P.* litigation of the early 1980s. A fair opportunity to learn no longer includes only exposure to content, provision of remedial education, and educator certification of exposure to content. It may involve a rich definition of what it means to be an educated person, such as this description of the desired outcomes of a public school education originally adopted in Kentucky and now used in several state courts and under consideration by several state legislatures. The Kentucky court declared that at a minimum,

education must have as its goal to provide each and every child with at least the seven following capacities:

(1) sufficient oral and written communication skills to enable students to function in a complex and rapidly changing civilization;

(2) sufficient knowledge of economic, social, and political systems to enable the student to make informed choices;

(3) sufficient understanding of governmental processes to enable the student to understand the issues that affect his or her community, state, and nation;

(4) sufficient self-knowledge and knowledge of his or her mental and physical wellness;

(5) sufficient grounding in the arts to enable each student to appreciate his or her cultural and historical heritage;

(6) sufficient training or preparation for advanced training in either academic or vocational fields so as to enable each child to choose and pursue life work intelligently; and

(7) sufficient levels of academic or vocational skills to enable public school students to compete favorably with their counterparts in surrounding states, in academics or in the job market. (*Rose v. Council for Better Education*, 1989, 212)

As courts have worked further to refine their specification of what a system of education must do to provide an adequate educational opportunity, the embrace of a definition of the outcomes of education of the type used in the *Rose* case reflects an approach that comes closer to adopting a perspective on education, more consistent with those of socioculturalists, using a richer understanding of the broad range of factors associated with providing an effective learning environment. Nonetheless, these evolving legal standards have far to go in addressing the broad range of issues described by the socioculturalists, and even further in finding ways to support the enactment of these visions. And, not even a majority of the states have embraced the notion that states have an obligation to provide an adequate education.

The more recent school finance court decisions, however, begin to address the question of learning opportunities in different ways, as judges and legislators are influenced by the now widely available test results. In the most recent case in Massachusetts, for example, the courts' consideration of issues related to OTL took into account such issues as funding, access to preschool and special education services, the state articulation of mandatory curriculum frameworks for local schools, and teacher quality. However, the use of a state accountability system based on test scores was persuasive evidence to the state's highest court that the state was meeting its obligation to provide education, even if there was persistent low performance on the tests for the most at-risk populations of students in the most poorly funded schools (*Hancock v. Driscoll* 2005; Pullin 2007). This suggests an assumption that the use of accountability testing presumes the existence of an OTL sufficient to meet at least the judges' notions of what must be done to adequately educate children.

What began many decades ago as an effort on the part of educators and social scientists to perfect the relationship between tests and curriculum has, in the twenty-first century, become an increasingly complex relationship between OTL and assessment, driven by the demands of external policy makers but often uninformed by recent work by social scientists and educators, some of which is represented in this volume.

In this era of NCLB implementation and aggressive state and local level education reform initiatives using testing, there is a particular imperative to more fully understand the relationship between OTL and assessment. Social scientists must further refine their conceptual framing of OTL as well as their methodologies for the study of OTL. The intersection of OTL and assessment has rich potential for cross-disciplinary collaboration. At the same time, policy researchers and policy makers must further explore their assumptions about the relationship between assessment and OTL. As the stakes associated with educational testing continue to increase for students, educators, and educational institutions, it is imperative to assess more closely the alignments among tests, instruction, and intended learning outcomes. The measurement of OTL is consequential for individual students seeking access to meaningful educational opportunities and for groups of students, be they ethnic or language minorities, students from families with low socioeconomic status, immigrant children, or children with disabilities (Guiton and Oakes 1995; Pullin 2002). A clearer understanding of how to ensure OTL in all its aspects is of paramount importance for educators, who struggle to provide appropriate services for students under the pressures of declining resources and increasing testing. Finally, a closer look at issues of testing and OTL will provide public policy makers with a better understanding of the complexities embedded in the effort to improve educational opportunities for all students.

References

American Educational Research Association, American Psychological Association, and National Council of Measurement in Education. 1999. *Standards for educational and psychological testing*. Washington, D.C.: American Educational Research Association.

Baxter, G. P. and R. Glaser. 1998. Investigating the cognitive complexity of science assessments. *Educational Measurement: Issues and Practice* 17(3): 37–45.

Black, P. and D. Wiliam. 1998. Assessment and classroom learning. *Assessment in Education* 5: 7–74.

Bloom, B. 1971. *Mastery learning*. New York: Holt, Rinehart, and Winston.

Brown v. Board of Education of Topeka Kansas, 347 U.S. 483 (1954).

Carnegie Forum on Education and the Economy. 1986. *A nation prepared: Teachers for the 21st century* (Report of the Task Force on Teaching as a Profession). Washington, D.C.: The Forum.

Carnoy, M., R. Elmore, and L. Siskin. 2003. *The new accountability: High schools and high stakes testing*. New York: RoutledgeFalmer.

Chapman, P. D. 1988. *Schools as sorters: Lewis M. Terman, applied psychology, and the intelligence testing movement, 1890–1930*. New York: New York University Press.

Cohen, D. K. and H. C. Hill. 2001. *Learning policy: When state education reform works*. New Haven: Yale University Press.

Cohen, D., S. Raudenbush, and D. Ball. 2003. Resources, instruction, and research. *Educational Evaluation and Policy Analysis* 25: 119–42.

Debra P. v. Turlington, 644 F. 2d 397 (5th Cir. 1981).

Elmore, R. 2002. Testing trap. *Harvard Magazine* 105: 35–37.

Elmore, R. 2004. *School reform from the inside out: Policy, practice, and performance*. Cambridge: Harvard Education Press.

Frederiksen, N. 1984. The real test bias: Influences of testing on teaching and learning. *American Psychologist* 39: 193–202.

Fuhrman, S., ed. 2001. *From the capitol to the classroom: Standards-based reform in the states (Yearbook of the National Society for the Study of Education)*. Chicago: National Society for the Study of Education.

Glaser, R. 1963. Instructional technology and the measurement of learning outcomes: Some questions. *American Psychologist* 18: 519–21.

Glaser, R. 1994. Criterion-referenced tests: Part I. Origins. *Educational Measurement: Issues and Practice* 13(4): 9–11.

Guiton, G. and J. Oakes. 1995. Opportunity to learn and conceptions of educational equality. *Educational Evaluation and Policy Analysis* 17: 323–36.

Haertel, E. H. 1989. Student achievement tests as tools of educational policy: Practices and consequences. In *Test policy and test performance: Education, language, and culture,* edited by B. R. Gifford, 35–63. Boston: Kluwer Academic Publishers.

Haertel, E. H. 1999a. Performance assessment and educational reform. *Phi Delta Kappan* 80: 662–66.

Haertel, E. H. 1999b. Validity arguments for high-stakes testing: In search of the evidence. *Educational Measurement: Issues and Practice* 18(4): 5–9.

Haertel, E. H. and R. C. Calfee. 1983. School achievement: Thinking about what to test. *Journal of Educational Measurement* 20: 119–32.

Haertel, E. H. and J. L. Herman. 2005. A historical perspective on validity arguments for accountability testing. In *Uses and misuses of data for educational accountability and improvement (yearbook of the National Society for the Study of Education),* issue 2, edited by J. L. Herman and E. H. Haertel, 1–34. Malden, Mass.: Blackwell.

Hancock v. Driscoll, 443 Mass. 428, 822 N.E. 2d 1134 (2005).

Heubert, J. P. and R. M. Hauser, eds. 1999. *High Stakes: Testing for tracking, promotion, and graduation.* Washington, D.C.: National Academy Press.

Kirp, D., M. Yudof, B. Levin, and R. Moran. 2001. *Educational policy and the law* (4th ed.). Stamford, Conn.: Wadsworth.

Kirst, M. W. and C. Mazzeo. 1996. The rise, fall, and rise of state assessment in California, 1993–96. *Phi Delta Kappan* 78: 319–23.

Koretz, D. 2005. Alignment, high stakes, and the inflation of test scores. In *uses and misuses of data for educational accountability and improvement (yearbook of the National Society for the Study of Education),* issue 2, edited by J. L. Herman and E. H. Haertel, 99–118. Malden, Mass.: Blackwell.

Lange, P. C., ed. 1967. *Programmed instruction in the schools: An application of programming principles in "individually prescribed" instruction (Yearbook of the National Society for the Study of Education),* issue 2, edited by H. G. Richey, M. M. Coulson, and P. C. Lange. Chicago: University of Chicago Press.

Linn, R. L. 1993. Educational assessment: expanded expectations and challenges. *Educational Evaluation and Policy Analysis* 15: 1–16.

Linn, R. L. 2000. Assessments and accountability. *Educational Researcher* 29(2): 4–16.

Madaus, G., ed. 1983. *The Courts, validity, and minimum competency testing.* Boston: Kluwer-Nijhoff.

Madaus, G. F. 1988. The influence of testing on the curriculum. In *Critical issues in curriculum (Yearbook of the National Society for the Study of Education),* issue 1, edited by K. J. Rehage, I. Westbury, and A. C. Purves, 83–121. Chicago: University of Chicago Press.

Madaus, G. F., D. Stufflebeam, and M. S. Scriven. 1983. Program evaluation: An historical overview. In *Evaluation models: Viewpoints on educational and human services evaluation,* edited by G. F. Madaus, M. S. Scriven, and D. Stufflebeam, 3–22. Norwell, Mass.: Kluwer Academic Publishers.

McDonnell, L. M. 1995. Opportunity to learn as a research concept and a policy instrument. *Educational Evaluation and Policy Analysis* 17: 305–22.

McDonnell, L. M. 2004. *Politics, persuasion, and educational testing.* Cambridge: Harvard University Press.

McGuinn, P. 2006. *No child left behind and the transformation of federal education policy, 1965–2005.* Lawrence: The University Press of Kansas.

McNeil, L. M. 2000. *Contradictions of school reform: The educational costs of standardized testing.* New York: Routledge.

Melnick, S. and D. Pullin. 2000, September/October. Can you take dictation? Prescribing teacher quality through testing. *Journal of Teacher Education* 51: 262–75.

Messick, S. 1984. The psychology of educational measurement. *Journal of Educational Measurement* 21: 215–37.

Mislevy, R. J. 1996. Test theory reconceived. *Journal of Educational Measurement* 33: 379–416.

Moss, P. A., D. Pullin, J. P. Gee, and E. N. Haertel. 2005. The idea of testing: psychometric and sociocultural perspectives. *Measurement: Interdisciplinary Research and Perspectives* 3: 63–83.

National Commission on Excellence in Education (NCEE). 1983. *A nation at risk: The imperative for educational reform.* Washington, D.C.: U.S. Government Printing Office.

National Council on Education Standards and Testing (NCEST). 1992. Raising standards for American education: A report to Congress, the Secretary of Education, the National Education Goals Panel, and the American people. Washington, D.C.: U.S. Government Printing Office.

National Research Council. 2001. *Testing teacher candidates: the role of licensure tests in improving teacher quality,* edited by K. Mitchell et al. Washington, D.C.: National Academy Press.

Office of Technology Assessment. 2002. *Testing in American schools: Asking the right questions* (OTA-SET-519). Washington, D.C.: U.S. Government Printing Office.

Popham, W. J. 1994. The instructional consequences of criterion-referenced clarity. *Educational Measurement: Issues and Practice* 13, no. 4: 15–18, 30.

Porter, A. 1995. The uses and misuses of opportunity-to-learn standards. *Educational Researcher* 24: 21–27.

Porter, A. 2002. Measuring the content of instruction: uses in research and practice. *Educational Researcher* 30: 3–14.

Porter, A. and J. Smithson. 2001. Are content standards being implemented in the classroom? A methodology and some tentative answers. In *From the Capitol to the classroom: Standards-based reform in the States (yearbook of the National Society for the Study of Education)*, issue 2, edited by S. H. Fuhrman, 60–80. Chicago: University of Chicago Press.

Pullin, D. 2002. Testing individuals with disabilities: Reconciling social science and social policy. In *Assessing Individuals With Disabilities*, edited by R. Ekstrom and D. Smith, 11–32. Washington, D.C.: American Psychological Association.

Pullin, D. 2004, Sept./Oct. Accountability, autonomy, and academic freedom in educator preparation programs. *Journal of Teacher Education* 55: 300–12.

Pullin, D. 2007, Winter. Ensuring an adequate education: Opportunity to learn, law and social science. *Boston College Third World Law Journal* 27: 83–130.

Resnick, L. B. and D. P. Resnick. 1992. Assessing the thinking curriculum: New tools for educational reform. In *Changing Assessments: Alternative Views of Aptitude,*

Achievement, and Instruction, edited by B. Gifford and M. O'Connor, 37–75. Norwell, Mass.: Kluwer.

Rose v. Council for Better Education. 790 S.W. 2d 186 (Kentucky Supreme Court, 1989).

Sax, G. and L. S. Collet. 1968. An empirical comparison of the effects of recall and multiple-choice tests on student achievement. *Journal of Educational Measurement* 5: 169–73.

Shavelson, R. J., G. P. Baxter, and J. Pine. 1992. Performance assessment: political rhetoric and measurement reality. *Educational Researcher* 21(4): 22–27.

Shepard, L. A. 2000. The role of assessment in a learning culture. *Educational Researcher* 29(7): 4–14.

Smith, M. and J. O'Day. 1993. Systemic school reform. In *Designing Coherent Education Policy*, edited by S. Fuhrman. San Francisco: Jossey-Bass.

Smith, E. R., R. W. Tyler, and the Evaluation Staff. 1942. *Appraising and Recording Student Progress*, vol. III. The Adventure in American Education Series. New York: Harper and Bros.

Spillane, J. 2004. *Standards deviation: How schools misunderstand educational policy*. Cambridge: Harvard University Press.

Terman, L. M. 1919. *The intelligence of school children*. Boston: Houghton Mifflin.

Tyler, R. W. 1949. *Basic principles of curriculum and instruction*. Chicago: University of Chicago Press.

Vinovskis, M. A. 1999. *History and educational policymaking*. New Haven: Yale University Press.

Wang, J. 1998. Opportunity to learn: The impacts and policy implications. *Educational Evaluation and Policy Analysis* 20: 137–56

Wiggins, G. 1992. Creating tests worth taking. *Educational Leadership* 49(8): 26–33.

Wilson, S. 2003. *California dreaming: Reforming mathematics education*. New Haven: Yale University Press.

3 A Sociological Perspective on Opportunity to Learn and Assessment

Hugh Mehan

OVERVIEW

This chapter reviews the major conceptions of opportunities to learn and assessment within the discipline of sociology. The traditional view of schooling as a meritocratic sorting device is contrasted with (1) the view of schooling that asserts schools (either wittingly or unwittingly) serve to reproduce the existing hierarchies of privilege; (2) the point of view that proposes that schools, peers, and families mediate the relations between structural constraints and human action; and (3) a resurgent democratic conception of schooling.

In contrast to the meritocratic conception of opportunity to learn (OTL) and assessment that asserts schools provide students with avenues to compete as individuals for valued resources, I present evidence that questions whether students have equal access to valued educational and cultural resources. This leads to defining OTL in terms of establishing the conditions within schools for the open flow of ideas and solving problems that are connected to the "real world." Multiple measures of students' academic performance – especially those such as portfolios and exhibitions – that assess learning in authentic contexts (see Gee, this volume, and Mislevy, this volume) are preferred over standardized tests as assessment tools.

Social equality is one of our nation's fundamental ideals. In the educational realm, this ideal has generally been expressed in terms of *an equality of opportunity to learn*. Regardless of the circumstances of one's background (e.g., social class, race, ethnicity, gender, or sexual orientation), members of our society are presumed to be provided with an opportunity to improve their station in life by doing well in school. Although social equality is an ideal in American society, the contribution of the school to achieving this ideal is a matter of debate. *Do* schools make a difference in people's lives by giving them opportunities to learn and therefore succeed in life? Or do schools unwittingly perpetuate inequality by providing greater opportunities to learn to certain segments of society and fewer opportunities to other segments? Or are the background characteristics associated with people – their race, class, and language status – more powerful determinants of success later in life than are the opportunities to learn provided to them in schools?

THE TRADITIONAL VIEW: THE SCHOOL IS A MERITOCRATIC SORTING DEVICE PROVIDING EQUAL OPPORTUNITIES TO LEARN

There has long been an egalitarian political and educational ideology in this country that views people's chances for success in life as primarily the result of a combination of talent, personal achievement, individual effort, and hard work. This "achievement ideology" derives in part from the British empiricist tenet that the individual's mind is a *tabula rasa* at birth, to be etched by learned experiences, unfettered by innate limitations or capabilities. Jefferson's bold assertion that, because of its fragility, a democratic society requires a well-educated citizenry has been reinforced by Horace Mann, John Dewey, and their followers' advice to develop schools that foster individuals' pursuit of individual social, economic, and political ends that will simultaneously benefit society at large. In general, the egalitarian perspective is optimistic with regard to the possibilities of change in people's lives. It acknowledges the influences of heredity, class, race, and language status but claims these factors do not limit opportunities to learn, human development, or social mobility.

Schools Provide Equal Opportunities to Learn

An important sociological manifestation of this ideology is the "functionalist" view of the school. In such presentations (e.g., Davis and Moore 1945; Dreeben 1968; Parsons 1959; Turner 1960) developed primarily in this country's post–World War II euphoria, the society is depicted as a system of positions or statuses that are roughly equivalent to occupations. These statuses are arranged in a hierarchical order in terms of their importance for the preservation and maintenance of society. The positions that are most important and require special, often abstract, skills for their performance are bestowed with the most prestige and rewards. The positions that are the least important and require only manual skills are accorded far fewer rewards and less prestige.

The occupational structure operates efficiently when the duties associated with the functionally most important positions are performed by the most qualified people. This matching of talent to positions cannot be left to social inheritance; that would waste precious talent, the functionalist argument continues. People without the requisite talent but born into high-class families or with the correct social connections might wind up in key positions, while people with important talent but born into low-income families or despised social groups might find themselves in less important positions. Therefore, efficient societies must have mechanisms to select and sort people into the appropriate occupational slots.

School has been the most conspicuous institution to fulfill the function of matching talent to positions in industrialized, capitalist societies.[1] Schools sort students by giving them the opportunities to learn cognitive skills – those needed for problem solving, logical inference, computation, and abstract reasoning. These general skills presumably will help students do well in successive layers of the school system and the world of work, but they are not intended to be the particular skills required for a certain job. The development of job-specific skills is to be left to employers after they hire employees.

The functionalist view of the role of school in society is grounded in the human capital conception of work (Becker 1975; Karabel and Halsey 1977). "Human capital" is a rather vague term referring to cognitive skills and capacity to learn. Employers are willing to pay more for the service of people with greater amounts of human capital because productivity is assumed to increase with the quality of labor. The school plays two main functions for developing human capital: providing students with opportunities to learn cognitive skills and assessing students' acquisition of them.

The view that status is, and should be, attained on the basis of hard work, effort and merit, and not passed on from one generation to another through inheritance, is intrinsic to the American egalitarian credo that I call here "the achievement ideology." It is therefore the responsibility of the school to provide all children with the equal opportunity to acquire the cognitive skills necessary for the pursuit of improved status – or at least protect against the loss of acquired status. In U.S. schools, the operation of a "contest mobility system" (Turner 1960), in which virtually everyone has a chance to compete for important positions, is said to foster equality of educational and economic opportunity. Competition is achieved by delaying and minimizing the for occupational positions as long as possible and building forgiveness into the system. Although people will eventually end up in different positions, they are all provided with equivalent opportunities to learn cognitive skills. Multiple pathways through the educational system provided through such mechanisms as GED programs and programs that encourage students to transfer from community colleges to four-year colleges and universities enable students to have second and even third chances to acquire requisite skills.

Schools Assess Students' Talents and Efforts

In addition to providing all students with equal opportunities to learn, schools perform a second function in industrialized, capitalist societies: They assess students' performance and sort them according to their performance. A stratified workforce, with mental work at the top of the hierarchy and manual labor at the bottom, is a "functional necessity" in industrialized, capitalist societies (Davis and Moore 1945). Doctors, lawyers, and political, business, and military leaders make plans, solve problems, assess profits and losses – all of which is abstract work requiring higher-order thinking skills. Service workers, factory workers, and manual laborers work more with their hands than with their heads – and thus do not require training in higher-order thinking skills. Schools assist the economic sector by sorting students so that they can be placed into the appropriate slots in the workplace. Students who do well in school and advance through the educational system are presumed to be well prepared for positions closer to the top of the economic hierarchy, whereas students who do not do well in school, or who leave early ("drop out"), are seen to be suitable for jobs at the lower end of the hierarchy. Indeed, students who drop out do others a service – because they reduce the competition for the precious few jobs at the top of the hierarchy (Fine 1991; Varenne and McDermott 1998).

This sorting function is facilitated by standardized tests and course grades. Standardized tests are the assessment instrument of choice for assessing students' performance because they solve the problem of subjective and nonuniform teacher evaluation. Uniformly, simply, and neatly applied, standardized tests presumably enable all children to be examined on the "same" material and have their scores compared with national norms and each other.

The use of objective tests and grades in this sorting operation is presumed to be rational and neutral – and hence meritocratic – because it is done on the basis of students' achieved characteristics (effort, hard work), not ascribed characteristics (socioeconomic status, race, gender). Furthermore, because schools are presumably making judgments on students' achievements and not their ascriptions, schools assist students in moving up the socioeconomic "ladder of success."

Summary

In the traditional view of schooling in the United States, OTL is defined in meritocratic, individualistic, and competitive terms. Students have an equal opportunity to learn because they are placed in environments where they can achieve through their effort and hard work. They have the opportunity to compete with peers for precious resources. They are judged on the basis of their individual performance on presumably objective measures such as tests. Athletic metaphors abound in this tradition: Students engage in "competitions" and "races for success." For example: "The contest mobility system is like a sporting event in which many compete for a few recognized prizes. The contest is judged to be fair only if all the players compete on an equal footing. The victory must be one solely on one's own efforts" (Turner 1960, 857).

The achievement ideology undergirding the meritocratic thesis defines educational success as a matter of individual effort and hard work. The corollary of this proposition is that academic failure or difficulty stems from a lack of effort and hard work. That is, placement in the lower rungs of the economic hierarchy is the fault of the individual who did not try hard enough. This mode of legitimating stratification blames individuals for their failure to attain a higher status and deflects attention from the system itself.

CRITICISMS OF THE MERITOCRATIC THESIS

Faith in the meritocratic thesis, which contends that schools provide equal opportunities to learn by granting all students access to cognitive skills, has been shaken in recent years. Many observers[2] have concluded that opportunities to learn are not equally distributed across all students; instead, they vary by race, class, gender, and language status.

Students' Ascribed Characteristics and Academic Achievement

In general, students who live in poor neighborhoods and attend schools with a higher concentration of underrepresented minority and limited English-proficient students score lower on every measure of academic achievement – reading proficiency, high school completion, college participation, and college completion rates. The following is but a sample of measures of academic achievement that differ by the race/ethnicity and social class of students.

Reading Proficiency

Twelve percent of African American students and 39% of white students scored "proficient" on the fourth grade reading test on the 2003 administration of the National Assessment of Educational Progress (Education Trust 2003a, 2003b). This disparity was recapitulated in California: Seventeen percent of Hispanic students, 21% of African American students, and 54% of white students scored "proficient" or "advanced" on the English Language Arts portion of the California Standards test in 2003 (Oakes 2003).

High School Completion, College Going, and College Completion

Twenty-one percent of Latino, 4.3% of Asian/Pacific Islander, 11.7% of African American, and 8.2% of white students aged sixteen to nineteen did not complete high school in 2000 (Census 2002 Supplemental Survey).

The combined verbal and math SAT scores of white students was 1,058, Latino 928, and African American 860 in 2000 (Harvey 2002).

Seventy-seven percent of African Americans, 59.6% of Hispanics, and 82.4% of whites aged eighteen to twenty-four completed high school in 2000 (Harvey 2002).

Sixty-one percent of African American, 53.1% of Hispanic, and 66.9% of white students aged 18 to 24 participate in college in 2000 (Harvey 2002).

Thirty-eight percent of African Americans, 46% of Hispanics, and 59% of whites aged 25 to 29 completed Division I colleges in 2000 (Harvey 2002).

Striking Correlates between Students' Characteristics and Educational Resources

The students who have the greatest scholastic needs are provided with the fewest resources that foster opportunities to learn. Poor, underrepresented minority, and students learning English as a second language are concentrated in schools where there are fewer *material* resources such as course offerings, laboratories, theatres, science, art, music equipment, and textbooks.

Fifty-eight percent of Asian, 46% of white, 40% of African American, 32% of Hispanic, and 28% of American Indian students took four years of English, three years each of social studies and mathematics, and two years of a foreign language in 1998 (NCES 2001).

Four percent of African American, 10% of Hispanic, and 66% of white students took advanced placement (AP) exams nationwide in 2002 (Jerald 2002).

Only 639 students across twelve comprehensive high schools in low-income neighborhoods of the Inglewood, California, school district sat for the AP exams in math and science in 1999, an average of fifty-three per school. Of these, only 117, or an average of fewer than ten exams at each school, achieved a passing score. By contrast, at five of the schools in the district's wealthiest neighborhoods, students took 890 math and science exams, an average of 178 per school. Of these, 629, or an average of 126 per school, earned a passing score (Oakes 2003). The Inglewood findings are recapitulated in San Diego. The four high schools in the poorest San Diego neighborhoods offer a total of seventeen AP courses, whereas the four high schools in San Diego's wealthiest neighborhoods offer fifty-one (Mehan and Grimes 1999). These differences in course offerings and test taking limit the opportunities of low-income students of color to learn.

Teachers who instruct poor, underrepresented minority and English language–learner (ELL) students have the fewest professional qualifications such as credentials and academic degrees: "One out of four secondary classes in core academic subjects (24%) is assigned to a teacher lacking even a college minor in the subject being taught. In the nation's high-poverty schools, that rate skyrockets to over one-third of classes (34%). . . . Similarly, 29% of classes in high-minority schools are assigned to an out-of-field teacher" (Jerald 2002, 4).

Students in high-poverty schools have more than twice the number of new teachers than low-poverty schools. Low-poverty schools have 12% new teachers; high-poverty schools have 26% new teachers (Mehan and Grimes 1999).

Furthermore, teachers in high-poverty schools are more likely to harbor negative attitudes about the ability of poor, underrepresented minority students and English learners to learn and achieve at the highest levels of performance. These negative attitudes become manifest in the subtleties of teacher–student interactions, the form of questions asked, praise or punishment offered, and access to instructional opportunities (Oakes 2003; Wilcox 1982).

Cultural and political processes operating across class, racial, and ethnic lines also constrain equal opportunities to learn. Well-to-do families have greater access to social networks that assist their children in gaining access to those "institutional agents" (Stanton-Salazar 2000; Stanton-Salazar et al. 2000) that assist them in gaining entrance to prestigious preparatory schools or colleges. They invest economic capital in private counselors and test-preparatory services that translate into educational capital and back into economic capital (McDonough 1997). They are better positioned to "game the system" by moving to neighborhoods with "good schools," sending their children to college-preporatory private schools, arranging for special consid-erations on high-stakes tests, defending particular definitions of merit that privilege their position, and the like (Cookson and Persell 1985; Powell 1996).

THE CONTRARIAN VIEW: THE SCHOOL IS A REPRODUCTION MACHINE THAT PERPETUATES SOCIAL INEQUALITIES

Facts like these have lead observers to question the claims that U.S. society is meritocratic and whether school functions as a rational sorting device, preparing students for the world of work based on their achievements. Recall Turner's (1960, 857) injunction about school as a contest mobility system: "The contest is judged to be fair only if all the players compete on an equal footing. The victory must be one solely on one's own efforts." The unequal distribution of educational resources suggests that all students are not com-peting on an equal footing. Students from low-income, ethnic, and language-minority backgrounds are unfairly handicapped in any "race for success" by their race, social class, and language status.

When critics extend this argument to its most extreme form, they say school is not just doing a bad job of sorting kids on the basis of achieve-ment and eventually will improve. They dismiss the possibility of progress in favor of a more radical and pessimistic view: School is not organized to provide equal educational opportunities to all students. Instead, it is pur-posefully organized to reproduce the status hierarchy that currently exists in U.S. society. Research and theorizing on the contribution of the school to the reproduction of inequality falls loosely into two main groups: one that emphasizes economic factors and one that emphasizes cultural factors in the reproduction of inequality.

The Reproduction of Inequality by Economic Means

One group of "reproduction theorists" (e.g., Bowles and Gintis 1976; Carnoy 1974; Wilcox 1982) interpret the social facts of unequal opportunities I sum-marized above in terms of orthodox Marxism blended with ideas from struc-tural/functionalism. For them, the core of the matter is the "the capitalist process of production ... [It] produces not only surplus value, but it also produces and reproduces the capitalist relation itself; on the one hand, the capitalist, on the other hand, the wage laborer" (Marx 1867/1976, 724). This "capitalist relation" is established, Bowles and Gintis claim, by the correspondence established between the organization of work and the organization of schooling. Schools prepare the sons and daughters of the elite to ascend to their place at the top of the economic hierarchy and to train the sons and daughters of workers to accept their lowly places in the economic hierarchy by purposefully offering them a differentiated curriculum.

Exposure to this differentiated curriculum is facilitated by neighborhood segregation and tracking within schools. When children attend neighborhood schools, children from workers' families and those from the elite are naturally separated. In schools that integrate students from different ethnic or social class backgrounds, students from low-income or ethnic-minority backgrounds are more likely to be assigned to low-ability groups within classrooms, vocational tracks, or special education programs, whereas students from more well-to-do backgrounds or white (and Asian) students are more likely to be placed in high-ability groups, college-preparatory classes, or gifted and talented (GATE) programs (Cicourel and Mehan 1985; Oakes 1985/2005).

Invidiously inherent in the differential exposure to material resources afforded by tracking systems is the recapitulation of the relations of authority that exist between manager and worker in the relations of authority between teacher and students (Wilcox 1982). Students in schools in working-class neighborhoods, low-ability groups, or vocational tracks are taught docility, rule following, passivity, and obedience to external authority. With fewer educational materials and poorly prepared teachers, they receive shallow and superficial instruction. Individuality and creativity are suppressed in favor of conformance to drill-and-practice rhythms and routines – which are just the skills needed in the majority of occupations in American society that require a passive and compliant labor force to perform jobs that demand little autonomy and responsibility. By contrast, students in schools in well-to-do neighborhoods or college-preparatory tracks are taught to work at their own pace, to make intelligent choices among alternatives, and to internalize and even generate norms rather than follow externally constraining ones. With rich educational materials and better prepared teachers, they receive challenging and rigorous instruction. The problem solving and higher-order thinking skills they develop will serve them well in professions or positions at or near the top of businesses.

This line of research dismisses the achievement ideology that says students can achieve to their capacity because they have been provided with an equal opportunity to learn in favor of a thesis that schools mystify people by convincing them that their success – or their failure – is a matter of their own doing. The legitimatization of the capitalist order requires that the population be convinced that the people in positions of power deserve to be there; likewise, people in lowly positions have reason to accept their fate. To make sense of students or schools labeled as "failing," we need "successful" students and schools to serve as point of contrast. "Legitimately identified success is made the ground against which failure stands out as 'the problem'" (Fine 1991; Varenne and McDermott 1998, 109). To legitimate a meritocracy, students are taught that people achieve success and earn rewards by trying hard and expending effort; so, too, they are taught that people achieve failure by not trying hard or expending effort.

Redefining Opportunities to Learn in Terms of the Resources Needed to Learn

This line of research, which calls our attention to the unequal distribution of educational resources in American education, has been incorporated into legal and political arguments attempting to redefine the criteria for assessing educational equality to include the *conditions* for learning. The Supreme Court decision in *Brown v. Board of Education* (1954) established the "fundamental importance of education" in American society because it highlighted the relationship between education and key social outcomes: citizenship, the inculcation of cultural values, and individuals' economic and social opportunities.

Since *Brown*, we have seen a flood of educational opportunity policies from the government and the courts, including school desegregation, compensatory programs, and special assistance for language minority and special education students (see Pullin, this volume). The so-called War on Poverty created programs such as Head Start and compensatory education to equalize opportunities for poor children. Public Law 94–142 required schools to develop "individual educational plans" for special education students and place them in the "least restrictive educational environment." In 1974, the U.S. Supreme Court decided in *Lau v. Nichols* that schools must provide special assistance to students whose first language is not English. The supreme courts in a number of states have ruled that state school finance systems that provide less money to schools that serve poor students are unconstitutional. Title VI of the Elementary and Secondary Education Act challenged the legality of ability grouping in racially mixed schools.

Also since *Brown*, a number of lawsuits have been filed that assert states are legally responsible for ensuring that all children in their jurisdiction have

access to the "bare essentials required of a free and common school education" – trained teachers, current textbooks, and adequate and safe facilities
(Rosenbaum et al. 2000b, 6 [quoted in Powers 2004]; see also Oakes 2002;
Rosenbaum 2000a). These cases argue that disparities in these educational
resources are fundamentally unfair. *Williams v. State of California* is one case
that reframed OTL to include the conditions of education. The plaintiffs
successfully petitioned the court to "order the State to develop a system that
prevents, detects, and cures unequal access to basic educational necessities"
(Rosenbaum et al. 2002, 324 [quoted in Powers 2004]). The lawsuit focused
on three specific conditions within schools and classrooms: the distribution
of credentialed teachers, the condition of facilities, and the quality and supply
of textbooks.

By focusing on "how dollars are actually used within classrooms and
schools to produce desirable educational outcomes" (Grubb and Goe 2002,
5), the *Williams* case and other legal challenges both affirm the promise of
equal educational opportunity that is at the heart of the *Brown* decision and
transform it by demanding the material redress of the deep inequities in the
distribution of educational resources in public education (Powers 2004).

Redefining Assessment: Using Multiple Measures

Because of their presumable objectivity, standardized tests have become the
key tool in the meritocratic vision of schooling. The "standards and accountability" approach that has dominated school reform in recent years gives a
prominent role to standardized tests in order to prod schools and districts
toward excellence. In its present instantiation, the No Child Left Behind Act of
2001 (NCLB) mandates that schools test students in literacy and math yearly
in elementary, middle, and high school. Starting in 2005–06, all schools will
have students tested yearly in literacy and math in grades 3 through 8 and at
least once in high school. If schools do not meet "annual yearly progress" goals
as measured by their students' performance on standardized tests, they are
subject to discipline and punishment. In the most extreme cases, underper-
forming schools that receive Title I funds face restructuring – that is, conver-
sion into charter schools or takeover by the state or a private company.

Supporters of this practice (e.g., Education Trust 2003a, 2003b; Hanushek
and Raymond 2004; Tucker and Codding 1998) call attention to its outcomes-
based definition of equality. Instead of measuring equal educational opportunity in terms of inputs (e.g., federal or state aid), NCLB measures equality in
terms of outputs (students' achievement, primarily on standardized tests).
Furthermore, supporters of NCLB assert that accountability systems give

the public substantial knowledge about the status of their local schools in comparison to state and national standards. In addition to enabling parents to make more informed choices about the education of their children, this knowledge also puts public pressure on low-performing schools to improve their quality or suffer the consequences. Publicity, in fact, has positively benefited low-performing schools. Many have made significant improvements after the spotlight was turned on them (Education Trust 2003a, 2003b). Carnoy and Loeb (2002) report that the greater the sanctions imposed by a state, the better black students (but not Latinos) did on high-stakes tests.[3]

Critics of the practice of using standardized tests in high-stakes accountability regimens (e.g., Amrein and Berliner 2002; Haney 2000; Kohn 2002; McNeill 1998) have lodged a number of complaints. By taking only standardized scores into account, most current accountability systems automatically reward schools in affluent areas because parents' income is highly correlated with students' academic performance (Betts et al. 2000; Haney 2000; Linn 2000; Powers 2004). Although using any single measure of student learning is not good practice, relying on short, timed, multiple-choice tests is especially problematic, critics say, because such tests do not measure the creativity, problem-solving ability, or critical thinking needed for lifelong learning and active participation in a democratic society; worse, they demoralize test takers who are not fluent in English.

From the teachers' point of view, high-stakes tests are not always aligned well with the state standards they are presumed to inform. Teachers, fearful of recriminations, dumb down their curriculum in order to "teach to the test," thereby subtracting precious time from much-needed instruction. For example, Pedulla et al. (2004) report that 76% of teachers facing the highest stakes and 63% of those encountering the lowest sanctions said that mandatory testing led to teaching in ways that contradicted their own ideas of sound educational practice. Worse, they change students' answers to inflate results (Amrein and Berliner 2002; Jacob and Levitt 2003). Teachers also complain that test results are not produced quickly enough to assist them in diagnosing students' learning needs and modifying curriculum and instruction accordingly.

High-stakes testing may have the unintended consequence of doing more harm than good. Its increased use seems to be correlated with increases in the proportion of students who drop out of school and decreases in the proportion who graduate (Amrein and Berliner 2002). The National Academy of Sciences (1999) reports that using tests to retain students in the same grade produces no lasting effects. Retaining students dramatically increases the likelihood that retained students will eventually drop out.

Student assessments, of course, are essential to realizing improvements in schools. One obvious way to hold schools accountable for academic performance without penalizing students unfairly is to measure progress toward a goal of excellence, not just comparing performance against an absolute standard. Another is to place more emphasis on comparisons of performance from year to year rather than from school to school; this practice allows for differences in starting points while maintaining an expectation of improvement for all (Linn 2000). Yet another is to use a portfolio of measures – test scores, students' course work, grades, exhibitions, teachers' recommendations – which is the position advocated by several groups (including the Civil Rights Project, the New York Performance Standards Consortium, the Coalition for Authentic Reform in Massachusetts, the American Evaluation Association, and the American Educational Research Association).[4]

The Reproduction of Inequality by Cultural Means

The "economic reproduction thesis" is not without its critics. It exaggerates the degree of integration between the demands of capitalist elites and the organization of schooling (Apple 1982; Giroux 1988; MacLeod 1987; McLaren 1997); it reduces to the same kind of functionalist argument it presumably replaced (Karabel and Halsey 1977); it does not examine the processes and practices of schooling and other cultural arrangements that reproduce inequalities (Mehan 1992); and it reduces human actors – students, teachers, parents, workers, and employers – to passive role players shaped exclusively by the demands of capital (MacLeod 1987; Mehan 1992).

Bourdieu (1985; Bourdieu and Passeron 1977; Bourdieu and Waquant 1992) has provided a more subtle account of inequality by proposing that cultural elements mediate the relationship between economic structures, schooling, and opportunities to learn. Distinctive cultural knowledge ("cultural capital") is transmitted by the families of each social class. As a consequence, children of the elite classes inherit substantially different cultural knowledge, skills, manners, norms, dress, style of interaction, and linguistic facility than do the sons and daughters of the lower classes. Students from elite classes, by virtue of a certain linguistic and cultural competence acquired through family socialization, are provided with the means of appropriating success in school. Children who read "good books," visit museums, attend symphonies, and go to the theater acquire an ease and familiarity with the dominant culture that the educational system implicitly requires of its students for an opportunity to learn.

Furthermore, the sons and daughters of the elite benefit from their families' connections to important and productive social relationships, or what

Bourdieu (1985) has called "social capital" (cf. Bourdieu and Passeron 1977). Social capital is understood by analogy to economic capital. In the same way that money can be exchanged for valued goods and services, a social relationship can be converted into valued outcomes, such as getting into college or acquiring employment. Participation in highly valued cultural activities also connects elite parents and their sons and daughters with each other, which, in turn, strengthens their ties to privileged social networks. Thus, social capital, like economic capital, can produce profits or benefits in the social world, can be converted into other forms of capital, can accumulate, and can reproduce itself in identical or expanded form (Bourdieu 1985).

In order for students to progress through the educational system and exercise control over their lives and their futures, they need to gain access to social capital, namely social networks. Within these networks are institutionally well-placed adults who either directly or indirectly provide institutional resources and opportunities. These "institutional agents" (Stanton-Salazar 2000; Vásquez, Stanton-Salazar, and Mehan 2000) are usually located within formal bureaucratic contexts (e.g., schools, government agencies, federally sponsored programs, colleges and universities, churches), but they also appear in voluntary civic and political associations and small-scale institutions in the neighborhood. Because of their privileged positions in social networks, institutional agents have the power to give or withhold knowledge about resources and opportunities under the control of their own institution or under the control of neighboring institutions (Vásquez et al. 2000). Thus, the power of institutional agents is derived from their ability to situate youth within resource-rich social networks by actively manipulating the social and institutional forces that determine who shall "make it" and who shall not. From the point of view of the student, then, gaining access to educational opportunities and life choices essentially entails gaining access to social networks.

The lack of success experienced by members of the working class in the occupational structure occurs not just because they lack material and economic resources; they also do not have the appropriate cultural capital and social connections to climb the occupational ladder. Knowledge of and familiarity with dominant uses of language, types of writing, and cultural and literary allusion transmitted through the family are required to gain and maintain access to and mastery of the curriculum (Gee, this volume). Without the right kind of cultural and social capital, students are limited in their chances to learn from educational material and interact profitably with teachers.

In sum, Bourdieu claims that schools contribute to the reproduction of inequality by organizing schooling so it rewards the cultural capital of the elite classes and systematically devalues that of the lower classes. This more nuanced view overcomes the economic determinism in Bowles and Gintis's (1976) position. Yet two problems remain. We are not shown in concrete social situations *how* the school devalues the cultural capital of the lower classes and valorizes the cultural capital of the upper classes. Furthermore, Bourdieu treats students as passive bearers of cultural capital provided by their parents and teachers. Fortunately, recent ethnographic work – some specifically influenced by Bourdieu's theoretical orientation and other work not directly influenced by it – gives us insight into how cultural capital works in specific contexts to provide opportunities to learn for some classes of students but not others.

Students' Contributions to Unequal Opportunities to Learn

A series of articulate ethnographies has begun to establish a balance between structural determinants, cultural processes, and social agency in explaining unequal opportunities to learn. While acknowledging that structural constraints inhibit opportunities to learn, they focus on students' own contributions to their difficulties and the cultural institutions that mediate structure and agency. Apple and Weis (1983), Foley (1990), MacLeod (1987, 1995), Weis (1990), and Willis (1979) revealed working-class youth in the United Kingdom and the United States who developed their deep insights into the economic condition of their social class under capitalism but rejected achievement ideology, subverted teacher and administrator authority, and disrupted classes because they could not envision success. Ogbu (1974, 1987, 1991) extends this analysis to "involuntary immigrants" (African American, Latino, and Native American students) who equate the achievement ideology with "acting white." Eschewing identification with this label, they disengage from the rhythms and rituals of schooling and oppose school rules, respect for external rewards, orderly work habits, and the demand for subordination associated with the achievement ideology. Tragically, their resistance contributes to their lowly status, first in the academic and later in the economic realm.

Although thoughtful critics have cautioned against homogenizing the experiences of working-class and underrepresented minority youth (Carter 2005; Horvat and O'Conner 2006), the agency attributed to struggling students in these ethnographic accounts certainly distinguishes them from the abstract theorizing and determinism of either Bowles and Gintis or Bourdieu. Unlike the students in Bowles and Gintis's rendition, who passively internalize mainstream values of individual achievement, or the students in Bourdieu's theory, who simply carry cultural capital on their backs or in their heads, these working-class students and students of color make real choices in their everyday lives. Although at first glance the working-class students' rebellious behavior, their low academic achievement, and high dropout rates seem to stem from lack of self-discipline, dullness, laziness, or inability to project themselves into the future, the actual causes are quite different. Their unwillingness to participate comes from their assessment of the costs and benefits of playing the game. It is not that schooling will not propel them up the ladder of success; it is that the chances are too slim to warrant the attempt. Given this logic, the oppositional behavior of Macleod's Hallway Hangers, Foley's *vatos*, and Willis's lads is a form of resistance to an institution that cannot deliver on its promise of equal educational opportunity for all students.

Cultural Processes Mediating Structural Constraints and Unequal Opportunities to Learn

Adding the notion of "students' resistance" to the lexicon employed to understand unequal opportunities to learn in schools, then, reveals the contributions social actors make to their own plight. As Ogbu (1991) has said, this line of research shows how victims contribute to their own victimization. A second step in building a comprehensive sociological theory of OTL involves incorporating the cultural processes that mediate the relationship between structural constraints and social agency. Peer groups, parents, and students' perceptions are three such influential mediating cultural processes.

Holland and Eisenhart (1990) found that the college peer group was a crucial cultural process in the construction of the traditional female identity that suppresses the academic identity offered by college. Talented women at "Bradford" and "Southern University" scaled back their aspirations for business and professional careers even though they had expressed high aspirations throughout their lives. The intervening cultural mechanism of the college peer group (a cultural meaning system arranged around romantic love) enticed academically oriented women and reinforced those who saw college only in instrumental terms – as a way to get a job or a husband.

The culture of romance is an escape with sad consequences. Although women used sexual attractiveness to escape dreary lives and avoid bumping up against the glass ceiling, they did not acquire the credentials that college had to offer. Therefore, such women wind up untrained for any good job and assured of economic dependence on men. Ironically, then, women's immersion in romance embedded them more deeply in the culture of male domination and female submission and in doubled work: waged and unwaged (Holland and Eisenhart 1990, 50).

MacLeod (1987, 1995) says that peer group affiliation coupled with parents' actions shaped the differential responses of the Brothers and the Hallway Hangers to similar socioeconomic circumstances. The Brothers thought that racial inequality had been curbed and educational opportunity had been improved because of the Civil Rights movement. Based on their perceptions, they conformed to school norms and pursued the achievement ideology. Family life also mediated. The parents of the Brothers wanted their children to have professional careers. Toward that goal, they exercised control over their sons, setting a relatively early curfew and expecting them to perform to a certain level at school; violations of academic expectations were punished by restrictions, and the punishments stuck. Members of the Brothers' peer group reinforced these actions. The parents of the Hallway Hangers did not act in this manner. They gave their sons free rein and did not monitor schoolwork. Peer groups reinforced parents' actions by not discouraging each others' resistance.

Lareau (1989, 2003; Lareau and Horvat 1999; Lareau and Shumar 1996), who has compared parent–school relations in working-class neighborhoods with those in upper middle–class neighborhoods, provides us with a detailed understanding of the way parents shape students' academic careers and their opportunities to learn while in school. Lareau and other researchers (especially Azmitia and Cooper 2002; Delgado-Gaitan 1990, 1991, 1994; Epstein 1992, 2001; Fine 1991; Reese et al. 1995; Valdez 1996) find that teachers in most schools value and encourage parent involvement, seeing it as a reflection of the concerns parents have for their children. Yet not all parents are able to respond evenly to school expectations for parent involvement. The quantity and quality of parental involvement is linked to the social and cultural resources, including disposable time and income, available to parents in different social class positions. Working-class parents struggle to put food on the table, arrange for housing, and negotiate often unsafe neighborhoods before they even think about responding to teachers' requests to volunteer in the classroom, attend back-to-school nights, or participate in school governance. Middle-income parents, with the occupational skills, prestige, and the all-important variable of *time*, have the resources to manage childcare, transportation, and schedules that enable them to meet with teachers, hire tutors for struggling students, and participate in school-sanctioned activities.

Accompanying this access to resources is a different cultural logic of raising children (Lareau 2003). Middle-income parents drench their children in organized out-of-school activities controlled by parents and other adults. Activities like ballet, soccer, music lessons, and gymnastics dominate the lives of middle-class children – and their parents. By ensuring that their children have these and other cultural experiences, middle-class parents exert a concerted effort in cultivating their children's development. Working-class and poor parents, by contrast, do not consider the concerted development of their children to be an essential part of good parenting. They see child development as the unfolding of a natural process.

The enactment of these cultural logics entail different consequences. Although both working-class and middle-class parents want their children to succeed in school and life, their social location leads them to deploy different strategies to achieve those goals. The strategies deployed by working-class parents – trusting teachers to educate their children, setting clear boundaries between adult and children, allowing children to control their leisure activities – does not enhance their children's opportunities to engage institutional agents (teachers, government officials) with confidence. The strategies deployed by middle-income parents – concerted cultivation of their children and additional exposure to culturally valued activities – does enhance their children's exposure to adults in important social institutions, including teachers in schools. Also, although middle-income parents seem strung out by their often frantic devotion to their children's extracurricular activities (Lareau 2003), it must be acknowledged that these children develop the very sense of confidence, ease, and familiarity with the dominant culture's norms, manners, and ways of speaking that Bourdieu says promotes students' social and cultural capital and, in turn, opportunities to learn and advancement through the educational and economic systems.

In sum, cultural processes within peer groups and families can serve as mediators between structural constraints and students' opportunities to learn. The fact that different groups of students and their parents react differently to objectively similar socioeconomic circumstances reveals that some reproduction theories are overly deterministic and underplay the role of cultural processes. The reaction of the Hallway Hangers and women seduced by the culture of romance vindicate Bourdieu's theory. Confronting a closed opportunity structure, they lowered their aspirations and openly resisted the educational institution and its achievement ideology. Yet neither Bowles and Gintis nor Bourdieu does as well in explaining the actions of the Brothers or women and new immigrants with high academic aspirations. The Brothers experienced the same *habitus* and were exposed to the same hidden curriculum of the school as were the Hallway Hangers, but the Brothers responded to it by eagerly adopting the achievement ideology and maintaining high aspirations for success.

These careful ethnographies, which focus our attention toward everyday life and away from abstract theorizing, forcefully inform us that externally constraining forces, such as those dominating the theories of Bowles and Gintis and Bourdieu and Passeron, when taken alone do not account adequately for the actions of people. Culturally grounded resources help people interpret patriarchal and socioeconomic constraints. Furthermore, comparisons of students' actions demonstrate quite clearly that individuals and groups respond to structures of domination in diverse and unpredictable ways.

Discontinuity between the Languages of the Home and the School

Students of language use in homes and schools (e.g., Cazden 1988; Erickson 2004; Erickson and Mohatt 1982; Gutiérrez 2006; Gutiérrez et al. 1995, 1999; Heath 1983; Lee 1995, 2000, 2001, this volume; Mehan 1979; Philips 1982; Shultz et al. 1982; Tharp and Gallimore 1988; Vogt et al. 1987) have suggested that recitation-type lessons in school may be compatible with the discourse patterns in middle- and upper-income Anglo families but incompatible with the discourse patterns of certain low-income and language minority group families. Typical public school classrooms demand individualized performance, emphasize competition among students, dispense praise and criticism in public, employ an interrogative format using "known information questions," and expect students to label objects and discuss them out of context. Whereas these discourse patterns are prevalent in the homes of middle- and upper-income families, they are not as prevalent in the homes of lower-income families. These discontinuities may, in turn, contribute to the lower achievement and higher drop-out rate among certain language minority students.

Although not cast in terms of Bourdieu's theory, these comparisons of language at home and at school show the interactional operation of certain aspects of cultural capital to produce opportunities to learn for some classes and not others. Because the language use of middle-income parents matches the often implicit and tacit demands of the classroom, middle-income children are being equipped with the very skills and techniques that are rewarded in the classroom. Likewise, because the language use of low-income parents does not match the discourse of the classroom, low-income children are not being provided with the cultural capital that is so valorized in the classroom.

BREAKING THE YOKE OF REPRODUCTION

In addition to describing the social and cultural processes and practices that contribute to the reproduction of inequality in American education, researchers have worked with practitioners to provide enhanced opportunities to learn, especially for those students ill served by the public school system. Their efforts include modifying classroom discourse, untracking and detracking schools, and enacting a democratic vision for schools.

Modifying Classroom Discourse to Develop Critical Thinking Skills

While providing a powerful antidote to cultural and biological deprivation explanations of unequal opportunities to learn, the cultural discontinuity account is not without its detractors. Critics (Foley 1990; Levinson et al. 1996; McLaren 1997; Ogbu 1991; Varenne and McDermott 1998) fear that its liberal assimilationist assumptions are inadequate to the real challenges of creating equity in a racialized capitalist order because this perspective can mistakenly reduce inequality to a problem of miscommunication. Critics argue that even if parents read more stories to their children at bedtime or teachers learned to respect language minority students' codes or learned to communicate effectively with them, structural inequities (e.g., glass ceilings, downsized corporations, and institutional discrimination) would remain.

Despite these disclaimers about cultural discontinuity as a theory to explain educational inequality, a vigorous set of policy recommendations has emerged from this body of work. The basic idea is to use students' home knowledge and language as a resource in classroom instruction. A first wave of intervention research based on sociolinguistic insights about the logic, grammaticality, and coherence of language variants incorporated the language and culture from disadvantaged groups to develop classroom instruction that was more culturally compatible. Delpit (1995), González et al. (2004), Gutiérrez and her colleagues (1995, 1999, 2006), Lee (1995, 2000, 2001, this volume), and Rosebery et al. (1992) represent a second wave of intervention research that uses language and culture as resources for developing fundamentally important academic skills, such as critical thinking in reading. These and other researchers (Cole 1996; Moll et al. 1992; Moll and González 2004; Vásquez 2004) do not want to simply build upon the strengths of home language to smooth classroom interaction; they want to empower students by linking cultural resources and critical thinking.

These approaches to classroom instruction that appropriate the language and cultural knowledge of low-income and language minority students are radical departures from the textbook memorizing or even experimental demonstrations found in most classrooms. Here we see students constructing literary and scientific understandings through an iterative process of theory building, hypothesis testing, and data collection. These students pose their own questions, generate their own hypotheses, and analyze their own data. These activities facilitate students' appreciation of responses that were different from their own, which Vygotskians and Piagetians alike agree is essential in learning to take the perspective of the other. Like real-life scientists and literary critics, these students challenge one another's thoughts, negotiate conflicts about evidence and conclusions, and share their knowledge in order to achieve an advanced understanding. Like adults in real-world situations, these students work in a community of practice in which the exploration of individual participants is guided and supported by the whole group (cf. Palincsar and Brown 1984).

Untracking

Tracking is the typical practice of educating students with different amounts of academic preparation. This practice holds instruction time constant while varying curriculum and instruction. Untracking is tracking's opposite; this practice holds curriculum and instruction constant while varying instructional time.

Rigorous Curriculum Accompanied by Academic and Social Supports

An elaborate version of untracking is the "Advancement Via Individual Determination" program, better known by its acronym AVID (Mehan et al. 1996). AVID is designed to help low-achieving students with high academic potential prepare for entrance into colleges and universities. The AVID approach to untracking places previously low-achieving students (who are primarily from low-income and ethnic or linguistic-minority backgrounds) in the same college-preparatory academic programs that high-achieving students (who are primarily from middle- or upper-middle-income and "majority" backgrounds) are in. Recognizing that the previously low-achieving students who are placed into college-preparatory classes may not have adequate preparation and that teachers in college-preparatory classes may not be prepared to teach this type of student, AVID has arranged a system of supports, or "scaffolds," to assist students in making the transition from low-track to high-track high school classes and preparing for college.

Among the most visible supports is a special elective in which AVID students are given explicit instruction in a special method of note taking that stresses specific techniques for compiling main ideas, abstracting key concepts, and identifying questions that guide analysis. Tutors from local colleges assist in class. Test-taking skills – equivalent to those taught in the Princeton Review or Kaplan courses well-to-do students frequent – including ways to eliminate distracting answers, techniques for approximating answers, and probabilities about the success of guessing – are also taught explicitly in AVID classrooms. By dispensing these academic techniques, AVID gives its students explicit instruction in the implicit or hidden curriculum of the school.

Institutional support of students augments this explicit socialization process. Dedicated teachers advocate on behalf of their AVID students. If students are absent, AVID teachers call them in the evening; they talk to students' academic teachers to monitor progress; they gather assignments for absent students; they call students at home to relay assignments and check on their well-being (Mehan et al. 1996). They even intervene in suicide attempts and resolve employment situations that affect students' academic performance (Stanton-Salazar et al. 2000).

AVID teachers also build bridges between high school and the college system by arranging tours of colleges and universities and by teaching students the intricacies of the college application process, assisting them in writing college essays, and completing college applications and financial aid forms. AVID teachers obtain information about college scholarships and hound students about meeting SAT test and application deadlines. Some particularly exuberant AVID teachers hand-carry completed applications to local colleges and advocate on students' behalf with admissions officers. Peer-group relations also support untracking. Within the social space demarcated for them, AVID students form new, academically oriented friendships and develop academic identities. The time that students spend together on trips to colleges, in collaborative study groups, and informal discussions with college tutors and guest speakers from local colleges and businesses strengthens the formation of academic identities.

The Academic and Social Consequences of Untracking

These institutional arrangements contributed to positive academic outcomes as measured by improved college attendance (Mehan et al. 1996) and performance on standardized tests (Watt et al. 2004). In addition to performing well academically, the African American and Latino students in AVID developed a reflective system of beliefs – a critical consciousness – about the limits and possibilities of the actions they take and the limitations and constraints they face in life. While acknowledging the importance of academic achievement for success later in life, AVID students studied did not subscribe to a romantic version of the achievement ideology. Having experienced the pain of prejudice and discrimination, Latinos and African Americans in AVID realized that their individual effort and hard work would not automatically lead to success. Furthermore, the African American and Latino students in AVID recognized that they must develop linguistic styles, social behavior, and academic skills that are acceptable to the mainstream. They developed these skills but without sacrificing the cultural identity they nurtured at home and displayed in their neighborhoods.

AVID students come from friendship groups in neighborhoods that are not always academically oriented. In order to manage the tension created by their participation in academics during school with their participation in life with friends after school, AVID students adopted a number of strategies. Some hid their academic activities entirely, both at school and with their local friends, but most worked to manage two identities. They engaged in academic pursuits with their AVID friends at school and engaged in recreational pursuits with their neighborhood friends after school and on weekends. These "border crossing strategies" seem to be effective for the Latino and African American students in AVID, just as they have been effective for recent immigrants to the United States (Gibson 1997; Valenzuela 1999).

From Untracking to Detracking

AVID selects students with high potential and midrange grades, places them in college-preparatory classes, and bolsters them with social supports. Approximately 15% of any given high school benefits from this practice. The existing system of social supports operates primarily during 180 hours of an elective class each academic year for 2 to 3 years. The practice of placing students in college-preparatory classes accompanied by a social support system is apparently adequate to elevate students with average to high GPAs and test scores to college eligibility. To enhance the opportunities of more students to learn at the highest levels, academic programs need to be deepened so that students spend more time being challenged academically. The social support system accompanying the academic program also has to be broadened so that students receive even more explicit socialization about the hidden curriculum of the school and social networks are thus expanded.

The Preuss School at the University of California San Diego has transformed the idea of *untracking* into *detracking* by expanding it quantitatively and then qualitatively. Established after the Regents of the University of California banned affirmative action, the Preuss School offers only a college preparatory curriculum in grades 6 through 12 to its 750-plus students, all of whom are selected by lottery from low-income backgrounds. The majority are from groups that are underrepresented in the university (McClure et al. 2006). Recognizing that many entering students will lack preparation for this rigorous instruction, the school provides students with a comprehensive system of academic and social supports. The academic supports include a longer school day (two more hours), longer school year (195 instead of 180 days), tutoring by UCSD undergraduates, and "Saturday Academies" for students who continue to struggle. In order to immerse students deeply as participants in a culture of learning, students serve as assistants in laboratories and apprentices in theater and dance. The social supports include psychological counseling, mentoring by community members, and parental involvement in school activities such as governance, supervising extracurricular activities, and participating in adult education classes (Alvarez and Mehan 2004).

Like their colleagues in AVID classrooms, Preuss teachers and counselors engage in an explicit socialization process in their classes that parallels the implicit socialization process that occurs in well-to-do families. They also build bridges between high school and the higher education system by arranging tours of colleges and universities and teaching students the intricacies of the college application process – assisting them in writing college essays and completing college applications and financial aid forms. Preuss teachers and counselors obtain information about college scholarships and hound students about meeting SAT test and application deadlines.

In Bourdieu's (1985) terms, the Preuss School connects low-income students with social networks, giving them some of the cultural capital at school that is similar to the cultural capital that more economically advantaged parents provide to their children at home through their family networks.

The Preuss School has graduated three classes: 80% of students in the first graduating class (2004), 87% of the class of 2005, and 78% of the class of 2006 have enrolled in colleges such as Berkeley, UCLA, UCSD, Harvard, MIT, Dartmouth, and Claremont. The remaining students are enrolled in community colleges, with an option to transfer to the University of California after two years (McClure et al. 2006). Future research will attempt to open up the "black box of schooling" to determine which combination of parent involvement, academic practices, and social supports contributes to the development of students' academic identities and successful college-going records.

In sum, providing students with rigorous curriculum accompanied by academic and social supports is vital to the success of untracking and detracking efforts. Placing previously low-tracked students in college preparatory classes gives them access to the academic track that leads to college. Academic placement itself is not sufficient, however. Scaffolds that expose the hidden curriculum and build bridges between high school and college help ensure that students who have not had experience with academically oriented classes succeed in them.

Schooling for a Democratic Society

A teacher used newspaper accounts of current events to invigorate classroom discussion. One such article reported that people were killed in mudslides in a South American country as a consequence of a "natural disaster." The teacher invited closer examination. The students discovered that only the homes of poor families were destroyed in the mudslides; the homes of more well-to-do families, which were built in nearby valleys, were untouched. The poor – unable to afford to live in the valleys – were forced to live on unstable hillsides – where, year after year, they were susceptible to the forces of nature. This teacher taught the students that this death by mudslide was more a function of unequal economic structures than natural forces. (Beane and Apple 1995, 14)

This teaching moment – which placed the analysis of a tragic event into a broad political, social, and economic context – exemplifies an educational movement that defines equal opportunities to learn in terms of providing students with learning experiences that promote the democratic way of life. Taking Dewey's (1916) injunctions about the relationship between democracy and education seriously, proponents of "democratic education" want to expose schools to the open flow of ideas; faith in the collective and individual capacity of people to create possibilities for resolving problems; concern for the welfare of others and the "common good"; and a concern for the dignity and rights of individuals and minorities. This conception of democracy as "a way of life" – an idealized set of values that must be lived – goes far beyond the meaning of democracy as a form of political governance involving the consent of the governed, participating in elections, and being represented by people elected to governmental office (Beane and Apple 1995, 6–7).

Although there are precious few of such schools in the United States, those that exist incorporate one or two features: the creation of democratic structures and processes by which life in school is carried out and/or the creation of a curriculum that gives students democratic experiences. Both the decision-making and curricular dimensions of democratic schools are exemplified by Sizer's Coalition of Essential Schools (CES) (Sizer 1992), especially its manifestation in Meier's Central Park East School (Meier 1995). The CES intends to create schools where the rigorous use of the mind for all students, without exception, is the highest priority. When democratic structures and processes have been created, committees, councils, and other schoolwide decision-making groups are opened not only to professional educators but also to young people, their parents, and other members of the school community. Meaningful participation in issues of governance involves decision making about curriculum, instruction, the distribution of funds, and the hiring and firing of administrators and teachers. A school created to give students democratic experiences features project-based learning; critical reflection and analysis to evaluate ideas, problems, and policies; performance-based assessment (in lieu of standardized tests for students to demonstrate mastery); and connecting the curriculum with real-world experiences. Space is made in the curriculum to study large-scale social problems such as global warming; the consequences of the population explosion; inequality among races, classes, and genders; and analysis of news that does or does not appear in papers or on television and the perspective from which it is presented (Carlson and Apple 1998; Giroux and McLaren 1994).

Yet this democratic impulse must always be on guard against co-option, the engineering of consent, and the excesses of populist governance. School-site management, while appearing to reverse centralized decision making, can devolve into localized struggles over minor matters when major policy and program decisions are actually made in distant places. Student participation can be relegated to meaningless, albeit symbolic, student-council debates over the color of crepe paper at school dances or how much to tax students for sports or bands. Ironically, local, populist politics do not always serve democratic ends. For example, we might still have racial segregation or schools only for the sons of the landed gentry or curriculum based on the moral teachings of fundamentalist protestants (as found in New England Primers or the McGuffey Readers) were those issues relegated to the local vote.

Finally – and most importantly – trying to create a democratic curriculum can foster conflict and backlash. The possibility of hearing a wide range of voices can threaten traditional conceptions of knowledge. Encouraging students to critically analyze issues raises the possibility that they may challenge dominant interpretations and call received wisdom into question (Beane and Apple 1995). Neither of these moves is popular with educators and citizens who see the function of education to be the unquestioned transmission of knowledge from generation to generation and the socialization of youth into existing forms of society.

CONCLUSIONS

At this point in the development of sociological theory and research on OTL and assessment, we have two major, competing visions of schooling. On the one hand is the optimistic, meritocratic vision that idealizes schooling as an institution that provides students with equal opportunities to learn based on their individual effort and hard work. On the other hand, we have the darkly pessimistic vision that asserts schools are (either wittingly or unwittingly) organized to reproduce the existing stratification in society that breaks out along social class, race, and gender lines. The time seems ripe to undo the seeming contradiction that schooling is *either* promoting educational equality *or* stifling the advancement of students from low-income backgrounds. What is magical about the achievement ideology is that the groups of people who have been denied equal opportunities to learn blame themselves – not the cultural apparatus of schooling – for their difficulties.

A helpful first step in resolving this apparent contradiction is stifling the determinism in reproduction theory and recognizing the transformative possibilities of cultural and institutional mediation; that is, the influence of peers, parents, and curricular practices. This involves more closely investigating just how modifying classroom discourse, untracking or detracking practices, and forming democratic schools actually forge more equitable opportunities to learn.

The ethnographies of successful interventions I reviewed above reveal several common features:

- They recognize that learning involves the construction of identities and the skill to participate as a member in many different settings (see Gee, Lee, and Moss, all this volume).
- Learning occurs when students have effective access to appropriate resources, such as well-prepared teachers, well-designed curricula, sufficient and current laboratory equipment, books, and technology, as well as comfortable and safe facilities (Pullin, this volume, expands on this theme; cf. Oakes 2003).
- The schools and their agents act collectively in a deliberate, intensive, and explicit fashion to generate a socialization process that produces the same sorts of strategies and resources deployed in privileged homes and institutions.

When these practices are instituted systematically, working-class youth and students of color enjoy some of the same advantages that accrue to their more privileged peers. Teachers who untrack or detrack students or engage in critical pedagogy present counterexamples to reproduction theorists' formulation that the school contributes to an immutable class structure. In these educational arrangements, students, most of whom are from low-income families and African American and Latino backgrounds, are being taught cultural capital, a commodity Bourdieu says is normally and "naturally" transmitted in elite families.

Teachers in untracked, detracked, and democratic educational environments play the role usually played by parents of elite students – informing them about the rules of the game and intervening on their behalf with administrators or teachers who resist their academic plans or desires. They also play the role usually played by private counselors or admissions offices at elite schools – advocating on their behalf with admissions officers or financial aid officers at colleges or universities. That is, they are actively constructing opportunities in ways that Bourdieu says are normally and "naturally" reserved for elite families.

If the sons and daughters of low-status students can *learn* the skills, manners, and norms presumably *inherited* by elite students, this raises questions about the class basis of cultural capital. If teachers can embed their low-status students in productive social networks, this raises questions about the unique privilege of social capital. Both of these activities raise the possibility of improved opportunities to learn.

If the sons and daughters of low-status families are acquiring cultural capital from their teachers and if the teachers of low-status students are activating social networks, then reproduction theorists must modify the rigid way in which they think about schools. Schools are not always and necessarily reproductive systems. We have described circumstances in which schools, or at least segments within schools, can be transformed to increase the possibility of social mobility by activating cultural capital and constructing social networks.

Before we celebrate the transformation of the schools from settings for the reproduction of social inequality into instruments of social equity, we must, of course, determine if the actions we have observed are substantial, long-term institutional changes. If we have only revealed changes on the margin, we do not have genuine mobility patterns but a cynical process of allowing a precious few members of the underclass through the gates so as to legitimate achievement ideology, while the great masses are kept down.

Notes

1. The military and religious institutions also fulfill this function, perhaps unwittingly.
2. Notably Coleman et al. 1966; Jencks et al. 1972; Bowles and Gintis 1976; Jencks et al. 1978; Jencks and Phillips 1998; Oakes 2003.
3. Although test scores improved, graduation rates did not, however, leading these authors to question the overall utility of high-stakes regimens.
4. The position of the American Evaluation Association (2002: 1) is: "High-stakes testing leads to under-serving or mis-serving all students, especially the most needy and vulnerable, thereby violating the principle of "do no harm." AERA (2000, 1)

based its position on the 1999 *Standards for Educational and Psychological Testing*: "Decisions that affect individual students' life chances or educational opportunities should not be made on the basis of test scores alone."

References

Alvarez, D. and H. Mehan. 2004. Providing educational opportunities for underrepresented students. In *Teaching all the children*, edited by D. Lapp. New York: Guilford Publications.

American Educational Research Association. 2000. AERA position on high stakes testing. http://www.aera.net/about/policy/stakes.htm.

American Educational Research Association, American Psychological Association, and the National Council on Measurement in Education. 1999. Standards for educational and psychological testing. Washington, D.C.: AERA.

American Evaluation Association. 2002. American Evaluation Association position statement on high stakes testing in preK-12 education. http://www.eval.org/hst3.htm.

Amrein, A. L. and D. C. Berliner. 2002. High-stakes testing, uncertainty, and student learning. *Education Policy Analysis Archives* 10. http://epaa.asu.edu/epaa/v10n18/.

Apple, M. W. 1982. *Education and power*. Boston: Routledge and Kegan Paul.

Apple, M. W. and L. Weis. 1983. *Ideology and practice in education: A political and conceptual introduction*. Philadelphia: Temple University Press.

Azmitia, M. and C. Cooper. 2002. Navigating and negotiating home, school and peer linkages in adolescents. Final Report: Project 3.3. www.crede.ucsc.edu/research/sfc/3.3_final.html.

Beane, J. A. and M. Apple. 1995. *Democratic Schools*. Alexandria, V.A.: ASCD.

Beane, J. A. and M. Apple. 1995. *Schooling for democracy*. New York: ASCD.

Becker, G. S. 1975. *Human capital: A theoretical and empirical analysis, with specific reference to education*, 2nd ed. New York: Columbia University Press.

Betts, J. R., K. S. Rueben, and A. Danenberg. 2000. *Equal resources, equal outcomes? The distribution of school resources and student achievement in California*. San Francisco: Public Policy Institute of California.

Bourdieu, P. 1985. The forms of capital. In *Handbook of theory and research for the sociology of education*, edited by J. G. Richardson, 241–58. New York: Greenwood.

Bourdieu, P. and J. P. Passeron. 1977. *Reproduction in education, society and culture*. London: Sage Publications.

Bourdieu, P. and J. D. Wacquant. 1992. *An invitation to a reflexive sociology*. Chicago: University of Chicago Press.

Bowles, S. and H. I. Gintis. 1976. *Schooling in capitalist America*. New York: Basic Books.

Brown v. Board of Education of Topeka Kansas 347 U.S. 483 (1954).

Carlson, D. and M. Apple, eds. 1998. *Power, knowledge, pedagogy: The meaning of democratic education in unsettling times*. Boulder: Westview Press.

Carnoy, M. 1974. *Education as cultural imperialism*. New York: David McKay.

Carnoy, M. and S. Loeb. 2002. Does external accountability affect student outcomes? A cross-state analysis. *Educational Evaluation and Policy Analysis* 24: 305–31.

Carter, P. 2005. *Keeping it real: School success beyond black and white*. New York: Oxford University Press.

Cazden, C. B. 1988. *Classroom discourse*. Portsmouth, N.H.: Heineman.

Cicourel, A. V. and H. Mehan. 1985. Universal development, stratifying practices and status attainment. *Social Stratification and Mobility* 4, 3–27.

Cole, M. 1996. *Cultural psychology.* Cambridge: Harvard Belknap.

Cookson, P. W., Jr. and C. H. Persell. 1985. *Preparation for power: America's elite boarding schools.* New York: Basic Books.

Census. 2002. *Supplemental survey.* Washington, D.C.: US Census Bureau.

Coleman, J. S., E. Q. Campbell, C. J. Hobson, C. McPartland, A. M. Mood, F. D. Weinfeld, and R. L. York. 1966. *Equality of educational opportunity.* Washington, D.C.: U. S. Office of Education.

Davis, K. and W. E. Moore. 1945. Some principles of stratification. *American Sociological Review* 10: 242–49.

Delgado-Gaitan, C. 1990. *Literacy for empowerment: The role of parents in their children's education.* London: Falmer.

Delgado-Gaitan, C. 1991. Involving parents in the schools: A process of empowerment. *American Journal of Education* 100: 20–45.

Delgado-Gaitan, C. 1994. Empowerment in Carpinteria: A five-year study of family, school and community. Baltimore: Center for the Research on Effective Schooling for Disadvantaged Students.

Delpit, L. 1995. *Other people's children: Cultural conflict in the classroom.* New York: W. W. Norton.

Dewey, J. 1916. *Democracy and education.* New York: Macmillan.

Dreeben, R. 1968. *On what is learned in school.* Reading, Mass.: Addison-Wesley.

Digest of Educational Statistics. 2001. Berkeley: National Center for Educational Statistics. Table 143.

Education Trust. 2003a. Latino achievement in America. Washington, D.C. edtrust.org.

Education Trust. 2003b. African American achievement in America. Washington, D.C. edtrust.org.

Epstein, J. 1992. School and family partnerships. In *Encyclopedia of Educational Research* 1139–51. New York: MacMillan.

Epstein, J. 2001. *School, family and community partnerships: Preparing educators and improving schools.* Boulder: Westview Press.

Erickson, F. E. 2004. *Talk and social theory.* London: Polity Press.

Erickson, F. E. and G. Mohatt. 1982. Participant structures in two communities. In *Doing the ethnography of schooling,* edited by G. D. Spindler, 132–75. New York: Holt, Rinehart and Winston.

Fine, M. 1991. *Framing dropouts: Notes on the politics of an urban public high school.* Albany: State University of New York Press.

Foley, D. E. 1990. *Learning capitalist culture: Deep in the heart of Tejas.* Philadelphia: University of Pennsylvania Press.

Gibson, M. A. 1997. Complicating the immigrant/involuntary minority typology. *Anthropology and Education Quarterly* 28: 431–54.

Giroux, H. A. and P. McLaren, eds. 1994. *Between borders: pedagogy and the politics of cultural studies.* New York/London: Routledge.

Giroux, H. A. 1988. *Schooling and the struggle for public life: Critical pedagogy in the modern age.* Minneapolis: University of Minnesota Press.

González, N., L. C. Moll, and C. Amanti, eds. 2004. *Theorizing practices: Funds of knowledge in households and classrooms.* Cresskill, N.J.: Hampton.

Grubb, N. and L. Goe. 2002. The unending search for equity: California policy, the "new" school finance, and the *Williams* case. http://www.decentschools.org.

Gutiérrez, K. D. 2006. Studying cultural practices in urban learning communities. *Human Development* 45: 312–21.

Gutiérrez, K. D., P. O. Baquedano-López, and C. Tejada. 1999. Rethinking diversity: Hybridity and hybrid language practices in the third space. *Mind, Culture and Activity* 6: 286–303.

Gutiérrez, K. D., B. Rymes, and J. Larson. 1995. Script, counterscript and underlife in the classroom: James Brown vs. *Brown v. Board of Education. Harvard Educational Review* 65: 445–71.

Haney, W. 2000. The myth of the Texas miracle in education. *Education Policy Analysis Archives* 8. http://epaa.asu.edu/epaa/v8n4.

Hanushek, E. A. and M. E. Raymond. June 2004. Does school accountability lead to improved student performance? NBER Working Paper No. 10591. Cambridge, Mass.: National Bureau of Economic Research.

Harvey, W. B. 2002. *Minorities in higher education.* Washington, D.C.: American Council on Education.

Heath, S. B. 1983. *Ways with words.* New York: Cambridge University Press.

Holland, D. and M. Eisenhart. 1990. *Educated in romance.* Albany: SUNY Press.

Horvat, E. McN and C. O'Conner. 2006. *Beyond acting white: Reframing the debate on black student achievement.* Lanham, Md: Rowman and Littlefield.

Jacob, B. A. and S. D. Levitt. 2003. Rotten apples: An investigation of the prevalence and predictors of teacher cheating. NBER Working Paper No. w9413. Cambridge, Mass: National Bureau of Economic Research.

Jencks, C. S., M. Smith, H. Acland, M. J. Bane, D. Cohen, H. Ginits, B. Heyns, and S. Michelson. 1972. *Inequality: A reassessment of the effect of family and schooling in America.* New York: Basic Books.

Jencks, C. S., S. Bartlett, M. Corcoran, J. Crouse, D. Eaglesfield, G. Jackson, R. McClelland, M. Olneck, J. Swartz, S. Ward, and J. Williams. 1978. *Who gets ahead? The determinants of economic success in America.* New York: Basic Books.

Jencks, C. S. and M. Phillip, eds. 1998. *The Black-white test score gap.* Washington, D.C.: Brookings Institution.

Jerald, C. D. 2002. *All talk no action: Putting an end to out of field teaching.* Washington, D.C.: The Education Trust.

Karabel, J. and A. H. Halsey, eds. 1977. *Power and ideology in education.* New York: Oxford University Press.

Kohn, A. 2002. *Education Inc: Turning learning into a business.* Portsmouth, N.H.: Heinemann.

Lareau, A. 2003. *Unequal childhoods: Class, race and family life.* Berkeley: UC Press.

Lareau, A. 1989. *Home advantage: Social class and parental intervention in elementary education.* London: Falmer Press.

Lareau, A. and E. M. Horvat. 1999. Moments of inclusions, class, cultural capital in family-school relationships. *Sociology of Education* 72: 37–53.

Lareau, A. and W. Shumar. 1996. The problem of individualism in family-school policies. *Sociology of Education* 69: 24–39.

Lee, C. D. 1995. A culturally based cognitive apprenticeship: Teaching African American high school students skills in literary interpretation. *Reading Research Quarterly* 50: 608–30.

Lee, C. D. 2000. Signifying in the zone of proximal development. In *Vygotskian perspectives on literacy research: Constructing meaning through collaborative inquiry*, edited by C. D. Lee and P. Smagorinsky, 191–225. New York: Cambridge University Press.

Lee, C. D. 2001. Is October Brown Chinese: A cultural modeling activity system for underachieving students. *American Educational Research Journal* 38: 97–142.

Levinson, B. A., D. E. Foley, and D. C. Holland, eds. 1996. *The cultural production of the educated person: Critical ethnographies of schooling and local practice*. Albany, N.Y.: State University of New York Press.

Linn, R. L. 2000. Assessments and accountability. *Educational Researcher* 29: 4–16.

MacLeod, Jay. 1987. *Ain't no makin' it: Lowered aspirations in a low-income neighborhood*. Boulder: Westview Press.

MacLeod, J. 1995. *Ain't no makin' it: Aspirations and attainment in a low-income neighborhood*. Boulder: Westview Press.

Marx, K. (1867 [1976]). *Capital*. London: Penguin.

McClure, L., J. L. Morales, R. Jacob-Almeida, and C. Richter. 2006. The Preuss School at UCSD: Student characteristics and academic achievement, class of 2005. http://create.ucsd.edu/Research_Evaluaton/.

McDonough, P. 1997. *Choosing colleges. How social class and schools structure opportunity*. Albany: State University of New York Press.

McLaren, P. 1997. *Revolutionary multiculturalism: Pedagogies of dissent for the new millenium*. Boulder: Westview Press.

McNeill, L. 1998. *Contradictions of reform*. New York: Routledge.

Mehan, H. 1979. *Learning lessons*. Cambridge: Harvard University Press.

Mehan, H. 1992. Understanding inequality: The contribution of ethnographic studies. *The Sociology of Education* 65: 1–20.

Mehan, H., L. Hubbard, I. Villanueva, and A. Lintz. 1996. *Constructing school success: The consequences of untracking low achieving students*. Cambridge: Cambridge University Press.

Mehan, H. and S. Grimes. 1999. The achievement gap in the San Diego City Schools. La Jolla: The San Diego Dialogue.

Meier, D. 1995. *The power of their ideas: Lessons for America from a small school in Harlem*. Boston: Beacon Press.

Moll, L. C. and N. Gonzalez. 2004. Engaging life: A funds of knowledge approach to multicultural education. In *Handbook of research on multicultural education*, 2nd ed., edited by J. A. Banks and C. A. McGee Banks. San Francisco: Jossey Bass.

Moll, L., C. Amanti, D. Neff, and N. Gonzalez. 1992. Funds of knowledge for teaching: Using a qualitative approach. *Theory into Practice* 31: 132–41.

National Academy of Sciences. 1999. *High stakes: Testing for tracking, promotion and graduation*. Washington, D.C.: NAS.

No Child Left Behind Act of 2001, 107th Cong., 1st sess., H.R.1.EH.

Oakes, J. 1985 [2005]. *Keeping track*, 2nd ed. New Haven: Yale University Press.

Oakes, J. 2002. Education inadequacy, inequality, and failed state policy: A synthesis of expert reports prepared for *Williams v. State of California*. http://www.decentschools.org.

Oakes, J. 2003. *Critical conditions for equity and diversity in college access*. Los Angeles, Calif.: UC ACCORD.

Ogbu, J. U. 1974. *The next generation: An ethnography of education in an urban neighborhood*. New York: Academic Press.

Ogbu, J. U. 1987. Variability in minority school performance: A problem in search of an explanation. *Anthropology and Education Quarterly* 18: 312–34.

Ogbu, J. U. 1991. Immigrant and involuntary minorities in comparative perspective. In *Minority status and schooling*, edited by M. Gibson and J. U. Ogbu. New York: Garland.

Palinscar, A. S. and A. Brown. 1984. Reciprocal teaching of comprehension-fostering and comprehension monitoring activities. *Cognition and Instruction* 1: 117–75.

Parsons, T. 1959. The school classroom as a social system. *Harvard Educational Review* 29: 297–318.

Pedulla, J., S. L. Abrams, G. Madaus, M. Russell, M. Ramos, and J. Miao. 2004. Perceived effects of state-mandated testing programs on teaching and learning: Findings from a national survey of teachers. Chestnut Hill: Center for the Study of Testing, Evaluation, and Educational Policy, Boston College.

Philips, S. U. 1982. *The invisible culture: Communication in classroom and community on the Warm Springs reservation.* New York: Longman.

Powell, A. G. 1996. *Lessons from privilege: The American prep school tradition.* Cambridge: Harvard University Press.

Powers, J. M. 2004. High-stakes accountability and equity: Using evidence from California's public schools accountability act to address the issues in *Williams v. State of California. American Educational Research Journal* 41: 763–96.

Reese, L., S. Balzano, R. Gallimore, and C. Goldenberg. 1995. The concept of *educación*: Latino family values and American schooling. *International Journal of Educational Research* 23: 57–81.

Rosebery, A. S., B. Warren, and F. R. Conant. 1992. *Appropriating scientific discourse: Findings from language minority classrooms* (Working Paper No. 1). Cambridge: Technical Educational Research Center.

Rosenbaum, M. D. et al. 2000a. Complaint for injunctive and declaratory relief. Papers filed with the Superior Court of the State of California. http://www.aclu-sc.org/attachments/w/Williams_vs_California_Complaint_1.pdf.

Rosenbaum, M. D. et al. 2000b. First amended complaint. Papers filed with the Superior Court of the State of California. http://www.decentschools.org.

Rosenbaum, M. D. et al. 2002. Plaintiffs' liability disclosure statement. Papers filed with the Superior Court of the State of California. http://www.decentschools.org.

Shultz, J., Florio, S., and F. Erickson. 1982. Where's the floor? *The Quarterly Newsletter of the Laboratory of Comparative Human Cognition* 4: 2–9.

Sizer, T. R. 1984. *Horace's compromise: The dilemma of the American high school.* New York: Houghton Mifflin.

Sizer, T. R. 1992. *Horace's school: Redesigning the American high school.* New York: Houghton Mifflin.

Sizer, T. R. 2004. *The red pencil.* New Haven: Yale University Press.

Stanton-Salazar, R. 2000. *Manufacturing hope and despair: The school and kin support networks of U.S.-Mexican youth.* New York: Teachers College Press.

Stanton-Salazar, R., O. Vásquez, and H. Mehan. 2000. Engineering success through institutional support. In *Academic achievement of minority students: Perspectives, practices and prescriptions*, edited by S. Gregory. Lanham, Md.: University Press of America.

Tharp, R., and R. Gallimore. 1988. *Rousing minds to life: Teaching, learning, and schooling in social context.* Cambridge: Cambridge University Press.

Tucker, M. S. and J. B. Codding. 1998. *Standards for our schools*. San Francisco: Jossey-Bass.

Turner, R. H. 1960. Sponsored and contest mobility and the school system. *American Sociological Review* 25: 855–67.

Valdez, G. 1996. *Con Respeto: Bridging the distances between culturally diverse families and schools: An ethnographic portrait*. New York: Teachers College Press.

Valenzuela, A. 1999. *Subtractive schooling: U.S.-Mexican youth and the politics of caring*. Albany: State University of New York Press.

Varenne, H. and R. P. McDermott. 1998. *Successful failure: The schools America builds*. Boulder: Westview Press.

Vásquez, O. A. 2004. *La Cláse Magica: Imagining optimal possibilities in a bilingual community of learners*. Tanwah, N.J.: Laurence Erlbaum.

Vásquez, O. A., R. Stanton-Salazar, and H. Mehan. 2000. Engineering success through institutional support. In *The Academic achievement of minority students*, edited by Shiela T. Gregory. Lanham, N.Y.: University Press of America.

Vogt, L. A., C. Jordan, and R. Tharp. 1987. Explaining school failure, producing school success: Two cases. *Anthropology and Education Quarterly* 18: 276–88.

Watt, K. M., C. M. Powell, and I. D. Mendisla. 2004. Implications of a comprehensive school reform model for secondary schools students under represented in higher education. *JESPAR* 9: 241–59.

Weis, L. 1990. *Working class without work*. London: Routledge and Kegan Paul.

Wilcox, K. 1982. Differential socialization in the classroom: Implications for equal opportunity. In *Doing the ethnography of schooling*, edited by G. D. Spindler, 268–309. New York: Holt, Rinehart and Winston.

Willis, P. 1979. *Learning to labor*. New York: Columbia Teachers College Press.

4   A Sociocultural Perspective on Opportunity to Learn

James Paul Gee

INTRODUCTION

The field of psychometrics has been predominant in work on testing and assessment. For the most part, psychometrics has been strongly influenced by traditional psychological assumptions about the mind and learning. Work that takes a sociocultural perspective has played a much smaller role and has heretofore made little contact with psychometrics. This chapter discusses contributions such a sociocultural perspective has to make to issues of assessment and testing, with a focus on an expanded notion of opportunity to learn (OTL). Ensuring that all learners have had equal OTL is both an ethical prerequisite for fair assessment and a solid basis on which to think about educational reforms that will ensure that all children can succeed at school. It is also a point at which mutually informing discussion can occur between people working in psychometrics and those working on sociocultural approaches to learning.

This section begins with a consideration of the traditional perspective in psychology, one that views knowledge and learning through the lens of mental representations in individuals' heads (Clancey 1997). Even in this traditional view, many of the types of issues that sociocultural perspectives emphasize also arise, although in a more backgrounded way. I will then turn to a more direct consideration of sociocultural perspectives, starting with the relationship between learners and their learning environments. In subsequent sections, I will spell out this relationship in terms of the connections between learning and learners' experiences in the world; how knowledge is distributed across people and their tools; the central importance of people's participation in shared talk and social practices; and the nature of the special varieties of language used in talk and participation when people learn in content areas in school – areas like math, science, social studies, and literature.

Finally, I will take up the nature of the relationship between culture and participation in school practices.

THE TRADITIONAL VIEW

A traditional way to view knowledge (e.g., Fodor 1975; Newell and Simon 1972; Pylyshyn 1984) is in terms of mental representations stored in the head ("mind/brain"). These representations are the way information from the world is stored and organized in the mind/brain and how it is processed or manipulated. Such a perspective leads to a focus on questions about how information gets into the head, how exactly it is organized in the head, and how it leaves the head when people need to use it. Indeed, these questions have played a central role in much educational research.

This traditional perspective leads rather naturally to a way of looking at the notion of OTL. Learners have had the same OTL if they have been exposed to the same information ("content"). If they have been exposed to the same content, then, according to this view, they have each had the opportunity to store this information in their heads; that is, to "learn it."

Even in this traditional view, complexities arise. For example, there is the problem of "prior knowledge." Most learning theorists agree that the representation of something new in someone's head varies in important ways – important for the material that is learned – on the basis of what is already in the person's head (Bransford, Brown, and Cocking 2000). This is because new information has to be integrated with prior knowledge to make sense, and new knowledge makes sense in different ways according to how it is integrated with such prior knowledge.

New information that cannot be tied to any prior knowledge is not learned well or at all. New information that is well integrated with prior knowledge is more deeply learned than new information that is only superficially integrated with prior knowledge. Thus, even in a traditional view, the notion of OTL would have to consider not just the information to which learners have been exposed, but also what prior knowledge they have brought to the new learning encounter, because this affects the type of learning that takes place or even if any learning occurs at all. Even according to a traditional view, therefore, there is an unavoidable historical dimension to learning and to questions about OTL. Looking at just the here and now will not work, even if traditional assumptions about knowledge and learning are taken into account.

A second complexity is what we might call the "power of representation problem." Some ways of representing information are better for some purposes than for others; some forms of representation are more efficient or effective than others. A list is one way to represent information, but a principle from which each member of the list can be deduced and from which new members of the list can be generated is more powerful for many purposes. For example, a list of English words ending in "-ness" (e.g., "goodness," "happiness," "sadness") is less efficient, for many purposes, than a generalization like: "adjective + ness = an abstract noun" coupled with a "blocking principle" in terms of which the generalization does not apply if a non-ness word already exists for the same meaning. Thus, there is no "tallness" because "height" already exists.

However, a learner cannot form a given representation unless he or she has the requisite "mental" representational resources. For example, a learner (or computer) innocent of linguistic ways to represent grammatical generalizations involving morphology would have to settle for a list of "-ness" words. Thus, even in the traditional view, learning and OTL cannot just be a matter of the information to which one was exposed. For true and equal OTL, learners must all have the capacity to form the required representations at the required degree of "power." Two learners exposed to English "-ness" words, one of whom has the grammatical representational resources to represent morphological generalizations and the other of whom does not, have not had the same opportunity to learn the same thing at the same level, even if they have been exposed to the same data. Of course, grammatical representational resources are, in large part, biologically endowed or at least learned in a relatively uniform way across individuals (Chomsky 1986), but no such thing is true in learning literacy, science, or other "content" areas in school, including learning grammar at a conscious level as a "content" area.

The power-of-representation problem shows that, even in the traditional view, we must consider which tools – in this case, tools in the sense of representational resources – the learner has brought to the learning encounter or picked up there along with information (data, content). This is, of course, a different sort of "prior knowledge" issue, in which the required prior knowledge is knowledge of powerful representational schemes. Such schemes are often tied to the disciplinary nature of what is being learned. For example, an academic domain like biology or linguistics has its own special representational resources (such as the one we just reviewed) in terms of which information is more effectively or powerfully dealt with in that domain. Thus, learning these domains – and talking about OTL in these domains – is not a matter of mere exposure to information, but also exposure to and practice with the requisite representational means of these domains.

This last point has obvious implications for testing and assessment. A test made up of a list of facts cannot tell us whether someone has used a list-like representation or a more principled representation to answer the questions on the test. It also cannot tell us whether the student has learned the representational schemes inherent in and partly definitive of the academic domain (in terms of which such facts are generated). It may also be said that a test of such facts puts more burden on those who have simply had to memorize the facts than it does on those who have had the opportunity to master the sorts of representational resources that allow these facts to be generated or inferred. On the other hand, a test that requires knowledge of such representational schemes is not fair if some students have only been exposed to the sorts of facts such schemes generate but not given the opportunity to develop those representational schemes themselves.

Once we grant the points above regarding representational resources, then, even in the traditional view, we have to concede a nonmental aspect to knowledge. In any academic domain, the representational resources it uses – the effective ones that learning the domain entails – are not just mental entities stored in experts' heads. These representational devices are also written down – inscribed – in public ways in terms of words, symbols, graphs, and so forth, on paper, and in machines and various tools the discipline uses. They are also available in the behavior and talk of other people who are experts in the domain. Surely an inability to understand and be able to use these public representational resources does not auger well – even in the traditional view – for the nature and quality of a learner's mental representations in the domain. Even learning the mental representations of a domain, according to the traditional view, must have something to do with learning to use and interact with the public ones.

A third complexity that arises, even within the traditional view, is one that we can see clearly if we consider an analogy with language acquisition. Language acquisition theorists have long pointed out that there is an important difference between "input" and "intake" (Corder 1967; Ellis 1997; Gass 1997). Input is data from the language to be learned to which the learner is exposed. If these data are not processed (not paid attention to and used) by the learner, they obviously have no effect. Intake is input that has been processed in ways that can lead to learning about the language to be acquired.

With any learning, there is an input/intake problem. Even if learners have been exposed to the same information (data, content) – thus, to the same input –it has not necessarily been intake for all of them. There are any number of reasons why input may not actually be intake for various learners. Of course, the "prior knowledge" problem discussed earlier can be one reason why, for some learners, certain sorts of input are not intake. Another important variable discussed in the second-language-acquisition literature (see Gee 2008 for a more general discussion) that can cause input not to be intake is that a learner resists using input for social, cultural, or emotional reasons – the learner resists learning because of some perceived threat or insult to his or her individual, social, or cultural sense of self.

In the second-language-acquisition literature, this matter is sometimes viewed this way: Each learner has an "affective filter" (Dulay, Burt, and Krashen 1982; Krashen 1983). When perceived threat is low, the filter is low and input is allowed to get in the head; that is, to become intake. When perceived threat is high, the affective filter is raised and input does not get in or is not properly processed; that is, it does not become intake. Obviously, if the learning situation itself is what is causing the affective filter to rise for some students, we have clear implications for OTL, because these students are not really exposed to the same information as are other students, as the information is now not intake for them.

The input/intake problem tells us, even in the traditional view, that we must go beyond purely cognitive considerations in thinking about learning and the notion of OTL. Learners whose "affective filters" have been raised have not had the same OTL as those learners whose filters have not been raised, despite the fact that they were exposed to the same information, the same input. For the former, the input is not intake – thus, it does not lead to learning. Because the affective filter is tied to social, cultural, and emotional considerations – to learners' views of themselves and their identities in relation to what is to be learned – such sociocultural and effective considerations arise even in traditional views of knowledge and learning.

Our discussion so far has sought to make clear that issues of the historical trajectory of one's learning, of the different public resources available to learners, and the nature of learners' social and cultural identities (and their interpretation of the learning situation in terms of those identities), issues often associated with sociocultural approaches to learning, arise even in the traditional framework that stresses mental representations. Even in the traditional approach, the notion of OTL would have to broaden well beyond mere exposure to the same information, data, or content.

THE SITUATED/SOCIOCULTURAL VIEW

We have seen that in the traditional view, knowledge is viewed in terms of mental representations stored in the head ("mind/brain"). We also have seen that complexities arise in this view, although they tend to be backgrounded in favor of studies of cognitive processing. We will turn now to an alternative to the traditional view. This alternative is based on a variety of related, but different, approaches to knowledge and learning stemming from research on situated cognition and sociocultural approaches to language and learning. This alternative emphasizes some of the complexities we discussed with the traditional view and other issues closely related to them.

There is no one accepted situated/sociocultural view, but rather a variety of different perspectives developed in work using different disciplinary lenses from areas like the learning sciences (e.g., Brown 1994), cognitive science (Clark 1997), sociolinguistics (e.g., Gee 1992, 1996, 2004), and cognitive anthropology (Lave and Wenger 1991) – just as there is, in reality, no single accepted formulation of the traditional view. However, to simplify matters, we will develop a perspective on situated/sociocultural work that seeks to capture some of the leading themes in the body of disparate work relevant to a situated/sociocultural viewpoint.

A situated/sociocultural viewpoint looks at knowledge and learning not primarily in terms of representations in the head, although there is no need to deny that such representations exist and play an important role. Rather, it looks at knowledge and learning in terms of a *relationship* between an individual with both a mind and a body and an environment in which the individual thinks, feels, acts, and interacts. Both the body and the environment tend to be backgrounded in traditional views of knowledge and learning.

Any environment in which an individual finds him or herself is filled with *affordances*. The term "affordance" (coined by Gibson 1977, 1979; see also Norman 1988) is used to describe the perceived *action possibilities* posed by objects or features in the environment. The affordances of an individual's environment are what the individual can perceive as feasible to, in, on, with, or about the objects or features in that environment. Of course, an affordance does not exist for an individual who cannot perceive its presence. Even when an affordance is recognized, however, a human actor must also have the capacity to transform the affordance into an actual and effective action. *Effectivities* are the set of capacities for action that the individual has for transforming affordances into action. An effectivity means that a person can take advantage of what is offered by the objects or features in the environment.

Focusing on affordance/effectivity pairs places the focus not on the individual or the environment but on a pairing of the two, a relationship between them. A hammer affords certain actions (e.g., hammering) better than others if one perceives the hammer in properly functional terms. Yet this affordance cannot be transformed into action unless the individual has the capacity to take up the hammer in the right way to transform its affordances into action.

A door that swings out has a set of affordances for movement of a certain sort that can be effected by individuals who have the capacity to push on the door in the way it best affords action.

If we apply this terminology to knowledge and learning in school, we can say that learning involves developing effectivity toward the affordances in specific sorts of environments – for example, in environments in which students are seeking to learn aspects of science, mathematics, social studies, literary criticism, and so forth. Learners must come to be able to perceive fruitful affordances and transform these action possibilities into appropriate actions in thought, word, and deed. In this perspective, studying learning is a matter of studying the relationship between learners and their environments. We have to ask what affordances are available in the environments of particular learners and what effectivities they have or are developing for transforming these affordances into action. We cannot ask only about what is in the learner's head.

Of course, other people (experts and peers) are one special category of "objects" in learners' environments. Different people with different sorts of knowledge and skills afford different learners quite distinctive possibilities of action through talk and shared practices, provided that learners can effect the transformation of these resources into fruitful action and interaction.

This perspective has direct implications for how we view OTL. According to this perspective, learners have not had the same OTL just because they have been exposed to the same information or content. The learning and assessment environment must afford them similar capacities of action. A learner for whom certain objects, people, or features of the environment are not affordances, either because the learner cannot perceive their possibilities for action or cannot effect that action, is not being exposed to the same environment as is a learner for whom these objects, people, or features are true affordances open to the learner's developed or developing effectivity. Notice, too, that there are issues of affordance/effectivity pairings for both learning environments and assessment environments, because both are places where learners have to act.

The affordance/effectivity distinction is only one way to say that thinking and learning are "situated", that is, that we can only understand and define them relevant to the relationships between individuals and specific environments or classes of environments. Yet environment is a complex term in this context. For human beings, the material world and our bodies are part of our environment; human-made tools and artifacts are part of our environment; and other people and their actions and talk are part of our environment. These three categories – each of which interacts and overlaps with the others – define three related emphases in work on situated/sociocultural approaches to knowledge and learning: embodiment, distributed cognition, and social practices.

EMBODIMENT

The traditional view of knowledge and learning that we discussed earlier is often connected with a closely related viewpoint that the meaning of a word is some general concept in the head that can be spelled out in something like a definition. For example, the word "bachelor" might be represented by a complex concept in the head that the following definition would capture: "a male who is not married."

However, today there are accounts of language and thinking that are different. Consider, for instance, these two quotes from some recent work in cognitive psychology:

... comprehension is grounded in perceptual simulations that prepare agents for situated action. (Barsalou 1999a, 77)

... to a particular person, the meaning of an object, event, or sentence is what that person can do with the object, event, or sentence. (Glenberg 1997, 3)

These two quotes are from work that is part of a "family" of related viewpoints which, for want of a better name, we might call the "situated cognition" family, which means that these viewpoints all hold that thinking is connected to and changes across actual situations and is not always or usually a process of applying abstract generalizations, definitions, or rules (e.g., Barsalou 1999a, 1999b; Brown, Collins, and Dugid 1989; Clancey 1997; Clark 1997, 2003; Engeström, Miettinen, and Punamaki 1999; Gee 1992; Glenberg 1997; Glenberg and Robertson 1999; Hutchins 1995; Latour 1999; Lave 1996; Lave and Wenger 1991; Wertsch 1998; Wenger 1998). Although there are differences among the different members of the family, they share the viewpoint that language and thinking are tied to *people's experiences of situated action in the material and social world*. Furthermore, these experiences are stored in the mind/brain not in terms of language ("propositions") but in something like dynamic images tied to perceptions both of the world and of our own bodies, internal states, and feelings. Increasing evidence suggests that perceptual simulation is indeed central to comprehension (Barsalou 1999a, 74).

Let us use a metaphor to make clear what this viewpoint means, a metaphor drawn from the realm of video games (Gee 2003, 2004; for similar perspectives not built on a video game metaphor see Holland and Quinn 1987; see

Strauss and Quinn 1997 for a perspective from anthropological psychology; see Barsalou 1999a, b; Glenberg 1997; Glenberg and Robertson 1999; Churchland 1995; Churchland and Sejnowski 1992; Clark 1989, 1997, 2003 for cognitivist perspectives). Video games like *Deus Ex, Half-Life, Age of Mythology, Rise of Nations,* or *Neverwinter Nights* involve a visual and auditory world in which a player manipulates a virtual character. Such games often come with editors or other sorts of software with which the player can make changes to the game world or even build a new game world. The player can make a new landscape, a new set of buildings, or new characters. The player can set up the world so that certain types of actions are allowed or disallowed. The player is building a new world by using, but modifying, the original visual images (really, the code for them) that came with the game.

One simple example of this is the way players can build new skateboard parks in a game like *Tony Hawk's Pro Skater.* Players must place ramps, trees, grass, poles, and other things in space so that they or other players can manipulate their virtual characters to skateboard in the park in a fun and challenging way. In the act, the player can create problems that other players must solve in order to skate the park successfully.

Imagine the mind works in a similar way. We have experiences in the world, including things we have experienced in dialogue with others. Let us use as an example experiences of weddings. These are our raw materials, like the game with which the gamer starts. Based on these experiences, we can build a simulated model of a wedding. We can move around as a character in the model as ourselves, imaging our role in the wedding, or we can "play" other characters at the wedding (e.g., the minister), imaging what it is like to be that person. The model we build is not "neutral"; rather, the model is meant to take a perspective on weddings. It foregrounds certain aspects of weddings that we view as important or salient. It backgrounds other elements that we think are less important or less salient and leaves some things out altogether.

However, we do not build just one wedding-model simulation and store it away once and for all in our minds. Rather, we build different simulations on the spot for different specific contexts we are in. In a given situation or conversation involving weddings, we build a model simulation that fits that context and helps us to make sense of it. Our models are specially built to help us make sense of the specific situations we are in, conversations we are having, or texts we are reading. In one case, we might build a model that emphasizes weddings as fun, blissful, and full of potential for a long and happy future. In another case, we might build a model that emphasizes weddings as complex, stressful, and full of potential for problematic futures.

We build our model simulations to help us make sense of things and prepare for action in the world. We can act in the model and test which consequences follow before we act in the real world. We can role-play other people in the model and try to see what motivates their actions or could follow from those actions before we respond to them in the real world. In fact, human beings tend to want to understand objects and words in terms of their "affordances" for actions. Take something as simple as a glass:

The meaning of the glass to you, at [a] particular moment, is in terms of the actions available. The meaning of the glass changes when different constraints on action are combined. For example, in a noisy room, the glass may become a mechanism for capturing attention (by tapping it with a spoon), rather than a mechanism for quenching thirst. (Glenberg 1997, 41)

Faced with the word "glass" in a text or a glass in a specific situation, the word or object takes on a specific meaning or significance based not just on the model simulation we build, but also on the actions with the glass that we see as salient in the model. In one case, we build a model simulation in which the glass is "for drinking"; in another it is "for ringing like a bell to get attention"; in another it is a precious heirloom in a museum that is "not for touching." Our models stress affordances for action so that they can prepare us to act or not act in given ways in the real world.

We think and prepare for action with and through our model simulations. They are what we use to give meaning to our experiences in the world, and they prepare us for action in the world. They help us give meaning to words and sentences, yet they are not language. Furthermore, because they are representations of experience (including feelings, attitudes, embodied positions, and various sorts of foregroundings and backgroundings of attention), they are not just "information" or "facts." Rather, they are value-laden, perspective-taking "games in the mind."

Of course, talking about simulations in the mind is a metaphor that, like all metaphors, is incorrect if pushed too far (see Barsalou 1999b for how a similar metaphor can be cashed out and corrected by a consideration of a more neurally realistic framework for "perception in the mind"). It should be pointed out, though, for those who find an analogy to games trivializing, that simulations are often used at the cutting edge of the sciences of complex systems to form and test hypotheses, test predictions, and generate analyses. Simulations involving multiple "players" are also widely used for learning in the military and in workplaces where people must learn to coordinate their skills with others.

Thus, meaning is not about general definitions in the head. It is about building specific models for specific contexts. Even words that seem to have very clear definitions, like the word "bachelor" that we used as an example at the beginning of this section, do not really have such clear definitions. Meaning is not about definitions but about simulations of experience. For example, what model simulation(s) would you bring to a situation in which someone said of a woman, "She's the bachelor of the group?" You might build a simulation in which the woman was attractive, at or a little older than marriageable age, perhaps a bit drawn to the single life and afraid of marriage, but open to the possibilities. You would see yourself as acting in various ways toward the woman and see her responding in various ways. The fact that the woman was not an "unmarried man" would not stop you from giving meaning to this utterance. Someone else, having had different experiences than you, would form a different sort of simulation. Perhaps the differences between your simulation and the other person's would be big, perhaps small. They are small if you and that person have had similar experiences in life and larger if you have not.

If we admit the importance of the ability to simulate experiences in order to comprehend oral and written language, we can see the importance of supplying all children in school with the range of necessary experiences with which they can build good and useful simulations for understanding subjects like science. Nearly everyone will have experiences of weddings and bachelors sufficient for building simulations with which to think and prepare for action. Not all learners have adequate experiences with concepts like reflection and refraction, atoms and molecules, or force and motion that will allow them to build simulations that can serve for thinking and meaning in science.

This is clearly an important issue regarding OTL. If some children have had experiences through which they can build and manipulate appropriate simulations in a domain and others have only interacted with oral and written words, the latter have only general and verbal understandings; they cannot assign the richer and more useful meanings to words and texts that the former can. They have not had the same opportunity to learn the material in as deep and meaningful a way.

One issue that arises when we think of meaning as situated in actual experiences people have had is generality. Of course generality is important, but in a situated viewpoint it is often (and sometimes best) attained, at least initially, bottom up by comparing and contrasting various specific experiences that can then serve as materials for building simulations that apply more generally to a domain. Let's consider a specific example. The science educator diSessa (2000) has successfully taught the algebra behind Galileo's principles of motion (principles related to Newton's laws) to children in sixth grade and beyond using a specific computer programming language called Boxer.

The students type into the computer a set of discrete steps in the programming language. For example, the first command in a little program meant to represent uniform motion might tell the computer to set the speed of a moving object at one meter per second. The second step might tell the computer to move the object, and a third step might tell the computer to repeat the second step over and over. Once the program starts running, the student will see a graphical object move one meter each second repeatedly, a form of uniform motion.

Now the student can elaborate the model in various ways. For example, the student might add a fourth step that tells the computer to add a value a to the speed of the moving object after each movement the object has taken (let us say, for convenience, that a adds one more meter per second at each step). Now, after the first movement on the screen (when the object has moved at the speed of one meter per second), the computer will set the speed of the object at two meters per second (adding one meter), and, then, on the next movement, the object will move at the speed of two meters per second. After this, the computer will add another meter per second to the speed, and on the next movement the object will move at the speed of three meters per second. This will repeat forever, unless the student has added a step that tells the computer when to stop repeating the movements. This process is obviously modeling the concept of acceleration. Of course, you can set a to be a negative number instead of a positive one and watch what happens to the moving object over time instead.

The student can keep elaborating the program and watch what happens at every stage. In this process, the student, with the guidance of a good teacher, can discover a good deal about Galileo's principles of motion through his or her actions in writing the program, watching what happens, and changing the program. The student is seeing, in an embodied way, tied to action, how a representational system that is less abstract than algebra or calculus (namely, the computer programming language, which is actually composed of a set of boxes) "cashes out" in terms of motion in a virtual world on the computer screen.

An algebraic representation of Galileo's principles is more general – basically, a set of numbers and variables that does not directly tie to actions or movements as material things. As diSessa points out, algebra doesn't distinguish effectively "among motion ($d = rt$), converting meters to inches ($i = 39.37 \times$ m), defining coordinates of a straight line ($y = mx$), or a host of other conceptually varied situations" (diSessa 2000, 32–33). They all just look alike. He goes on to point out that "[d]istinguishing these contexts is critical in learning, although it is probably nearly irrelevant in fluid, routine work for experts," (diSessa 2000, 33) who, of course, have already had many embodied experiences using algebra for a variety of different purposes of their own.

Once learners have experienced the meanings of Galileo's principles about motion in a situated and embodied way, they have understood one of the situated meanings for the algebraic equations that capture these principles at a more abstract level. Now these equations are beginning to take on a real meaning in terms of embodied understandings. As learners see algebra spelled out in additional specific material situations, they will come to master it in an active and critical way, not just as a set of symbols to be repeated in a passive and rote manner on tests. As diSessa puts it:

Programming turns analysis into experience and allows a connection between analytic forms and their experiential implications that algebra and even calculus can't touch. (diSessa 2000, 34)

Abstract systems originally got their meanings through such embodied experiences for those who really understand them. Abstraction (at least in many important cases) rises gradually out of the ground of situated meaning and practice and returns there from time to time, or it is meaningless to most human beings.

DISTRIBUTED KNOWLEDGE

In the study of knowledge and learning, a situated/sociocultural perspective takes as its unit of analysis not the person alone, but "person plus mediating device" (Brown, Collins, and Dugid 1989; Wertsch 1998). A mediating device is any object, tool, or technology that a person can use to enhance performance beyond what could be done without the object, tool, or technology. It obviously makes little sense to ask how high a pole vaulter can jump without a pole. Furthermore, poles made of different material enable different types of jumps (Wertsch 1998). What learners can understand and accomplish with diSessa's Boxer program as a mediating device is obviously different than what they can do without it.

When people use mediating devices, knowledge is distributed, some of it existing in their heads, some of it existing in the ways in which they can coordinate themselves (as bodies and in terms of social practices) with the tools they are using, and some of it existing in the tools themselves. Other people are also "tools" for learners when and if the learners can interact with them so as to gain and produce mutual knowledge. One problem for the traditional view of knowledge and learning – the view that focuses on mental representations – is that almost all human thought and interaction is mediated by objects, tools, technologies of various sorts, or other people.

In fact, it is clear that a mental representation itself is a mediating device. A learner who has internalized geometry as a form of mental representation can understand and use the laws of the pendulum better and more deeply than one who has not (in fact, using geometry is how Galileo discovered these laws). However, once we concede this fact, it is clear, too, that public representations – like geometry on paper or diSessa's Boxer program – are just as important as mental representations in serving as mediating devices. If we are interested in learning and OTL, we must ask which mediating devices are available, how they are made public, and how they come to be used.

People are smarter when they use smart tools. Better yet, people are smarter when they work in smart environments; that is, environments that contain, integrate, and network a variety of tools, technologies, and other people, all of which store usable knowledge. When we ask where knowledge resides in such smart environments, the answer is that it is distributed across the insides of individuals' heads, their bodies, their tools and technologies; other people; and the ways in which all of these are integrated and linked together in a network. This perspective is common now in businesses and work-places, less so in schools (Gee, Hull, and Lankshear 1996; Hagel and Brown 2005).

People are always parts of environments, whether they are particularly smart ones or not. They always think and act as part of larger systems that contain more than their own heads do. This perspective has been well captured by work in activity theory. The Russian psychologist Vygotsky (1978) argued that human beings do not react directly to or interact directly with the environment. Rather, human reactions and interactions are mediated by signs (language and other symbol systems) and tools. Vygotsky went on to argue that people learn how to use these mediating devices primarily through social interaction. Through participation in common activities with already adept others, people internalize the workings of their culture, their language, and various symbols, artifacts, norms, values, and ways of acting and inter-acting. The furniture of the human mind first exits publicly in the world of social interaction and participation.

For activity theorists, the proper unit of analysis in studying activity, cer-tainly including learning, is an *activity system*; that is, a group ("community," though without any connotation of people personally having to feel close to

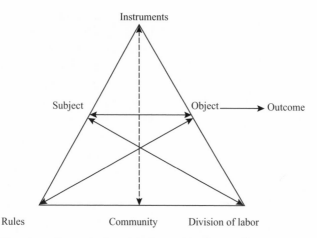

Figure 4.1. Conceptual model of an activity system (Engeström 1987, 78).

each other) of actors who have a common object or goal of activity (Cole and Engeström 1993; Engeström 1987). An activity system as a unit of analysis connects individual, sociocultural, and institutional levels of analysis. The study of activity ceases to be just the psychology of an individual, focusing instead on the interaction of individuals and systems of artifacts in institutional settings that develop across time.

Figure 4.1 (from Engeström 1987) models the integrated elements of an activity system. The whole system has certain intended and unintended "outcomes." The outer triangle contains the integration of "instruments" (various tools and technologies), "rules" (norms of use), and "division of labor" (the differential expertise of different actors in the system). Various other relationships in the model capture the diverse ways in which "subjects" (actors), the "object" (goal) of the activity system, and the "community" (various types of actors in the system) interrelate with each other and with the instruments, rules, and division of labor.

To see the model at work, consider the example of a doctor working at a clinic (example taken from Center for Activity Theory and Developmental Work Research 2003). The object (goal) of the doctor's work is the health problems of his or her patients. The outcomes include both intended ones like improvements in health and unintended ones like patients getting lost in the midst of overcrowding in the clinic. The instruments include tools like x-rays, laboratory tests, and medical records as well as medical knowledge that is partly internalized and partly stored in books and tools. The community consists of the various actors who constitute the staff of the clinic and its patients. The division of labor determines the tasks and powers of the doctors, nurses, aides, patients, and other actors in the system. Finally, various rules and norms regulate how, when, and where various actions and interactions take place, as well as the use of time, how outcomes are measured and assessed, and the criteria for rewards.

The same activity system will look different if we take the point of view of another subject (actor) in the system; for example, a nurse. Both the doctor and the nurse share the same overall object (goal), the health care of the patients, but they do not necessarily construe it in the same way. Different actors, because of their different histories and different positions in the division of labor, may very well construe the object and the other components of the activity system in different – sometimes quite different – ways. Yet they still must coordinate their different interpretations of the object (goal) and the activity system as a whole to ensure that the system operates, however well or poorly. This coordination requires continual overt and tacit negotiation, carried out in word and deed, among the various actors in the system.

An activity system does not exist by itself; it interacts within a network of other activity systems. For example, our clinic may receive various rules and instruments from management, another activity system, and in turn, the clinic produces outcomes for other activity systems, such as insurance companies.

If we take an activity-system view of students in a classroom, we cannot ask only about the individual student. We have to ask what sort of activity system the student is in, what his or her role is in it, what the system looks like from his or her perspective, what it looks like from the perspective of other actors (e.g., the teacher, other students) in the system, and what other systems interact with the one the student is in. From an opportunity-to-learn perspective, we must consider more than the information to which the learner has been exposed. All of the other elements in the system need to count as well, including the ways in which all of these elements mediate the learner's knowledge and performance.

PARTICIPATION

In situated/sociocultural work, activity systems have often been analyzed in terms of the notion of a "community of practice" (Lave and Wenger 1991; Wenger 1998). In communities of practice, people share a set of practices, often carried out collaboratively, related to carrying out a common endeavor. Newcomers pick up both overt and tacit knowledge through a process of guided and scaffolded participation in the community of practice, a process that has been compared to apprenticeship.

The term "community of practice" – which is now common in the business literature as a way to reform work (Gee, Hull, and Lankshear 1996; Wenger 1998; Wenger, McDermott, and Snyder 2002) – has been used to cover a variety of different social configurations in which shared practices and participation are central (for a critique of the notion of "community of practice," see Gee 2004 and Barton and Tusting 2005). Not all of these fit the sometimes "warm" connotations of the word "community." Nonetheless, the central ideas are that people learn new practices through participation with others, that they are networked with others and with various tools and technologies in ways that allow them to accomplish more than they could by themselves, and that knowledge is stored as much in the network and the practices of the group as it is in any one person's head.

Communities of practice – in workplaces and in some educational instantiations – are beginning to take on a distinctive shape. Some salient features are listed below. These features have commonly been mentioned in literature seeking to reform modern workplaces to make them smarter, but they have all been applied to reform in schools as well and are found in one form or another in classrooms that place a premium on students generating knowledge through participation in authentic practices in areas like science and mathemetics (DuFour and Eaker 1998; Fink and Resnick 2001; Fullan and Hargreaves 1991):

(1) Members of the community of practice are affiliated with each other primarily through a common endeavor and shared practices and only secondarily through ties rooted in shared culture, race, class, gender, or ability. These latter ties – as well as other forms of diversity – are not seen as dividers but are leveraged as differential resources for the whole group in carrying out its common endeavors and practices.

(2) The common endeavor is organized around a whole process (involving multiple but integrated functions), not single, discrete, or decontextualized tasks carried out outside of or without knowledge of the wider contexts that give them meaning.

(3) Members of the community of practice must all share extensive knowledge. By "extensive knowledge," I mean that members must be involved with many or all stages of the endeavor; able to carry out multiple, partly overlapping, functions; and able to reflect on the endeavor as a whole system, not just their part in it. This shared extensive knowledge also involves shared norms, values, and ways of acting

and interacting that allow the community of practice to carry out its endeavors.

(4) Members of the community of practice also each have intensive knowledge; that is, specialized and deep knowledge that goes beyond the group's shared extensive knowledge, which they have built up and can supply to others who do not share it when they need aspects of it for their own work.

(5) Much of the knowledge in the community of practice is *tacit* (embodied in members' mental, social, and physical coordinations with other members, and with various tools and technologies) and *distributed* (spread across various members, their shared sociotechnical practices, and their tools and technologies) and *dispersed* (available offsite from a variety of different sources).

(6) The role of leaders is to design communities of practice, continually resource them, and help members turn their tacit knowledge into explicit knowledge to be used to further develop the community of practice, while realizing that much knowledge will always remain tacit and situated in practice.

In such communities of practice, people are committed through their immersion in practice, because it is the practice itself that gives them their identity. Diverse individual skills and cultures are recruited as resources for the community, not as identities that transcend the community of practice itself.

It is clear that an activity-system perspective, with its links to the notion of a community of practice, treats people, including learners in school, as actors and not just as passive recipients of information (Greeno and Gresalfi, this volume). What people do in an activity system or a community of practice is not entirely a result of what is going on inside their heads but is contingent on interactions among all the elements of the system in which they are acting and interacting. As Greeno (1997, 8) has stated, "just presenting hypotheses about the knowledge someone has acquired, considered as structures in the person's mind, is unacceptably incomplete, because it does not specify how other systems in the environment contribute to the interaction."

It is also clear from our discussion of activity systems and communities of practice that the notion of *participation* in social interaction is foundational. This is so for several reasons. First, according to this perspective, following Vygotsky's (1978) ideas about the Zone of Proximal Development, learning starts when learners are first able to accomplish with others through participation in interaction what they cannot yet accomplish on their own. Such skills are said to be in the learner's Zone of Proximal Development, and these are the skills that will soon become individual accomplishments. By the time they become individual accomplishments, learners will have internalized these skills in terms of the schemes they have seen publicly at work in their social interactions with others using various sign systems and tools. These skills, in this sense, retain a social element.

Second, we have seen earlier that the meanings of words and signs, if they are to be truly useful, must be situated in experiences that learners have had that they can simulate in their minds and from which they can eventually build simulations that are more generally applicable. Yet learners can only come to see how words and signs fit particular patterns of experience if they see these words used in specific situations in ways that make clear how they apply. Thus, models of language in use in specific situations from masters and more expert peers is crucial for learning how to situate the meanings of words and signs in specific ways – otherwise, learners have only general verbal definitions as meanings that are hard to apply in specific situations.

Third, participation in social practices not only makes meanings public, but it also allows us to ask how we can position learners in the interaction so as to allow them to be active generators of knowledge (Greeno 1997, 1998; Greeno and Gresalfi, this volume). We saw, at the outset of this chapter, that even with the traditional "in the head" approach to knowledge and learning, there is the problem that some representations are much more powerful than others. When learners must generate knowledge as part and parcel of social practice, they must use more powerful representational systems in their heads and on paper – the sorts of representations that yield new results and do not just store already-provided information. However, to produce such knowledge, learners must be given both the authority for and the resources with which to build knowledge (tools and interactions with masters and more expert peers). In turn, placing participation in talk and other social practices at the center of learning allows us to investigate the affordances and constraints of different forms of participation, a crucial question that hardly arises in the traditional view. To the extent that different forms of talk and social interaction lead to different affordances and constraints for different learners, we confront, once again, a key concern for thinking about equitable opportunities to learn.

Fourth, one of the most important tools for learning in the content areas like mathematics and science is mastery of the specialist varieties of language these areas use, varieties that, as a family, are often referred to as (forms of) "academic language" (Schleppegrell 2004). Specialist varieties of language are crucial tools (mediating devices) for creating meanings in the academic content areas. In this sense, learning in the content areas is a form of language development, and like all forms of language development, it is for the most part dependent on specific forms of social interaction with masters (people who know the form of language) and peers (Halliday and Matthiessen 1999). In fact, we know a good deal about how varieties of language are acquired, knowledge that can be applied to learning in the content areas in a situated/ sociocultural perspective (Gee 2004; Schleppegrell and Colombi 2002). Let us turn, then, to the issue of language and learning.

ACADEMIC REGISTERS

Although people tend to think of a language like English as one entity, actually it's not one but many entities (Gee 2004, 2005). There are many different varieties of English. Some of these are different dialects spoken in different regions of the country or by different sociocultural groups. Some are different varieties of language used by different occupations or for different specific purposes; for example, the languages of carpenters, lawyers, or video game players.

Every human being, early in life, acquires a vernacular variety of his or her native language. This form is used for face-to-face conversation and for "everyday" purposes. Different groups of people speak different dialects of the vernacular, connected to their family and community. Thus, a person's vernacular dialect is closely connected to his or her initial sense of self and belonging in life.

After the acquisition of their vernacular variety has begun, people often also go on to acquire various nonvernacular specialist varieties of language used for special purposes and activities. For example, they may acquire a way of talking (and writing) about fundamentalist Christian theology, video games, or bird watching. Specialist varieties of language are different – sometimes in small ways, sometimes in large ways – from people's vernacular variety of language. Linguists often refer to these specialist varieties of language, tied to specific tasks and identities, as "registers" (Halliday and Martin 1993).

One category of specialist varieties of language is what we can call academic varieties of language; that is, the varieties of language connected to learning and using information from academic or school-based content areas (Gee 2002; Halliday and Matthiessen 1999; Schleppegrell 2004; Schleppegrell and Colombi 2002) The varieties of language used in (different branches) of biology, physics, law, or literary criticism fall into this category.

Some texts are, of course, written in vernacular varieties of language; for example, some letters, e-mail, and children's books. The vast majority of texts in the modern world, though, are not written in the vernacular but in some specialist variety of language. People who learn to read the vernacular often have great trouble reading texts written in specialist varieties of language. Of course, there are some texts written in specialist varieties of language (e.g., nuclear physics) that many very good readers cannot read.

Specialist varieties of language, whether academic or not, often have both spoken forms and written ones, and these may themselves differ from each other. For example, a physicist or computer scientist can write in the language of physics or computer science and speak a version of it, too (e.g., in a lecture).

It is obvious that once we talk about learning to read and speak specialist varieties of language, it is hard to separate learning to read and speak this way from learning the sorts of content or information that the specialist language is typically used to convey. That content is accessible through the specialist variety of language and, in turn, that content is what gives meaning to that form of language. The two – content and language – are married (Halliday and Matthiessen 1999).

Of course, one key area where specialist varieties of language differ from vernacular ones is vocabulary. Yet they also often differ in syntax and discourse features as well ("syntax" means the internal structure of sentences; "discourse" in this context means how sentences are related to each other across a text and what sorts of things can or cannot be said in a particular type of text). For example, suppose someone is studying the development of hornworms (cute green caterpillars with yellow horns). Contrast the vernacular sentence "Hornworms sure vary a lot in how well they grow" with the (academic) specialist sentence "Hornworm growth exhibits a significant amount of variation."

The specialist version differs in vocabulary (e.g., "exhibits"), but it also differs in syntactic structure. Verbs naming dynamic processes in the vernacular version (e.g., "vary," "grow") show up as nouns naming abstract things in the specialist version ("variation," "growth"). The vernacular sentence makes the hornworms (cute little caterpillars) the subject/topic of the sentence, but the specialist sentence makes hornworm growth (a measurable trait for hornworms) the subject/topic. A verb–adverb pair in the vernacular version ("vary a lot") turns into a verb plus a complex noun phrase in the specialist version ("exhibits a significant amount of variation").

Although we do not have space to pursue the matter fully here, specialist varieties of language also differ from vernacular varieties at the discourse level. We can see this even with our two sentences. Note that the specialist version does not allow an emotional word like "sure" that occurs in the vernacular version. We would not usually write or say, "Hornworm growth sure exhibits a significant amount of variation." There is nothing wrong with this sentence syntactically. We just don't normally speak or write this way in this variety of language. It doesn't "go with" the other things we say or write in this variety. At the cross-sentential level, specialist languages use many devices to connect, contrast, and integrate sentences across stretches of text that are not used as frequently, or exactly in the same way, in vernacular varieties of language (like the phrase "at the cross-sentential level" at the beginning of this sentence).

Specialist languages draw, of course, on grammatical resources that exist also in vernacular varieties of language. For example, any vernacular variety of English can make a noun (like "growth") from a verb (like "grow"). Yet to know the specialist language, you have to know that this is done regularly in such a variety; you have to know why (its function in the specialist language); and you have to know how and why doing this goes together with a host of other related processes (for example, using a subject like "hornworm growth" rather than "hornworms" or avoiding emotive words like "sure"). Any variety of a language uses certain patterns of resources, and to know the language, you have to be able to recognize and use these patterns (Halliday 1973, 1985a, 1985b; Halliday and Martin 1993; Halliday and Matthiessen 1999). This is much like recognizing that the pattern of clothing "sun hat, swimsuit, and thongs" means someone is going to the beach.

Earlier we stressed the close connections between meaning and experience. Yet our experiences of talk, dialogue, and social interaction with other people are a large part of what teaches us how words and other signs apply to reality. Let us consider for a moment how people learn the meaningful functional features of their everyday language. Note, however, that we are not talking about the acquisition of "core grammar" (the basic design features that all languages share at least parameters for), an innate competence for human beings (Chomsky 1986). We are talking about how people learn which discourse and pragmatic functions words and syntactic structures can carry out within the social groups of which they are members. Consider, in this regard, the following quote from Michael Tomasello (1999):

... the perspectival nature of linguistic symbols, and the use of linguistic symbols in discourse interaction in which different perspectives are explicitly contrasted and shared, provide the raw material out of which the children of all cultures construct the flexible and multi-perspectival – perhaps even dialogical – cognitive representations that give human cognition much of its awesome and unique power. (p. 163)

Let's briefly explore what this means. From the point of view of the theory Tomasello is developing, the words and grammar of a human language exist to allow people to take and communicate alternative perspectives on experience (see also Hanks 1996). That is, words and grammar exist to give people alternative ways to view one and the same state of affairs. Language is not about conveying neutral information; rather, it is about communicating perspectives on experience and action in the world, often in contrast to alternative and competing perspectives: "We may then say that linguistic symbols are social conventions for inducing others to construe, or take a perspective on, some experiential situation" (Tomasello 1999, 118). This is not to say, by the way, that some perspectives are not better or worse than others, only that language allows its users to state and debate different perspectives or interpretations of the world about them.

This is not surprising, because we have argued already that people give meaning to language by running simulations of our previous experiences. We see that language is already built to convey perspectives on experience, not to offer neutral viewpoints detached from how people actually see things. Human language is built to support human thinking, both of which are perspectival.

Let's give some examples of what it means to say that words and grammar are not primarily about giving and getting information, but rather about giving and getting different perspectives on experience. You open Microsoft's Web site: Are products you can download from the site without paying a price for them "free," or are they being "exchanged" for prior Microsoft purchases (e.g., Windows)? Saying "the download was free because I already owned Windows" is a different perspective on the same sort of experience than "the download was paid for when I bought Windows." If I use the grammatical construction "Microsoft's new operating system is loaded with bugs," I take a perspective in which Microsoft is less agentive and responsible than if I use the grammatical construction, "Microsoft has loaded its new operating system with bugs."

These are all examples from daily life. However, such perspective taking is equally important for the specialist varieties of language used in the content areas in school – a type of language development that occurs after children's early socialization into their native vernacular dialects. Earlier we discussed diSessa's programming language for capturing some specific applications of Galileo's laws of motion. These laws, and diSessa's specific symbolic instantiation of them, take a perspective on the material world that is quite different from the perspectives we tend to use everyday language for to take on that same world. Furthermore, other symbolic forms take yet a different perspective on much the same phenomena (e.g., geometrical expression of the laws of motion). Learners don't really understand any of these symbolic expressions unless they see what perspective they are designed to take on reality; that is, how they imply the world *is* and what the symbolic forms allow us to do to/with the world. The best way to see this is to participate in social interactions and activities in which these symbolic forms are used in ways that make clear what they mean and how they apply.

How do children learn how words and grammar line up to express particular perspectives on experience? Here, interactive, intersubjective dialogue with more advanced peers and masters appears to be crucial. In such dialogue, children come to see, from time to time, that others have taken a different perspective on what is being talked about than they have. At a certain developmental level, children have the capacity to distance themselves from their own perspectives and (internally) simulate the perspectives the other person is taking, thereby coming to see how words and grammar come to express those perspectives (in contrast to the way in which different words and grammatical constructions express competing perspectives).

Later, in other interactions or when thinking, the child can rerun such simulations and imitate the perspective-taking the more advanced peer or adult has done by using certain sorts of words and grammar. Through such simulations and imitative learning, children learn to use the symbolic means that other persons have used to share attention with them:

In imitatively learning a linguistic symbol from other persons in this way, I internalize not only their communicative intention (their intention to get me to share their attention) but also the specific perspective they have taken. (Tomasello 1999, 128)

Tomasello also points out (1999, 129–30) that children come to use objects in the world as symbols at the same time (or with just a bit of a time lag) as they come to use linguistic symbols as perspective-taking devices on the world. Furthermore, they learn to use objects as symbols (to assign them different meanings encoding specific perspectives in different contexts) in the same way they learn to use linguistic symbols. In both cases, the child simulates in his or her head and later imitates in his or her words and deeds the perspectives his or her interlocutor must be taking on a given situation by using certain words and certain forms of grammar or by treating certain objects in certain ways. Thus, meaning for words, grammar, and objects comes out of intersubjective dialogue and interaction: "... human symbols [are] inherently social, intersubjective, and perspectival" (Tomasello 1999, 131).

The same dialogic, socially interactive process of language acquisition that shapes children's early understanding of the meaningful functions of their everyday language applies to their learning later specialist varieties of language that are crucial for school success. Learners need to participate in social interactions and activities in which they can make good guesses about what perspectives on reality the language and other symbol systems they see in use are being used to take. They need to be able to simulate these in their minds and try them out in interactions, hopefully in contexts that do not punish them for initially unsuccessful or partially flawed attempts.

If students fail to know the languages of the content areas, no really deep learning can occur, although they memorize and recite facts they don't fully understand and cannot themselves use in proactive ways. If children do not start early on the acquisition of academic forms of language, they are swamped by the later grades and high school and beyond, where language demands in the content areas become intense and complex. Again, we face a crucial opportunity-to-learn issue: Have all children in a given learning environment had equal opportunity to learn the specialist forms of language vital for thought and action in the domain they are seeking to learn?

CULTURE

A sociocultural approach places a premium on learner's experiences, social participation, use of mediating devices (tools and technologies), and position within various activity systems or communities of practice. The word "culture" has taken on a wide variety of different meanings in different disciplines. Nonetheless, it is clear that, as part and parcel of our early socialization in life, we each learn ways of being in the world, of acting and interacting, thinking and valuing, and using language, objects, and tools that crucially shape our early sense of self. A situated/sociocultural perspective amounts to an argument that students learn new academic "cultures" at school (new ways of acting, interacting, valuing, and using language, objects, and tools) and, as in the case of acquiring any new culture, the acquisition of these new cultures interacts formidably with the learners' initial cultures (in Gee 1996, 2005, I use the term "Discourse" – with a capital "D" – instead of "culture").

So far we have discussed the kinds of specialized experiences, tools, forms of participation, and varieties of oral and written language that are found in school and elsewhere in public settings like academics, workplaces, and institutions for which schools are meant to prepare people. Our early socialization in life gives us what we might call our "vernacular" culture; that is, the ways of being, doing, acting, interacting, and using language, objects, and tools that we associate with being an "everyday" ("nonspecialized") person belonging to specific social groups. Each of us has a culturally different way of being an "everyday" person, and it is this identity that we bring to school when we start the process of learning the specialized ways associated with formal schooling and academic content areas.

As we saw earlier, linguists have long made a distinction between a person's "vernacular" dialect (which is different for different geographical and social groups) and the specialized varieties of language ("registers") like those used in the content areas in school and in academic disciplines (Labov 1972; Milroy and Milroy 1985). We can broaden this distinction to consider not only people's vernacular dialects but also their vernacular cultural ways as a whole (Barton 1994). Just as one's vernacular dialect is the core basis on which new varieties of language are learned, so, too, one's vernacular culture is the core basis on which new cultures at school are learned.

We argued earlier that we humans give meanings to things and plan for action by building perspectival simulations in our minds based on the sorts of experiences we have had. Yet each of us has had different experiences – and learned different perspectives on those experiences – in our early enculturation. These home- and community-based ways of building meaning interact with and form the initial base for the child's new experiences at school and in academic content areas, the experiences with which the child will learn to build school-based models of the world.

The same is true in the other areas we have discussed. Children come to school with culturally specific, favored methods of participating in interactions and activities and using language and mediating devices (objects, tools, and technologies) of various sorts (Lee, this volume). These methods also interact with the new, school-based methods the child must learn.

The specialized forms of language and interaction that the child finds at school can resonate with and bridge to the child's vernacular cultural ways and thereby enhance learning. Alternately, they can lack such resonance or fail to create such bridges, thereby raising the child's affective filter and ensuring that school-based input is not actually intake. A great deal of the literature in the sociocultural area is devoted to this topic (e.g., Delpit 1995; Heath 1983; Scollon and Scollon 1981; Taylor 1983; Taylor and Dorsey-Gaines 1987). It has been shown, for instance, that the home-based practices of many middle-class families involve actions, interactions, and ways with words that resonate with practices that occur at school (e.g., Delpit 1995; Gee 1996; Heath 1983; Ochs et al. 1992). For example, practices in which children engage in early pretend readings of books or give scaffolded reports at dinnertime to their parents about some activity they have done that day have been shown to facilitate early success with early school literacy practices. Allowing children to develop "islands of expertise" with regard to subjects like trains or dinosaurs, for which they tend to give and hear school-related explanatory language, is another practice that appears to facilitate early school success (Crowley and Jacobs 2002).

In all of these cases and many others like them, children are not only practicing early versions of school-based practices but are doing so as part and
parcel of being socialized into their vernacular culture. These children come
to associate school and school-based ways with their home and community-
based identities, thanks to the initial overlap between home and school practices. This is a powerful form of affiliation.

There is also ample literature demonstrating that children from groups
that have tended to fare less well in school also engage in complex and sophisticated language and interactional practices at home. For example, the complex and often poetic verbal practices of many African American children
have been well documented (e.g., Delpit 1995; Gee 1996; Labov 1972, 1974;
Rickford and Rickford 2000; Smitherman 1977). However, too few schools
make use of early school-based practices that resonate with these vernacular
practices and build on them, thereby failing to build the initial strong sense
of affiliation with school that often occurs for other children.

The same issues that arise for children's entry into school continue to
apply throughout the school years. However, young people bring to school
not only their vernacular language and culture but also their peer-based cultures (Shuman 1986). Some of these themselves involve specialist varieties of
language and culture ("discourses") connected not to school "content" but
to their own peer-based and community identities – for example, if they have
become adept at hip-hop or anime. The language and practices associated
with hip-hop or *Yu-Gi-Oh* (an anime card game, video game, and television series) are quite complex – indeed, "specialist" and often "technical."
However, they are not school based. Schools, therefore, face the issue of how
to bridge – and not denigrate – not just children's home-based cultures but
their peer-based and "popular cultural" cultures as well.

Schools can make use of students' cultural knowledge and practices and
link to their cultural senses of self or they can ignore – or worse, denigrate –
these and risk raising the learner's affective filter. Work like that of Lee (1993,
1995, 1997, 2001, this volume) has amply demonstrated that such resonance
and links can be made and can make for real school success, even in high
school. Lee has built a curriculum that allows African American students
to use and research their own vernacular dialects (dialects well studied by
professional linguists) and vernacular verbal practices of using metaphor
and other tropes. The students also study specialized practices in domains
like rap, which have integral links to their vernacular culture. These studies,
which are academic in their own right, serve, too, as a mediating device for the
students' later studies of standard school-based fare involving, for example,
literary critical studies of African American and other novelists.

Lee has also demonstrated that classroom interaction, talk, and participation can be enacted in ways that resonate with some African American students' home- and community-based discourse practices (i.e., ways of making sense through language in social interaction). At the same time, these classroom practices involve deep learning of school-based content via the types of situated and participatory learning we have discussed earlier in this chapter and, together with Lee's overall curriculum, eventually lead as well to the acquisition of more specialized registers and school-based ways with words. What Lee is doing is, of course, no more than what schools do often at an unconscious level for more privileged children from other cultural groups – those more often associated with so-called "mainstream" middle-class children's homes.

Surely two children have not had the same opportunity to learn if schooling or a given assessment is built on resonances with one child's vernacular culture and not on the other's. Worse yet, two children have not had the same OTL if, however unconsciously, schooling or assessment ignores, dismisses, or demeans the one child's home- and community-based sense of self and ways with words, deeds, and interactions.

CONCLUSIONS: ASSESSMENT

Current assessments often don't mean what we often think they do. For example, the well-known phenomenon of the "fourth-grade slump" – the common situation in which children who have passed early reading tests cannot "read to learn" by the time more complex language demands, connected with academic content areas, are made in the fourth grade – shows that early reading tests do not mean children are learning to read in any academically useful way (Chall, Jacobs, and Baldwin 1990; see also the Research Round-Up section of the Spring 2003 issue of *American Educator*).

If we think of learners in terms of developmental trajectories (Greeno and Gresalfi, this volume) in the space of academic content learning and the learning of the complex forms of academic language associated with different content areas, teachers and policy makers alike need assessments that tell them where learners are in their trajectories and whether they are on course for successful progress in the future. Even certain forms of "failure" may be indicative of progress (e.g., when young children start saying "goed" instead of "went," demonstrating that they are catching on to the existence of an underlying rule system rather than just memorizing forms), and certain forms of "success" may not really portend success, as is so well shown by the fourth-grade slump.

Assessing the development of learners rather than static stores of skills and information that may not be meaningful in terms of the course of development means that we must ensure that all learners are given the resources and environments necessary for development in school. Americans believe that schooling is a right for all children. Thus, it makes sense to argue that children have certain rights with regard to learning and assessment; that is, rights to conditions that if unmet mean assessment is meaningless or unfair and full development impossible. This chapter, while overemphasizing certain sociocultural approaches to learning, has discussed a number of these "rights," each couched in terms of the notion of OTL.

In summary, we can state the following rights we would argue each child has with regard to OTL. When these rights are not honored, assessments are meaningless and unfair, unless their point is to tell us that the learners' rights were not honored.

1. Classrooms must offer learners not just the same "content" but also equal affordances for action, participation, and learning.

2. Because comprehension requires the ability to simulate relevant experiences in the mind, all learners must be offered the range of necessary experiences with which they can build good and useful simulations for understanding in the content areas (e.g., science, mathematics, social studies, history).

3. Learning for humans is mediated by "smart tools"; that is, representations, technologies, and other people networked into knowledge systems. Thus, learners must be offered equal access to such smart tools.

4. Learning takes place within activity systems, systems that, in school, should be a form of a community of practice. Thus, we must consider more than the information to which the learner has been exposed. All the other elements in the system need to count as well, including access to the forms of participations and social interaction that make one an agent and knower in the system.

5. Content learning in school requires learning new forms of language and the identities, values, content, and characteristic activities connected with these forms of language (e.g., the language of literary criticism or of experimental biology). Every learner has the right for these "new cultures" to be introduced in ways that respect and build on the learner's other cultures and indigenous knowledge, including his or her home-based vernacular culture and peer-based and "popular culture" cultures ("Discourses").

There are, of course, other such rights connected to authentic OTL. Yet caring about these rights means caring – in research, teaching, and assessment – about the trajectories of learners as they develop within content areas in school as part of communities of practice, engaged in mind, body, and culture, and not just as repositories of skills, facts, and information.

References

Barsalou, L. W. 1999a. Language comprehension: Archival memory or preparation for situated action. *Discourse Processes* 28: 61–80.

Barsalou, L. W. 1999b. Perceptual symbol systems. *Behavioral and Brain Sciences* 22: 57–660.

Barton, D. 1994. *Literacy: An introduction to the ecology of written language*. Oxford: Blackwell.

Barton, D. and K. Tusting. 2005. *Beyond communities of practice: Language power and social context*. Cambridge: Cambridge University Press.

Bransford, J., A. L. Brown, and R. R. Cocking. 2000. *How people learn: Brain, mind, experience, and school: Expanded edition*. Washington, D.C.: National Academy Press.

Brown, A. L. 1994. The advancement of learning. *Educational Researcher* 23: 4–12.

Brown, A. L., A. Collins, and P. Dugid. 1989. Situated cognition and the culture of learning. *Educational Researcher* 18: 32–42.

Center for Activity Theory and Developmental Work Research. 2003. The activity system. http://www.edu.helsinki.fi/activity/pages/chatanddwr/activitysystem/.

Chall, J. S., V. Jacobs, and L. Baldwin. 1990. *The reading crisis: Why poor children fall behind*. Cambridge: Harvard University Press.

Chomsky, N. 1986. *Knowledge of language: Its nature, origin, and use*. New York: Praeger.

Churchland, P. M. 1995. *The engine of reason, the seat of the soul*. Cambridge: MIT Press.

Churchland, P. S. and T. J. Sejnowski. 1992. *The computational brain*. Cambridge: Bradford/MIT Press.

Clancey, W. J. 1997. *Situated cognition: On human knowledge and computer representations*. Cambridge: Cambridge University Press.

Clark, A. 1989. *Microcognition: Philosophy, cognitive science, and parallel distributed processing*. Cambridge: MIT Press.

Clark, A. 1997. *Being there: Putting brain, body, and world together again*. Cambridge: MIT Press.

Clark, A. 2003. *Natural-born cyborgs: Why minds and technologies are made to merge*. Oxford: Oxford University Press.

Cole, M. and Y. Engeström. 1993. A cultural-historical approach to distributed cognition. In *Distributed cognition: Psychological and educational considerations*, edited by G. Salomon, 1–46. Cambridge: Cambridge University Press.

Corder, S. P. 1967. The significance of learners' errors. *International Review of Applied Linguistics* 5: 160–70.

Crowley, K. and M. Jacobs. 2002. Islands of expertise and the development of family scientific literacy. In *Learning conversations in museums*, edited by G. Leinhardt, K. Crowley, and K. Knutson, 333–56. Mahwah, N.J.: Lawrence Erlbaum.

Delpit, L. 1995. *Other people's children: Cultural conflict in the classroom.* New York: The New Press.

diSessa, A. A. 2000. *Changing minds: Computers, learning, and literacy.* Cambridge: MIT Press.

DuFour, R. and R. Eaker. 1998. *Professional learning communities at work: Best practices for enhancing student achievement.* Bloomington, Ind.: Solution Tree.

Dulay, H., M. Burt and S. Krashen. 1982. *Language two.* Oxford: Oxford University Press.

Ellis, R. 1997. *Second language acquisition.* Oxford: Oxford University Press.

Engeström, Y. 1987. *Learning by expanding. An activity theoretical approach to developmental research.* Helsinki: Orienta Konsultit.

Engeström, Y., R. Miettinen, R.-L. Punamäki, eds. 1999. *Perspectives on activity theory.* Cambridge: Cambridge University Press.

Fink, E. and L. Resnick. 2001. Developing principals as instructional leaders. *Phi Delta Kappan* 82: 598–606.

Fodor, J. A. 1975. *The language of thought.* Cambridge: Harvard University Press.

Fullan, M. and A. Hargreaves. 1991. *What's worth fighting for in your school?* New York: Teachers College Press.

Gass, S. M. 1997. *Input, interaction, and the second language learner.* Mahwah, N.J.: Lawrence Erlbaum.

Gee, J. P. 1992. *The social mind: Language, ideology, and social practice.* New York: Bergin and Garvey.

Gee, J. P. 1996. *Social linguistics and literacies: Ideology in Discourses,* 2nd ed. London: Routledge/Taylor & Francis.

Gee, J. P. 2002. Literacies, identities, and discourses. In *Developing advanced literacy in first and second languages: Meaning with power,* edited by M. Schleppegrell and M. Cecilia Colombi, 159–75. Mahwah, N.J.: Lawrence Erlbaum.

Gee, J. P. 2003. *What video games have to teach us about learning and literacy.* New York: Palgrave/Macmillan.

Gee, J. P. 2004. *Situated language and learning: A critique of traditional schooling.* London: Routledge.

Gee, J. P. 2005. *An introduction to discourse analysis: Theory and method,* 2nd ed. London: Routledge.

Gee, J. P. 2008. *Social linguistics and literacies: Ideology in discourses,* 3rd ed. London: Routledge/Taylor and Francis.

Gee, J. P., G. Hull, and C. Lankshear. 1996. *The new work order: Behind the language of the new capitalism.* Boulder: Westview.

Gibson, J. J. 1977. The theory of affordances. In *Perceiving, acting, and knowing: Toward an ecological psychology,* edited by R. Shaw and J. Bransford, 67–82. Hillsdale, N.J.: Lawrence Erlbaum.

Gibson, J. J. 1979. *The ecological approach to visual perception.* Boston: Houghton Mifflin.

Glenberg, A. M. 1997. What is memory for? *Behavioral and Brain Sciences* 20: 1–55.

Glenberg, A. M. and D. A. Robertson. 1999. Indexical understanding of instructions. *Discourse Processes* 28: 1–26.

Greeno, J. 1997. On claims that answer the wrong questions. *Educational Researcher* 26: 5–17.

Greeno, J. 1998. The situativity of knowing, learning, and research. *American Psychologist* 53: 5–26.

Hagel, J. and J. S. Brown. 2005. *The only sustainable edge: Why business strategy depends on productive friction and dynamic specialization.* Boston: Harvard Business School Press.

Halliday, M. A. K. 1973. *Language in a social perspective: Explorations in the functions of language.* London: Edward Arnold.

Halliday, M. A. K. 1985a. *Spoken and written language.* Victoria: Deakin University.

Halliday, M. A. K. 1985b. *An introduction to functional grammar.* London/Baltimore: Edward Arnold.

Halliday, M. A. K. and J. R. Martin. 1993. *Writing science: Literacy and discursive power.* Pittsburgh: University of Pittsburgh Press.

Halliday, M. A. K. and C. M. I. M. Matthiessen. 1999. *Construing experience through meaning: A language-based approach to cognition.* New York: Continuum.

Hanks, W. F. 1996. *Language and communicative practices.* Boulder: Westview Press.

Heath, S. B. 1983. *Ways with words: Language, life, and work in communities and classrooms.* Cambridge: Cambridge University Press.

Holland, D. and N. Quinn, eds. 1987. *Cultural models in language and thought.* Cambridge: Cambridge University Press.

Hutchins, E. 1995. *Cognition in the wild.* Cambridge: MIT Press.

Krashen, S. D. 1983. *Principles and practices in second language acquisition.* Oxford: Pergamon Press.

Labov, W. 1972. *Language in the inner city: Studies in Black English vernacular.* Philadelphia: University of Pennsylvania Press.

Labov, W. 1974. The art of sounding and signifying. In *Language in its social setting*, edited by W. Gage, 84–116. Washington, D.C.: Anthropological Society of Washington.

Latour, B. 1999. *Pandora's hope: Essays on the reality of science studies.* Cambridge: Harvard University Press.

Lave, J. 1996. Teaching, as learning, in practice, *Mind, Culture, and Activity.* 3: 149–64.

Lave, J. and E. Wenger. 1991. *Situated learning: Legitimate peripheral participation.* New York: Cambridge University Press.

Lee, C. D. 1993. *Signifying as a scaffold for literary interpretation: The pedagogical implications of an African American discourse genre.* Urbana, Ill.: National Council of Teachers of English.

Lee, C. D. 1995. A culturally based cognitive apprenticeship: Teaching African American high school students skills in literary interpretation. *Reading Research Quarterly* 30: 608–31.

Lee, C. D. 1997. Bridging home and school literacies: Models for culturally responsive teaching, a case for African American English. In *A handbook for literacy educators: Research on teaching the communicative and visual arts*, edited by J. Flood, S. B. Heath, and D. Lapp, 334–45. New York: Macmillan.

Lee, C. D. 2001. Is October Brown Chinese? A cultural modeling activity system for underachieving students. *American Educational Research Journal* 38: 97–141.

Milroy, J. and L. Milroy. 1985. *Authority in language: Investigating language prescription and standardisation.* London: Routledge.

Newell, A. and H. A. Simon. 1972. *Human problem solving.* New York: Prentice-Hall.

Norman, D. A. 1988. *The design of everyday things.* New York: Basic Books.

Ochs, E., R. Smith, D. Rudolph, and C. Taylor. 1992. Storytelling as a theory-building activity. *Discourse Processes* 15: 37–72.

Pylyshyn, Z. 1984. *Computation and cognition.* Cambridge: MIT Press.

Research round-up. Spring 2003. *American Educator.*

Rickford, J. R. and R. J. Rickford. 2000. *Spoken soul: The story of Black English.* New York: John Wiley.

Schleppegrell, M. 2004. *Language of schooling: A functional linguistics perspective.* Mahwah, N.J.: Lawrence Erlbaum.

Schleppegrell, M. and M. C. Colombi, eds. 2002. *Developing advanced literacy in first and second languages: Meaning with power,* 159–75. Mahwah, N.J.: Lawrence Erlbaum.

Scollon, R. and S. W. Scollon. 1981. *Narrative, literacy, and face in interethnic communication.* Norwood, N.J.: Ablex.

Shuman, A. 1986. *Storytelling rights: The uses of oral and written texts by urban adolescents.* Cambridge: Cambridge University Press.

Smitherman, G. 1977. *Talkin and testifin: The language of Black America.* Boston: Houghton Mifflin.

Strauss, C. and N. Quinn. 1997. *A cognitive theory of cultural meaning.* Cambridge: Cambridge University Press.

Taylor, D. 1983. *Family literacy: Young children learning to read and write.* Portsmouth, N.H.: Heinemann.

Taylor, D. and C. Dorsey-Gaines. 1987. *Growing up literate: Learning from inner city families.* Portsmouth, N.H.: Heinemann.

Tomasello, M. 1999. *The cultural origins of human cognition.* Cambridge: Harvard University Press.

Vygotsky, L. S. 1978. *Mind in society: The development of higher psychological processes.* Cambridge: Harvard University Press.

Wenger, E. 1998. *Communities of practice: Learning, meaning, and identity.* Cambridge: Cambridge University Press.

Wenger, E., R. McDermott, and W. M. Snyder. 2002. *Cultivating communities of practice.* Cambridge: Harvard Business School Press.

Wertsch, J. V. 1998. *Mind as action.* Oxford: Oxford University Press.

5 Individualizing Assessment and Opportunity to Learn

Lessons from the Education of Students with Disabilities

Diana C. Pullin

Students with disabilities are a group for whom opportunity to learn (OTL) and educational assessment present special issues of public policy and challenges for educational research and practice. These challenges highlight both the powerful prospects for improving schools and the significant limitations inherent in current practice. One commentator has suggested that "when read critically, special education provides the structural and cultural insights that are necessary to begin reconstructing public education for the historical conditions of the twenty-first century and, ultimately, for reconciling it with its democratic ideals" (Skrtic 1991, 206).

Children with disabilities were a group long excluded from our nation's schools. In 1974, Congress estimated that more than a million children with disabilities were not in school (Hehir and Gamm 1999; Pullin 1999). When a commitment was made to educate this population, it was embedded in a series of state and federal legal protections that define access to educational opportunity in a manner quite different from the opportunities afforded to students without disabilities. Although our system of educating students with disabilities is far from perfect in either design or implementation, examination of the treatment of students with disabilities[1] affords a different lens for viewing the challenges associated with providing every child with a full and fair opportunity to learn utilizing appropriate and meaningful testing and assessment.

Almost nine percent of the students in the country, more than six million children and youth, received special education services in 2002 under the federal Individuals with Disabilities Education Act (IDEA); almost half of these students were those placed in the category of individuals with specific learning disabilities (U.S. Department of Education 2004). Another, smaller group of students with mild disabilities who received supportive services but did not need special education was also served by our schools (Pullin

2002, 2006). All of these students afford a unique perspective to inform our considerations of new ways of approaching OTL and assessment. Because of their history of exclusion from our nation's schools, legal requirements afford students with disabilities access to diagnostic testing to assess their individual needs as learners, special procedural protections to regulate their relationships with educators, structured mechanisms for parental participation, individualized educational program documents defining the terms and conditions of their schooling, and different treatment when it comes to the implementation of high-stakes accountability testing and assessment.

This chapter proposes that the special case of students classified with disabilities provides insight into new ways of understanding and reconceptualizing OTL and assessment. It considers the ways in which the perspectives offered in this volume suggest some necessary new approaches for the education and assessment of students with disabilities as well as some implications for students in general education. Drawing from sociological, sociocultural, and situative perspectives represented in this volume, it discusses the procedures and practices for classifying disability status and eligibility for special services, defining OTL for students with disabilities, and the uses of assessment for placement, programming, and accountability for these students. It considers as well the roles of parents and educators in using assessment and in promoting OTL. It highlights the ambiguities associated with the bureaucratized response to externally imposed individual rights and the possibilities arising from a system calling for a more individualized, learner-centered, collaborative model for teaching and learning. The chapter suggests that research and theoretical perspectives, public-policy choices about both assessment and opportunity to learn, local-level practices in the provision of educational opportunities, and the implementation of assessment requirements can be enhanced through consideration of the contrasts between general and special education.

THE LEGALIZATION OF SPECIAL EDUCATION

The articulation of specific legal rights for individuals with disabilities arose from efforts to compel public services to this population and to incorporate them into schools, society, and the economic community (Hehir and Gamm 1999; Pullin 1999). However, these laws create what Minow (1990) characterizes as "dilemmas of difference." The pursuit of equality for students with disabilities required differential treatment, but that different treatment also stigmatized and isolated them. The social and legal constructions of difference allowed mandated access to educational opportunity but further separated students labeled as having disabilities from the nondisabled. At the same time, the legal provisions concerning the education of students with disabilities gave them access to different OTL and assessment systems that are, in some respects, more closely aligned with the sociocultural/situative perspectives described elsewhere in this volume.

The education of children with disabilities is governed by three federal laws and by parallel provisions in the laws of each state. The most significant federal legislation is the Individuals with Disabilities Education Act (IDEA) (2005), which provides federal financial assistance to states for students who have disabilities and require special education. As a condition for receiving federal funding, states and local school districts are required to meet procedural requirements about how services are delivered and substantive requirements to ensure that each eligible child receives education and supportive services designed to meet the student's individual needs for an appropriate education. In addition to this law, two federal civil rights statutes exist that bar discrimination against individuals with disabilities. Section 504 of the Rehabilitation Act is a broad prohibition against discrimination on the basis of disability, and the Americans with Disabilities Act (ADA) bars discrimination and requires affirmative steps to insure that individuals with disabilities are afforded a full and fair opportunity to participate in society.

As a result of these legal protections, students participate in a defined system of assessment to identify disabilities and individual educational needs; a mechanism for structuring learning opportunities for individuals; a system for parental involvement in individual educational decision making; and a system of accountability through assessment. Consideration of the extent to which these systems for students with disabilities impact the learning opportunities and assessment practices initiated by schools provides a useful perspective on educational practices impacting all students.

ASSESSING FOR EDUCATING STUDENTS WITH DISABILITIES

By legal mandate, formal classification based on individual testing and assessment is required as a precondition for participation in either the IDEA special education system or Section 504 supplemental services. In some other Western cultures, educational failure is attributed to the system rather than to the student. By contrast, in the United States, for most students with disabilities, the disability label is the consequence of schools' social, or cultural, practices that identify a problem within a student requiring differential treatment (Florian and Pullin 1999; Mehan, Hertweck, and Meihls 1986). To some extent, disability labels are the result of cultural practices designed to explain how some students do not fit into the social organizations we call schools (Hudak and Kihn 2001; McDermott 1993; Varenne and McDermott 1998). Indeed, special education represents the most sophisticated of our schools' sorting practices. Assessment for placement in school and for educational decision making plays a more significant role in educating students with disabilities than it does for other students.

The traditional conception of disability in schools in this nation is that it is the result of fixed traits within a child making the child qualitatively different than peers who are nondisabled (Florian and Pullin 1999; NRC 2002; Pullin, in press). This conception is open to challenge on many counts. Disability classification is a social and cultural phenomenon more than a matter of science (Varenne and McDermott 1998). In the United Kingdom, for example, there is explicit recognition that learning difficulties may not result from within-child factors (Florian and Pullin 1999). In the United States, however, disabilities are most often seen as inherent in a child. Some, however, have argued that the U.S. system relies on disability classifications to identify children who are a poor fit in a cultural system. In this view, disability, particularly the nonmedical disability, is a cultural construct used to manage those who don't perform well in school, particularly on tests or in deportment. There is often a fine line separating those classified with a disability from other students, particularly when the classification is one as subjective as specific learning disability (McDermott 1993). The consequences of these practices are particularly striking given that the overwhelming majority of students served under IDEA (48.3% in 2002) were those labeled with the most subjective of classifications: specific learning disabilities (U.S. Department of Education 2004).

Assessment to determine access to special education has often been the focal point in addressing cultural conflicts within schools resulting from immigration, racial desegregation requirements, efforts to address delinquency or other behaviors, access to employment, or other social factors (NRC 2002). School professionals play a critical role in initial referral to determine whether a disability exists, usually triggering the special education assessment process. Teacher bias about gender roles, race, ethnicity, socioeconomic status, or language background can inappropriately impact referral decisions. Lack of teacher expertise in special education matters is also a crucial factor, particularly as the shortage of qualified special educators is severe. As a result, there have been numerous concerns about deficiencies in the processes that might initiate a disability classification for a student (McDermott 1993; Mehan et al. 1986; NRC 2002).

The creation of a legally driven classification system has created a category of students who receive legally mandated special status within our educational system. Eligibility for this protected category status is fraught with cultural and professional distinctions that may or may not make sense for an individual child. Students fall within or outside the classification according to many essentially arbitrary factors (Gartner and Lipsky 1987; Mehan et al. 1986). However, once a student is placed within this system, formal structures exist for individually designing opportunities to learn.

Formal classification in this system rests heavily on traditional testing and assessment practices to determine disability status and special education eligibility (Salvia, Ysseldyke, and Bolt 2007). The diagnostic tools and practices used to generate disability labels are subject to challenge on many fronts, including concerns about the validity and reliability of the instruments used (Pullin 2002, 2005).

Although assessment for classification relies heavily upon standardized and often group-administered tests, the intent of diagnostic assessment is to inform an individualized educational placement and programming decision. These classification decisions are heavily criticized on several grounds. Many students are never diagnosed or are assessed incorrectly. The highest-incidence disabilities, particularly the specific learning disabilities and mild to moderate retardation, are identified currently through highly subjective means that can result in overreferral for evaluation because of such factors as teacher incapacity, the pressures imposed by external accountability testing, or manipulation by either parents or educators (Kelman and Lester 1997; NRC 2002). Over- or underrepresentation of cultural minority students often results (Losen and Orfield 2002; NRC 2002; Oswald et al. 1999). In recent years, about 12% of white students were identified for special education, compared with 14% of African Americans, 13% of Native Americans, 11% of Hispanics, and only 5% of Asian and Pacific Islanders (NRC 2002). Gender also plays a role in classification decisions, with boys often overrepresented in placements. At the same time, there are pockets of disproportionately high rates of mild disability categorizations in affluent communities (NRC 2002), perhaps because families perceive benefits associated with the individualized focus of the programming, access to accommodations for accountability or higher education admissions testing, or in the 504 plans or IEPs for students with disabilities.

In its original conceptualization, the legalization of special education mandated services for children excluded from school or from meaningful education because of disabilities. Most of those impacted were children with low-incidence, medically based types of disabilities and those with a label that was then defined as mental retardation. Over time, the legalization of special education came to be used not just to ensure access for students with significant disabilities but to create opportunities for those in previously unrecognized or more judgmentally based disability categories. Over the years, the categories of disabilities recognized under these legal provisions have expanded considerably, especially in the more judgmental, milder, and higher-incidence categories such as specific learning disabilities, attention deficit hyperactivity disorders, or autism spectrum disorders (Government Accountability Office 2005; NRC 2002; U.S. Department of Education 2004). This expansion of students identified as having disabilities and attendant opportunities for misclassification may become a more significant problem as schools scramble to meet accountability mandates of the No Child Left Behind Act of 2001 (NCLB) and seek the option of excluding some students with disabilities from accountability requirements, as discussed below.

Some of the shifts in classification are attributable to increases in the diagnostic capabilities of those assessing these students (see, for example, Shaywitz 2003). Some are the consequence of local educators' responses to the challenges of teaching students who don't meet expected norms. Some increases are attributable to as yet unclear environmental, medical, or other changes in our world. Yet some of these changes are also, to some extent, the result of the vigilance of concerned and empowered parents. The addition of the category of specific learning disabilities to the categories of children eligible under the federal special education laws reflected an enhancement of knowledge and diagnostic practices for defining new types of learning needs as well as a cultural shift in which categorizations became both more subjective and judgmental and, at the same time, more socially acceptable. The inclusion of the specific learning disability category in IDEA was soon followed by a decrease of about 25% in the number of students labeled as mentally retarded and an increase in students labeled with specific learning disabilities, which doubled (NRC 2002).

In 2004, when reviewing the IDEA, Congress determined that too many students were being classified into special education. It embraced a concept, based on the research of some special educators (NRC 2002; Salvia et al. 2007; Vaughn and Fuchs 2003), that instructional interventions, applied systematically and for a short time early in a child's schooling immediately after learning problems were identified, could eliminate the need for disability classification. This approach highlighted the fluidity of the disabilities designation for the largest group of students in the system.

The disability categories and diagnostic labeling that schools use are based on drawing sometimes artificial, highly variable distinctions between students who are characterized as disabled and those characterized as nondisabled (McDermott 1993; NRC 2002). A student might be categorized, and educated, quite differently in one state than he or she would in another. The result is, first of all, an impact on the diagnostic categorization of students who are really more appropriately placed on a continuum of individual learning needs, at the far end of which significant special programs and services are required (NRC 2002). However, once the disability label is applied and a distinction, no matter how artificial, is drawn to identify a child as eligible for special education or supportive services, a panoply of legal requirements is brought in to play. The result impacts OTL, particularly in the contemporary context of high-stakes testing for individual and institutional accountability. Many more students might be eligible for the programs and services associated with special education if the classifications were managed with even more flexibility. Indeed, most students might be found to have some special need.

The combination of legal requirements and the cultural, social, and educational phenomena surrounding the treatment of disabilities in our schools means that there is now more attention paid, for this population of students, to the educational challenges discussed elsewhere in this volume. It means at the very least a structure and process in place that calls for more attention, and more individualized attention, to the variations in children's educational needs. Yet once a disability and the need for special education or supportive services are identified, how does it affect the OTL provided to a child?

STRUCTURING OTL FOR STUDENTS WITH DISABILITIES

First, it should be noted that in addition to the difficulties of identifying students with disabilities, there are considerable challenges associated with the provision of special education services and the resulting opportunities to learn, or lack thereof. Federal funding has never been sufficient to meet the original share of costs that Congress promised to pay in the mid-1970s. A severe shortage of qualified personnel has long existed. Also, many of the instructional strategies research has shown to be effective are simply not used in schools (NRC 2002).

Context plays a critical role in educating any child; this is particularly true for students with disabilities. A key element of the context for these children is a set of legal protections unavailable to other students. The primary mechanism for addressing the education of students with disabilities is the IDEA. At the heart of the IDEA are requirements that every student with a disability who needs special education must receive an *appropriate* education, which must be described in a written individualized education program (IEP) uniquely formulated for that student in consultation between educators and parents. The IEP sets out diagnostic and performance information on the student and then describes the program, services, settings, goals, and annual review plans for the education of the student, including descriptions of how the student will participate in state or local assessment programs. For students who have disabilities that require supportive services or accommodations rather than special education services, the provisions of the implementing regulations under Section 504 require that they receive an appropriate education. As a result, many school districts write "504 plans" for these students, which can be somewhat analogous to the IEP. IEPs and 504 plans are documents that become, for students with disabilities, a road map to describe how OTL will be afforded, a road map that simply does not exist for the vast majority of nondisabled students.

The law mandates the participation of a team of educators in formulating an IEP or a 504 support plan, and ordinarily, more than one educator is required to implement it. Collaborative team decision making about educational approaches for an individual student during the classification and IEP formulation are, therefore, critical components of determining learning opportunities and, in many cases, implementing the components of the IEP (Salvia et al. 2007; Skrtic 1991). These types of collaborative approaches to teaching and learning are increasingly seen as fundamental to the delivery of meaningful educational opportunities for any type of student (Shulman and Shulman 2004; Spillane, Reiser, and Reimer 2002).

What, then, is OTL for students with disabilities? It is first a structure and a set of processes to which other students do not generally have access. These processes begin when a student is first identified as someone who has a medically identifiable disability or who may be struggling in a regular classroom or may respond to progressively intensive intervention approaches in the classroom. After a detailed individual evaluation of capabilities, once a student is identified as having a qualifying disability, schools are required to initiate the IEP or 504 plan process. Although many schools have turned to technology to facilitate this process, even using it to generate students' plans or IEPs, the process is individualized. To at least some extent, then, a student's needs must be specifically considered, and at least some general way for addressing those needs must be stated. Thus, the focus is not on placement into special education but on the benefits resulting from special education (Hehir and Gamm 1999; NRC 1997, 2002). Although it has now been made clear that these provisions do not need to be designed to maximize a student's potential, they must be designed to allow a student a reasonable opportunity to make educational progress (Alexander and Alexander 2005; Pullin 1999; Turnbull and Turnbull 1998). Students with disabilities are entitled to a wide range of instructional and supportive services, including special programs in local schools, supportive services like speech or physical therapy, and compensatory education services beyond the usual age of school attendance, all individually designed to ensure them an appropriate education (Alexander and Alexander 2005; Pullin 1999; Turnbull and Turnbull 1998). The IEP and 504 plans, therefore, range widely and include such factors as transition plans to facilitate progression from K–12 schooling to higher education or the workplace. The IDEA has been used successfully to obtain public funding to pay for private specialty school placements for students with disabilities who cannot be appropriately be educated in their public school, to limit disciplinary exclusion of students with disabilities from education programs, and to obtain school payment for transportation, health aides, hearing aids, nursing services, and a myriad of other provisions deemed necessary to ensure the provision of appropriate education (Alexander and Alexander 2005; Turnbull and Turnbull 1998).

The IEP is, however, a procedural and largely content-free mechanism that has been described by some researchers as bureaucratic and paperwork-focused rather than substantive, a notion Congress embraced to some extent in 2004 when it reviewed the IDEA (Christiensen and Dorn 1997; IDEA 2005; Skrtic 1991). The provision of meaningful opportunities to learn would require not simply a structure for individualized educational programming, but also the commitment and capability of educators and a context in which the program could be effectively implemented to benefit a student. In addition to the IEP documents, which can be simply a dysfunctional bureaucratic response to a legal mandate (Skrtic 1991), this would require more attention at the individual level to the provision of the types of meaningful educational experiences that would enhance an individual's educational trajectory and future productivity.

In many, perhaps most, instances, the special education system and the general education system as well fail to be sufficiently adaptable to appropriately serve the needs of individual learners and to allow teachers their full opportunity to implement appropriate professional practices (Skrtic 1991). Yet for students with disabilities, unlike students in general education, the IEP or 504 plan mechanism affords the opportunity to identify and address an individual student's learning needs and to define the opportunities the individual requires in order to benefit from education.

PARENTS' ROLES IN SPECIAL EDUCATION

Included within the conditions for creating meaningful OTL are sufficient relationships between school and home and school and community to

appropriately foster teaching and learning and broader conceptions of desirable knowledge (Honig, Kahne, and McLaughlin 2001). For students with
disabilities, the legal mandates affecting OTL call for parental agreement to
have a child evaluated to determine the existence of a disability and then for
parent involvement in the formulation of a child's IEP. The law requires that,
if possible, parents and a team of educators meet to devise and then meet
regularly to review the IEP. Students with disabilities can even participate in
the formulation of plans to afford them a meaningful opportunity to learn
by participating in IEP meetings (Test et al. 2004), although there is evidence
that this is not yet widely perceived as effective (Mason, Field, and Sawilowsky
2004).

In addition to the IEP requirements, IDEA also includes procedural
requirements to minimize the chances of erroneous disability labeling and
to enhance the provision of appropriate programs and services. Included in
the IDEA are administrative and court processes to allow opportunities for
parents to challenge school decisions concerning children. The IEP and the
504 plan can serve as a lever against recalcitrant schools for families with the
resources and time to pursue a relationship with their child's school to define
an educational plan for a child. Also, the importance of the procedural protections spelled out in IDEA and the role of parents in the IEP design process
has been clearly recognized by different types of policy makers.[2]

The content of an IEP rests largely on agreements between the family and
local school authorities, promoting school accountability to families without
treading too intrusively into the professional discretion of educators (Handler
1986; Neal and Kirp 1986). The parental rights and due-process protections
spelled out in the IDEA have their limits, however. If parents don't participate,
there are procedures to allow schools to step into the breach. If parents and
school officials disagree on what is appropriate for a child, an impartial
administrative hearing officer or a court can make the decision on what is
appropriate. Based on recognition of the specialized knowledge and expertise
of educators and a long tradition of judicial deference to educators, judges
regularly refuse to substitute their judgment for that of educators in special
education litigation (NRC 1997; Pullin 1999). This is so despite the fact that
the procedural protections of IDEA can fail to take into account the power
differential between families and professional educators (Handler 1986). For
example, in many instances, parents in inner-city schools are not encouraged
by educators to participate in IEP meetings (NRC 2002). For some families,
the resources, the time, or the capacity to influence the conditions of their
children's learning and confront the power of school authorities through the
processes spelled out in the law are missing. For these families, the IEP or

the 504 plan present an unattainable, perhaps even unknown, avenue for the pursuit of educational opportunity.

The phenomenon of middle-class parent involvement in the educational and other school activities of their children, the phenomenon Mehan characterizes as "concerted development" (this volume), has played a role in the evolution of special education. In some respects, the participation of privileged parents in special education decision making and disputes is simply yet another opportunity for reproduction of inequality. Although lower-income and less educated parents may have less time and fewer resources to participate in the parental roles envisioned by IDEA, many middle-class parents have seized the opportunity. Also, the cultural and social capital of privileged parents (Mehan, this volume) empowers them in the IEP or 504 planning process and in the due process provisions of the laws when parents are unsuccessful in persuading the IEP team or local school officials on the appropriate treatment for a child.

Although there are disagreements within the field on the measurable effectiveness of special education and supportive services, the current special education system has the benefit of targeting resources and attention to students in need (NRC 2002; Skrtic 1991). The mere existence of the IEP and parental participation provisions of special education law create a structure allowing those parents who do wish to pursue a special education program for their children at least a defined chance to structure an individualized mechanism for ensuring that a child's educational needs are met and at least some steps taken to ensure that appropriate educational opportunities are afforded. These mechanisms alone, no matter how imperfectly they are executed, create structures for individualized teaching and learning that begin to address some of the rich range of issues identified elsewhere in this volume as critical to meaningful OTL.

EDUCATORS' OPPORTUNITIES TO LEARN

However, the existence of structures designed to support learning opportunities are not sufficient. Meaningful OTL, the provision of the resources, supports, and occasions students need to enhance their achievement, requires, among other factors, sufficient "opportunity to teach" on the part of teachers and other educators (Darling-Hammond 2005; Elmore 2004; Shulman and Shulman 2004; Spillane 2004). The capability of both special and general educators to effectively deliver meaningful educational opportunities to students with disabilities is a growing concern (IDEA 2004). There is a severe shortage of qualified teachers for students with disabilities (NRC

2002). There are also concerns that special education teachers lack sufficient content knowledge in the academic domains (IDEA 2004). The
mere presence of a student in a system of special education or a general
education classroom does not ensure educational opportunity. Classrooms
and schools must be organized to afford meaningful participation opportunities. Educators must be prepared to implement effective approaches
that allow students to build in meaningful ways on their prior knowledge and experiences when exposed to instruction and experiences reasonably designed to lead to domain-specific expertise. Teachers of students
with disabilities, particularly accomplished teachers of students with significant disabilities, are highly adept at operating with a continuous feedback
loop utilizing dynamic, informal assessment information on student trajectories of progress in knowledge acquisition and the impact of specific
teaching interventions (Salvia et al. 2007). Many teachers are not similarly
effective.

In addition to the ideal of home–school collaboration in the formulation of programs and plans for the education of students with disabilities,
the system also is designed to promote collaboration among educators. The
design of IEPs is to be facilitated by a set of education professionals and
intended to jointly determine student needs and appropriate programming
(IDEA 2004). This element of collaboration among education professionals,
including both service providers and administrators and diagnosticians like
school psychologists, would be rare in general education. The evidence is not
clear, however, that the IEP is sufficiently useful for teachers in helping them
design and deliver effective instruction (Shriner 2000).

Congress' most recent review and revision of the IDEA in 2004 resulted in
its determination that special education has been impeded by a culture of low
expectations and insufficient use of proven, research-based methods of teaching and learning (IDEA 2004). Early intervention is of critical importance
(Hehir and Gamm 1999; NRC 2002) both in terms of ameliorating conditions
that might eventually lead to a disability classification or limiting the impact
of a disability, and there is a need for more professional development in the
implementation of these approaches (NRC 2002).

Special educators, like all other educators, need to benefit from opportunities to learn more effective approaches to their professional responsibilities. A growing body of literature demonstrates the critical importance of
the capacity of educators and schools to deliver high-quality education in
a standards-based, accountability-focused environment. This calls for policies and practices designed to allow educators the opportunity to learn and
adopt the approaches required for effective pedagogy (Cohen and Hill 2001;

Elmore 2004, 1996; Firestone, Schorr and Monfils 2004; McDonnell 2004; Shulman and Shulman 2004).

ACCOUNTABILITY ASSESSMENT FOR STUDENTS WITH DISABILITIES

The IEP and Section 504 and the structural and procedural mechanisms provided by law were the primary focus in the education of students with disabilities for almost twenty-five years. As a result, the success or lack of success of special education was determined student by student, with little accountability to the general public (NRC 1997). In the 1997 revision of IDEA, in the face of growing interest at both the state and federal levels in the use of standards-driven accountability systems, Congress required that students with disabilities participate in state and local accountability systems and that their IEPs specify both how that participation would occur and the educational programs and services needed to facilitate each student's participation in this testing and assessment. The extent of this participation was further detailed and emphasized in NCLB and the 2004 reauthorization of IDEA. These initiatives were designed to address the policy goals of allowing public access to information on the success of schools in educating students with disabilities and ensuring that their education was standards driven.

The federal government has recognized that too often in the past, students with disabilities were excluded from learning opportunities and that high-stakes accountability systems could play a role in ameliorating this problem (U.S. Dept of Education 2003). States have also recognized that some students with disabilities were never taught academic skills and concepts, even at very basic levels (Massachusetts Department of Education 2003). Courts have taken note of these new assessment-driven approaches. For instance, some courts have suggested that the best assessment of whether a student with disabilities is receiving an appropriate education is the use of "objective, if not standardized, standards" (*Helms v. School District* 1984, 825).

In the period after the 1997 IDEA changes were made, states began efforts to refine the necessary conditions for allowing students with disabilities to fully participate in test-based accountability systems in the states and local schools. These changes impact consideration of both OTL and assessment. For IDEA students and presumably for students with 504 plans, OTL in a high-stakes accountability testing context has a new meaning. Academic content standards and public accountability requirements are beginning to impact individualized educational choices, even for students with the most significant disabilities (Nagle and Crawford 2004; Zatta and Pullin 2004).

The practical and technical challenges associated with including students with disabilities in the increasingly important testing systems have, however, been considerable.

When students with disabilities participate in testing or assessments, they must be afforded reasonable accommodations during the test. A test accommodation is any variation in the standardized administration of a large-scale test in response to a student's disability (AERA, APA, NCME 1999). Typically, these accommodations include such things as extended time for test administration, large-print or Braille versions of a test, or the use of a sign interpreter or a scribe. These accommodations are usually the same accommodations students have written into their IEPs or their 504 plans for their educational activities. To that extent, the assessment accommodations mirror the OTL provisions of the student's educational plan.

Evidence is accumulating that the use of accommodations is increasing the participation of students with disabilities in both testing programs and educational experiences that focus on the content covered on tests. These students are also more likely than they were in the past to receive a regular high school diploma as a result of participation in the tests (Ysseldyke, Dennison, and Nelson 2004).

For those IDEA students with disabilities significant enough to effectively limit their ability to participate in testing or assessment with accommodations, a system of alternate assessments is being created (Saliva et al. 2007). Often, these alternate assessments address a different set of content or performance standards than those used in the general assessment (Pullin 2005). These alternate approaches take several possible forms: out-of-grade testing to administer a test more appropriate for a student's attainment than his or her usual age-level test; portfolios of student work or the collection of a body of evidence about success in attainment of standards and goals set out in a student's IEP; performance assessments; checklists; and an approach somewhat resembling more traditional paper-and-pencil assessments, most often filled out by teachers on the basis of one-on-one assessments of students (Lehr and Thurlow 2003). The most common approach in alternate assessment is the use of a portfolio assessment linked to grade-level expectations, scored with the same achievement level descriptors as the general assessment. Another approach relies upon the collection by a child's teacher of a "body of work," examples of work generated in daily classroom activities. Most of these submissions are graded by teachers in the state in which the data were gathered rather than by an outside testing company (Thompson and Thurlow 2003).

Some of the alternate assessment approaches take into account issues of participation discussed elsewhere in this volume. For example, the extent to which a student with a significant disability requires assistance in performing an assessed task is taken into account in scoring. These approaches, refined considerably, coupled with the types of portfolio and body-of-work approaches used for students with significant disabilities, begin to approach the models described by Mislevy (this volume). These would more meaningfully inform the provision of OTL with rich and thick descriptors from assessments invoking a wide variety of evidence beyond a single test score – the types of multiple sources of evidence in conjunction with a single test score as required by standards for appropriate test practice (AERA 2000; AERA, APA, NCME 1999). This richer and broader set of assessment evidence, used dynamically, can inform pedagogic choice to enhance student progress in the acquisition of domain-specific knowledge.

These approaches have had the effect, in some instances, of altering the content of special education away from the low-level, functional-life-skills approaches traditional for students with more severe disabilities in favor of more academic content associated with the curricular standards articulated for general education (Lehr and Thurlow 2003; Pullin 2005; Quenemoen, Thompson, and Thurlow 2003; Zatta and Pullin 2004). The result of requiring assessment participation by students with disabilities has resulted in changes in practice to enhance the quality of educational opportunities afforded many of these students (Thompson and Thurlow 2003; Ysseldyke, Dennison, and Nelson 2004). On the other hand, there is limited evidence of the psychometric quality of these alternate approaches (Minnema et al. 2004). Also, many of these alternate approaches are associated with a diminution of opportunities to learn. For example, one study found students being assessed on out-of-grade level tests that did not accurately match either their academic abilities or their instruction (Minnema, Thurlow, and Warren 2004). Recent changes in federal requirements are designed to reduce these types of practices (U.S. Department of Education 2007).

The accommodated and alternate approaches to assessment entail a number of psychometric, pedagogic, and fairness challenges for which there often are not clear solutions (Pullin 2005; Quenemoen, Thompson, and Thurlow 2003; Thompson and Thurlow 2003). Yet these approaches, particularly the use of portfolios or "body of evidence" collections of actual student work, are approaches to assessment that often overlap heavily with the IEP (Quenemoen, Thompson, and Thurlow 2003). As a result, many policy makers feel that the resulting evidence provides a useful insight into whether instruction was sufficient or IEPs were appropriately designed.

For students with significant disabilities, assessments can be informed by the sociocultural, sociological, situative, and cognitive science approaches discussed elsewhere in this volume. For these students, the administration of an alternate assessment often means the opportunity to participate in a form of assessment that is individualized, highly contextual, oriented toward promoting the eventual independence of the individual, and potentially tightly linked to the OTL particularly defined for that student in the IEP (Quenemoen, Thompson, and Thurlow 2003).

Consideration of the consequences of assessment are critical to an inquiry on accountability: To what extent does accountability testing rationalize inequality more than it ameliorates it (Howe 1997) for students with disabilities? A first look at the current contexts of testing in the United States suggests that students with disabilities may be the beneficiaries of a structure at least intended to afford them equity. Yet there are also concerns that high-stakes assessment may compel schools to inappropriately classify students into special education. In one study of urban special education, it was reported that not a single school in the study sample had achieved adequate yearly progress for students with disabilities (Nagle and Crawford 2004). The same study reported a trend toward moving students with disabilities toward more segregated placements, away from the least restrictive and more inclusive placements called for by the IDEA.

Consideration of the fairness of accountability testing for students with disabilities requires fairness and equity in both the assessment and curriculum (Gipps 1994). Given the complexities of schooling, there is no such thing as a completely fair assessment, but assessment can be, in Gipps' view, fairer, particularly the more individualized and contextualized it is. In this respect, students with disabilities, particularly those in alternate assessments, may have an advantage over students in general education, given the individualization mandated for special education and the goal of aligning the nature of the assessment with the curricular opportunities afforded those students (Salvia et al. 2007).

The use of accountability results for schools, states, or groups of students presents a more complicated set of challenges. Under NCLB, schools and states are to aggregate the data on performance of students with disabilities into overall student performance data. These data are also to be disaggregated, along with those for other traditionally disadvantaged students. The goal for including alternate assessments in school, district, and state accountability results is to ensure that students with disabilities have access to the opportunities to learn created by a standards-driven, assessment-based accountability system (Koretz and Barton 2003–2004; Quenemoen and Thurlow, 2002). However, the constructs being measured on different assessments and the scores and score scaling used may be incompatible (Pullin 2002, 2005).

In alternate assessment, with its unique scoring practices, summative data for students is sometimes hard to understand or perhaps even justify. The use of summative performance assessments enhances the validity of data concerning individuals but diminishes at least some of the opportunities to engage in institutional or cross-site comparisons. If assessments cannot validly and reliably be placed on a common metric, comparisons are meaningless. Also, if the criteria being assessed are themselves biased or value-laden, as they most certainly always are, the inferences to be made from assessment scores privilege a particular notion of educational attainment (Howe 1997). When considering the attainment of individuals with significant disabilities and what they bring to their classrooms, current definitions of content and performance standards guarantee failure for many.

There is a lack of systematic evidence about the impact on educational opportunities for students with disabilities as a result of participating in large-scale assessments (Koretz and Barton 2003–2004), although some studies are beginning to report that alternate assessment expanded teachers' perceptions of what students with disabilities can and should learn (Quenemoen, Rigney, and Thurlow 2002; Zatta and Pullin 2004), increased expectations for students with disabilities (Ysseldyke, Dennison, and Nelson 2004), and exposed special education teachers for students with significant disabilities to academic curriculum standards for the first time (Zatta and Pullin 2004). Studies of the impact of state standards indicate that local educators are responsive but that the changes occur most often in the curriculum content rather than in the pedagogy used in classrooms (Sipple, Killeen, and Monk 2004).

At the same time, there are now increasing reports of some of the unintended negative consequences associated with disaggregated data on students with disabilities in high-stakes testing. Some otherwise high-performing schools are now identified as low-performing solely on the basis of the scores from students with disabilities (Pullin 2005). When the stakes are high for schools and educators, as they are under NCLB and many state laws, these sorts of phenomena bear close observation, particularly in terms of ensuring integrity for OTL and in assessment for all students.

As a result of accommodations and alternate assessments, there are for students with disabilities efforts toward more effective integration of instruction and assessment, and research is beginning to find these effects (Ysseldyke, Dennison, and Nelson 2004; Zatta and Pullin 2004). The goals for the changes in IDEA in 1997 and NCLB in 2002 are beginning to have the effect of integrating students with disabilities into education reforms and accountability initiatives. At the same time, however, as the challenges of educating and assessing these students has become clearer and political pressures have mounted against NCLB and the federal government's implementation of it, the U.S. Department of Education has taken a series of steps to move back from full inclusion of all students with disabilities in these initiatives, granting states the opportunity to exclude students with the most significant cogni-. tive disabilities from the calculations of schools' adequate yearly progress in achievement (Pullin 2005; U.S. Department of Education 2007). The department has continued to expand the flexibility it gives states concerning the assessment of students with disabilities, now allowing five options for these students: participation in the general state assessment no different from that of students without disabilities; participation in the general assessment with appropriate accommodations; alternate assessment based on grade-level academic achievement standards; alternate assessment based on modified, less rigorous achievement standards; and alternate assessment based on alternate academic achievement standards (U.S. Department of Education 2007). The NCLB policy goal of educating *all* students to high standards has not been renounced, but the federal government's continual revisions of the rules concerning students with disabilities reflect an increasing number of individualized approaches to educating and assessing these students as well as an incremental increase in the extent to which they are slowly being moved back into differential status in the operation of the accountability system.

OPPORTUNITIES TO LEARN IN ACTION

Independent of the special education laws, there are some other legal protections to ensure access to OTL for all children. There are currently two primary sources for these protections, first in interpretations of the applicability of the federal constitution and second in the court interpretations of the provisions of some state constitutions (see Pullin and Haertel, this volume). Both sets of protections apply to all students, those with disabilities and those who have no disabilites. The federal courts have found that when a state requires passing a test in order to receive a high school diploma, it is incumbent on the state to ensure that the test only covers content that students have had a fair opportunity to learn (Heubert and Hauser 1999). In addition, a number of state constitutions have been found to require the provision of an adequate OTL for all public school students, according to the descriptions of the outcomes of an adequate education set out in the *Rose* case (1989) in Kentucky (see Pullin and Haertel, this volume). The authors of other chapters in this volume would consider the *Rose* standards at least a good beginning at defining an educated individual. The definition has a utility in assessing the learning opportunities for all students, including students with disabilities. This standard is different from that articulated for students with disabilities, although it has been argued that once a state has a broad adequacy standard like this, students' IEPs and 504 plans should be prepared in conjunction with these standards.

It is also now becoming common for courts to declare that if a state constitution has a guarantee for access to education like that in Kentucky, the state's content or curriculum standards should be congruent with that definition (*Hancock v. Driscoll* 2005). Furthermore, results of student performance on state tests might then be used to determine whether or not schools were in fact offering the opportunity to learn required by state law. It is early in the process of articulating and evaluating these claims, but the outcomes of these inquiries will have considerable impact on the opportunities to learn of all students, with or without disabilities.

Viewing the OTL provided to students with disabilities from the perspectives described in this volume highlights the distinctive treatment these students are supposed to receive in our schools when the system is working at its best as intended by the laws. Successful teaching and learning must focus on the empowerment of actively involved learners and recognition of the importance of the relationship between the learner and the learning environment. As learning is situated, OTL is not just exposure to particular content, and the enhancement of OTL is not achieved simply by exposing students to more content or even to particular high standards of academic-content knowledge. Rather, the authors of this volume argue that the provision of a rich learning and assessment environment affording a student appropriate capacities of action is required to allow the student to think, feel, act, and interact powerfully with content knowledge and meaningfully apply that knowledge.

Good teachers understand and use these newer approaches to learning and assessment for all types of students and in all types of settings in both general and regular education, even without legal mandates about how children are to be educated. If the elements in a learning setting mediate learners' acquisition of knowledge and enhanced performance capabilities, the education of students with disabilities presents the opportunity to come closer to adopting a sociocultural approach because of the legal mandates in operation. In many, but not all, respects, the IEP or 504 plans provided students with disabilities with focuses upon some of the components required for the empowerment of learners and recognition of the importance of particular types of learning environments in fostering meaningful educational accomplishment. Also, the accommodated assessment or alternate assessment of students with disabilities in high-stakes testing programs is an arena in which traditional psychometric and nontraditional approaches to teaching and accountability assessment have intersected, at least to some extent.

The education of students with disabilities does not come close to fully representing the rich and broad understandings of learning and assessment informed by sociocultural, sociological, and situative perspectives discussed elsewhere in this volume. There are also a number of problems associated with the quality of programs and services students with disabilities receive and with the isolation and low expectations they are often saddled with by educators and their same-age peers. However, in some important respects, the legal framework for the education of students with disabilities provides some useful lessons for examining learning and assessment issues for all students and some insights into how to provide adequate education for all students. Education of students with disabilities recognizes first that the provision of educational programs and services must be individualized and provided in a context appropriate for a particular child. These services must be designed and delivered collaboratively, usually by teams of educators and in cooperation with parents. Assessment is used to define the nature of a student's learning needs. Once a student is determined to have a disability, assessment must be linked to instructional components and characteristics that will allow the student to progress on a trajectory of acquisition of important knowledge and capabilities.

For the student who is not classified into the disability-based education system, these structures for the provision of OTL and these approaches to assessment are not mandated. Yet, given the very subjective manner in which students are classified or not classified into a category like the large group of students labeled with specific learning disabilities, access to the system of opportunities and structures of participation and protections created by disabilities law is determined by what are most often very unscientific judgments (McDermott 1993; Mehan et al. 1986).

The educational systems and processes resulting from state and federal special education and disability rights laws have, in some respects, created new variations in the reproduction of inequality. On the other hand, these systems have also created a structure for educational decision making related to OTL and assessment that creates a salutary approach to individualizing educational decision making, structuring learning opportunities, enhancing parent participation, and using perhaps more meaningful systems of assessment. For students without disabilities, the mandated structures and rights to access learning opportunities are not nearly so specific.

For some time now, it has been asserted that many of the instructional interventions that are used for students with mild disabilities could be equally beneficial for students who have not been identified with a disability (Skrtic 1991). Our legally mandated special education system is far from perfect. Most students with disabilities are a long way from receiving the full range of appropriate educational opportunities they require. There are insufficient qualified teachers and insufficient teaching in techniques research has shown to be most beneficial. Over- and underrepresentation of racial and language minorities and of one gender or the other characterize certain disability categories (Hehir and Gamm 1999; NRC 2002). Students with disabilities are twice as likely to drop out of school as their nondisabled peers, particularly in urban settings (Hehir and Gamm 1999). Some of these disparities can be attributed to poverty, health and nutrition, and sociocultural issues. Yet clearly many, if not most, of these disparities can be explained only by inadequate professional systems and practices (NRC 2002).

Placement into the system of special education can too often become a dead end for a student, even after thirty years of law-based mandates for equity and enhanced education. The disaggregated test scores now being reported for students with disabilities provide glaring evidence that there is still far to go in educating these students effectively to high standards (Pullin 2005). Yet states have already begun to embrace approaches from the special education system for assisting students from general education settings who are also failing to succeed in the test-driven system of education reform. Massachusetts, for example, promotes the use of an "individual student success plan" (ISSP) for students who are not performing well enough on the state test to qualify for a high school diploma. The ISSP resembles in many ways an IEP or a 504 plan and sets forth, based on input from educators working with the student, the student's strengths and weaknesses, multiple assessment data, instructional supports required, benchmarks to assess progress, and documentation of parent communication (Massachusetts Department of Education 2004a). For students who continue to fail the high-stakes test required for high school graduation, Massachusetts has an appeals system in which failing test scores can be offset with multiple measures of other indicia of student success sufficient to justify the award of a high school diploma (Massachusetts Department of Education 2004b).

Our system of education and assessment for students with disabilities and for all students will be required to change in the face of the current press for test-driven, high-stakes educational change. How the system will change remains open to debate. Our ambitions for assessment (of any type of student, typical or not) may exceed our capacities to provide all that policy makers, parents, the public, and education practitioners desire. Although we know more than our present public policies may acknowledge about effective teaching and learning, we still have far to go to provide every student with a meaningful opportunity to learn. There is clearly much more work to be done to ensure full and fair OTL for all students and to design and implement the appropriate assessment systems to accompany that teaching and learning. The current system for educating students with disabilities through either special education or supportive services is far from perfect. Yet it offers many useful lessons on different methods to assay the problems of determining appropriate uses of assessment and the provision of meaningful opportunities to learn. It establishes that schools can be organized to attend to an individualized, context-driven delivery of education, perhaps including even the sorts of response to intervention that could keep a child from being labeled with a disability. The disability label has many potential stigmatizing effects associated with it, and many special education programs can be dead ends in which adequate education is far from attainable. Yet the special education system, at its best, is data driven, focuses on the specific learning needs of individuals, provides guidance to educators acting collaboratively in addressing the individualized needs of learners, and considers the contexts of learning. It provides mechanisms to encourage parent involvement, includes a chance for external scrutiny of the decisions made about a child, and encourages the use of assessment to insure not only individual, but institutional accountability. In some respects, it is difficult to understand why more children, or all children, are not offered many of the same learning opportunities without having to bear the burdens associated with obtaining a disability label. Indeed, in some respects, the recent use of individualized plans to help low-performing nondisabled students prepare to succeed on accountability tests is one version of this use of a special education-like approach to providing learning opportunities. At the same time, the system of special education itself needs to be more responsive to the teaching and learning perspectives represented in this volume. Also, those creating and using the accommodated and alternate assessments used with increasing frequency for students with disabilities would be well served to consider the teaching, learning, and assessment issues highlighted throughout this volume.

Notes

1. Another special-needs population with particular challenges concerning both assessment and opportunity to learn is the population of English language learners (see NRC 2004). The focus of the current chapter on other special-needs populations in no way seeks to dismiss the particular challenges confronting students with limited English proficiency nor the educators who work to address their needs. A developing literature on this population (see, for example, Abedi, Hofstetter, and

Lord 2004) offers an additional perspective on the issues covered not only in this chapter but throughout this volume. Students with disabilities are focused on here because the requirements for educating them are more systematized and there is more information about this population (Thurlow, Minnema, and Treat 2004).

2. For example, one federal circuit court of appeals has determined that a denial of parental participation in the IEP process, in itself, can result in a loss of educational opportunities and, thus, the denial of the free and appropriate public education a student is entitled to under IDEA (see *Knable v. Bexley City School District* 2001).

References

Abedi, J., C. Hofstetter, and C. Lord. Spring 2004. Assessment accommodations for English language learners: Implications for policy-based empirical research. *Review of Educational Research* 74: 1–28.

Alexander, K. and M. Alexander. 2005. *American public school law*, 6th ed. Belmont, Calif.: Thomson.

American Educational Research Association. 2000. *Position statement of the American Educational Research Association on high-stakes testing in preK-12 education*. Washington, D.C.: American Educational Research Association.

American Educational Research Association, the American Psychological Association, and the National Council on Measurement in Education (AERA, APA, NCME). 1999. *Standards for educational and psychological testing*. Washington, D.C.: American Educational Research Association.

Christiensen, C. and S. Dorn. Summer 1997. Competing notions of social justice and contradictions in special education reform. *The Journal of Special Education* 31: 181–98.

Cohen, D. K. and H. C. Hill. 2001. *Learning policy: When state education reform works*. New Haven: Yale University Press.

Darling-Hammond, L. 2005. *Instructional leadership for systemic change: The story of San Diego's reform*. Lanham, Md.: ScarecrowEducation.

Elmore, R. 1996. Getting to scale with good educational practice. *Harvard Educational Review* 66: 1.

Elmore, R. 2004. *School reform from the inside out*. Cambridge: Harvard Education Press.

Firestone, W. A., R. Y. Schorr, and L. F. Monfils, eds. 2004. *The ambiguity of teaching to the test: Standards, assessment and educational reform*. Mahwah, N.J.: Lawrence Erlbaum.

Florian, L. and D. Pullin. 1999. Defining difference: A comparative perspective on legal and policy issues in education reform and special educational needs. In *Comparative perspectives on education reform and students with disabilities*, edited by M. McLaughlin and M. Rouse. London: Routledge.

Gartner, A. and D. Lipsky. 1987, November. Beyond special education: Toward a quality system for all students. *Harvard Educational Review* 57: reprinted in *Special education at the century's end: Evolution of theory and practice since 1970* (1992), edited by T. Hehir and T. Latus, 123–57. Cambridge: Harvard Educational Review.

Gipps, C. 1994. *Beyond testing: Towards a theory of educational assessment*. New York: Routledge Falmer.

Government Accountability Office. 2005, January 14. *Special education: Children with autism*. Washington, D.C.: GAO. GAO–05–220.

Hancock v. Driscoll, 443 Mass. 428, 822 N.E. 2d 1134. 2005.

Handler, J. 1986. *The conditions of discretion: Autonomy, community, bureaucracy.* New York: The Russell Sage Foundation.

Hehir, T. and S. Gamm. 1999. Special education: From legalism to collaboration. In *Law and school reform: Six strategies for promoting educational opportunity,* edited by J. Heubert, 205–43. New Haven: Yale University Press.

Helms v. School District No. 3 of Broken Arrow, 750 F. 2d 820 (10th Cir. 1984).

Heubert, J. and R. Hauser. 1999. *High stakes: Testing for tracking, promotion, and graduation.* Washington, D.C.: National Academy Press.

Honig, M., J. Kahne, and M. McLaughlin. 2001. School-community connections: Strengthening opportunity to learn and opportunity to teach. In *Handbook of research on teaching,* 4th ed., edited by V. Richardson, 998–1028. Washington, D.C.: American Educational Research Association.

Howe, K. 1997. Understanding equal educational opportunity: Social justice, democracy, and schooling. *Advances in Contemporary Educational Thought,* vol. 20. New York: Teachers College Press.

Hudak, G. and P. Kihn. 2001. *Labeling: Pedagogy and politics.* New York: Routledge-Falmer.

Individuals with Disabilities Education Act (IDEA). 2004. 20 U.S.C. 1401 et seq.

Kelman, M. and G. Lester. 1997. *Jumping the queue: An inquiry into the legal treatment of students with disabilities.* Cambridge: Harvard University Press.

Knable v. Bexley City School District, 238 F. 3d 755 (6th Cir. 2001).

Koretz, D. and K. Barton. 2003–2004. Assessing students with disabilities: Issues and evidence. *Educational Assessment* 9 1/2: 29–60.

Lehr, C. and M. Thurlow. 2003. *Putting it all together: Including students with disabilities in assessment and accountability systems* (Policy Directions No. 16). Minneapolis: University of Minnesota, National Center on Educational Outcomes. Retrieved August 20, 2004, from http://education.umn.edu/NCEO/OnlinePubs/Policy16.htm.

Losen, D. J. and G. Orfield. 2002. *Racial inequity in special education.* Cambridge: Harvard Education Press.

Massachusetts Department of Education. 2003, September 22. Concerns and questions about alternate assessment. Retrieved August 27, 2004, from http://www.doe.mass.edu/mcas/alt/.

Massachusetts Department of Education. 2004a. Individual student success plans – Guidance document for districts. Retrieved July 4, 2005, from http:// www.doe.mass.edu/.

Massachusetts Department of Education. 2004b. MCAS performance appeals. Retrieved July 4, 2000, from http://5 at www.doe.mass.edu/.

Mason, C., S. Field, and S. Sawilowsky. 2004. Implementation of self-determination activities and student participation in IEPs. *Exceptional Children* 70: 441–51.

McDermott, R. P. 1993. The acquisition of a child by a learning disability. In *Understanding practice,* edited by S. Chaiklin and J. Lave, 269–305. New York: Cambridge University Press.

McDonnell, L. 2004. *Politics, persuasion, and educational testing.* Cambridge: Harvard University Press.

Mehan, H., A. Hertweck, and J. Meihls. 1986. *Handicapping the handicapped: Decision-making in students' educational careers.* Stanford: Stanford University Press.

Minnema, J., M. Thurlow, and S. Warren. 2004, September. Understanding out-of-level testing in local schools: A first case study of policy implementation and effects. Out-of-level Testing Project Report 11. Minneapolis: University of Minnesota, National Center on Educational Outcomes. Retrieved August 20, 2004, from http://education.umn.edu/NCEO/OnlinePubs/OOLT11.html.

Minnema, J., M. Thurlow, R. Moen, and G. Van Getson. 2004, September. States' procedures for ensuring out-of-level test instrument quality. Out-of-level Testing Project Report 14. Minneapolis: University of Minnesota, National Center on Educational Outcomes.

Minow, M. 1990. *Making all the difference: Inclusion, exclusion, and American law.* Ithaca: Cornell University Press.

Nagle, K. and J. Crawford. 2004, April. Opportunities and challenges: Perspectives on NCLB from special education directors in urban school districts. EPPRI Issue Brief Six. College Park: Educational Policy Reform Research Institute, The University of Maryland.

National Research Council (NRC). 1997. *Educating one and all: Students with disabilities and standards-based reform*, edited by L. M. McDonnell, M. J. McLaughlin, and P. Morison. Washington, D.C.: National Academies Press.

National Research Council (NRC). 2002. *Minority students in special and gifted education*, edited by S. Donovan and C. Cross. Washington, D.C.: National Academies Press.

National Research Council (NRC). 2004. *Participation of English language learners and students with disabilities in NAEP and other large-scale assessments*, edited by K. Hakuta and A. Beatty. Washington, D.C.: National Academies Press.

Neal, D. and D. Kirp. 1986. The allure of legalization reconsidered: The case of special education. In *School days, rule days: The legalization and regulation of education*, edited by D. Kirp and D. Jensen. Philadelphia: Falmer Press.

No Child Left Behind Act of 2001, 107th Cong., 1st sess., 20 U.S.C. 4301. et seq.

Oswald, D. P., M. J. Coutinho, A. M. Best, and N. N. Singh. 1999. Ethnic representation in special education: The influence of school-related economic and demographic variables. *The Journal of Special Education* 32: 194–206.

Pullin, D. 1999. Whose schools are these and what are they for? The role of the rule of law in defining educational opportunity in American public education. In *Handbook of educational policy*, edited by G. Cizek, 3–29. San Diego: Academic Press.

Pullin, D. 2002. Testing individuals with disabilities: Reconciling social science and social policy. In *Assessing individuals with disabilities in educational, employment, and clinical settings*, edited by Committee on Disabilities, American Psychological Association. Washington, D.C.: American Psychological Association.

Pullin, D. 2005. When one size does not fit all – the special challenges of accountability testing for students with disabilities. In *Uses and misuses of data for educational accountability and improvement (Yearbook of the National Society for the Study of Education)*, issue 2, edited by J. L. Herman and E. H. Haertel. Malden, Mass.: Blackwell.

Pullin, D. 2006. Ensuring an adequate education: Opportunity to learn, law and social science. *Boston College Third World Law Journal 27*: 83–130.

Pullin, D. In press. Stigma, stereotypes and civil rights in disability classification systems. In *Issues in the classification of children in education: Perspectives and purposes of classification systems*, edited by M. McLaughlin and L. Florian.

Quenemoen, R., S. Rigney, and M. Thurlow. 2002. *Use of alternate assessment results in reporting and accountability systems: Conditions for use based on research and practice* (Synthesis Report 43). Minneapolis: University of Minnesota, National Center on Educational Outcomes. Retrieved August 20, 2004, from http://education.umn.edu/NCEO/OnlinePubs/Synthesis43.html.

Quenemoen, R., Thompson, S., and M. Thurlow. 2003, June. *Measuring academic achievement of students with significant cognitive disabilities: Building understanding of alternate assessment scoring criteria* (Synthesis Report 50). Minneapolis: University of Minnesota, National Center on Educational Outcomes. Retrieved August 20, 2004, from http://education.umn.edu/NCEO/OnlinePubs/Synthesis50.html.

Quenoemoen, R. and M. Thurlow. 2002. *Including alternate assessment results in accountability decisions* (Policy Directions No. 13). Minneapolis: University of Minnesota, National Center on Educational Outcomes. http://education.umn.edu/NCEO/OnlinePubs/Policy13.htm.

Rose v. Council for Better Educ., Inc. 1989. 790 S.W.2d 186 (Ky.).

Salvia, J. and J. Ysseldyke, with S. Bolt. 2007. *Assessment in special and inclusive education.* Boston: Houghton Mifflin.

Shaywitz, S. 2003. *Overcoming dyslexia: A new and complete science-based program for reading problems at any level.* New York: A. Knopf.

Shriner, J. 2000, Winter. Legal perspectives on school outcomes assessment for students with disabilities. *Journal of Special Education* 33: 232–39.

Shulman, L. S. and J. H. Shulman. 2004, March. How and what teachers learn: A shifting perspective. *Journal of Curriculum Studies* 36: 257–71.

Sipple, J., K. Killeen, and D. Monk. 2004, Summer. Adoption and adaptation: School district responses to state imposed learning and graduation requirements. *Educational Evaluation and Policy Analysis* 26: 143–68.

Skrtic, T. 1991, May. The special education paradox: Equity as the way to excellence. *Harvard Educational Review* 61:2. Reprinted in *Special education at the century's end: Evolution of theory and practice since 1970* (1992), edited by T. Hehir and T. Latus, 203–72. Cambridge: Harvard Educational Review.

Spillane, J. 2004. *Standards deviation: How schools misunderstand education policy.* Cambridge, Mass.: Harvard University Press.

Spillane, J., B. Reiser, and T. Reimer. 2002, Fall. Policy implementation and cognition: Reframing and refocusing implementation research. *Review of Educational Research* 72: 387–431.

Test, D., C. Muson, C. Hughes, M. Konrad, M. Neal, and M. Wood. 2004. Student involvement in Individualized Education Program meetings. *Exceptional Children* 70: 391–412.

Thompson, S. and M. Thurlow,. 2003. *State special education outcomes: Marching on.* Minneapolis: University of Minnesota, National Center on Educational Outcomes. Retrieved August 20, 2004, from http://education.umn.edu/NCEO/OnlinePubs/StateReport.html.

Thurlow, M., J. Minnema, and J. Treat. 2004. *A review of 50 states' online large-scale assessment policies: Are English language learners with disabilities considered? (ELLs with Disabilities Report 5).* Minneapolis: University of Minnesota, National Center on Educational Outcomes. Retrieved June 5, 2007, from http://education.umn.edu/NCEO/OnlinePubs/ELLsDisReport5.html.

Thurlow, M., R. Moen, and J. Altman. 2006. Annual performance reports: 2003–2004 state assessment data. Minneapolis: University of Minnesota, National Center on Educational Outcomes. Retrieved June 5, 2007, from http://www.education.umn.edu/NCEO/.

Turnbull, H. and A. Turnbull. 1998. *Free appropriate public education*, 5th ed. Denver: Love.

U.S. Department of Education. 2003. Title I – Improving the Academic Achievement of the Disadvantaged; Part II; Final Rule, 68 Fed. Reg. 68698 (2003) (to be codified at 34 CFR Part 200).

U.S. Department of Education. 2004. Twenty-sixth annual report to the Congress on the implementation of the Individuals with Disabilities Education Act. Washington, D.C. Retrieved April 3, 2007, from http://www.ed.gov/about/reports/annual/osep/2004/index.html.

U.S. Department of Education. 2007, April 9. Title I – Improving the Academic Achievement of the Disadvantaged; IDEA; Final Rule, 72 Fed. Reg. 17748–01 (to be codified at 34 CFR Parts 200 and 300).

Varenne, H. and R. McDermott. 1998. *Successful failure: The school America builds.* Boulder: Westview Press.

Vaughn, S. and L. Fuchs. 2003. Redefining learning disabilities as inadequate response to instruction: The promise and potential problems. *Learning Disabilities Research and Practice* 18: 137–46.

Ysseldyke, J., A. Dennison, and R. Nelson. 2004, May. *Large-scale assessment and accountability systems: Positive consequences for students with disabilities.* (Synthesis Report 51). Minneapolis: University of Minnesota, National Center on Educational Outcomes. Retrieved January 1, 2005, from http://education.umn.edu/NCEO/OnlinePubs/Synthesis51.html.

Zatta, M. and D. Pullin. 2004, April. Education and alternate assessment for students with significant cognitive disabilities: Implications for educators. *Education Policy Analysis Archives* 12: 1–27. www.epaa.asu.edu/epaa/v12n16/.

6   Cultural Modeling as Opportunity to Learn

Making Problem Solving Explicit in Culturally Robust
Classrooms and Implications for Assessment

Carol D. Lee

The cornerstone of assessment is localized in the face-to-face interactions in daily classroom instruction. Daily instruction involves understanding how learning inside disciplines should be organized to respond to the needs of particular learners. This chapter examines how opportunity to learn (OTL) can be structured in classrooms serving culturally diverse students in ways that (1) build on fundamental propositions in cognition; (2) focus on generative topics, concepts, and forms of problem solving within subject matters; and (3) scaffold forms of knowledge and ways of using language emerging from students' everyday experiences in families and communities. The basic argument is that reconceptualizing forms of assessment in the absence of reconceptualizing instruction will yield few results.

In this chapter, OTL means students have a right to rigorous instruction that:

1) is organized in ways to build on and expand forms of prior knowledge they construct from their experiences outside school and across their years of schooling;

2) provides them with models of expertise (e.g., models of more expert problem solving) and in-time feedback on the progress of their learning in ways that are usable and motivating; and

3) focuses on powerful and generative topics, concepts, and problem-solving strategies within academic subject matters and across their years of schooling in ways that help them make sense of how their learning is useful in the world.

In order for these opportunities to take root, several important issues must be addressed. First, we must have good operational definitions and illustrations

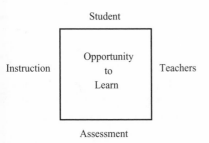

Figure 6.1. Dimensions of opportunity to learn.

of learning within subject matters from a developmental perspective. Second, we must find better ways to align external assessments of accountability at the aggregate level with the content of instruction, including ways of displaying competence in classrooms that are consistent with our conceptions of good learning. Third, and perhaps most important, we must see this problem as four sides of an OTL quadrangle that focuses on students, teachers, instruction, and assessment. How do we think about students' opportunities to learn; teachers' opportunities to learn; instruction as an opportunity for joint learning by teachers and students; and assessment as an opportunity for students, teachers, and the public to learn. Figure 6.1 captures these four dimensions of OTL. The cases discussed in this chapter offer insights into some, but not all, of these dilemmas.

In order to organize instruction in the ways I have described, one must have a deep understanding of what is required to engage in complex problem solving within subject matters and an equally deep understanding of the kinds of cultural knowledge that students from diverse backgrounds bring with them as they move from their lives outside school into classrooms (Lee 2001, 2007; Lee, Spencer, and Harpalani 2003). These forms of cultural knowledge include propositional knowledge about topics and natural as well as social phenomena, ways of using and understanding language(s), and social knowledge of human intentionality (i.e., what makes people tick). In addition to these forms of shared or distributed cultural knowledge, students also have knowledge of themselves, particularly of themselves as learners and social beings who seek particular kinds of social relationships with other human beings (Spencer 2006). Classrooms are dynamic spaces in which the cultural practices of the subject matter as well as the knowledge and dispositions of students and teachers are negotiated. How these negotiations take place creates or inhibits opportunities to learn for both students and teachers (Gutiérrez, Rymes, and Larson 1995).

One rationale for the design of instruction in ways that accomplish the ends I have described is derived from basic concepts about how people learn. There are at least three orientations to human learning that are relevant to the design of the kind of culturally robust instruction I have described so far: schema and related theories focusing on individual acts of cognition (Chi 1978; Rumelhart 1980); a distributed view of cognition (Perkins 1993; Salomon 1993); and a situated view of cognition (Lave and Wenger 1991; Rogoff and Lave 1984). Each of these orientations to how people learn offers useful insights that can inform culturally robust instruction. At the same time, there are persistent stereotypes and assumptions about particular human cultural groups that can also constrain how researchers and practitioners think about these cognitive orientations with relation to particular populations (Hernstein and Murray 1994; Jensen 1969). Thus, our ways of thinking about how people learn can either expand or constrain opportunities to learn, depending on our perspectives.

The first orientation is a *schema theoretic orientation* that focuses on individual cognition (Rumelhart 1980). This orientation addresses the powerful role that prior knowledge – in the form of schema-in-the-mind – plays in new learning (Steffensen, Joag-Dev, and Anderson 1979). This fundamental proposition is problematized with respect to students from black and brown communities, whose home language is other than "mainstream" academic English, or who come from low-income communities. In the United States, such students have historically in the United States been viewed as lacking appropriate prior knowledge for complex, discipline-specific academic learning (Bereiter and Engelmann, 1966). These persistent assumptions have historically undermined opportunities to learn for such students (Baron, Tom, and Cooper 1985; DeMeis and Turner 1978; Rist 1970).

The second is a *distributed view of cognition* that focuses on how thinking and learning are jointly constructed among people and artifacts (Pea and Gomez 1992; Perkins 1993; Salomon 1993). A distributed view of cognition draws attention to interactional processes among people and things in settings and is important for conceptualizing how students work with each other in classrooms and what kinds of material resources are available to support instruction. As with the schema theoretic orientation, this distributed view of cognition is undermined in light of persistent deficit assumptions regarding black and brown students and those from low-income backgrounds (Hernstein and Murray 1994; Stotsky 1999). Often, these students are evaluated not merely on the basis of individual displays of knowledge (i.e., the schema theoretic orientation) but on assumptions about routine practices that are shared within their communities and families (Orr 1987). For example, typical modes of interacting and particularly of using language may be viewed as deficits that are more likely to interfere with learning (Stotsky 1999).

The third is a *situated view of cognition* that takes people, artifacts, setting, and interactions within and across settings and time as elements of dynamic systems in which people learn (Lave and Wenger 1991; Rogoff and Lave 1984; Vygotsky 1978, 1981; Wertsch 1985). Under the best circumstances, this orientation focuses our attention additionally on alignment across grade levels, the role of students in influencing the course of what happens in classrooms, and the influences of the general school culture on the academic experiences of students. However, this situated view of cognition can also be problematized with respect to black and brown students and those from low-income backgrounds. From this situated perspective, these students have repeated experiences in school where in daily face-to-face interactions, the goals of instruction communicate that what they are doing in subject matters is not about deep thinking and has no value outside the local classroom. These students are also more likely to be in classrooms where there are few artifacts (physical or conceptual) that can augment and extend their thinking about problems in the subject matter. Also, time is more likely to be the enemy of these students in schools – the longer they stay in school, the less they achieve (Campbell, Hombo, and Mazzeo 2000). The cumulative effects of poor schooling socialize dismal views of the academic enterprise. The accumulated cultural capital within communities of origin are rarely used as resources in the classroom. These effects of time often fuel stereotypes and influence a culture of low expectations by teachers and administrators.

However, just as limited conceptions of how people learn can constrain opportunities to learn, more expansive views of learning can enhance instruction in ways that meet the criteria I have described in the opening section of this chapter. The role of prior knowledge, the nature of interactions in classrooms, the supports for learning embedded in materials used in classrooms, and systematic analyses of the demands of learning in specific subject matters have serious implications for both instruction and assessments, particularly for students – black, brown, and low-income – who currently struggle in our public schools.

In this chapter, I will illustrate the kind of teaching and learning that takes an expansive view of human learning in two academic domains: response to literature and science education. Such an expansive view of human learning takes seriously the prior knowledge and experiences of students, what I am calling *culturally robust instruction.* I address response to literature because in the middle to high school curricula, it is highly underconceptualized. People typically think that this is a domain in which building on students' everyday experience and prior knowledge would be easiest. However, in the absence of a well-specified conception of the domain, one cannot gain leverage for students' lives outside school because one doesn't understand the specific functions particular kinds of prior knowledge may serve. I address science education because it is one of the academic domains assumed to be least responsive to youths' everyday experiences. The ability to talk and read the languages of literature and science in order to solve recurrent and novel problems in both domains is of central importance. I turn to two programs of research that embody the principles of generativity, rigor, and relevance I have described for culturally robust instruction. Each research program uses fundamental constructs and propositions from the three cognitive orientations – schema theoretical models focusing on individual acts of cognition, distributed cognition focusing on how learning occurs through interaction with others, and situated cognition focusing on the role of settings, people, artifacts, and time in coordination with one another. Each research program wards against the negative stereotypes that can distort how these three cognitive orientations may be taken up in practice.

In each of the interventions described next, classrooms are organized to make particular kinds of literacies public, explicit, and accessible. In the Cultural Modeling Project, the target is using literary reasoning to access canonical works of literature. In the Chèche Konnen Project, the target is using scientific reasoning to construct arguments about scientific phenomena. Although the subject matters differ, the literacy demands are similar. Both require learning the kinds of questions that are deemed worth asking, making close observations, noting and imposing meaning on patterns, garnering evidence to support claims, weighing alternative explanations, and translating arguments into the language of the discipline.

THE CULTURAL MODELING PROJECT: THE CHALLENGE OF TEACHING READING COMPREHENSION

The Cultural Modeling Project calls for a close examination of what is required to engage in subject-matter reasoning (Lee 1995a, 1995b, 2000, 2001, 2002, 2003b, 2005, 2007). Empirical studies in this project to date have focused primarily on reasoning in response to literature. Such reasoning requires the reader to display certain habits of mind – a willingness to: (1) attend to language play as an end in itself; (2) impose coherence, even when there appears to be none; and (3) suspend disbelief in order to enter an imaginative subjunctive world while ascribing models of human intentionality to the actions of actors in that world. In addition, the reader is expected to notice prototypical patterns of plot types, character types, and archetypal themes as well as disruptions of a literal rendering that signal prototypical types of interpretive problems, such as symbolism, irony, satire, and use of unreliable narration (Booth 1974, 1983; Lee 2003b; Rabinowitz 1987; Smith and Hillocks 1988; Wolf 1995). Because the world of literature is largely about imagination and innovation, readers are also expected to recognize and act on disruptions to any of these expected patterns, because literary authors will play with us as readers, leading us down one path and then surprising our expectations.

In terms of OTL, there are several recurring problems that students, particularly black and brown students and students from low-income backgrounds, generally face (Lee 2003b). Methods for problem solving in the ways I have described are rarely made explicit. Literature anthologies are not organized around these recurring problems (Smith and Hillocks 1988). Secondary English teachers are quite adept readers themselves but do not have training in making this literary landscape visible (Grossman 2001). In addition, prevalent deficit assumptions can inhibit teachers' abilities to make what they do understand about these problem-solving processes public to certain groups of students (Anyon 1981; Rist 1970).

In the following section, I will illustrate a case of instruction that addresses the dilemmas I have outlined. It addresses a generative problem of reading in the subject matters. It scaffolds prior knowledge that students, in particular black and brown students, bring to classrooms from their everyday experiences. It makes public and explicit the reasoning required to carry out authentic tasks in the subject matter by modeling from students' life experiences. It structures classroom talk and other displays of understanding by making connections between the ways students use language in their everyday experiences and the particular ways of using academic language to construct subject matter–specific arguments. I hope with this illustration to draw attention to what this kind of teaching means for teacher knowledge – and by extension, teachers' opportunities to learn – for assessments – and by extension, both teachers', students', and the public's opportunities to learn.

Teaching Generative Knowledge

In the domain of response to literature, determining what is worth teaching is contested territory (Grossman 2001; Lee 1995c, 2007). This is in part because of the fundamental epistemology that underlies response to literature. Literary readers and critics do not value the notion of a single right answer to a question (Fish 1980; Tompkins 1980). Yet despite the openness regarding response, Applebee has repeatedly documented the stability of the English Language Arts curriculum (Applebee 1993). There is a stable staple of canonical works and authors, with Shakespeare at the helm. With minor changes, literature anthologies are organized at the freshman year by traditional conceptions

	African American	Latino	White
Make Generalizations	95%	97%	98%
Partial Skills	66	68	87
Understand Complicated Information	17	24	46
Learn from Specialized Materials	1	2	8

Figure 6.2. NAEP reading for 17-year-olds, 1999 (Campbell, Hombo, Mazzeo, 2000).

of genre (i.e., short story, novel, poetry, and drama); at the sophomore and junior years by chronology (the traditional American and British literature survey courses); and by theme at the senior year (focusing on archetypal themes like love, justice, and courage). I and others have argued that none of these ways structures opportunities for students to learn generative literary patterns in any explicit way (Applebee, Burroughs, and Stevens 2000; Lee 2003b, 2004; Smagorinsky and Gevinson 1989; Smith and Hillocks 1988). By virtue of this curriculum's organization, students' opportunities to learn are severely curtailed. I would argue that Figure 6.2, with results from the National Assessment of Educational Progress in reading for seventeen-year-olds, attests to the fact that how we teach reading in subject matters at the high school level is not working well for most students. The most rigorous tasks on the National Assessment of Educational Progress include subject matter–specific texts, including selections from literary works. Fewer than ten percent of all seventeen-year-olds appear competent at this most rigorous level.

Space will not allow for a full explication of my analysis of the domain of response to literature (Lee 2003b, 2007). However, I can illustrate my point with one example. Symbolism is an interpretive problem that readers will face whether reading a Toni Morrison novel, an Emily Dickinson poem, or a Chekhov play. It is a prototypical problem that cuts across genres, national literatures, authors, and themes. Thus, if a student is able to detect when a literal interpretation of a statement in the text should be rejected, reconstruct a warrantable figurative interpretation, note patterns within and across statements, and impose significance to those patterns as symbolic (i.e., representing a larger proposition than the literal), the student is able to understand symbolism when he or she meets it. In the Cultural Modeling literature curriculum, instruction focuses on generative topics, such as symbolism, irony, satire, and unreliable narration, among others.

Although this example is specific to the domain of response to literature, the principle of teaching generative knowledge is foundational to OTL (Perkins 1992). There is consistent research documenting the ways in which students from low-income backgrounds and students of color are more likely to be taught so-called basic skills than complex and domain specific forms of reasoning (Darling-Hammond 1985, 1987, 1999; Irvine 1990; Lee and Slaughter-Defoe 1995). To the extent that every state is required to hold schools accountable for rigorous academic standards – a policy that rolls out on the ground in the form of greater, largely multiple-choice tests – not teaching generative knowledge within subject matter seriously curtails students' opportunities to learn (Lee 2003a). In the area of response to literature, particularly at the secondary level, determining what is generative knowledge is not well articulated, by contrast with fields like mathematics, the sciences, and the social studies.

Scaffolding Students' Prior Knowledge in Order to Make Reasoning Explicit

Decades of work in the science of learning consistently document the important role of prior knowledge in learning (Bransford, Brown, and Cocking 1999). These findings are problematized in light of the continuing deficit stereotypes regarding students who are poor, black, and brown, and who speak first languages other than English. In light of the ethnic, racial, and linguistic diversity represented in U.S. schools, understanding the range of kinds of knowledge and life experiences that this diverse array of students brings to school is a significant challenge for the field of education; it is equally important to understand how these forms of knowledge and life experiences intersect with the demands of learning within subject matters (Lee, Spencer, and Harpalani 2003). This is an especially pressing challenge at the secondary school level, where the knowledge in subject matters tends to be more removed from everyday experience (DiSessa 1982).

The Cultural Modeling Framework provides a set of guiding principles for thinking about links between subject matter knowledge and the knowledge of everyday experience, with a particular focus on students who have been historically underserved by public education. The links may include related concepts in the everyday sphere that may be either naïve versions or even misconceptions of a target concept in the academic domain. Guided practice in analyzing points of similarity and difference is an important pedagogical strategy to help students understand the academic target more fully. Other links may include everyday practices that require modes of reasoning, dispositions, and habits of mind that are similar to those required to problem solve in the academic domain. Again, guided practice in analyzing how one reasons in the everyday context, demonstrating consistently across time how

reasoning is similar, related, or different across contexts is a useful pedagogical tool. However, these practices are only useful if one is able conceptually
to connect models and modes of reasoning in the everyday context with
generative models and modes of reasoning in the subject matter.

In the case of response to literature, I have noted that one recurrent problem is detecting and making sense of symbolism. My research has focused
on African American students, particularly adolescents who are speakers
of African American English. Such students routinely engage in a form of
talk called signifying (Smitherman 1977). Signifying is a form of ritual insult
that always involves figuration, double entendre, and playing with the aes-
thetic features of language (Mitchell-Kernan 1981; Morgan 1998). These students routinely construct and deconstruct symbols as they engage in this
form of language play. In a similar vein, adolescents across ethnic, racial,
and socioeconomic-status groups (although this cultural practice has strong
roots in African American youth culture) are deeply engaged with hip-hop
culture (Kitwana 2002; Rose 1994). The rap music at the center of this cultural community is often quite literary (Morrell 2002). Young people, when
listening to rap, looking at rap videos, popular films, television programs,
and advertising, are interpreting figurative tropes, such as symbolism, satire,
irony, and use of unreliable narration. They are engaged in forms of reasoning that are very akin to literary reasoning. In each of these instances,
the knowledge youth are using is tacit. Because it is tacit, without explicit
instruction, they are generally not able to expand on their own the arenas
in which they use it to include reasoning about canonical literary texts (Lee
1993, 1995a, 2000). As illustrated in the next section, in Cultural Modeling
classrooms, instructional talk focuses on the systematic examination of what
are called cultural data sets. Cultural data sets involve tasks rooted in the
everyday experiences of students, when the reasoning required is related to
the reasoning required for a target academic task that will follow.

A necessary prerequisite for enhancing students' opportunities to learn is
guided practice in making explicit the reasoning required for complex problem solving in subject matters by connecting such reasoning with practices
and concepts with which students are already familiar. This proposition is
true of all learners, but it is especially important for students who have long
histories of underachieving in school.

Structuring Classroom Talk

Classroom talk is the primary medium through which learning is negotiated
inside classrooms. It is useful to note that this is not necessarily the case in
all learning settings. For example, Barbara Rogoff observes what she calls

intent participation as young Mayan girls learn the complex art of weaving from their mothers and other women (Rogoff et al. 2003). This learning, Rogoff argues, is largely through observation. I am certain that one can find routine cases of learning through observation in the everyday lives of students, particularly those from low-income backgrounds. In fact, learning a first language occurs largely through observation compared with predominantly through explicit instruction. However, talk still reigns as the primary mode of communication in classrooms.

All settings offer what Gumperz and Hymes call contextualization cues (Gumperz and Hymes 1972). Contextualization cues are what we recognize as signals for how we are to participate. In the case of classrooms, the national language or version of a national language (i.e., social language and/or register); the rules for entering conversations and for appropriate tone, gesture, body language, and use of space; the kinds of supports for participation in the tasks at hand – all of these contribute to what sense students make of their role in that classroom. How talk and participation are structured and what supports are available greatly impact how much energy and attention students garner to take part or not.

In Cultural Modeling, classroom talk centers on how students come to know what they think they know, what evidence they use to support claims, and whether there are competing explanations. I have labeled such talk "metacognitive instructional conversations" (Lee 1998). In these classrooms, talk about one's thinking may take place in African American English vernacular, Spanish, or Hmong. This variety of languages of communication is made available to students because the goal at this point in instruction is to create a community that values attending to how it reasons and what it reasons about. As these modes of reasoning become more routine, conscious, and explicit, students are supported in translating that reasoning to forms of communication that are valued in the academic subject matter. This includes not just a generic Standard English, but rather speaking and writing in appropriate genres (especially in the crafting of oral and written arguments). I argue here that a really important criterion for OTL is explicit and long-term support for learning how to translate. In this vein, I draw on what we have learned about second-language acquisition (Gee 1994; Hymes 1980). Learning an academic language (i.e., the languages of history, physics, algebra, literary criticism) is similar in many ways to learning a new language. In many respects, learning to tackle multiple forms of assessment (multiple choice, open-response, projects and performances) is a problem of translation; learning how to understand what each format is asking of one and how to search one's memory for data, concepts, strategies, and modes of reasoning that may be relevant to one's conception of the task.

In the following example, I illustrate the following features of culturally robust instruction I have described in Cultural Modeling classrooms:

- focusing on generative knowledge within a discipline;
- making problem solving explicit;
- drawing on students' prior knowledge and experiences; and
- situating instruction within a medium of communication that builds on the full linguistic repertoires of students.

In the final section of this chapter, I will discuss how local assessments were developed to measure growth in Cultural Modeling classrooms.

In Cultural Modeling, cultural data sets are used to elicit students' tacit knowledge. Cultural data sets pose problems situated in the everyday experiences of students and require modes of reasoning analogous to the targeted new learning. The analysis of cultural data sets provides the foundation for what I have called metacognitive instructional conversation. The goal of such conversations is to prompt students to make discipline-specific modes of reasoning public and explicit and to help students understand relationships between what they already know and what we want them to learn in the context of subject matter–specific problem solving. In the following example, a class of high school seniors is analyzing the significance of the image of the mask in the rap song "The Mask" by the Fugees (1996). These are the particular stanzas in question:

Chorus:
M to the A to the S to the K
Put the mask on your face just to make it next day
Brothers be gamin' ladies be claimin'
I walk the street and camouflage my identity

My posse uptown wear the mask
My crew in the Queens wear the mask
Stick up kids with the Tommy Hill wear the mask
Yeah everybody wear the mask, but how long will it last

Stanzas:
I thought he was the wonder, I was stunned by his lips,
Takin' sips of an Amaretto Sour with a twist
Shook my hips to the base line, this joker grabbed my waistline
Puttin' pressure on my spine trying to get elbow to wine

I backed up off him and I caught him with five fingers to his face
I had to put him in his place, this kids invading my space
Then I recognized the smile, but I couldn't place the style

So many fronts in his mouth I thought he was the golden child
Then it hit me, that's Tariq from off the street around my grams
I hadn't seen him since sixteen when he got booked for doin' scams
I tried to walk away, but then he wouldn't let me leave
He ran up quick behind me askin', hey what happened to Steve
Steve was like this kid I went with back in grammar school
I chuckled knuckle-head I seen him yesterday he's cool
"Bust it, so who you checkin' now, probably some intellectual"
I kept the conversation straight, but he kept tryin' to make it sexual
Then his old lady tried to play me, waved her hands up in my face
Yo, I told her check your man cuz, you actin' out of place

The teacher is a masterful instructor. She does not listen to rap music, which positions the students from the beginning of instruction as genuine sources of authority. They are explaining to the teacher the symbolism of the reference to the character of Tariq as "the golden child." The transcript is reprinted from *Culture, Literacy and Learning: Taking Bloom in the Midst of the Whirlwind* by Carol Lee (2007).

(1) **T:** What does he mean here, so many fronts in his mouth I thought he was the golden child.

(2) **S Ellen, Alicia, Fatima:** Gold teeth.

(3) **T:** But . . .

(4) **Ellen:** That's like a big front anyway, cuz he got all this gold, all up in his mouth, and he just makin it his business to smile and let it be noticed.

(5) **T:** But who is the golden child?

(6) **Fatima:** The golden child that little boy who . . .

(7) **Ellen:** Eddie Murphy played

(8) **Alicia:** In that movie (laugh)

(9) **T:** So he's referring to something in a movie?

(10) **Alicia:** Yeah. (pause) You know how the golden child had all the power in the movie. (waits for a response) OK (laughs).

(11) T: I'm listening.

(12) Alicia: It was the movie. You ever seen the movie *The Golden Child*?

(13) T: Umm, umm (no).

(14) Ellen: Oh well that's ... (laughs)

(15) Alicia: It was the movie where this little boy he had all the power. But I don't really think that he just directly referring to it. He just indirectly. Everybody know the Golden Child had all the power. But he said that he had all these fronts in his mouth and he's the Golden Child ...

(16) Ellen: Right, Golden Child, except you know he got gold teeth.

(17) Alicia: ... He had all this gold in his mouth like he this Golden Child.

(18) T: And what would you have needed to know in order to come to that conclusion? What you just said ...

(19) Alicia: I just need to know all the fronts in his mouth. When she said mouth, I knew.

(20) Ellen: Right. Once she said that you knew what that meant.

(21) T: And what else would a person need to know in order to come to the conclusion that you just came to? What little bits of information would a person need? And where are you getting your answers from?

(22) Alicia: From stuff we already knew.

(23) T: So you're using prior knowledge.

(24) Ellen: They say in here how they...

(25) Alicia: We were usin our context clues, we were like when we see the word mouth then you know it's automatically it's something that got to do with, got to be in his mouth.

(26) T: I'm saying that to you because a piece of my knowledge that's missing is, I don't know anything about the Golden Child. So I'm in the same position that you're in sometimes when you approach these novels. I may know what the author's talking about because I can hook it on to something, and that's why if you can prove it, instead of saying there's no right or wrong answer, you have a reason for coming up with that. And I don't know what he's talking about, to be honest with you. That's why I listen to you.

(27) Ellen: He just talkin a lot about bringing attention to sayin he got a lot of gold in his mouth. He might not necessarily mean the Golden Child. Cuz that don't have a lot to do with his mouth.

(28) T: So the Golden Child would be like a symbol?

(29) Ellen: Right.

(30) T: Representing...

(31) Ellen: But not a symbol as being the Golden Child for his teeth, for having gold teeth.

(32) Alicia: It's figurative language. It's like if I be like Ellen, you star bright something, that's a another way of sayin she real light skinned. You know, that's figurative language.

(33) T: Umm hmm.

(34) Ellen: (Laughs) No, it's all right, it's all right.
(35) Alicia: I mean no, cuz you know, so she can understand this. Cuz if you called me little black star, you know.

In turns six through eight, ten, twelve, and fourteen through seventeen, the students assume the role of teacher, explaining where the reference to the golden child comes from and the subtle differences between the image in the movie and how it is being used in the song. The teacher assumes a unique role in prodding the students to make the knowledge on which they tacitly draw public and explicit in turn eighteen. The students' response in turns nineteen through twenty are localized to this particular song, but the teacher wants the students to be able to generalize the strategies they are using beyond this local context, as can be seen in turn twenty-one. It is important to note that when the teacher revoices Ellen's response in turn twenty, from Ellen's reference to "stuff we already knew" to the more formal register of "using prior knowledge," she is scaffolding in ways that facilitate transfer from the everyday text to the canonical texts that will follow. This process of revoicing in an academic register leads Alicia to also employ a similar register when she says, "We were using our context clues." In turn twenty-six, the teacher expands on the meta-point of the exchange, helping the students to anticipate its relevance for the canonical texts that will follow. Here she also invokes an important epistemological stance that is also a crucial stance for the problem solving that will be required as the students move into the canonical texts; namely, that multiple perspectives are invited and that these perspectives will be weighed on the basis of evidence. It is clear from what they are doing with this and the other cultural data sets that the evidence will be both textual and real world. They are using both in the analysis of the symbolism of "The Mask." In addition, in this same line she is willing to acknowledge another foundational epistemological stance; that is, that uncertainty is a good thing. We cannot engage in truly complex reasoning without being willing to tolerate uncertainty. This acknowledgement on the part of the teacher invites additional nuanced explication by the students. In turns twenty-seven, thirty-one, and thirty-two, Ellen and Alicia make a literary distinction in which they correct the teacher. It is precisely because the cultural data set is one for which they actually have greater prior knowledge than the teacher that the students are willing and in fact able to assume teaching roles in which they make visible a complex problem that is clearly within what Vygotsky (1978) calls their zones of proximal development (e.g., that which they can accomplish with support). Finally, in turns thirty-two, thirty-four, and thirty-five, they signify (e.g., African American English genre of ritual insult) on each other.

This example of a meta-cognitive instructional conversation within Cultural Modeling provides an example of what culturally robust instruction that is subject matter-specific looks like on the ground. The features of this instructional dialogue characterized how students learned during both the modeling and transfer phases of instruction, when students were applying similar strategies, epistemological stances, and modes of argumentation with regard to canonical works of literature.

CHÈCHE KONNEN: SENSE MAKING IN SCIENCE AND TEACHER LEARNING

Chèche Konnen (CCK) is a research collaborative headed by Beth Warren and Ann Rosebery of TERC (Technology, Education and Research Center) in Cambridge, Massachusetts (Ballenger 1997; Conant 1996; Rosebery, Warren, and Conant 1992). The group includes educational researchers, teacher-researchers, and scientists who have worked together for more than fifteen years. The fundamental questions with which CCK wrestles are similar to those engaged with Cultural Modeling. However, the domain is scientific reasoning. The students are elementary aged, and most are Haitian, Cape Verdean, Ethiopian, or from other African, East Indian, and Asian immigrant populations. Students come from diverse ethnic backgrounds and speak a wide array of national languages, including Portugese, Spanish, Haitian-Creole, Chinese, Korean, Hindi, Gujarati, Vietnamese, Amharic, Tigrina, and Cape Verdean Creole.

Chèche means "search for knowledge" in Haitian-Creole. The work of CCK squarely addresses the criteria for OTL outlined in this chapter: the right to instruction that (1) draws and builds on learners' prior knowledge; (2) models expert problem solving and practice and provides in-time feedback on performance; and (3) focuses on generative topics, concepts, and problem-solving strategies in ways that help students make sense of how their learning is useful in the world. CCK addresses these opportunities to learn both for teachers and students. It seeks to understand how the discourse practices and life experiences of students from ethnic/racial and language-minority groups serve as meaningful resources for learning scientific argumentation and key generative topics in science.

Working collaboratively with classroom teachers and scientists, CCK designs science instruction in ethnically and linguistically diverse elementary classrooms. The collaborative research group examines videotapes of instruction in these classrooms in order to understand the sense-making processes demonstrated by students about scientific phenomena, with a particular focus on how these sense-making processes reflect ways of talking and reasoning in the everyday lives of these children outside school. They have also examined the practices of working scientists and concluded that there are many points of similarity between the sense-making practices of these children and those used by scientists. For example, they find that many of these students engage in what they call "embodied imagining," influenced by studies of embodied cognition, when students imagine that they are inside the scientific phenomenon being studied (Lakoff and Nunez 2000). CCK cites research documenting how scientists imagine themselves inside a scientific phenomenon as a way of exploring how a phenomenon may unfold when observation and measurement are not available (Ochs, Gonzales, and Jacoby 1996). Other sense-making practices include forms of argumentation, imagining, narrative, and analogical reasoning. For example, Hudicourt-Barnes, a longtime member of CCK who began as a teacher-researcher and is now a full-time researcher on the project, describes how *bay odyans*, a Haitian-Creole discourse practice, and *diskisyon*, a form of argumentation in Haitian-Creole, are used by Haitian immigrant students to construct scientific arguments in their classrooms. In these classrooms, where the linguistic resources are integral to the work of students, instructional talk includes performative features (e.g., intonation, humor, theatrical use of gesture) that are not typical in the discourse of typical science classrooms and are very similar to findings by Lee and others about uses of African American English vernacular in classrooms (Foster 1987; Lee 1995b, 2005; Smitherman 2000; Taylor 1982). These findings are also consistent with other research on English language learners (ELLs) that documents the myriad meta-linguistic resources of students who have access to more than one language (Baquedano-Lopez 1997; Gutiérrez, Baquedano-Lopez, and Tejeda 1999; Lam 2000; Orellana et al. 2003; Valdes 2002).

It is common in CCK classrooms for teachers to design what Clement (1989) and colleagues call "bridging analogies" to model a scientific concept or process through the examination of an artifact, a practice, or an event from the everyday experiences of students. These anchors reflect the everyday experiences of students who are generally African or Caribbean immigrants from low-income backgrounds. In one powerful example, the production of sound on the African drum is the anchor for a careful study of the inscription of sound waves (Conant 1996). The class is a combined seventh and eighth grade transitional bilingual classroom. The class is conducted in both English and Haitian-Creole. The teacher is Josianne Hudicourt-Barnes, who is Haitian-American, then a teacher-researcher and now a researcher on the project. Her goal is to help students understand how amplitude and frequency are represented as sound waves. She initially uses a standard science-reform approach by having students use a computer-based program that displays the inscription of sound waves on a computer screen in response to a sound input. Originally, Hudicourt-Barnes expected that the use of a tuning fork as part of a hands-on science curriculum would engage students. However, their response was limited to a traditional IRE (initiation–response–evaluation) pattern of classroom talk (Mehan 1979), in which students largely responded to her questions rather than initiating their own. She then switched to anchor the students' exploration of sound inscriptions through the African drum.

The drum plays an important role in traditional Haitian culture, and these students were preparing for a school performance involving drumming. They were very familiar with the patterns for producing different sounds on the drum and the differences in the physical construction of drums (such as the circumference of and materials from which the head of the drum were made). They were also familiar with the Haitian-Creole words for different sounds on the drum. The teacher brought in a Haitian drummer to augment students' knowledge about the technical aspects of African drumming. A quality of learning in science that far surpassed what the traditional reform approach accomplished was made achievable by the combination of the following: Haitian-Creole discourse patterns available to them in this classroom; their knowledge of African drumming, augmented by drawing on community resources, or what Molls calls cultural "funds of knowledge" (Moll and Gonzales 2004); their identification with the practice of drumming; and the affordances that these forms of knowledge and the artifact of the drum itself made possible. Students initiated questions about relationships between the circumference of the drumhead, the position of the hand on the drum (i.e., angle), the velocity with which the hand hit the drum, the differential impact of different tools used to hit the drum, and the inscription of the amplitude of the sound wave. They investigated how the production of sounds involving two hands captured both amplitude and frequency in the inscription of sound waves. Students produced a poster that captured a classic drum sound, its name in Haitian-Creole, the inscription of sound waves produced by that sound, and an explanation of the relationships between the inscription and the production of the sound. As one group of students presented these findings, another student, Ketler, challenged the validity of the findings: "If, if, if that's the way the things are, they have to go do it again so I can see if that's the way the things really are" (Conant 1996, 9). The ensuing debate among the students focused on the role of replicability as a criterion for the validity of scientific findings.

CCK has conducted a number of studies to assess the impact of this kind of culturally responsive science instruction. It has designed tasks to elicit students' scientific understanding of concepts and their abilities to reason using scientific argumentation. It has also used released items from the National Assessment of Educational Progress (NAEP) and the Massachusetts Comprehensive Assessment System (MCAS) in science to assess student learning. In pre–post measures, it has found that students make significant progress from the beginning of instruction. In both talk-aloud protocols and use of released items from NAEP and MCAS, it has found that students typically surpass the performance levels of older students (Rosebery et al. 2005).

There is no question that this kind of instruction requires that teachers have deep content and pedagogical content knowledge. Teacher knowledge and attitudes have consistently proven to be important predictors of student academic success (Ball 2006; Darling-Hammond 1987, 1999; Foster 1997; Ladson-Billings 1994). Thus, teachers' opportunities to learn are the flip side of students' opportunities to learn. CCK approaches teacher professional development in the same way it approaches student learning. Teachers are encouraged to examine their own experiences with scientific phenomena and to interrogate their assumptions about what counts as adequate explanations of understanding regarding scientific concepts and problem solving. This is collaborative work that involves educational researchers, teachers, and teacher-researchers as well as practicing scientists. In the process, all stakeholders carefully examine what students say and do in these culturally responsive science classrooms in order to (1) deconstruct the deep structure that underlies what students say that may not be obvious and (2) interrogate their own understanding of core ideas in science. This work with teachers is long term and involves interrogating core ideas in physics (e.g., the atomic hypothesis, motion, and forces) and biology (e.g., evolutionary theory, ecological succession).

An important part of this work with teachers, which CCK terms "interrogating meaning," involves examining the meaning of technical language in scientific domains as it relates to the ways in which such language is used in everyday use. For example, "purpose" and "adaptation" in evolutionary theory and "pressure" in physics have decidedly different meanings in scientific and everyday contexts. This allowed teachers to situate their examinations of the discipline-specific meanings of vocabulary in relation to their own everyday experiences. This approach fostered teachers' learning to use their own experiences in the physical and natural world as anchors for thinking about scientific phenomena. Considering that most elementary school teachers have little formal training in science, it is significant that they have opportunities to see the connections between their own experiences in the natural world and core concepts and problem-solving processes in science. It is important to note that, for teachers, this parallels the right of students to have instruction that builds on their prior knowledge and everyday experiences. This OTL through the examination of both practice and one's own everyday experiences has important consequences for fundamental epistemologies. CCK teachers came to understand science as an open-ended pursuit to understand the natural world rather than as a set of unchanging facts that were accessible only to certain people.

The corpus of videotapes and student work in the CCK archives is vast. Teachers in CCK examine both artifacts of their own practice and those of other members of the group. Extended discussion with the diverse array of stakeholders – teachers, educational researchers, and practicing scientists and mathematicians – over long periods of time has led to fundamental restructuring of teachers' knowledge. This restructured content and pedagogical content knowledge led teachers to (1) address big ideas in science; (2) engage children in practices similar to those the teachers used in their own learning in science; (3) use children's questions and confusion to build curriculum; (4) incorporate children's cultural knowledge and discourse practices into classroom science; (5) broaden classroom discussions to include conversations in which students clarified everyday and scientific usages of words and discourse more generally; (6) teach students to interrogate scientific texts based on their own experiences and questions; and (7) use children's questions as a sign of their efforts to grapple with the complexity of scientific ideas rather than as simple confusion (Beth Warren, personal communication).

IMPLICATIONS FOR ASSESSMENT

I argued in the opening of this chapter that OTL included opportunities for teachers and students to learn from instruction. Assessments are generally viewed as tools through which, ideally, both teachers and students are able to evaluate what has been learned. I have illustrated so far examples of how instruction can be organized to address the demands of generativity, rigor, and relevance and have argued that we must attend to the organization of instruction if we have any hope of enhancing OTL for all, especially those most vulnerable in our schools and society. In this section, I want to problematize what many of our current assessment tools make visible about what students know. The quality of assessments, especially high-stakes accountability assessments of achievement, influence instruction by articulating what qualities of knowledge are valued and influence the public and practitioner's perceptions of what students know and are able to do. I focus here on literacy assessment in part because literacy is my field, but also because at the middle and high school levels, we have very few robust assessments of reading, especially reading in the content areas. I will illustrate some of these assessment dilemmas of reading in the content areas by looking at response to literature as an exemplar.

The problem of reasoning in response to literature is further complicated, particularly at the secondary school level, by a lack of adequate assessments of this ability. General achievement tests may include some literary selections. The dominant mode is the use of multiple-choice questions and timed readings, neither of which reflect in any authentic way what real readers do with complex, canonical works of literature. Scores on such assessments rarely disentangle skills in either comprehension or strategy use in relation to subject-matter reading. For example, the differences between reading in history, science, and literature have been well documented (Lemke 1998; Wineburg 1991; Wineburg and Grossman 1998). A student's ability to comprehend challenging primary-source documents in history and science are clearly good indicators of his or her understanding of these subject matters. Such abilities should also be reasonable predictors of reading habits across the life course. Do the results from the assessments in reading we typically now use say anything about whether it is reasonable to expect that after graduation, a given student may be more likely to go to either the public library or a Barnes and Nobles to read a Stephen Jay Gould or a Lerone Bennett or a Toni Morrison? Would not such lifelong habits be a good unto themselves? Would they not likely contribute to the broader civic good (Gutmann 1987)?

I recently examined the 2004 released test items from the Massachusetts Comprehensive Assessment System (MCAS) under the objectives for reading in English Language Arts (see http://www.doe.mass.edu/mcas) (Lee and Spratley, in press). The following question was used as an open-response

Table 6.1.[1]

	Narrator	Action	Rosa	Action
1	1. Amazed 2. Nervous 3. Scared 4. In love 5. Insecure		Intimidates	
2	1. In love	1. Narrator decided Rosa should be his wife 1a. Met eyes with Rosa/couldn't breathe/pulse stopped		
3	1. In love 2. Wants her as his wife 3. Happy	1. Narrator is dumbstruck and bewitched by her 3. Speaks to Rosa and can't think of anything to say		
4	1. Awe and dumbstruck 2. Too shy to speak 3. Afraid to lose her 4. Loss of control 5. Loses confidence and assertiveness	1. Shortness of breath 2. Goes mute		

item to test comprehension of a selection from Isabel Allende's *The House of the Spirits*.

The narrator has many different reactions when he is near Rosa. Identify two of these reactions and explain what they reveal about the narrator. Use relevant and specific information from the excerpt to support your answer.

The selection was titled "Rosa Beautiful" and was from the first chapter of the novel. The actual selection was not included in the released items because of copyright restrictions. First, it was clear that I could evaluate the student responses without having deeply read the selection. Second, it was obvious that a student could get the highest score, four, on his or her response with a fairly vacuous response by simply lifting several examples from the selection. Third, on further analysis, I concluded that, based on the released items, the student who scored the highest score of four and the next-to-lowest score of one both had inferred the same number of internal states to the protagonist, all of which were valid interpretations; plus, the student who scored the one had also imputed an internal state to the other main character, Rosa. Table 6.1

summarizes the internal states attributed to the protagonist by students scoring at each level in the responses released by the state to illustrate how such
open items were evaluated. One is the lowest, and four is the high score.

The primary difference in the answers receiving the highest and the next-
to-lowest scores had to do with length, form, and provision of examples
from the text. Other students who were closer to this format achieved higher
scores, even though their reasoning (in response to the question defined as
imputing appropriate internal responses to the protagonist) did not have the
same depth as that of the student who had the next-to-lowest score. The
appendix to this chapter has the full responses for each score as released by
the Massachusetts State Board of Education.

The examples in students' answers were about an emotional response that
is very common across the human experience; that is, having an explicit internal response to seeing someone you like a lot. In the full text itself (i.e., the
chapter from the book), the feelings of Rosa's suitor are problematized; the
nuances are explored. However, in this single open-response question to
the selection and across the multiple-choice questions, rarely are students
asked to consider or wrestle with a significant problem of literary reasoning.
There are several examples in the multiple-choice questions that ask students
to select a correct answer for a piece of text that is figurative or identify the
literary technique being used (in this question, hyperbole) in one multiple-
choice question. In this case, though, it appears that the multiple-choice
questions are potentially more rigorous than the open-response question.
However, the multiple-choice questions about figuration in the text do not
capture what really good readers do; that is, weigh competing explanations
and argue from textual evidence and real-world knowledge, including knowledge of the author and other texts and the pros and cons of these competing
explanations. That is not a task on the MCAS tenth-grade test on literature.
This is the tenth-grade examination that all Massachusetts high school students must pass in order to graduate from high school. It should be noted
that the MCAS is currently under revision.

This problem of inauthentic assessments (even those which purport to
be more authentic such as the MCAS and the New York Regents Exam),
especially in the area of reading comprehension generally and subject-matter
reading comprehension specifically, is even more complex. It should be noted
that compared with typical standardized achievement tests, the MCAS and
the New York Regents Exam are both more authentic and more rigorous,
including more complete versions of real texts. However, when compared
with what it means to read in the real world, the objectives are really not
rigorous. The tasks do not reflect what is required to carry out complex

reasoning in the subject matters. The New York Regents Exam does include a more authentic set of reading tasks in its Social Studies section, where students are asked to compare and contrast primary source documents in history (Lee and Spratley, in press). Unfortunately, this content area test is an anomaly. Try reading Toni Morrison's *Beloved* in a timed task. Although it is laudable that states like Massachusetts and New York are attempting to create more rigorous assessments and exit standards, black and brown students and students from low-income backgrounds are not fairing well on these assessments at all.

In response to this dearth of authentic rigorous assessments for literature at the middle and high school levels, the Cultural Modeling Project developed its own assessments (Lee 1993, 2007; Lee and Spratley, in press). Identifying existing instruments that would authentically capture complex literary reasoning was and continues to be difficult. Across several iterations, the Cultural Modeling Project has developed its own assessments while still documenting changes in scores on standardized measures. The assessments developed by the project include, in fact, full short stories that were not part of the curriculum unit, stories in which the generative problem of the instructional unit was a major interpretive problem in the story. Questions were developed using a taxonomy for comprehension in fiction developed by Hillocks (Hillocks and Ludlow 1984): key detail, basic stated information, simple implied relationship, complex implied relationship, and author's generalization. Most standardized reading assessments at the middle and high school levels categorize the products of comprehension as literal understanding, the ability to make inferences while reading and to extrapolate propositions from the text, and vocabulary understanding. Although these are clearly fundamental demands of reading as outcomes to be measured, they suffer from two limitations. First, scores in these areas tell teachers and students virtually nothing about why students are having problems in a given area, such as making inferences. Second, there are useful distinctions to be made between what is involved in extrapolating from a work of literature and from a particular kind of primary source document in history. Results from the assessments typically used shed virtually no light on either of these issues, both of which are crucial if assessments are to inform instruction and provide information that both teachers and students can use to improve.

The taxonomy developed by Hillocks is geared specifically to reading fiction. Each category represents a hierarchical sequence in levels of difficulty. For example, if a reader cannot identity a key detail in the text, he or she is not going to be able to make inferences. If a reader cannot make inferences when the information needed is constrained to several contiguous sentences or within a single paragraph, he or she will likely not be able to make more complex inferences that require identifying and imposing patterns on pieces of information that are distributed across the text. Thus, results from assessments built around something like the Hillocks taxonomy for fiction can serve a predictive function by identifying the foundational skills needed to solve more complex problems of comprehension. We do not have comparable taxonomies for reading comprehension within other content areas in the K–12 curriculum.

In order to address these problems, the Cultural Modeling Project developed its own assessments for response to literature. In the first iteration, items were subjected to Rasch analysis (Wright and Masters 1982; Wright and Stone 1979) in order to document that the question types represented different levels of difficulty (Lee 1993, 1995a). Tests were not timed. I used these criteria in the development of assessments because they represented more authentically what is entailed in the practice of literary interpretation in real-world contexts, in contrast to the arbitrary limitations of timed tests for literary comprehension and to address the critiques I have made in this chapter of assessments like the MCAS. It is interesting to note that although students did make gains on standardized achievement tests required by the school district and state, they still achieved at higher standards on the assessments developed by the project (Lee 2007). Although I recognize that the criticism could be raised that the explanation lies in the Cultural Modeling assessments being easier, I tend to reject such critiques because the texts themselves were longer and more complex than those typically found on the standardized achievement tests (certainly more complex than the texts in the Test of Academic Proficiency [TAP] used by the district where the school was located). The question types actually sampled a wider range of competencies than are generally assessed on standardized achievement tests. We consistently found that students who scored often in the bottom quartile of standardized assessments of reading comprehension demonstrated qualitatively different competencies both on our assessments as well as in the quality of their participation in classroom discussions and work.

In reviewing the Massachusetts' summary of statewide results in the prior year (Driscoll 2004), officials said:

Between 2003 and 2004, the percentage of African American, Asian, and Hispanic students performing at the *Proficient* and *Advanced* levels in English Language Arts rose in grades 3, 4, 7 and 10. At the same time, there was a general decline in the percentage of African American, Asian, and Hispanic students performing at the *Warning/Failing* level. The only exceptions were for African American students at

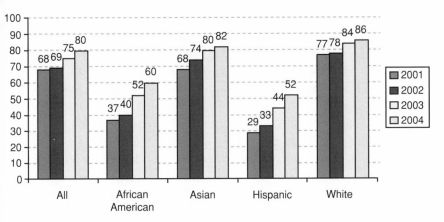

Figure 6.3. MCAS 2004 results by race/ethnicity.[2]

grade 3 and Asian students at grade 7, where that percentage remained unchanged since 2003, and for African American students at grade 7, where that percentage increased slightly. (p. 4)

Yet if one reviews the actual data charts that report results by ethnicity and race, it is abundantly clear that African American and Hispanic students lag behind their European American peers at levels that are disconcerting (Figure 6.3).

I believe there is a public logic that goes something like this: "We need rigorous academic standards and assessments that will ensure we can know who is able and who is not. *X* is such a test. Our students are doing well on this assessment. Therefore, our students are achieving." The general scores in Massachusetts for 2004 indicate that 80% of all students and 88% of regular students (those who are do not have limited English proficiency or are not labeled learning disabled) earned a competency determination on the first attempt at the tenth-grade MCAS. Of the 2005 graduates, 94% passed the MCAS before graduation. This is a noteworthy achievement, but its significance is muted when one considers the overall rigor of the assessment.

One of the few good aspects of the No Child Left Behind (NCLB) legislation is the requirement that schools disaggregate test scores by ethnicity/race and income. The problem with this legislation and the general response to the persistent lag in achievement of black and brown students is that there is no fundamental, systemic change in instruction or assessment. Under

NCLB, disaggregated scores are made public. Parents are told they can send their child to another, better-performing school, except that in a great many districts with large proportions of black and brown students, there are not enough high-performing schools to accommodate either students who do not make what is euphemistically called adequate yearly progress or schools with significant numbers of teachers who are deemed "qualified." Some fear that the NCLB legislation is a prelude to widespread vouchers. Yet as the history of vouchers in Milwaukee, Wisconsin, testifies, there are not enough (nor are there ever likely to be enough) private or charter schools to accommodate the number of students who need access to better-performing schools (Van Dunk and Dickman 2004). The same was true in Chicago, when under NCLB, school test results indicated the number of children who were eligible to transfer to better-performing schools. The problem was that there were not enough seats available in schools making adequate yearly progress to accommodate any but a very small percentage of those students who were eligible. Again, we have a band-aid response to a gushing wound.

CONCLUSIONS

I intend with these examples to examine the problem of OTL, in this case opportunity to learn to read well by subject-matter criteria, as situated in classrooms, in assessments, and in public policy. Most of the attention on OTL has focused on the use of results from external assessments to provide the public with evidence that students are learning. Requirements from NCLB are built on this proposition. When the results from assessments reveal that students are not making what is called adequate yearly progress, families have the option of transferring children to higher-performing schools. However, this policy masks the fundamental reasons why students are not learning and also hides the fact that these assessments often are not really measuring rigorous learning. I have attempted to demonstrate with the brief example from the MCAS in secondary English Language Arts that what is deemed a rigorous assessment may not really tap deep understanding.

OTL involves a matrix of interrelated competencies that must be developed in tandem. These minimally include the development of assessments that adequately tap what it means to engage in complex reasoning within and across subject matters; teachers' knowledge of subject matter, pedagogical content knowledge, language acquisition and language socialization, and child and adolescent development; and students' abilities to make generative connections between their everyday experiences and ways of using language and the technical concepts, vocabulary, forms of argumentation, and problem solving in the academic subject matters – minimally. Through the examples of the Cultural Modeling Project and Chèche Konnen, I have attempted to illustrate how the organization of learning environments in ways that scaffold the everyday experiences and ways of using language of ethnic/racial and language-minority groups, particularly those from low-income backgrounds, provide opportunities to learn, for both students and teachers, that result in robust learning.

Notes

1. Massachusetts Department of Education. 2004. Massachusetts Comprehensive Assessment System: Release of Spring 2004 Test Items (with answer key). http://www.doe.mass.edu/mcas/2004/release/.
2. Massachusetts Department of Education. 2004, June. Massachusetts Comprehensive Assessment System: Progress report on students attaining the competency determination statewide and by school and district: Classes of 2004 and 2005. www.doe.mass.edu/mcas/results.html?yr=04.

References

Anyon, J. 1981. Social class and school knowledge. *Curriculum Inquiry* 11: 3–42.

Applebee, A. 1993. *Literature in the secondary school: Studies of curriculum and instruction in the United States (NCTE Research Report No. 25)*. Urbana, Ill.: National Council of Teachers of English.

Applebee, A., R. Burroughs, and A. Stevens. 2000. Creating continuity and coherence in high school literature curricula. *Research in the Teaching of English* 34: 396–429.

Ball, A. 2006. *Multicultural strategies for education and social change: Carriers of the torch in the United States and South Africa*. New York: Teachers College Press.

Ballenger, C. 1997. Social identities, moral narratives, scientific argumentation: Science talk in a bilingual classroom. *Language and Education* 11: 1–14.

Baquedano-Lopez, P. 1997. Creating social identities through Doctrina narratives. *Issues in Applied Linguistics* 8: 27–45.

Baron, R., D. Y. H. Tom, and H. M. Cooper. 1985. Social class, race and teacher expectations. In *Teacher expectations*, edited by J. B. Dusek. Hillsdale, N.J.: Erlbaum.

Bereiter, C. and S. Engelmann. 1966. *Teaching disadvantaged children in pre-school*. Englewood Cliffs, N.J.: Prentice Hall.

Booth, W. 1974. *A rhetoric of irony*. Chicago: University of Chicago Press.

Booth, W. 1983. *A rhetoric of fiction*. Chicago: University of Chicago Press.

Bransford, J., A. Brown, and R. Cocking. 1999. *How people learn: Brain, mind, experience and school*. Washington, D.C.: National Academy Press.

Campbell, J. R., C. M. Hombo, and J. Mazzeo. 2000. *NAEP 1999 trends in academic progress: Three decades of student performance*. Washington, D.C.: National Center for Educational Statistics.

Chi, M. T. H. 1978. Knowledge structures and memory development. In *Children's thinking: What develops*, edited by R. Siegler, 73–96. Hillsdale, N.J.: Erlbaum.

Clement, J. 1989. Using bridging analogies and anchoring intuitions to deal with students' preconceptions in physics. *Journal of Research in Science Teaching* 30: 1241–57.

Conant, F. 1996. Drums in the science lab. *Hands On* 19: 7–10.

Darling-Hammond, L. 1985. *Equality and excellence: The educational status of Black Americans.* New York: The College Board.

Darling-Hammond, L. 1987. Teacher quality and inequality. In *Access to knowledge,* edited by P. Keating and J. Goodlad. New York: College Entrance Examination Board.

Darling-Hammond, L. 1999. *Teacher quality and student achievement: A review of state policy evidence.* Seattle: Center for the Study of Teaching and Policy.

DeMeis, D. K. and R. R. Turner. 1978. Effects of students' race, physical attractiveness and dialect on teachers' evaluations. *Contemporary Educational Psychology* 3: 77–86.

DiSessa, A. 1982. Unlearning Aristotelian physics: A study of knowledge-base learning. *Cognitive Science* 6: 37–75.

Driscoll, D. P. 2004, September. *Spring 2004 MCAS Tests: Summary of state results.* Malden: Massachusetts Board of Education.

Fish, S. 1980. *Is there a text in this class? The authority of interpretive communities.* Cambridge: Harvard University Press.

Foster, M. 1987. "It's cookin' now": A performance analysis of the speech events of a Black teacher in an urban community college. *Language in Society* 18: 1–29.

Foster, M. 1997. *Black teachers on teaching.* New York: The New Press.

Fugees. 1996. The mask. *On the Score.* Holland: Ruffhouse Records.

Gee, J. P. 1994. First language acquisition as a guide for theories of learning and pedagogy. *Linguistics and Education* 6: 331–54.

Grossman, P. 2001. *Research on the teaching of literature: Finding a place,* 4th ed. New York: Macmillan Press.

Gumperz, J. J. and D. Hymes. 1972. *Directions in sociolinguistics: The ethnography of communication.* New York: Holt.

Gutierrez, K., P. Baquedano-Lopez, and C. Tejeda. 1999. Rethinking diversity: Hybridity and hybrid language practices in the Third Space. *Mind, Culture, and Activity* 6: 286–303.

Gutierrez, K., B. Rymes, and J. Larson. 1995. Script, counterscript, and underlife in the classroom: James Brown versus Brown v. Board of Education. *Harvard Educational Review* 65: 445–71.

Gutmann, A. 1987. *Democratic education.* Princeton: Princeton UP.

Hernstein, R. J. and C. Murray. 1994. *The bell curve: Intelligence and class structure in American life.* New York: Free Press.

Hillocks, G. and L. Ludlow. 1984. A taxonomy of skills in reading and interpreting fiction. *American Educational Research Journal* 21: 7–24.

Hymes, D. 1980. *Language in education: Ethnolinguistic essays.* Washington, D.C.: Center for Applied Linguistics.

Irvine, J. 1990. *Black students and school failure.* New York: Praeger.

Jensen, A. 1969. How much can we boost IQ and scholastic achievement? *Harvard Educational Review* 39: 1–123.

Kitwana, B. 2002. *The hip hop generation: Young Blacks and the crisis in African American culture.* New York: Basic Civitas.

Ladson-Billings, G. 1994. *The dreamkeepers.* San Francisco: Jossey-Bass.

Lakoff, G. and R. Nunez. 2000. *Where mathematics comes from: How the embodied mind brings mathematics into being.* New York: Basic Books.

Lam, E. 2000. L2 literacy and the design of the self: A case study of a teenager writing on the internet. *TESOL Quarterly* 34: 457–81.

Lave, J. and E. Wenger. 1991. *Situated learning.* New York: Cambridge University Press.

Lee, C. D. 1993. *Signifying as a scaffold for literary interpretation: The pedagogical implications of an African American discourse genre.* Urbana, Ill.: National Council of Teachers of English.

Lee, C. D. 1995a. A culturally based cognitive apprenticeship: Teaching African American high school students' skills in literary interpretation. *Reading Research Quarterly* 30: 608–31.

Lee, C. D. 1995b. Signifying as a scaffold for literary interpretation. *Journal of Black Psychology* 21: 357–81.

Lee, C. D. 1995c. Viewpoints: Symposium on the usefulness of literacy research. *Research in the Teaching of English* 29: 335–8.

Lee, C. D. 1998. *Supporting the development of interpretive communities through metacognitive instructional conversations in culturally diverse classrooms.* Paper presented at the Annual Conference of the American Educational Research Association.

Lee, C. D. 2000. Signifying in the zone of proximal development. In *Vygotskian perspectives on literacy research: Constructing meaning through collaborative inquiry,* edited by C. D. Lee and P. Smagorinsky, 191–225. New York: Cambridge University Press.

Lee, C. D. 2001. Is October Brown Chinese? A cultural modeling activity system for underachieving students. *American Educational Research Journal* 38: 97–142.

Lee, C. D. 2002. *When and where I enter: Understanding and choreographing instructional discourse based on African American English discourse patterns.* Paper presented at the Annual Meeting of the American Educational Research Association, New Orleans.

Lee, C. D. 2003a. Cultural modeling and the challenges of Chicago high school reform. In *Chicago high school reform,* edited by V. Lee. Chicago: Consortium on Chicago School Reform.

Lee, C. D. 2003b. *Cultural modeling and pedagogical content knowledge: The case of the teacher of literature.* Paper presented at the Annual Meeting of the American Educational Research Association, Chicago.

Lee, C. D. 2004. Literacy in the academic disciplines and the needs of adolescent struggling readers. *Voices in Urban Education* 3.

Lee, C. D. 2005. Double voiced discourse: African American Vernacular English as resource in Cultural Modeling classrooms. In *New literacies for new times: Bakhtinian perspectives on language, literacy, and learning for the 21st century,* edited by A. Ball and S. W. Freedman. New York: Cambridge University Press.

Lee, C. D. 2007. *Culture, literacy and learning: Taking bloom in the midst of the whirlwind.* New York: Teachers College Press.

Lee, C. D. and D. Slaughter-Defoe. 1995. Historical and sociocultural influences on African American education. In *Handbook of research on multicultural education,* edited by J. Banks and C. Banks, 348–71. New York: Macmillan.

Lee, C. D., M. B. Spencer, and V. Harpalani. 2003. Every shut eye ain't sleep: Studying how people live culturally. *Educational Researcher* 32: 6–13.

Lee, C. D. and A. Spratley. In press. *Reading in the disciplines and the challenges of adolescent literacy.* New York: Carnegie Foundation of New York.

Lemke, J. 1998. Multiplying meaning: Visual and verbal semiotics in scientific text. In *Reading science: Critical and functional perspectives on discourse of science,* edited by J. R. Martin and R. Veel, 87–113. New York: Routledge.

Mehan, H. 1979. *Learning lessons.* Cambridge: Harvard University Press.

Mitchell-Kernan, C. 1981. Signifying, loud-talking and marking. In *Mother wit from the laughing barrel,* edited by A. Dundes, 310–328. Englewood Cliffs, N.J.: Prentice-Hall.

Moll, L. and N. Gonzales. 2004. Engaging life: A funds of knowledge approach to multicultural education. In *Handbook of research on multicultural education,* 2nd ed., edited by J. Banks and C. A. M. Banks. New York: Jossey-Bass.

Morgan, M. 1998. More than a mood or an attitude: Discourse and verbal genres in African American culture. In *African-American English: Structure, history, and use,* edited by S. S. Mufwene, J. R. Rickford, and G. Bailey. New York: Routledge.

Morrell, E. 2002. Toward a critical pedagogy of popular culture: Literacy development among urban youth. *Journal of Adolescent and Adult Literacy* 46: 72–78.

Ochs, E., P. Gonzales, and S. Jacoby. 1996. When I come down I'm in the domain state: Grammar and graphic representation in the interpretive activity of physicists. In *Interaction and grammar,* edited by E. Ochs, E. Schegloff and S. Thompson, 328–69. New York: Cambridge University Press.

Orellana, M., J. Reynolds, L. Dorner, and M. Metaleza. 2003. In other words: Translating or "para-phrasing" as a family literacy practice in immigrant households. *Reading Research Quarterly* 38: 12–34.

Orr, E. W. 1987. *Twice as less: Black English and the performance of Black students in mathematics and science.* New York: Norton.

Pea, R. D. and L. Gomez. 1992. Distributed multimedia learning environments. *Interactive Learning Environments* 2: 73–109.

Perkins, D. 1992. *Smart schools: Better thinking and learning for every child.* New York: The Free Press.

Perkins, D. 1993. Person-plus: A distributed view of thinking and learning. In *Distributed cognitions: Psychological and educational considerations* edited by G. Salomon, 88–110. New York: Cambridge University Press.

Rabinowitz, P. 1987. *Before reading: Narrative conventions and the politics of interpretation.* Ithaca: Cornell University Press.

Rist, R. 1970. Student social class and teacher expectations: The self-fulfilling prophecy in ghetto education. *Harvard Educational Review* 40: 411–51.

Rogoff, B. and J. Lave. 1984. *Everyday cognition: Its development in social context.* Cambridge: Harvard University Press.

Rogoff, B., R. Paradise, R. Mejía Arauz, M. Correa Chávez, and C. Angelillo, et al. 2003. Firsthand learning through intent participation. *Annual Review of Psychology* 54: 175–204.

Rose, T. 1994. *Black noise: Rap music and Black culture in contemporary America.* Hanover, N.H.: Wesleyan University Press.

Rosebery, A. S., B. Warren, C. Ballenger, and M. Ogonowski. 2005. The generative potential of students' everyday knowledge in learning science. In *Understanding mathematics and science matters,* edited by T. Romberg, T. Carpenter, and D. Fae. Mahwah, N.J.: Erlbaum.

Rosebery, A. S., B. Warren, and F. R Conant. 1992. Appropriating scientific discourse: Findings from language minority classrooms. *The Journal of Learning Sciences* 2: 61–94.

Rumelhart, D. 1980. Schemata: The building blocks of cognition. In *Theoretical issues in reading comprehension: Perspectives from cognitive psychology, linguistics, artificial intelligence and education,* edited by R. Spiro, B. Bruce, and W. Brewer, 33–58. Hillsdale, N.J.: Erlbaum.

Salomon, G. 1993. *Distributed cognitions: Psychological and educational considerations.* New York: Cambridge University Press.

Smagorinsky, P. and S. Gevinson. 1989. *Fostering the reader's response: Rethinking the literature curriculum, grades 7–12.* Palo Alto, Calif.: Dale Seymour Publications.

Smith, M. and G. Hillocks. 1988. Sensible sequencing: Developing knowledge about literature text by text. *English Journal,* October: 44–49.

Smitherman, G. 1977. *Talkin and testifyin: The language of Black America.* Boston: Houghton Mifflin.

Smitherman, G. 2000. *Talkin that talk: Language, culture and education in African America.* New York: Routledge.

Spencer, M. B. 2006. Phenomenology and ecological systems theory: Development of diverse groups. In W. Damon and R. M. Lerner, eds., *Handbook of child psychology,* 6th ed., vol. 1, 829–93. New York: Wiley.

Steffensen, M., C. Joag-Dev, and R. Anderson. 1979. A cross-cultural perspective on reading comprehension. *Reading Research Quarterly* 15: 10–29.

Stotsky, S. 1999. *Losing our language: How multicultural classroom instruction is undermining our children's ability to read, write, and reason.* New York: Free Press.

Taylor, M. 1982. *The use of figurative devices in aiding comprehension for speakers of Black English.* Urbana: University of Illinois.

Tompkins, J. 1980. *Reader-response criticism: From formalism to post structuralism.* Baltimore: Johns Hopkins University Press.

Valdes, G. 2002. *Expanding the definitions of giftedness: The case of young interpreters from immigrant countries.* Mahwah, N.J.: Lawrence Erlbaum.

Van Dunk, E. and A. M. Dickman. 2004. *School choice and the question of accountability: The Milwaukee experience.* New Haven: Yale University Press.

Vygotsky, L. 1978. *Mind in society: The development of higher psychological processes,* edited by M. Cole et al. Cambridge: Harvard University Press.

Vygotsky, L. 1981. The genesis of higher mental functions. In *The concept of activity in Soviet psychology,* edited by J. Wertsch. Armonk, N.Y.: M. E. Sharpe.

Wertsch, J. 1985. *Vygotsky and the social formation of mind.* Cambridge: Harvard University Press.

Wineburg, S. 1991. Historical problem solving: A study of the cognitive processes used in the evaluation of documentary and pictorial evidence. *Journal of Educational Psychology* 83: 73–87.

Wineburg, S. and P. Grossman. 1998. Creating a community of learners among high school teachers. *Phi Delta Kappan* 73: 684–9.

Wolf, D. P. 1995. *Reading reconsidered: Literature and literacy in high school.* New York: College Entrance Examination Board.

Wright, B. D. and G. Masters. 1982. *Rating scale analysis.* Chicago: MESA Press.

Wright, B. D. and M. H Stone. 1979. *Best test design.* Chicago: MESA Press.

APPENDIX

Graded responses to open-response question about Allende's *The House of the Spirits*, with MCAS criteria for scoring.

Throughout the excerpt from the House of Spirits by Ismbal Allenda, the narrator has many reactions to Rosa's beauty. One of these reactions is shortness of breath and another was going mute. Both reactions reveal information about the narrator. When Rosa walks by the narrator on the streetcar, and looks at him, the narrator "couldn't breathe and [his] pulse stopped." This response shows the narrator is in complete awe and dumbstruck by Rosa's beauty. He does not think clearly because his entire being is entrapped in her gaze and he has no control over her beauty. Later, the narrator is within speaking distance of Rosa and he "stood there mute mouth gaping." Again, the narrator is in awe of Rosa's beauty. He is too shy to speak and too afraid to lose her if he does. Her beauty leaves the narrator with loss of control over his own being. He forgets what to do or how to act. When faced with Rosa's beauty he loses the confidence and assertiveness he sent with the letters and flowers. Rosa clearly changes the narrator and causes him to react strangely around her.

Grade 4 (Highest score)

Response is a complete, clear, and accurate identification and explanation of two of the narrator's reactions and what they reveal about him. Relevant and specific textual evidence, presented through direct quotation, paraphrase, or a combination of both methods, is included in the response.

The narrator has many different reactions when he is near Rosa. For example when she passes by him to go to the store he is "dumbstruck", and "bewitched" by her and her every move. This reaction tells us that the narrator has fallen in love with Rosa and wants her as his wife. Another reaction we see is when the narrator finally gets to speak to Rosa and he can't think of anything to say. This particular reaction tells us that the narrator is so happy to just get a chance to speak to her that it has consumed his whole mind and he doesn't know what he wants to say.

Grade 3

Response is a fairly complete, clear, and accurate identification and explanation of two of the narrator's reactions and what they reveal about him. Relevant but often general textual evidence, presented through direct quotation, paraphrase, or a combination of both methods, is included in the response.

The narrator before he even knew Rosa, decided then and there that she was the only woman in the world who was worthy to be his wife. This reaction means that he has completely fallen for Rosa. Another reaction would be when the narrator met eyes with Rosa, he described it as part of me died. I couldn't breathe and my pulse stopped in its tracks.

Grade 2

Response is a partial, possibly unclear, identification and explanation that, in attempting to identify and explain two of the narrator's reactions and what they reveal about him, offers either a mix of accurate and inaccurate evidence or simply a piece or two of accurate evidence by itself. Some relevant but general and vague textual evidence, presented through direct quotation or paraphrase, is included in the response.

The narrator is amazed by Rosa but also also nervous and scared. She intimidates him with her beauty. I think it shows that the narrator is in love with her but insecure about himself.

Grade 1

Exhibiting varying degrees of clarity, response is a minimal identification and explanation that, in attempting to identify and explain two of the narrator's reactions and what they reveal about him, consists of largely inaccurate evidence, a general statement about the narrator's reactions, or a few snippets of detail. Little, if any, relevant textual evidence (either through direct quotation or paraphrase) is included in the response.

Identify two of these reactions and explain what they reveal about the narrator.
The narrator is a girl name Rose Rose. Nana is a beautiful girl I can still remember the exact moment when Rose the Beautiful entered my life like a distracted angel who stole my soul as she went by she was with he nana and another child probably one of her younger sisters. I don't generally spend my time thinking about women but only a fool could have failed to sport that apparition who caused a stir wherever she went and tied up traffic with her incredible green hair which make run wen I see her green hair after that I came back ask her out.

Grade 0

Response is incorrect, irrelevant, or contains insufficient evidence to show any understanding of the narrator's reactions and what they reveal about him.

7   Opportunities to Learn in Practice and Identity

James G. Greeno and Melissa S. Gresalfi

Following Suchman, (1985), Lave, (1988), Lave and Wenger (1991), Hutchins, (1995a), Engeström, (1999), and others, we take a *situative* perspective in our research and, in this chapter, regarding opportunity to learn (OTL).[1] Conducting analyses of learning with this perspective involves defining *activity systems* as the unit of analysis, which includes one or more persons interacting with each other and with material and informational resources that are present in the setting. The main emphasis of the situative perspective is on how learning by individuals and groups is accomplished through interaction between elements of an activity system. Of course there are changes in the participating individuals' mental structures, including schemata, but these are not the primary focus of our analyses. In this view, learning by an individual in a community is conceptualized as a trajectory of that person's participation in the community – a path with a past and present, shaping possibilities for future participation. Learning by a group or community is also conceptualized as a trajectory – a path that corresponds to change in the community's practices.

A SITUATIVE PERSPECTIVE ON LEARNING

Individuals Learning in a Community

Lave and Wenger (1991) outlined a situative framework on learning by considering the trajectories of individuals' participation as they become members of a *community of practice*. As individuals initially join a new activity, their involvement is limited to *peripheral participation*. Learning occurs as individuals participate in the practices of the community; changes in their participation reflect their increased capabilities and "know-how" as they are entitled and expected to act with greater initiative and responsibility. In other words, learning occurs as individuals' participation becomes increasingly similar to that of experienced old-timers. A crucial contribution of this framework is the acknowledgement that the ways that individuals are positioned with respect to others and the content of the activity is inseparable from their engagement with the content itself. Thus, learning involves participation with both interpersonal and informational aspects of an activity. The individual's trajectory of learning can be considered in terms of his or her engagement with the practices of the community as he or she moves from peripheral to more central participation.

A trajectory is usually defined as a path that an object follows as it moves through a physical or conceptual space. We adapt this concept to characterize changes in an individual's ways of participating over time in a community. An important aspect of this metaphor for learning is that trajectories are generated dynamically, partially according to general patterns and partially in interaction with specific circumstances that arise. (An analogy is the trajectory of a golf ball hit off a tee. The activity system includes the golfer, a club, the ball, the landscaping of the hole, the wind conditions, and so on. General properties of the ball's trajectory are determined by the magnitude and direction of the impact of the club when it strikes the ball, the gravitational field, and the friction of air. Yet its trajectory can be altered significantly by a sudden gust of wind during its flight.)

Considering learning as a trajectory serves some useful conceptual and analytical purposes. It encourages a focus on learning as a process occurring over time, which necessarily includes both consistencies and changes in the direction of the trajectory. It supports analyses of the affordances of learning settings that influence trajectories of participation. Primarily, though, it provides a conceptualization of learning in which trajectories are considered as changes in participation that occur in and are results of interactions between many factors, including characteristics of learners in relation to the resources and practices of the activity systems in which learning takes place (pursuing the golf ball analogy, the trajectory of the ball is considered an event at the level of the system, which includes the golfer, the ball, the golfer's swing, the force vector at the moment of impact, the conditions of air pressure and wind currents during its flight, etc.).

Analyzing learning in this way requires making a fundamental shift from the ways learning has been conceptualized traditionally. Rather than a process of acquiring structures, learning is considered as a process in which individuals participate more proficiently in practices that have structure. This shift in emphasis has significant implications for the ways we think about learning and the ways we identify or account for problems with learning (such as the persistent achievement gap between students of different races, ethnicities, and social class) and solutions to these problems (such as tracking or increasing remediation programs).

In our work, we focus on two aspects of student learning: informational, involving students' interactions with information, concepts, and principles of subject-matter domains; and interpersonal, involving students' interactions with each other, a teacher, and other people. We understand all activity as embodied and interactive with material systems, which can include constructing and manipulating models that are designed to incorporate subject-matter concepts and principles. In terms of information, students' trajectories can progress toward better understanding of concepts and principles of a domain, or it can progress toward more skillful performance of routine procedures or recitations, or both. In its interpersonal aspects, a student's trajectory can progress toward more engaged and successful contributions to a group's work or increased focus and concentration on independent work.[2]

Some Important Characteristics of Activity Systems

We consider opportunities to learn as situated by conceptualizing OTL as *affordances* for changing participation and practice. In this view, understanding a learner's trajectory involves hypotheses about affordances that are available to the learner to participate in particular ways. Affordances (the term was contributed by Gibson 1979) are relational. An affordance for an individual in an activity system includes the resources and practices of the system, that individual's access to those resources and practices, and the dispositions and abilities of the individual to participate in a way that supports her or his activity and learning in some way (Norman 1988). Affordances are not all-or-none; rather, they vary along a continuum. When we say that an activity affords some aspect of participation for some individuals, we mean that it makes it relatively easy for those individuals to participate in that way.

In our situative view, opportunities to learn are characteristics of activity settings. Lave and Wenger (1991) discussed opportunities to learn in terms of whether the necessarily peripheral participation of newcomers is *legitimate*. In legitimate peripheral participation (LPP), newcomers' responsibilities, albeit limited, are meaningful and make tangible contributions to the community's functions. LPP also requires resources for understanding functions and meanings of activities, including access to information about how one's activities fit into the larger functions of the community. Lave and Wenger's discussion included two cases of apprenticeships that contrasted in terms of the ways they created access to legitimate opportunities to learn.

In African tailor shops studied by Lave, apprentices participated integrally in making clothing, with initial responsibility for performing simple operations, followed by progression along a trajectory of performing increasingly complex aspects of the trade. By contrast, in some Chicago meat-cutting and -packaging plants studied by Marshall (1972), apprentice butchers were assigned the work of wrapping pieces of meat that had been cut by experienced butchers in a separate room, so the apprentices lacked access to even observing the skills that butchers need for their work.

In terms of our situative framing, the learning environment of the apprentice tailors afforded a trajectory of becoming competent and responsible in the making of clothes. The curriculum respected the capabilities that the apprentices had at different points of their learning, giving them tasks that were within their zones of proximal development (Vygotsky 1978). The tasks they were given were meaningful, contributing tangibly to the production of the shop. They had access to direction and guidance by their supervisors, and they worked side by side with more experienced tailors, with opportunities to observe their work practices. Their learning was a trajectory in which they progressed in achieving fuller participation in the productive activities of making clothes. By contrast, the apprentice butchers were not afforded a trajectory of becoming competent and responsible in the cutting of meat. Their task of wrapping already-cut pieces contributed to the productivity of the group, but they did not have access to participating in a sequence of increasingly complex and responsible tasks or even to observing the activities of more experienced workers as a resource for learning the practices that constitute the work of fully qualified butchers.

It is important to note that the situated nature of learning does not necessarily mean that what is learned is bounded solely within a specific activity system. Individuals can learn in one setting in a way that changes their participation in a different setting, particularly when the new setting has similar constraints and affordances as the initial context that are perceived by the learner (Greeno, Smith, and Moore 1993). For example, elementary teachers in a professional development project, Cognitively Guided Instruction, participated in activities of analyzing videotapes of students solving simple mathematical problems, focusing on thinking strategies that students employed. There was a trajectory of their participation in the workshop, of course, but the trajectory of some teachers' classroom activity also changed, in which their interactions with students involved greater attention to the thinking strategies of their students, not just whether they could produce correct solutions (Fennema et al. 1993). The workshop activities were designed to support this change in trajectory. Teachers were shown videotapes of students solving problems, which were discussed as examples of students' thinking strategies. They were asked to provide their analyses of examples and predict how students they observed solving one problem were likely to work on other problems with the same structure. We take this to be a case of transfer of learning across settings, because the success of some teachers' learning with these activities was probably greater than would have been the case if they had only participated in discussions of the theoretical analyses of student thinking that were the scientific basis for designing the workshops.

Learning by Communities of Practice

Learning by groups and communities can also be described in terms of their trajectories. A trajectory of group learning involves change in its practices. Learning by a group implies learning by its individual members – if the practices that an individual participates in change, then the individual's participation must also adapt in some way. This does not negate the validity of analyses of learning as a property of the group activity. Analyses of learning by a group and analyses of learning by one or more of its individual members can both be carried out; they involve focusing analyses at different levels.

A group's learning trajectory may progress in a variety of ways; for example, toward more effective collaborative activity of achieving mutual understanding in its subject-matter domain or toward more effective practices for performing and learning procedural skills of its domain. Thus, its changes in practice can become more inclusively collaborative or more rigidly restrictive, including some students in collaboration and learning and marginalizing others.

In an example of positive group learning led and reported by Engeström (2001), workers in two departments of a health care system convened, reached an understanding of a problem involving a lack of coordination of the treatment patients were receiving in the two departments, and developed new practices designed to provide better coordination of information and treatment. Their learning trajectory altered their practices regarding coordination of their activities, including changes in their discourse involving different understanding of the contradiction in their initial practices and a change in the practices they were committed to following in their work. Although, to be sure, the participation of individual members in both departments shifted as a result of these new, emergent understandings, it was the learning and renewed coordination between the two groups that was especially significant.

Successful learning by a class involves change in practices corresponding to progress in the understanding and use of concepts and representations in a subject-matter domain. In our situative perspective, a curriculum is a sequence of activities that affords both discussion and use of some concepts and methods of a subject matter to become more advanced. Most obviously, a classroom's practices change as information and concepts are added to its common ground, supporting changes in the content of its discourse, as students proceed through their curriculum. As they progress, the teacher and the students have new information that they use in talking about and making sense of new ideas. As a consequence, the practices of the classroom, specifically in terms of the ways participants can make sense of new information, change. Opportunities to learn for a classroom include resources and practices that can support the extension and transformation of those practices. What's more, these practices and resources are self-supporting, as an opportunity to learn (when taken up) can also become a practice of the classroom that marks the way the system has changed over time.

One example of classroom learning[3] comes from a curriculum for rational numbers designed by Moss and Case (1999). Working with rational numbers, they built on findings by Confrey (1994) and others, which showed that young children have significant understanding of simple multiplicative operations of doubling and halving quantities and, somewhat less firmly, of tripling or dividing into thirds. They hypothesized that by middle–elementary school, children also have significant understanding of percentage fractions, based on their familiarity with a decimal monetary system. Based on these findings and conjectures, they designed activities that provided opportunities to learn about fractions, decimals, and percents through the coordination of two dimensions of information, one involving physical quantities and the other involving symbolic representations of fractions.

Moss and Case's (1999) curriculum makes strong use of embodied cognition, with students interacting with material systems in ways that exemplify the quantitative concepts that they can learn to coordinate with numerical representations. Material systems included fractions of linear distances along the floor that children enacted by walking partway from one end to another of a line and fractions of vertical columns that were filled or covered. Building on students' initial understanding of concepts such as halves (50%) and halves of halves (25% and 75%), they supported students in making connections between these different representations. Teaching with the curriculum was successful, with fourth-grade children learning to solve problems and explain meanings of numerical and quantitative symbols and operations better than a comparable group of students taught in a standard curriculum.

The trajectory of learning developed by Moss and Case (1999) was designed according to a cognitive model of conceptual growth, with students building on ideas that they already understood to form new conceptual understandings. However, we can also conceptualize the students' learning as a trajectory of changing participation with material resources. The activities of the curriculum included interaction with objects, talk about their quantitative properties, and use of mathematical representations. The students' discourse, including talk about quantities and use of representations, progressed in its use of increasingly advanced mathematical concepts and principles in the domain of rational numbers. Initially, the students were able to talk about fractional quantities of distances, heights, and so forth. In the learning activities of the curriculum, they advanced to talking about and constructing representations of percentages corresponding to those fractional quantities, supported in part by their knowing how to talk about money. Then they participated in activities in which they learned to talk about and represent fractions that correspond to percentages. At each point along the trajectory, learning activities were designed to afford students' progress toward adding some aspect of mathematical discourse to the practices they had already developed. The affordance of each activity was designed so that participating in the discourse of the activity would use mathematical concepts and methods beyond those already developed but would be within the capability of students to extend their discourse with the supports of material resources (physical distances and heights) and relevant concepts that they knew (fractional quantities of money). In addition, the activities were designed to afford opportunities for students to engage with mathematical concepts in an intentionally embodied way – such as walking distances, measuring amounts, or dividing real quantities. These activities thus afforded an opportunity for students to *experience* these mathematical ideas – "halving" became not just an operation on symbols that refer to numbers but an embodied experience of walking half as far, pouring out half of a container of water, and so forth.

Another example of a classroom trajectory of learning comes from Bowers, Cobb, and McClain (1999), who analyzed students' learning of a mathematical practice involving use of a computer representation that supported understanding of place-value concepts in addition and subtraction. The place-value concept was realized in computer graphics that depicted single pieces of candy, rolls of ten pieces, and boxes of ten rolls. The embodied cognition of the activities involved interacting with the computer displays; that is, the students operated on images via the computer interface rather than manipulating physical pieces of candy directly. Even so, the coordination of quantitative concepts and symbolic representations of numbers and arithmetic operations was supported by activities in which the two modes of representation were related. As Bowers et al. illustrated, learning a specific representational practice with understanding requires engaging in patterns of discourse that need to be learned by students with their teacher in a classroom group. Thus, the trajectory of the group moved toward a change in this discourse practice over time. Bowers et al. also provided analyses of individual learning, showing transitions in the participation of individuals who participated in this practice differently at particular moments in time.

Groups or communities, especially in classrooms, often have trajectories that operate at more than one level. In addition to changes in discourse and specific methods in the subject matter of the kind we have discussed, practices such as general methods of solving problems and representing information are learned and adopted, becoming parts of the class's practices for doing their work. For example, over the course of a year, students and their teacher may develop understandings about the ways that they will be expected and obligated to make sure that their solutions are sensible and comprehensible to others. In discussing these changes, Yackel and Cobb (1996) distinguished between general social norms, sociomathematical norms, and (technical) mathematical practices, all of which can change as aspects of a classroom's learning trajectory.

Changes in general discourse practice can also occur if the class adopts changes in its patterns of explanation and argumentation that are characteristic of its subject-matter discipline. This was one of the goals that Lampert (1990, 2001) described for her teaching as she tried to create a classroom wherein student work would resemble that of mathematicians. For example, Lampert (1990) noted that she wanted to encourage a "courageous and modest" way of interacting that involved being entitled, obligated, and empowered to share mathematical assertions and ideas, even when they were not completely developed, while simultaneously being open to listening to others' arguments and refutations about what is mathematically true.

A SITUATIVE PERSPECTIVE ON OTL

Aspects of Activity

Clearly, one of the most crucial aspects of understanding OTL comes from the activity system in which students are participating. Classroom activities are generally organized as tasks, so OTL depends on the tasks that students have to work on. To understand the OTL that tasks afford, we distinguish a task's topic, cognitive demands, and the agency of students' participation in the task.

The topic of a classroom task is the component of a subject-matter curriculum that the task addresses, such as an operation on rational numbers in Moss and Case's (1999) curriculum or adding or subtracting multidigit numbers in base-ten arithmetic, as in Bowers et al.'s (1999) study.

The cognitive demands of a task (Doyle and Carter 1984) depend in part on its topic but on other factors as well, because tasks on the same topic may involve engaging in dramatically different activities that include varied informational resources. Tasks can involve correctly performing specified procedures or recalling information that has been presented previously. Alternatively, tasks can involve generating explanations of procedures or factual information in relation to general concepts and principles of the domain. It is important to recognize that cognitive demands of a task for a student or class depend on both the content of the task and what the student(s) already know(s). A problem may be solved by applying a well-defined procedure, and if a student knows the procedure and recognizes its applicability (e.g., when a student is given a series of problems that all can be solved using the same procedure that recently has been reviewed), the cognitive demand of that task for the student is low. However, if that student does not know the procedure or does not recognize its applicability, he or she could be required to engage in significant generative interpretation and problem solving. This is directly related to our earlier claim that affordances for action are relational; students' histories of participation shape their attunement to affordances in a setting and in a task but also reshape the nature of the affordances themselves.

Stein et al. (2000) examined tasks assigned in middle-school mathematics classes in a mathematics education reform program called QUASAR and characterized those tasks in terms of the cognitive demands required for their successful completion. Lowest-level tasks required only that students recite something from memory. Second-level tasks required correct performance of a procedure but without the need to relate the procedure to general concepts. The third level, called *procedures with connections*, required students to attend to concepts that made the procedures meaningful, and the fourth level, called *doing mathematics*, required students to consider meanings of concepts and methods explicitly. Despite the potential of tasks, however, Stein et al. noted that in many of the classrooms they observed, the cognitive demand of tasks was frequently systematically decreased as students and the teacher worked on tasks together. Specifically, it was very typical for a task to create opportunities for students to engage with procedures by making connections between ideas. In the end, however, because of interactions that glossed over explanations or focused on correct answers without justifications, such tasks created opportunities only for students to correctly perform a procedure.

The cognitive demands of tasks are related to a second issue that we consider in our work: the agency of students' participation with a task. As we use the term, agency refers to the kind of action students can and need to perform in completing a particular mathematical task. Pickering (1995) distinguished between two types of agency that can be exercised in intellectual domains. *Disciplinary agency* refers to actions taken by an individual or group in which the outcome is determined by properties of an established procedure or method (if the procedure or method is performed correctly). For example, someone exercises disciplinary agency when he or she uses the quadratic formula[4] to solve a quadratic equation. The function specifies which numbers get slotted into particular parts of the equation, and the actual solution of the equation is a well-established series of procedural moves, such as starting by simplifying the quantity underneath the radical. *Conceptual agency* refers to actions by an individual or group in which the outcome is determined by choices made by the actor(s); for example, in formulating a question, choosing a method, or explaining a solution conceptually. When working on a task, an individual may complete an action with disciplinary agency by recalling a fact or definition from a text or performing an action according to an accepted procedure. Alternately, a person may propose or question a formulation of a problem or an approach to solving it or propose or question a conceptual interpretation of something the group has done.

The levels of cognitive demand of tasks discussed by Stein et al. (2000) differ in the kinds of agency Pickering distinguished. Recalling facts or definitions and executing procedures involves disciplinary agency; there are correct answers, and a student either gets it right or doesn't. Performing procedures with connections[5] and especially doing mathematics generally involve conceptual agency, with students positioned to take initiative in constructing meaning from and understanding the methods and concepts that are the subjects of their learning.

The cognitive demands and therefore the kinds of agency that students are afforded in classrooms make a very significant difference in their opportunities to learn. If students' activities are limited to exercising disciplinary agency and completing tasks with low levels of cognitive demand, they are afforded learning trajectories that involve acquiring skill but not progressing toward full participation in activities involving generative and authoritative use of concepts and principles. In a perfect world, students would spend most of their time working on tasks that involve engaging in what Pickering called a "dance of agency," wherein they would oscillate between thinking about how to solve a problem using the conceptual tools at their disposal (conceptual agency) and then actually implementing those tools in order to discover whether their conjecture about a possible solution is correct (disciplinary agency). Unfortunately, it seems that many classroom tasks mainly afford students opportunities only to exercise disciplinary agency, because they are assigned problems that involve primarily practicing a known procedure.

The distinction we make between elements of OTL would not be useful without evidence that these distinctions have implications for what students actually learn. The studies reviewed below illustrate how OTL, in the content of the tasks and in the way tasks are implemented with respect to the kinds of agency they afford, make a difference in terms of what students come to know and think about mathematical content and about the domain more broadly.

In Stein et al.'s (2000) results, students whose classrooms had more tasks with high-level cognitive demands had stronger OTL, as indicated by their higher scores on assessments of their learning, especially for learning mathematical concepts and principles. Work by Boaler (1997/2002) illustrates the role that different activity systems (including dramatically different tasks) can play in creating opportunities to learn mathematics. Boaler followed a cohort of students in two British secondary schools in working-class neighborhoods during a three-year period, focusing on mathematics teaching and learning. At one school, called Amber Hill, students were afforded opportunities to learn mathematical procedures, as teachers presented mathematical content didactically and students mainly practiced procedural skills aimed at preparing them to do well on standardized tests. At the other school, called Phoenix Park, students were afforded opportunities to learn to solve problems using mathematical tools, as students mainly worked on investigations that required the use of mathematical concepts and methods in the context of solving an open-ended problem. The students were not told how to solve particular problems and were encouraged to consider the strengths or usefulness of different procedures on their own. Teachers at Phoenix Park taught procedures, but only when they could be used by students in their work. Boaler concluded that the students in the two schools learned different forms of mathematical knowledge, with students at Phoenix Park learning to use mathematics much more generally and generatively. We would say that this resulted from their having had distinctively different OTL. The OTL at Amber Hill supported learning mathematics as a set of procedures, with success defined as ability to perform specified procedures correctly, limited to disciplinary agency. The OTL at Phoenix Park supported learning mathematical concepts and procedures as resources for understanding, reasoning, and solving problems; that is, to act with significant conceptual agency. The contrast in outcomes was demonstrated especially well when students were given open-ended assessment tasks. When students were asked to design a flat (i.e., an apartment), Phoenix Park students considered issues such as the sizes and locations of different rooms that should be included and proceeded meaningfully, using mathematics to advance their design work. Amber Hill students made less progress on the problems, treating them as occasions where they should be able to identify procedures they thought they were expected to perform.

A final example of strong OTL comes from work by Engle and Conant (2002). They reported findings from a fifth grade classroom organized according to Brown and Campione's (1994) Fostering Communities of Learners program. Each group of four to five students studied an endangered species and wrote a report about its condition, including its habitat and biological features related to its endangerment and survival. In one of the groups studying whales, an issue arose regarding whether its study should include orcas, which the group members had heard "are really dolphins" from a staff member at a marine park where they had taken a field trip. When one of the students opined that they should eliminate orcas from their study, another student became vociferously upset. One of the teachers directed the students to discuss the matter and decide what to do. Their discussion lasted twenty-seven minutes, and the topic continued to engage the students during the several weeks in which the class completed their projects. Engle and Conant asked what conditions in the classroom practice could be responsible for this remarkable instance of productive disciplinary engagement. They suggested four factors of classroom practice: The students had authority for their positions in the debate; they were accountable for explaining and supporting their positions; there were ample resources available to them to conduct their inquiry; and the classroom practice encouraged problematizing substantive issues and positioning students as responsible agents in resolving issues that arose.

Engle and Conant's (2002) analysis is consistent with, and expands on, our idea that high levels of cognitive demand and conceptual agency are significant factors in supporting OTL through participation. The students were engaged in tasks that had high levels of cognitive demand, carrying out a biology assignment using what they considered to be alternative claims about the proper classification of a species, formulating arguments based on anatomical features, and evaluating the authority of sources, including the marine park staff and textbooks. Their discussions were rife with conceptual agency; they interpreted and evaluated their sources and argued the significance of the evidence. Engle and Conant's analysis thus suggests that attending to factors such as authority, accountability, resources, and problematizing in design of learning environments creates OTL that progresses toward generative, meaningful participation in practices of inquiry and use of knowledge and understanding.

OTL as It Relates to Individuals

We have discussed ways in which different learning environments, especially classrooms, differ in the affordances they provide for learning. However, affordances are relationships between characteristics of resources in an environment and characteristics of learners. Therefore, in a single classroom, affordances for learning are not the same for all individuals. For example, an explanation given by a teacher that affords increased understanding for one learner may for another learner afford increased effectiveness at resisting participating in discussions about meanings of concepts. On the other hand, individuals with similar dispositions for participating in some way, such as discussing meanings of concepts with other learners, are afforded that kind of participation more strongly in some learning environments than they are in others. That is, a learner may participate actively in conceptual discussions and become more effective in such participation in an activity setting that is organized to afford that kind of participation and learning, while a similar learner may not participate in that way in a setting where having conceptual discussions is not afforded as strongly.

The strength of the affordance for a kind of participation can also vary within a given activity system. The affordance for a person to do something at any given moment depends on, for example, what other people are doing or what the person is attending to at the time.

As we consider the relation between actions by an individual and the sequence of actions that occur in an episode of activity, two key ideas become relevant: the ways that individuals become *positioned* in interaction and the *identities* they develop through their participation. Positioning focuses on aspects of the organized activity system; it refers to ways in which aspects of the system afford opportunities for different individuals to contribute differently. Identity refers to patterns in the ways individual students take up opportunities to learn that are presented to them.

In any episode of interaction, each participant is positioned in relation to the other participants, the material and informational resources in the situation, and the subject-matter domain in some way (Harré and van Langenhove 1999). The system of these positionings at any moment of interaction can be thought of as a participant structure (Phillips 1972). At any point in time, someone is taking or has taken the lead, others are expressing agreement, deferring to the leader's authority, or questioning or challenging the information, opinion, or proposal that is offered, and so on. Different OTL is afforded to each individual from moment to moment, depending on how he or she is positioned in the interaction. For example, in the following episode, from a study of two eighth-grade algebra classes (Gresalfi 2004), four students were positioned relative to each other and to the subject matter such that some students were positioned as subject-matter "experts" and were afforded opportunities to talk about and explain their mathematical thinking, while other students were positioned as "confused" and were afforded opportunities to listen to and record the thinking of others. In addition, in this group, being an "expert" meant that you were difficult to understand, making you qualitatively different from those who were confused. The positionings that occurred in this group can be clearly seen in this interaction but were also the result of months of classroom history (the following excerpt comes from an episode of group work recorded eight months into the school year). In this episode, the students were working on revisions from a test that they had just gotten back. They were working on the following problem: *A garden is currently 4 m wide and 7 m long. If the area of the garden is to be doubled by increasing the width and the length by the same number of meters, find the new dimensions of the garden.*

82	Monica:	OK. (*to Jacob*) Which one did you do, did you do the second one?
86	Jacob:	(*leaning over to look at Fathia's paper, says to Monica*) She got a higher grade than you. I did the first one and second one
89	Elise:	That's what I did, and I totally didn't get it. So wait, how do you do them?
91	Jacob:	(*banging on the table*) OK, for the first one
	Jacob:	(*to Elise*) twice the area of the garden is gonna be . . . fifty-six, meters squared (*looking at Elise*)
94	Monica:	Fifty-six, why is it fifty-six?
95	Jacob:	Because the original area is twenty-eight, right?
96	Elise:	OK, so /wait
97	Monica:	/um, this is what I did, could you tell me what's WRONG with it? (*pushing her paper towards Jacob, and smiling, Elise laughs*)
100	Jacob:	Can I, can I, can you look at your work so I can explain it?
101	Monica:	(*leans forward and smiles, resting her forehead on her left hand, looking at Jacob*)
103	Elise:	OK, OK, so, what he said, OK, I'll translate
104	Monica:	No, but OK, so this is what I did

105	Jacob:	OK, Elise, I'll talk to you, and /you talk to her
106	Elise:	/(*holding up her right hand,*
107		*palm facing Jacob*) shh shh shh – no be QUIET, I'm translating.
109	Elise:	(*leaning over and talking to Monica*) So, the garden is currently (thirty four)

In this interaction, Jacob immediately was positioned as the "expert," in part by virtue of the fact that he had answered this question correctly on the test. Both Elise and Monica turned to him for help and explanation but put the onus for their understanding on Jacob. This can be seen specifically in lines ninety-eight and ninety-nine, when Monica asked Jacob to do the work of uncovering her error and explaining what mistake she made. A bit later in the conversation, Jacob was positioned as being incomprehensible, seen in line 104 when Elise suggested that she translate Jacob's explanation. This positioning was not resisted by Jacob but was enthusiastically taken up, with Jacob offering to talk to Elise, who would translate to other group members. This positioned both Jacob and Elise as capable of understanding and Monica and Fathia as requiring more explanation. In the end, it was Jacob and Elise who did the work of sense-making in solving the problem by explaining how they translated the text of the problem to a series of mathematical procedures (through this positioning, they were afforded the opportunity to engage with the task by exercising conceptual agency). By contrast, Monica and Fathia were afforded the opportunity to record the procedures Jacob and Elise shared and thus were afforded the opportunity to exercise only disciplinary agency.

In an activity setting that extends over time, such as a classroom, patterns of interaction develop such that the ways that different individuals participate have some degree of stability. In our work thus far, we have found the concept of *participatory identity* (Holland et al. 1998) to be particularly useful in considering students' patterns of participation over time. Identity formation, as we understand it, is a two-way process between the individual and what he or she brings to an interaction and the resources and consequent opportunities of a particular activity setting (Greeno 2001; Wenger 1998). An individual's identity corresponds to the expectations of others and of him- or herself about his or her ways of participating in the activity setting (Cobb, Gresalfi, and Hodge, forthcoming; Gee 2001; Sfard and Prusak 2005). Specifically, we operationalize participatory identity by considering the emerging patterns in the opportunities that an individual takes up in the context of particular activity systems and the opportunities that are created in that system (Gresalfi 2006).

Gresalfi (2004) studied participatory identities of individual students in two eighth-grade algebra classes and presented eight case studies. Her analysis illustrated the ways students' dispositions toward working on mathematics alone, engaging socially with other students, or engaging with other students socially about their mathematical work interacted with the opportunities created in the classrooms for students to engage with other students and with mathematical content. A difference between the teachers in the two classrooms involved their emphasis on collaborative activity. In the classroom where collaborative work was emphasized and coached, the identities of some students shifted during the school year, becoming more responsive to opportunities to interact with other students to reach mutual understandings of solutions to problems. In the classroom with less emphasis on collaboration, students with strong dispositions to work alone maintained that pattern throughout the year, while those who started the year with a significant disposition for collaborative work became less inclined to collaborate and did so only in more procedural ways, such as by sharing answers rather than rationales.

Identities are often associated with ethnic, class, and gender membership. In our situative view, these memberships are crucial aspects of opportunities to learn. Because of the organization of many classroom activity structures, membership often conflicts with, and thus limits, students' participation in practices of learning (Delpit 1988; Erickson 1992; Ladson-Billings 1997). An important part of participatory identity in a classroom is one's identification of the subject matter and practices as meaningful and important for one's growth and development. Individuals who are viewed by others and themselves as alien in the community or as excluded from the life trajectories for which school learning is designed (c.f. D'Amato 1992; Ogbu 1992) are cut off from the opportunities to learn that are provided for students who are understood to be in the school's mainstream. Programs such as Lee's (this volume), Robert Moses's Algebra Project (Moses and Cobb 2001), Jerry Lipka's mathematics project with Up'ik communities (Lipka, Mohatt, and the Ciulistet Group 1998), and Eric Gutstein's social justice curriculum (Gutstein 2003) are examples of programs that seek to redesign the tasks of instruction so they support a participation structure with significant conceptual agency by *all* students.

A SITUATIVE PERSPECTIVE ON ASSESSMENT

In a situative perspective, assessments are activities in which students participate, just as they do in all of the other activities of a classroom system.

Assessments are activities that produce information that is used for evaluating some aspect of a group's or an individual's participation.

In this broad sense, all interaction involves assessment. In every moment of interaction, participants produce information that reflects their current understanding of each others' statements and intended meanings, and this information plays a major role in the way the interaction progresses. In this sense, assessment is inherent in all interactions, although the function of assessment is, for the most part, tacit. When participants in an interaction evaluate their progress or each others' contributions explicitly, they engage in deliberate assessment. When they construct material records that represent evaluations, they engage in documentary assessment (Jordan and Putz 2004; for further discussion of this distinction, see Moss, Girard, and Greeno, this volume).

The situative perspective views all activity as interaction in which a person or group participates in a practice that uses resources in the environment. Cognition is considered as distributed; that is, the activity that occurs is understood primarily as performance of the activity system, including contributions of material and informational resources as well as those of human participants. For example, Hutchins (1995b) analyzed performance of the cockpit of a commercial airplane, considered as an activity system, which remembered reliably to adjust the flaps and slats of the airplane during descents. The achievement of reliable remembering was accomplished in part by the pilots, but understanding the reliability of the system required including informational cues that were placed so that they were visible and salient at the times when adjustments needed to be made. Another analysis by Hutchins (1995a) involved the navigation room of a large navy ship entering a harbor. This activity system had to plot the position of the ship at frequent intervals to provide guidance in steering the ship to avoid collisions. Normally, the position plots were accomplished by an efficient system that included support of electronic systems, but in a case that Hutchins described, the ship's electrical power failed. Hutchins described the crew's successful adaptation to this loss of computational support. The position plots were accomplished, but by a very different cognitive process, which became more efficient over a series of plots.

Hutchins's studies were not presented as assessments, but they can be interpreted as assessments. Records could be kept of frequencies with which the flaps and slats were adjusted, as they must be, as airplanes descended. The scores would be nearly perfect. Someone could interpret this as indicating that airline pilots have very good memories. Hutchins would argue against this attribution to the human participants in the cockpit system. In his perspective, the achievement should be credited to cockpits as distributed cognitive systems. As a thought experiment, imagine a test in which pilots or pilot candidates are required to write, in a limited amount of time, a list of operations they must perform during a descent. Further, imagine that performance on the written test is not perfect, particularly in having some pilots omit the operation of adjusting flaps and slats. What would we be justified in concluding from such a result about the pilots' memory for performing that operation? From a cognitive perspective, explanation of the difference would appeal to differences between the contexts for the cognitive processes of remembering, probably noting that requirements for remembering are simpler in the cockpit than in the written test. The situative perspective, focusing on the performance of activity systems, would consider how the cockpit system includes affordances for the action of remembering to adjust the flaps and slats at the appropriate time.

We hope that the distinction between testing memory by recording performance of cockpits and by giving a written test seems ridiculously obvious. We find it interesting, though, that many assessment practices use performances on written tests as proxies for knowing how to act in very different activity systems, such as the administration of a written test in order to be granted a driver's license. More germane to school assessment, written tests are the primary means of evaluating students' learning in subject-matter disciplines, neglecting assessments that could provide information about their knowing how to formulate questions and problems, evaluate evidence, formulate and evaluate arguments, judge the validity and significance of conclusions, and other important aspects of knowing including knowing how to use conceptual and representational resources of domains.

From a situative perspective, assessments that purport to measure students' knowledge in simple quantitative terms, without taking the assessment activity into account, simply do not make sense. Measuring knowledge is subject to an analogous constraint to one that applies to measuring the velocity of an object moving in space. Since Galileo (1632/1967), physicists have recognized that the velocity of an object is meaningless except in relation to a specified frame of reference.[6] The situative perspective assumes that knowing has the same property. It is fundamentally relative to a frame of reference in which it observed and interpreted. The frame of reference for an assessment of someone's knowing is the activity system in which the person participates in generating information that is used in evaluating what he or she knows. For example, in the navigation room that Hutchins (1995a) studied, an assessment of the crew's efficiency in plotting the ship's positions could be made under normal conditions, with the support of its electronic systems. Very different information was obtained about the crew's capability when the conditions changed and it had to plot positions without electronic support. It is pointless to ask which of these would be a truer measure of the crew's knowing how to plot the ship's positions. Each is a valid measure, but it is meaningful only in relation to the frame of reference that differed significantly between the two circumstances.

Situative Studies of Assessment Systems

In the situative perspective, research on assessment considers activities and practices, not just psychometric properties of data that are produced. We briefly review two such studies.

In collaboration with two elementary-school teachers, Hall, Knudsen, and Greeno (1996) studied mathematics assessment activities in a fifth-grade classroom taught by one of the teachers who collaborated in the study. The teachers were beginning their participation in a longitudinal development and research project involving educational uses of computing, portfolio assessment, and student writing. Hall et al. studied two assessment activities in the fifth-grade class. One was a chapter test of the kind that is common in elementary mathematics classrooms. The other was an activity of designing and constructing a geometry tutorial for younger children (second and third grades) using a HyperCard stack.

The teachers and Hall et al. (1996) examined video records of classroom activity and developed an analytic framework for characterizing classroom assessment practices and understanding how practices facilitated meaningful assessments of student learning, or did not. The framework specifies six issues:

- activities that make up the assessment and how contingencies between activities produce information about learning;
- forms of participation that are available for students in the activities;
- lines of communication that are open between participants;
- the subject matter of the assessment;
- the media of assessment, including patterns of interaction and documents that record information about student activity and performance; and
- types of information that are produced.

Applying these categories to the two assessment activities of a chapter test and constructing a tutorial resulted in some clear contrasts, as would be expected. Students were afforded multiple forms of participation in the tutorial assessment and limited participation in the chapter test. The information generated in the chapter test was limited to correct or incorrect answers and, finally, to the number of correct answers by each student, while the tutorial assessment included records of explanations and alternative definitions considered and constructed by students. The (limited) information generated in the chapter test was more portable beyond the classroom.

Smith (2004) provided another example of a situative study of assessment in two eighth-grade mathematics classrooms. The classrooms were taught by the same teacher with different curricula, one with a traditional textbook and the other with a progressive, standards-based curriculum called *Mathematics in Context* (National Center for Research in Mathematical Sciences Education and Freudenthal Institute, 1997–1998). Smith reported that the teacher articulated somewhat different learning goals for the students in the two classes, aspiring to a more expansive set of goals for the students using the more progressive curriculum, "e.g., developing number sense, learning to solve many kinds of problems, learning to question things, being able to justify their thinking, becoming intelligent consumers, developing confidence" (p. 67), in line with the more conceptually demanding tasks provided in that curriculum. Classroom activities reflected these different goals, and the teacher monitored the students' conceptual understanding as they worked on problems. However, the assessments that resulted in documentary records of student learning were limited to numbers of correct or satisfactory solutions of problems in both classes. Although the students who used *Mathematics in Context* worked on more complex tasks, the teacher's feedback on their papers was mainly limited to judgments about whether their work was satisfactory, with little guidance for ways they could have presented stronger solutions. In terms of Hall et al.'s (1996) framework, although the students' work had more information about their mathematical thinking, this information was not reflected in the teacher's responses or made a part of the documentary record that resulted from the process. Smith reported that as a result of these findings, revised guidelines for assessment were included in the teachers' guides provided with the *Mathematics in Context* curriculum.

These studies illustrate the situated nature of knowing, even in its most simplified or static form: a simple written assessment. Understanding or being able to use information from an assessment requires knowing both how a person has performed, and the activity in which he or she has performed. This challenges current notions of measurement and accountability, because scores are reported without any information about the nature of the assessment tool (much less the nature of the activity with which students were engaging at the time). Significant changes to our current assessment system will require changes in the nature of what is reported, including going beyond unqualified use of representations of knowledge that are derived from situations that bear little or no resemblance to the activities in which knowledge is constructed and used.

Implications for Assessment Practices

Assessment practices have very significant effects on students' learning (e.g., Black and Wiliam 1998), and therefore the nature of assessment is a crucial issue for OTL. Black and Wiliam showed that classrooms with formative assessment practices, where deliberate assessment is conducted to inform decisions about ongoing learning activities, had superior student learning. It follows, then, that productive formative assessment must be one of the standards for classrooms to meet in order to provide acceptable OTL. Results of situative analyses, such as those of Hall et al. (1996) and Smith (2004), discussed earlier, emphasize that OTL in assessment activities depends on ways that students participate in those activities, not just on the items and tasks that are included in tests or other performance assessments.

In addition to their consequences for OTL, different assessment practices also position students very differently in ways that involve moral issues of treating students justly. Wiggins (1993) advocated a bill of rights for students to protect them against harms that current practices of testing often inflict, including entitlement to question grades and test practices without fear of retribution, opportunities for students to explain or justify answers marked as wrong that they believe to be well founded, feedback that informs students about their progress toward well-specified standards, and policies that provide incentives and opportunities for improving performance and seeing progress.

We believe that there is a principle involved in several of the rights that Wiggins advocated – that every student should be entitled to contribute meaningfully to the case that is made regarding her or his success in learning. Learning trajectories are, and should be, varied, because there are many different aspects of participation that are needed and valuable. The ways in which individuals progress should not be evaluated against a single standard, except for a set of capabilities that all members of our society should be expected to have the opportunity to develop. Yet every student should be entitled and expected to develop in ways that go beyond minimum standards, and these trajectories vary in many ways, as they should. Each learner's perspective should be represented significantly in the information that accumulates as the account of her or his development and learning. In addition, every student is entitled to have access to the rules governing, and expectations

for, competent performance. As Delpit (1988) has noted, the expectations for
what constitutes competent performance are often implicit and not equally
clear to all students, as a consequence of alignment or misalignment between
classroom cultural practices and home cultural practices. Thus, students do
not always have equal access to information about the requirements for successful performance, which may lead to differences in learning trajectories
that are not consequences of students' desire or effort to engage with the
content and ideas of the curriculum.

UNDERSTANDING ACCESS TO OTL

The organization of a classroom activity system creates opportunities for
students to exercise different types of agency and thus to engage differently
with each other, the teacher, and the subject-matter domain. Opportunities
to learn are affordances for participation, which are relations between characteristics of activity systems and characteristics of participants. Whether or
not students can or do take up these opportunities and why they might or
might not do so is an important aspect of the learning that actually occurs
and should be considered in any theory of learning.

Regarding topics of instruction, differences between students in what they
already know and can do often produce differences in whether or not they
can take up opportunities to learn. If a teacher uses technical terms or refers
to procedures that are known by some but not all of the students, the students
who know those terms or procedures are positioned to take up that OTL,
while others are not. School curricula that emphasize sequences of tasks
organized to require specific previous learning create a dilemma in which
there will be some students who are poorly prepared to participate in the
tasks that are assigned (and hence can learn only that they are inadequate) or
some students for whom the assigned tasks do not extend their knowledge
and capability (and hence can learn only that they are "smart") – usually both
deficiencies occur. These curricula create negative OTL by guaranteeing that
significant numbers of students *won't* learn; that is, they will fail (Varenne
and McDermott 1998). Not all school learning has this feature, at least to
the same extent. The programs that we described earlier, by Moss and Case
(1999), in the QUASAR classrooms that maintained high levels of cognitive
demand (Stein et al. 2000), by the teachers in Phoenix Park studied by Boaler
(1997/2002), in Fostering Communities of Learners (Brown and Campione,
1994), and many other programs that are designed and conducted similarly,
are much more equitable in terms of the access they create for all students to
essential leaning resources and, therefore, to OTL.

Regarding cognitive demands, tasks that afford conceptual connections or "doing" the subject matter for some students probably do not for others, unless practices in the classroom are effective in distributing the functions of understanding and meaning-making equitably. Several practices have positive effects on distributing opportunities to participate meaningfully among students. For example, Lampert's (1990, 2001) students work in groups, and it is understood that when the group has arrived at an answer, every student needs to be prepared to explain the group's answer to the class (Lampert 2001; Hall and Rubin 1998). Cohen (e.g., 1986) developed methods of distributing roles in student work groups when teaching using *complex instruction*, with the effect of reducing inequalities of status in the groups' activity. In the Fostering Communities of Learners classrooms we studied (e.g., Engle and Conant 2002), individual students in each group were responsible for developing different sections of the report, providing a distribution of expertise and authority based on their respective knowledge of different substantive aspects of their projects. We find this latter method especially promising, because it positions every student with authority and accountability on the topic of her or his specialization.

Regarding affordances for disciplinary and conceptual agency, individuals in the classroom may be differentially likely to take up opportunities to propose and question courses of action and their interpretation. One aspect of these differences has been discussed in the psychology of motivation by Dweck (1999; Dweck and Leggett 1988), Ames (1992; Ames and Archer 1988), and others. In analyses focused on individual students' motivations, Dweck and Legett (1988) distinguished between students with learning orientations and students with performance orientations. A learning orientation disposes a student to engage in challenging tasks, believing that effort in such tasks will result in learning and becoming "smarter." A performance orientation, in a student who has low confidence, disposes students to avoid challenging tasks because of concern about being exposed as being intellectually deficient. We expect that a student with a strong learning orientation would be more likely than a student with a strong performance orientation to take up opportunities to act with conceptual agency by offering ideas or questioning others' proposals in class or group discussions. However, Ames and Archer (1988) demonstrated that these goal orientations can be made more or less salient by specific situational demands. For example, if social comparison is made salient, students are more likely to focus on ability and are thus likely to engage in behaviors that will yield favorable judgments or avoid unfavorable judgments of their competence. On the other hand, if the classroom emphasizes and rewards effort, improvement, and participation, a mastery orientation is likely to be elicited, and students will be more likely to believe that effort leads to success, to pursue challenging tasks, and to try harder in the face of failure (Ames 1992). A further distinction from Herrenkohl and Wertsch (1999) is between mastery and appropriation; that is, mastery emphasizes acquiring skill to perform routine procedures correctly, and appropriation emphasizes developing generative capabilities to use concepts and methods in the student's own voice, involving greater conceptual agency.

In our situative view, we would consider these aspects of orientation as characteristics of individual students' participation in the activity systems of classrooms; that is, of the interactions of characteristics of individual students and characteristics of classroom practices. We consider the orientations of individual learners and of classrooms or groups to be jointly constructed in interactions.

Finally, the construction of agency in learning is not something that happens uniformly for all students in a classroom or group. Classrooms and groups construct affordances for agency that differ from student to student and indeed, from moment to moment in classroom interaction. These differences can have significant effects on the OTL that is afforded to different students.

CONCLUSION: SOME REQUIREMENTS FOR APPRAISING OTL

We propose considering OTL as affordances for student participation that support trajectories toward stronger valued capabilities and dispositions. We hypothesize that these affordances include tasks with high levels of cognitive demand involving meaningful social interaction and significant contact with concepts and principles of subject-matter domains; participation structures that involve exercising significant conceptual agency; and adequate skills and knowledge for routine procedures and information.

If this view of OTL is adopted, there are some obvious challenges facing efforts to appraise[7] it. Of course, appraisals of OTL need to provide evidence regarding the subject-matter topics that are in the contents of learning activities. They also need to provide evidence about the levels of cognitive demand in the tasks in which students participated. Tasks differ both in their potential and actual levels of cognitive demand, and evidence is needed regarding the levels that are achieved in the actual conduct of tasks.

Appraisals also need to provide evidence regarding the kinds of agency that are afforded to students in their learning activities. If students are to learn to take initiative and be generative in activities that use the concepts and principles of a discipline, they need to be positioned in their learning activities with that kind of agency. We hypothesize that positioning with conceptual agency is a critical supporting factor for most students in developing participatory identities that support productive participation. Having conceptual agency does not preclude acquiring skills and knowledge for using procedures and information routinely; indeed, positioning with conceptual agency can provide motivation for practicing routine skills and knowledge by providing contexts where they are useful.

Appraising OTL in these ways changes the obligations of educators and school systems more broadly. On the part of educators, both teachers and teacher educators will need to invest significant effort in identifying what to include in appraisals of OTL and how to measure their presence or absence. This would include, we suspect, collaborations among multiple groups of teachers and other educators. Making these changes could only happen with support from the context in which teachers are working – their school, the district, and broader institutions of schooling (Gamoran et al. 2003). Specifically, teachers and teacher educators would need the material, informational, and social supports required to make these changes and sustain them by shifting and recasting current notions of assessment.

We have a conjecture: To make progress toward an understanding of OTL that will support appraising it meaningfully, we will need to be able to model affordances in ways that identify contributions to them from the classroom environment, from teaching, and from individuals and groups of students. Models of affordances will necessarily identify trade-offs, in which stronger support in the environment can compensate for weaker support by learners, and vice versa. With such models, it will be possible to identify levels of contribution of practices and other resources in learning environments in relation to characteristics of students who learn there. As a consequence, such models could have implications for our success in meeting the needs of all students as we specify a model of learning that includes both individuals and aspects of the activity system in which they are participating.

Appraisal systems for OTL should include formulation of standards, but these should not be expected to designate specific practices or resources that are required in every learning environment. Instead, individuals and organizations will develop practices and provide resources that provide affordances for learning in different ways. Accountability for meeting standards will require an individual or organization to make a case for its practices and use of resources in relation to a model of affordances it has adopted and that is supported in the knowledge of the field. Clearly, making such a case that might be useful across students or across a school would require supporting teachers and schools in making these significant changes in their practice.

Of course, these ideas are far from the prevalent notions of OTL, which seem to be limited to the content topics of learning activity. Moving toward inclusion of affordances for participation with high levels of cognitive demand and conceptual agency would require considerable change in the commitments of our society for its educational system. As researchers, we can offer to evaluate the prospect of such a change and support it with our research efforts.

ACKNOWLEDGMENT

Greeno's contribution to this writing was supported by a grant from the Spencer Foundation. Gresalfi's contribution was supported by a grant from the National Science Foundation.

Notes

1. There are several terms in use that refer to perspectives that have similar conceptual and methodological commitments to the one we call situative. These include socio-cultural, activity–theoretic, and distributively cognitive. We believe that groups of researchers who use these several labels differ mainly in emphasis on different aspects of activity. Our situative perspective emphasizes both informational and interpersonal aspects of interaction, such as contributions of material systems, and histories of individual positioning in the environment. In this chapter, we consider the subject-matter contents of activity, especially discourse, in quite a bit of detail, using concepts and methods of the cognitive theory of comprehension (e.g., Kintsch 1998). We also draw on ecological psychology (e.g., Gibson, 1979; Reed 1996) and situation theory (Barwise and Perry 1983) in framing analyses of activity, considered as interactions of individuals with each other and with environmental systems, in terms of relational concepts, especially affordances and constraints.

2. Trajectories can also move in nonproductive directions – toward ways of partici-pating that are not likely to lead to increased academic learning or understanding. For example, students' trajectories can progress toward more skillful avoidance of engagement with tasks in the subject-matter domain, toward stronger resis-tance to collaborative interaction, or toward more effective disruption of classroom activities.

3. The classroom examples that we discuss involve mathematics, partly because this is the domain in which we have done most of our research and therefore are in closest touch within these studies, and partly to complement other chapters that concentrate on examples of literacy learning.

4. The quadratic formula is: $(-b \pm \sqrt{(b^2 - 4ac)})/2a$, given $ax^2 + bx + c = 0$.

5. Procedures with connections may involve significant conceptual agency if students are expected to take initiative in constructing the connections. If they are given by a teacher or textbook without significant student initiative, then, of course, they only involve disciplinary agency.

6. Galileo used an example of someone on the deck of a ship observing a ball of wax sinking in a vertical tube of oil. In the frame of reference of the ship, the ball moves vertically downward at some speed. The ship is sailing around the perimeter of a

circular lake, and in the frame of reference of someone standing on the shore, the path of the ball is a helix with a very large diameter and a small height. Asking what the path of the ball is makes no sense unless the frame of reference is specified.

7. We use "appraisal" rather than "assessment" to refer to evaluative studies of OTL, hoping it will be easier for readers to discern when we are discussing studies that provide information about OTL and when we are discussing studies that provide information about students' learning.

References

Ames, C. 1992. Classrooms: Goals, structures, and student motivation. *Journal of Educational Psychology* 84: 261–71.

Ames, C. and J. Archer. 1988. Achievement goals in the classroom: Students' learning strategies and motivation processes. *Journal of Educational Psychology* 80: 260–7.

Barwise, J. and J. Perry. 1983. *Situations and attitudes.* Cambridge: MIT Press.

Black, P. and D. Wiliam. 1998. Inside the black box: Raising standards through classroom assessment. *Phi Delta Kappan* 80: 139–48.

Boaler, J. 2002. *Experiencing school mathematics: Traditional and reform approaches to teaching and their impact on student learning, revised and expanded edition.* Mahwah, NJ: Lawrence Erlbaum Associates. (Originally published 1997)

Bowers, J. S., P. Cobb, and K. McClain. 1999. The evolution of mathematical practices: A case study. *Cognition and Instruction* 17: 25–64.

Brown, A. L. and J. C. Campione. 1994. Guided discovery in a community of learners. In *Classroom lessons: Integrating cognitive theory and classroom practice*, edited by K. McGilly. Cambridge: MIT Press.

Cobb, P., M. Gresalfi, and L. Hodge. Forthcoming. *An interpretive scheme for analyzing the identities that students develop in mathematics classrooms.*

Cohen, E. G. 1986. *Designing groupwork: Strategies for the heterogeneous classroom.* New York: New Press.

Confrey, J. 1994. Splitting, similarity, and rate of change: A new approach to multiplicative and exponential functions. In *The development of multiplicative reasoning in the learning of mathematics*, edited by G. Harel and J. Confrey, 293–332. Albany, N.Y.: SUNY Press.

D'Amato, J. 1992. Resistance and compliance in minority classrooms. In *Minority education: Anthropological perspectives*, edited by E. Jacob and C. Jordan, 181–207. Norwood, N.J.: Ablex.

Delpit, L. D. 1988. The silenced dialogue: Power and pedagogy in educating other people's children. *Harvard Educational Review* 58: 280–98.

Doyle, W. and K. Carter. 1984. Academic tasks in the classroom. *Curriculum Inquiry* 14: 124–49.

Dweck, C. S. 1999. *Self-theories: Their role in motivation, personality, and development.* Philadelphia: Psychology Press.

Dweck, C. S. and E. L. Legett. 1988. A social-cognitive approach to motivation and personality. *Psychological Review* 95: 256–73.

Engeström, Y. 1999. Activity theory and individual and social transformation. In *Perspectives on activity theory*, edited by Y. Engeström, R. Miettinen and R. Punamaki. New York: Cambridge University Press.

Engeström, Y. 2001. Expansive learning at work: Toward an activity theoretical recon-ceptualization. *Journal of Education and Work* 14: 133–56.

Engle, R. A. and F. Conant. 2002. Guiding principles for fostering productive disci-plinary engagement: Explaining an emergent argument in a Community of Learners classroom. *Cognition and Instruction* 20: 399–483.

Erickson, F. 1992. Transformation and school success: The policies and culture of edu-cational achievement. In *Minority education: Anthropological perspectives*, edited by E. Jacob and C. Jordan, 27–51. Norwood, N.J.: Ablex.

Fennema, E., T. P. Carpenter, M. Franke, and D. Carey. 1993. Learning to use children's mathematics thinking: A case study. In *Schools, mathematics, and the world of reality*, edited by R. B. Davis and C. A. Maher. Boston: Allyn and Bacon.

Galileo, G. 1632/1967. *Dialogue concerning the two chief world systems*. Berkeley: Univer-sity of California Press.

Gamoran, A., C. W. Anderson, P. A. Quiroz, W. G. Secada, T. Williams, and S. Ashman. 2003. *Transforming teaching in math and science: How schools and districts can support change*. New York: Teachers College Press.

Gee, J. P. 2001. Identity as an analytic lens for research in education. In *Review of Research in Education*, vol. 25, edited by W. G. Secada. Washington, D.C.: American Educational Research Association.

Gibson, J. J. 1979. *The ecological approach to visual perception*. Boston: Houghton Mifflin.

Greeno, J. G. 2001. *Students with competence, authority, and accountability: Affording intellective identities in classrooms*. New York: College Board.

Greeno, J. G., D. R. Smith, and J. L. Moore. 1993. Transfer of situated learning. In *Transfer on trial: Intelligence, cognition, and instruction*, edited by D. K. Detterman and R. J. Sternberg, 99–167. Norwood, N.J.: Ablex.

Gresalfi, M. S. 2004. *Taking up opportunities to learn: Examining the construction of participatory mathematical identities in middle school students*. Palo Alto: Stanford University.

Gresalfi, M. S. 2006, April. *Opportunities for whom? Classroom practices and the partic-ipatory identities of differentially successful students*. Paper presented at the American Educational Research Association.

Gutstein, E. 2003. Teaching and learning mathematics for social justice in an urban, Latino school. *Journal for Research in Mathematics Education* 34: 37–73.

Hall, R. P., J. Knudsen, and J. G. Greeno. 1996. A case study of systemic aspects of assessment technologies. *Educational Assessment* 3: 315–61.

Hall, R. and A. Rubin. 1998. There's five little notches in here: Dilemmas in teaching and learning the conventional structure of rate. In *Thinking practices in mathematics and science learning*, edited by J. G. Greeno and S. V. Goldman, 189–236. Mahwah, N.J.: Erlbaum.

Harré, R. and L. van Langenhove. 1999. *Positioning theory: Moral contexts of intentional action*. Oxford: Blackwell Publishers.

Herrenkohl, L. and J. V. Wertsch. 1999. The use of cultural tools: Mastery and appro-priation. In *Development of mental representation: Theories and applications*, edited by I. Sigel, 415–35. Mahwah, N.J.: Lawrence Erlbaum.

Holland, D., D. Skinner, J. G. Lachicotte, and C. Cain. 1998. *Identity in cultural worlds*. Cambridge: Harvard University Press.

Hutchins, E. 1995a. *Cognition in the wild*. Cambridge: MIT Press.

Hutchins, E. 1995b. How a cockpit remembers its speed. *Cognitive Science* 19: 265–88.

Jordan, B., and P. Putz. 2004. Assessment as practice: Notes on measures, tests, and targets. *Human Organization* 63: 346–58.

Kintsch, W. 1998. *Comprehension: A paradigm for cognition*. Cambridge: Cambridge University Press.

Ladson-Billings, G. 1997. It doesn't add up: African American students' mathematical achievement. *Journal for Research in Mathematics Education* 28: 697–708.

Lampert, M. 1990. When the problem is not the question and the solution is not the answer: Mathematical knowing and teaching. *American Educational Research Journal* 27: 29–63.

Lampert, M. 2001. *Teaching problems and the problems of teaching*. New Haven: Yale University Press.

Lave, J. 1988. *Cognition in practice: Mind, mathematics and culture in everyday life*. New York: Cambridge University Press.

Lave, J. and E. Wenger. 1991. *Situated learning: Legitimate peripheral participation*. New York: Cambridge University Press.

Lipka, J., G. V. Mohatt, and the Ciulistet Group. 1998. *Transforming the culture of schools: Yup'ik Eskimo examples*. Mahwah, N.J.: Lawrence Erlbaum.

Marshall, H. 1972. Social constraints on learning. In *Learning to work*, edited by B. Greer. Beverly Hills: Sage Publications.

Moses, R. P. and C. E. Cobb. 2001. *Radical equations: Math literacy and civil rights*. Boston: Beacon Press.

Moss, J. and Case, R. 1999. Developing children's understanding of the rational numbers: A new model and an experimental curriculum. *Journal for Research in Mathematics Education* 30: 122–47.

National Center for Research in Mathematical Sciences Education, and Freudenthal Institute. (1997–1998). *Mathematics in Context*. Chicago: Encyclopedia Britannica.

Norman, D. A. 1988. *The psychology of everyday things*. New York: Basic Books.

Ogbu, J. U. 1992. Adaptation to minority status and impact on school success. *Theory into Practice* 31: 287–95.

Phillips, S. 1972. Participant structures and communicative competence: Warm Springs children in community and classroom. In *Functions of language in the classroom*, edited by C. Cazden, D. Hymes, and V. John, 370–94. New York: Teachers College Press.

Pickering, A. 1995. *The mangle of practice: Time, agency, and science*. Chicago: University of Chicago Press.

Reed, E. 1996. *Encountering the world: Toward an ecological psychology*. Oxford: Oxford University Press.

Sfard, A. and A. Prusak. 2005. Telling identities: In search of an analytic tool for investigating learning as a culturally shaped activity. *Educational Researcher* 34: 14–22.

Smith, M. E. 2004. Practices in transition: A case study of classroom assessment. In *Standards-based mathematics assessment in middle school*, edited by T. A. Romberg, 60–79. New York: Teachers College Press.

Stein, M. K., M. S. Smith, M. A. Henningsen, and E. Silver. 2000. *Implementing standards-based mathematics instruction: A casebook for professional development*. New York: Teachers College Press.

Suchman, L. 1985. *Plans and situated action: The problem of human-machine communication.* Cambridge: Cambridge University Press.

Varenne, H. and R. McDermott. 1998. *Successful failure: The schools that America builds.* Boulder: Westview.

Vygotsky, L. S. 1978. *Mind and society: The development of higher psychological processes.* Cambridge: Harvard University Press.

Wenger, E. 1998. *Communities of practice: Learning, meaning, and identity.* Cambridge: Cambridge University Press.

Wiggins, G. P. 1993. *Assessing student performance: Exploring the purpose and limits of testing.* San Francisco: Jossey-Bass.

Yackel, E. and P. Cobb. 1996. Sociomathematical norms, argumentation, and autonomy in mathematics. *Journal for Research in Mathematics Education* 27: 458–77.

8   Game-Like Learning

An Example of Situated Learning and Implications for Opportunity to Learn

James Paul Gee

KNOWLEDGE: AS NOUN AND VERB

The theory of learning in many schools today is based on what I would call the "content fetish" (Gee 2004). The content fetish is the view that any academic area (whether physics, sociology, or history) is composed of a set of facts or a body of information and that the way learning should work is through teaching and testing such facts and information.

However, for some current learning theorists, "know" is a verb before it is a noun, "knowledge" (Barsalou 1999a, 1999b; Bereiter and Scardamalia 1993; Clark 1997; Glenberg 1997; Glenberg and Robertson 1999; Lave and Wenger 1991; Rogoff 1990). Any actual domain of knowledge, academic or not, is first and foremost a set of activities (special ways of acting and interacting so as to produce and use knowledge) and experiences (special ways of seeing, valuing, and being in the world). Physicists *do* physics. They *talk* physics. And when they are being physicists, they *see* and *value* the world in a different way than do non-physicists. The same applies for good anthropologists, linguists, urban planners, army officers, doctors, artists, literary critics, historians, and so on (diSessa 2000; Lave 1996; Ochs, Gonzales, and Jacoby 1996; Shaffer 2004).

Yet if much decontextualized, overt information and skill-and-drill on facts does not work as a theory of learning, neither does "anything goes," "just turn learners loose in rich environments," "no need for teachers" (Kirschner, Sweller, and Clark 2006). These are the progressive counterpart of the traditionalists' skill-and-drill, and they, too, are problematic as a theory of learning. Learners are novices, and leaving them to float among rich experiences with no guidance only triggers human beings' great penchant for finding creative but spurious patterns and generalizations that send them down garden paths (Gee 1992, 2001). The fruitful patterns or generalizations in any domain are those that are best recognized by those who already know how to look at the domain and how the complex variables at play in the domain interrelate with each other. This is precisely what the learner does not yet know.

Here we reach a central paradox of all deep learning. It won't work to try and tell newcomers everything. We don't know how to put it all into words, because a domain of knowledge is first and foremost made up of ways of doing, being, and seeing, ways complex enough that they outrun our abilities to put them all into explicit formulations. When we do put what we know into explicit words, learners often can't retain them or even really understand them fully because they have not done the activities or had the experiences to which the words refer. This should worry advocates of overt instruction.

Yet as we have already said, simply turning learners loose to engage in the domain's activities won't work either, because newcomers don't know how to start, where to look for the best leverage, and which generalizations to draw or how long to pursue them before giving them up for alternatives. Of course, we can hardly expect learners to reinvent for themselves domains that took thousands of people and hundreds of years to develop. This should worry advocates of immersion.

This paradox has lead some educators, over the last few years, to search for what I would call "post-progressive pedagogies"; that is, pedagogies that combine immersion with well-designed guidance (e.g., Brown 1994; Lehrer 2003; Lehrer and Schauble 2005; Martin 1990). One area, perhaps surprisingly, where learning today works very much in this fashion, that is, by combining immersion and guidance in intelligent ways, is modern video games (Gee 2003a, 2004). Indeed, there has been much interest during the last few years in the role that good video games and related types of simulations can play in learning inside and outside schools (e.g., Barab et al. 2005; Barab et al. in press; Gee 2003a, 2005; Jenkins and Squire 2004; Shaffer 2007; Squire 2005, 2006; Steinkuehler 2004, 2006).

Below I will give some examples of the role game-like learning can play in post-progressive pedagogies and the ways such learning can speak to issues of equity and oppotunity to learn (OTL). Before I do so, I will point out that the dilemma we discussed earlier – between knowledge as information and knowledge as activity and experience – is related to another dilemma familiar from recent research on cognition: the dilemma between general, abstract, and verbal understandings, on the one hand, and situated understandings, on the other.

GENERAL VERSUS SITUATED UNDERSTANDINGS

A situated understanding of a concept or word implies the ability to use the word or understand the concept in ways that are customizable to different specific situations of use (Brown, Collins, and Dugid 1989; Clark 1989, 1993, 1997; Gee 2004). A general or verbal understanding implies an ability to explicate one's understanding in terms of other words or general principles but not necessarily an ability to apply this knowledge to actual situations. Thus, although verbal or general understandings may facilitate passing certain kinds of information-focused tests, they do not necessarily facilitate actual problem solving. Research in cognitive science has shown, for example, that it is perfectly possible to understand Newton's laws as formulas, realizing their deductive capacities in a general way, but not be able to actually draw these deductions and apply them to a concrete case in actual practice to solve a real-world problem (Chi, Feltovich, and Glaser 1981; Gardner 1991).

Let me quickly point out that all human understandings are, in reality, situated. What I am calling verbal understandings are, of course, situated in terms of other words and, in a larger sense, the total linguistic, cultural, and domain knowledge a person has (Gee 2006). Yet they are not necessarily situated in terms of methods of applying these words to actual situations of use and varying their applications across different contexts of use. Thus, I will continue to contrast verbal understandings with situated ones, with the latter implying the ability to do and not just say.

Situated understandings are the norm in everyday life. Even the most mundane words take on different meanings in different contexts of use. Indeed, people must be able to build these meanings on the spot in real time as they construe the contexts around them. For instance, people construct different meanings for a word like "coffee" when they hear something like "The coffee spilled, get the mop" versus "The coffee spilled, get a broom" versus "The coffee spilled, stack it again." Indeed, such examples have been a staple of connectionist work on human understanding (Clark 1993).

Verbal and general understandings are top-down. They start with the general; that is, with a definition-like understanding of a word or a general principle associated with a concept. Less abstract meanings follow as special cases of the definition or principle. Situated understandings generally work in the other direction; understanding starts with a relatively concrete case and gradually rises to higher levels of abstraction through the consideration of additional cases.

The perspective I am developing here, one that stresses knowledge as activity and experience before knowledge as facts and information and situated as opposed to verbal understandings, has many implications for the nature of learning and teaching, as well as for the assessment of learning and teaching. Recently, researchers in several different areas have raised the possibility that what we might call "game-like" learning through digital technologies can facilitate situated understandings in the context of activity and experience grounded in perception (Games-to-Teach Team 2003; Gee 2003a; McFarlane, Sparrowhawk, and Heald 2002; Squire 2003). I turn first to an application of what I consider game-like learning that uses no real game, then to a game made explicitly to enhance school-based learning, then to a commercial game that enhances deep learning in a crucially important way, and finally to a game-like simulation, built into an overall learning system, that uses many of the same learning principles as the commercial game. I will then conclude with some remarks on implications, especially for issues of assessment and OTL.

GAME-LIKE LEARNING: ANDY DISESSA

Andy diSessa's (2000) work is a good example, in science education, of building on and from specific cases to teach situated understandings. Further, diSessa's approach bears similarities to the game-like learning we will discuss in the next section. DiSessa has successfully taught children in sixth grade and beyond the algebra behind Galileo's principles of motion by teaching them a specific computer programming language called Boxer.

The students write into the computer a set of discrete steps in the programming language. For example, the first command in a little program meant to represent uniform motion might tell the computer to set the speed of a moving object at one meter per second. The second step might tell the computer to move the object. A third step might tell the computer to repeat the second step over and over again. Once the program starts running, the student will see a graphical object move one meter per second repeatedly, a form of uniform motion.

The student can elaborate the model in various ways. For example, the student might add a fourth step that tells the computer to add a value a to the speed of the moving object after each movement the object has taken (let us say, for convenience, that a adds one more meter per second at each step). Now, after the first movement on the screen (when the object has moved at the speed of one meter per second), the computer will set the speed of the object at two meters per second (adding one meter), and then, on the next movement, the object will move at the speed of two meters per second. After this, the computer will add another meter per second to the speed, and on the next movement, the object will move at the speed of three meters per second. And so forth forever, unless the student has added a step that tells the computer when to stop repeating the movements. This process is obviously modeling the concept of acceleration. Of course, you can set a to be a negative number instead of a positive one and watch what happens to the moving object over time instead.

The student can keep elaborating the program and watch what happens at every stage. In this process, the student, with the guidance of a good teacher, can discover a good deal about Galileo's principles of motion through his or her actions in writing the program, watching what happens, and changing the program. What the student is doing here is seeing in an embodied way, tied to action, how a representational system that is less abstract than algebra or calculus (namely, the computer programming language, which is actually composed of a set of boxes) "cashes out" in terms of motion in a virtual world on the computer screen.

An algebraic representation of Galileo's principles is more general, basically a set of numbers and variables that do not directly tie to actions or movements as material things. As diSessa points out, algebra doesn't distinguish effectively "among motion ($d = rt$), converting meters to inches ($i = 39.37 \times m$), defining coordinates of a straight line ($y = mx$), or a host of other conceptually varied situations" (diSessa 2000, 32–33). They all just look alike. He goes on to point out that "[d]istinguishing these contexts is critical in learning, although it is probably nearly irrelevant in fluid, routine work for experts" (diSessa 2000, 33), who, of course, have already had many embodied experiences in using algebra for a variety of different purposes of their own.

Once learners have experienced the meanings of Galileo's principles about motion in a situated and embodied way, they have understood one of the situated meanings for the algebraic equations that capture these principles at a more abstract level. Now these equations are beginning to take on a real meaning in terms of embodied understandings. As learners see algebra spelled out in more such specific material situations, they will come to master it in an active and critical way, not just as a set of symbols to be repeated in a passive and rote manner on tests. As diSessa puts it:

Programming turns analysis into experience and allows a connection between analytic forms and their experiential implications that algebra and even calculus can't touch. (diSessa 2000, 34)

DiSessa does not actually refer to his work with Boxer as game-like learning, though some people pushing the design of actual games for learning have been inspired, in part, by his approach to learning and science education

(Gee 2003a). Indeed, Boxer produces simulations that are, in many respects, game-like and that certainly can entice from learners the sort of flexible consideration of possibilities that play can inspire. However, I turn now to an actual game designed to enhance situated learning that goes beyond verbal understandings.

Supercharged!

Kurt Squire and his colleagues (Squire et al. 2004; see also Jenkins, Squire, and Tan 2003; Squire 2003) have worked on a computer game called *Supercharged!* to help students learn physics. *Supercharged!* is an electromagnetism simulation game developed in consultation with MIT physicist John Belcher by the Games-to-Teach project at MIT (run by Henry Jenkins; see www.educationarcade.org). Players use the game to explore electromagnetic mazes, placing charged particles and controlling a ship that navigates by altering its charge. The game play consists of two phases: planning and playing. Each time players encounter a new level, they are given a limited set of charges that they can place throughout the environment, enabling them to shape the trajectory of their ship.

Each level contains obstacles common to electromagnetism texts. These include points of charge, planes of charge, magnetic planes, solid magnets, and electric currents. Each of these obstacles affects the player's movement according to laws of electromagnetism. The goal of the game is to help learners build stronger *intuitions* for electromagnetic concepts based on perceptual and embodied experiences in a virtual world where these concepts are instantiated in a fairly concrete way.

Squire et al. (2004) report some results that are part of a larger design experiment examining the pedagogical potential of *Supercharged!* in three urban middle school science classrooms with a good deal of cultural diversity. In this study, the experimental group outperformed the control group on conceptual examination questions. Post-interviews revealed that both experimental and control students had improved their understanding of basic electrostatics. However, there were some qualitative differences between the two groups. The most striking differences were in students' descriptions of electric fields and the influence of distance on the forces that charges experience. For example, one girl, during her post-interview, described an electric field as:

The electric[ity] goes from the positive charge to the negative charge like this [drawing a curved line from a positive charge to a negative charge]. I know this because this is what it looked like in the game and it was hard to move away or toward it because the two charges are close together so they sort of cancel each other out. (p. 510)

In the control group, the students also performed well in drawing what an electric field looked like, although their reasons for their explanations revealed a different type of thinking:

INTERVIEWER: Ok, what do you think the electric field looks like around a positive charge?
ALEX: It has lines going outward from it like this [drawing lines with arrows pointing outward].
INTERVIEWER: Why do you think it looks like that?
ALEX: I don't know. The teacher said so and showed us a picture and that was what it looked like. (p. 510)

It appears that students in the experimental group were recalling experiences and challenges that were a part of the game play of *Supercharged!*, whereas students in the control group were relying more on their ability to memorize information. Playing *Supercharged!* enabled some students to confront their everyday (mis)conceptions of electrostatics as they played through levels that contradicted these conceptions. Students used representations of electric fields depicted in the game as tools for action.

Squire (2004) conclude that:

These initial findings suggest that the primary affordances of games as instructional tools may be their power for eliciting students' alternative misconceptions and then providing a context for thinking through problems. Adept game players appropriate game representations as tools for thinking, which, for some students such as Maria, were later taken up in solving other physics problems. (p. 510)

Yet Squire and his colleagues also acknowledge that the teachers came to realize that students were initially playing *Supercharged!* without a good deal of critical reflection on their play. The teachers then created log sheets for their students to record their actions and make predictions, which reinforced the purpose of the activity and encouraged students to detect patterns in their play. Later, the teachers provided even more structure, using the projector to display game levels, encouraging the class to interpret the events happening onscreen and make predictions about how they thought the simulation would behave. This additional structure added more focus to students' play and allowed the teacher to prompt deeper reflection on game play.

We see here, then, a good example of a post-progressive pedagogy, a well-integrated combination of embodied immersion in rich experience (the game wherein the learner virtually enters an electromagnetic field) and scaffolding and guidance, both through the design of the game itself as a learning resource and through teachers making the game part of a larger coherent learning activity system. The argument is not for games in and of themselves but as part of a well-designed learning activity system.

Full Spectrum Warrior

There are a plethora of people today who want to make "serious games" for learning (for more information, see www.seriousgames.org or www.educationarcade.org). However, I believe we need to pay serious attention to how good commercial games deliver learning as part and parcel of enjoyable game play. Good commercial games are more or less forced to incorporate good principles of learning (Gee 2003a). Today's video games are long, complex, and hard – and avid players would not have it any other way. Game designers face the same sorts of challenge our schools do: how to get people to learn something and learn it well, even enjoy learning it, when it is long and difficult. Games that can't be learned, or games that don't motivate people to learn them, don't get played, and the companies that make them go broke.

I have argued that deep learning involves, first and foremost, activity and experience, not facts and information. Yet something interesting happens when one treats knowledge primarily as activity and experience, not facts and information: The facts come free. A large body of facts that resist out-of-context memorization and rote learning comes free of charge if learners are immersed in activities and experiences that use these facts for plans, goals, and purposes within a coherent knowledge domain (Shaffer 2004).

We also discussed a central paradox of all deep learning. It won't work to try and tell newcomers everything, but simply turning learners loose to engage in the domain's activities won't work either. I have already said that good commercial games would be out of business by now if they weren't good at getting themselves learned well, so game designers have already offered elegant solutions to this paradox. Unfortunately, our schools are still locked into endless and pointless battles between "traditionalism" and "progressivism," between overt teaching and immersive learning, between skill-and-drill and activities, as though these were the only two alternatives.

Because we don't have the space here to explicate the theory of learning behind each category of game, I will talk about just one such theory relevant to several categories and, perhaps, most relevant to those interested in making serious games. Many good commercial video games are based on a theory of learning I will call "distributed authentic professionalism," a theory that resolves our paradox quite nicely (see also Shaffer 2004, 2007). Let's look at one such game: *Full Spectrum Warrior* (Pandemic Studios, for PC and Xbox).

Before I begin, let me hasten to say that I am well aware that this game is ideologically laden. It carries messages, beliefs, and values about war, warfare, terrorism, cultural differences, the U.S. military, and the role of the United States and its army in the modern, global world. I don't agree with some of these messages, beliefs, and values, but all that needs to be left to the side for now. It is not that these issues are not important. Right now, my only goal is to understand the game *Full Spectrum Warrior* as an example of a particular type of game recruiting a particular type of learning.

Full Spectrum Warrior has its origins in a U.S. Army training simulation, but the commercial game retains only about 15% of what was in the Army's simulation (Buchanan 2004, 150). *Full Spectrum Warrior* teaches the player (yes, it is a teacher) how to be a professional soldier. It demands that the player think, value, and act like one to "win" the game. You cannot bring just your game-playing skills, the skills you use in *Castlevania*, *Super Mario*, or *Sonic Adventure 2 Battle*, to this game. You do need these, but you need another set of skills as well. These additional skills are a version of the professional practice of modern soldiers – the professional skills of a soldier commanding a dismounted light infantry squad composed of two teams.

In *Full Spectrum Warrior*, the player uses the buttons on the controller to give orders to the soldiers, as well as to consult a GPS device, radio for support, and communicate with command. The instruction manual that comes with the game makes it clear from the outset that players must think, act, and value like a professional soldier to play the game successfully: "Everything about your squad . . . is the result of careful planning and years of experience on the battlefield. Respect that experience, soldier, since it's what will keep your soldiers alive" (p. 2).

Yet there is something else beyond values that is important here: The virtual characters in the game (the soldiers in the squads), on the one hand, and the real-world player, on the other hand, control different parts of the domain of professional military expertise. We get the whole domain only when we put their knowledge together. The knowledge is *distributed* between them. A human being (the player) shares knowledge with a virtual reality (the soldiers).

Full Spectrum Warrior is designed in such a way that certain sorts of knowledge and certain types of skill are built right into the virtual characters, the soldiers (and into the enemies, as well). Other sorts of related knowledge must be learned and used by the player:

The soldiers on your teams have been trained in movement formations, so your role is to select the best position for them on the field. They will automatically move to the formation selected and take up their scanning sectors, each man covering an arc of view. (p. 15)

Thus, the virtual characters (the soldiers) know part of what needs to be known (various movement formations), and you, the player, know another part (when and where to engage in such formations). Thus is true of every aspect of military knowledge in the game. Your soldiers know different things than you know, have mastered different bits of professional military practice than the bits you need to master to play the game. The game only works when the two different bits are put together – thought about and acted on – as a whole by the player who uses the virtual soldiers as smart tools or resources.

The player is immersed in activity, values, and ways of seeing, but the player is scaffolded by the knowledge built into the virtual characters and the weapons, equipment, and environments in the game. The player is also scaffolded by some quite explicit instruction given "just in time," when it can be understood in action and through experiences that make clear what the words really mean in context. The learner is not left to his or her own devices to rediscover the foundations of a professional practice that took hundreds of years to develop. Our paradox is solved.

There are some caveats. I have used the word "professional," a word that unfortunately brings to mind high-status people who are paid well for specialist skills. Yet that is not what I mean. I am referring to what I will now call "authentic professionalism." Authentic professionals have special knowledge and distinctive values tied to specific skills gained through a good deal of effort and experience. They do what they do not for money, but because they are committed to an identity in which their skills and the knowledge that generates them are seen as valuable and significant. They don't operate just by well-practiced routines; they can think for themselves and innovate in their domains when they have to. Finally, professionals welcome challenges at the cutting edge of their expertise (Bereiter and Scardamalia 1993). Good carpenters, good skateboarders, and good musicians are authentic professionals just as much – and sometimes more so – as are good doctors, lawyers, and professors. Later, when I discuss the game *Madison 2020*, I will give a specific example of what it means to have even young children thinking and learning in professional domains (Shaffer 2007).

Many good video games involve the same formula as *Full Spectrum Warrior*. They distribute authentic professional expertise between the virtual character(s) and the real-world player, something we can represent by the formula

Virtual Characters ← Authentic Professional Knowledge → Player.

For example, the game *Thief: Deadly Shadows* involves the professional identity of a master thief. Thieving expertise is distributed among the virtual character (Garrett) and the real-world player. *Tony Hawk's Underground* involves the professional identity of a skateboarder.

Many will object to *Full Spectrum Warrior* because of its ideology (values and worldview). Indeed, many will also object to the ideology of *Thief* and *Tony Hawk's Underground*. What all of these games exemplify, though, is that there is no real learning without some ideology. Adopting a certain set of values and a particular worldview is intimately connected to performing the activities and having the experiences that constitute any specific domain of knowledge. Physicists hold certain values and adopt a specific worldview because their knowledge making is based on seeing and valuing the world in certain ways. The values and worldview of astrologists comport badly with those of an astronomer; the values and worldview of a creationist comport badly with those of an evolutionary biologist. What we hope, of course, is that school exposes students to multiple and juxtaposed ideologies in a critically reflective context.

As one masters *Full Spectrum Warrior* through scaffolded activity based on distributed knowledge, facts – many of them – come free. All sorts of arcane words and information that would be hard to retain through rote drill become part of one's arsenal (tools), through which activity is accomplished and experience understood. For example, I now know what "bounding" means in military practice, how it is connected to military values, and what role it plays tactically to achieve military goals. If you knew only what it meant in terms of a verbal definition, your understanding could not begin to compete with mine.

Full Spectrum Warrior (and *Thief* and *Tony Hawk*) share knowledge and skill between a virtual character or characters (and objects and environments) and the player. In the act, by the end of the game, they allow the player to have experienced a "career," to have a story to tell about how his or her professional expertise grew and was put to tactical and strategic uses.

A good school-based learning experience that followed the *Full Spectrum Warrior* model would have to pick its domain of authentic professionalism well, intelligently select the skills and knowledge to be distributed, build in a related value system as integral to learning, and give explicit instruction only "just in time" or "on demand." David Shaffer's "epistemic games," one of which we will discuss below, exemplify this approach.

AUGMENTED BY REALITY: *MADISON 2020*

In their *Madison 2020* project, David Shaffer and Kelly Beckett at the University of Wisconsin have developed, implemented, and assessed a game-like simulation that simulates some of the activities of professional urban planners (Beckett and Shaffer 2004; see also Shaffer et al. 2004). This game (and I will call it a game because it functions very much like a game in the learning environment in which it is used) and its learning environment incorporate many of the same deep learning principles that we have seen at play in *Full Spectrum Warrior*.

Shaffer and Beckett's game is not a stand-alone entity but is used as part of a larger learning system. Shaffer and Beckett call their approach to game-like learning "augmented by reality," because a virtual reality – that is, the game simulation – is augmented or supplemented by real-world activities; in this case, further activities of the sort in which urban planners engage. Minority high school students in a summer enrichment program engaged with Shaffer and Beckett's urban planning simulation game, and, as they did so, their problem-solving work in the game was guided by real-world tools and practices taken from the domain of professional urban planners.

As in the game *SimCity*, in Shaffer and Beckett's game, students make land-use decisions and consider the complex results of their decisions. However, unlike in *SimCity*, they use real-world data and authentic planning practices to inform those decisions. The game and the learning environment in which it is embedded is based on David Shaffer's theory of *pedagogical praxis*, a theory that argues that modeling learning environments on authentic professional practices – in this case, the practices of urban planners – enables young people to develop deeper understandings of important domains of inquiry (Shaffer 2004). The emphasis, however, is not on professions as vocations but as domains of expertise that recruit important ways of knowing and producing knowledge; thus, Shaffer calls his games "epistemic games" (Shaffer 2007).

Shaffer and Beckett argue that the environmental dependencies in urban areas have the potential to become a fruitful context for innovative learning in ecological education. Although ecology is, of course, a broader domain than the study of interdependent urban relationships, cities are examples of complex systems that students can view and with which they are familiar. Thus, concepts in ecology can be made tangible and relevant.

Cities are composed of simple components, but the interactions among those components are complex. Altering one variable affects all the others, reflecting the interdependent, ecological relationships present in any modern city. For example, consider the relationships among industrial sites, air pollution, and land property values: Increasing industrial sites can lead to pollution that, in turn, lowers property values, changing the dynamics of the city's neighborhoods in the process.

Shaffer and Beckett's *Madison 2020* project situated student experience at a micro level by focusing on a single street in their own city (Madison, Wisconsin):

Instead of the fast-paced action required to plan and maintain virtual urban environments such as *SimCity*, this project focused only on an initial planning stage, which involved the development of a land use plan for this one street. And instead of using only a technological simulation [i.e., the game, JPG], the learning environment here was orchestrated by authentic urban planning practices. These professional practices situated the planning tool in a realistic context and provided a framework within which students constructed solutions to the problem. (Beckett and Shaffer 2004, 11–12)

The high school students Shaffer and Beckett worked with had volunteered for a ten-hour workshop (run over two weekend days) focused on city planning and community service. At the beginning of the workshop, the students were given an urban planning challenge: They were asked to create a detailed redesign plan for State Street, a major pedestrian thoroughfare in Madison, a street quite familiar to all of the students in the workshop. Professional urban planners must formulate plans that meet the social, economic, and physical needs of their communities. To align with this practice, students received an informational packet addressed to them as city planners. The packet contained a project directive from the mayor, a city budget plan, and letters from concerned citizens providing input about how they wished to see the city redesigned. The directive asked the student city planners to develop a plan that would, in the end, have to be presented to a representative from the planning department at the end of the workshop.

Students then watched a video about State Street, featuring interviews with people who expressed concerns about the street's redevelopment aligned with the issues in the informational packet (e.g., affordable housing). During the planning phase, students walked to State Street and conducted a site assessment. Following the walk, they worked in teams to develop a land-use plan using a custom-designed, interactive geographic information system

(GIS) called MadMod. MadMod is a model built using Excel and ArcMap (Environmental System Research Institute 2003) that lets students assess the ramification of proposed land use changes.

MadMod – the "game" in the learning system – allows students to see a virtual representation of State Street. It has two components, a decision space and a constraint table. The decision space displays address and zoning information about State Street using official two- or three-letter zoning codes to designate changes in land use for property parcels on the street. As students made decisions about changes they wished to make, they received immediate feedback about the consequences of changes in the constraint table. The constraint table showed the effects of changes on six planning issues raised in the original information packet and the video: crime, revenue, jobs, waste, car trips, and housing. Following the professional practices of urban planners, in the final phrase of the workshop, students presented their plans to a representative from the city planning office.

MadMod functions in Shaffer and Beckett's curriculum like a game much in the way *SimCity* does. In my view, video games are simulations that have "win states" in terms of goals players have set for themselves. In this case, the students have certain goals, and the game lets them see how close or far they are from attaining those goals. At the same time, the game is embedded in a learning system that ensures those goals and the procedures used to reach them are instantiations of the professional practices and ways of knowing of urban planners.

Shaffer and Beckett show, through a pre-/post-interview design, that students in the workshop were able to provide more extensive and explicit definitions of the term "ecology" after the workshop than before it. The students' explanations of ecological issues in the post-interview were more specific about how ecological issues are interdependent or interconnected than in the pre-interview. Concept maps that the students drew showed an increased awareness of the complexities present in an urban ecosystem. Thus, students appear to have developed a richer understanding of urban ecology through their work in the project.

One hundred percent of the students said the workshop changed the way they thought about cities, and most said the experience changed the things they paid attention to when walking down a city street in their neighborhoods. Better yet, perhaps, Shaffer and Beckett were able to show transfer: Students' responses to novel, hypothetical urban planning problems showed increased awareness of the interconnections among urban ecological issues. All these effects suggest, as Shaffer and Beckett argue, "that students were able to mobilize understanding developed in the context of the redesign of one local street to think more deeply about novel urban ecological issues" (p. 21).

Let me begin to relate my remarks above more directly to assessment issues by using another commercial game as an example. It involves people playing real-time strategy video games like *Rise of Nations*, *Age of Empires*, or *Age of Mythology* (Gee 2003a, 2004), which are arguably the most complicated videogames made.

In real-time strategy games (so-called "RTS" games), a player takes a given civilization (e.g., in *Rise of Nations*, the Russians, Chinese, British, Indians, Incas, etc.) from its earliest days as a simple village to the rise of modern cities through a variety of ages (e.g., in *Rise of Nations*, the Classical Age, the Medieval Age, the Gunpowder Age, the Industrial Age, the Modern Age, and the Information Age). Players must build many different types of buildings and cities; discover and collect resources like timber, gold, minerals, and oil; build different types of soldiers, armies, and military apparatuses, as well as priests and scholars; establish new territories through movement (across land and sea), war, or diplomacy; set and collect taxes and engage in trade; establish religious and educational institutions; and build wonders and monuments. As a player builds up resources, knowledge, and achievements, he or she can choose to move into ever more modern ages, upgrading all buildings, soldiers, and apparatus. Of course, a player can also choose to stay in an earlier age, build up massively in that age in certain respects, and defeat civilizations that are more "modern."

The player must do all this in competition with other civilizations (as many as five or six) played by the computer or other real people. There is a premium on time, because everyone operates in real time; each person acts while all of the other players are acting, so speed can be one strategy for victory (although one can also choose to "turtle"; that is, build more slowly but secure one's territory through fortifications or diplomacy). Players can establish different conditions for victory – for example, most territory gained, defeat and colonization of other civilizations, diplomatic conditions, or the success of a civilization on grounds other than military (e.g., economy or wonders built).

Such a game, although complex, is certainly no more complicated than math or science in school when learners are playing it as an actual enterprise (practice) and not just as memorizing facts. In fact, as I go through this discussion, I would like the reader to imagine replacing my example – I will use the game *Rise of Nations* – with something like "doing experimental science" (e.g., with fast-growing plants) or "reading and researching a topic with others – for example, using the jigsaw method – well enough to teach it to peers," activities that might well go on in elementary school. I want the reader to ask, "Why shouldn't learning school subjects be more like playing *Rise of Nations*? Why shouldn't assessment work in school the way it does in *Rise of Nations*?" I am not saying necessarily that it should; I am saying we should ask why it shouldn't.

Let's say now we wanted to assess Janie on her playing of *Rise of Nations*. At one level, there is no need to view assessment as in any way separate from playing the game. If Janie has managed to get to a new age, we know for sure that she can play the game; if she can get to later and later ages, we know she can play it well; if she can hold her own against other players, we know she is very good indeed (of course, we have to be sure she doesn't cheat, although with video games, what is called "cheating" often involves a good deal of knowledge about the game and forms of collaboration that we might very well approve of, but that is a topic for another day; see Consalvo 2007). If we are picky and demand to know whether Janie is "proficient," then the game can be set to various difficulty levels, making the computer opponents harder and harder to beat – if Janie still holds her own, we know she is "proficient" – in fact, very good. So does she.

Why, then, would we need any assessment apart from the game itself? One reason – indeed, a reason Janie herself would – is that Janie might want to know, at a somewhat more abstract level than moment-by-moment play, how she is doing and how she can do better. She might want to know which features of her activities and strategies in the game are indicative of progress or success and which are not. Of course, the game is very complex, so this won't be any particular score or grade. What Janie needs is a formative or developmental assessment that can let her theorize her play and change it for the better, and this is what the game gives her.

At the end of any play session in *Rise of Nations*, the player does not just get the message "you win" or "you lose," but rather a dozen charts and graphs detailing a myriad of aspects of her activities and strategies across the whole time span of her play (and her civilization's life). This gives Janie a more abstract view of her play; it models her play session and gets her to see her play session as one "type" of game, one way to play the game against other ways. It gives her a meta-representation of the game and her game play in terms of which she can become a theoretician of her own play and learning. From this information, she does not learn just to be faster or "better"; she

learns how to think strategically about the game in ways that allow her to
transform old strategies and try out new ones. She comes to see the game as
a system of interconnected relationships.

Here are the charts and graphs Janie will see after each session of play.
Janie will see herself compared, at each stage of the game play, with the other
players (real people or the computer) in each chart and graph:

1. Achievements: Games (shows victory type [conditions under which
   victory was achieved], high score [total points of the winner, points
   are summarized over all the features in the charts and graphs below],
   map type [terrain chosen, some are harder than others], and game
   time [how long the session lasted]);
2. Achievements: Score (shows total score and scores for army, combat,
   territory, cities, economy, research, wonders);
3. Achievements: Military (shows largest army, number of units built,
   units killed, units lost, buildings built, buildings lost, cities built, cities
   captured, cities lost);
4. Achievements: Economy (shows food collected, timber collected,
   wealth collected, metal collected, oil collected, rare resources, ruins
   bonuses, resources sent, resources received);
5. Achievements: Research (shows when Classical Age, Medieval Age,
   Gunpowder Age, Industrial Age, Modern Age, Information Age each
   achieved, library research, miscellaneous research, unit upgrades);
6. Achievements: Glory (shows most citizens, most caravans, most scholars, most cities, most territory, most wonders held, forts built, units
   bribes, survival to finish);
7. Achievements: Player speed (shows player speed, hotkeys pressed,
   mouse clicks, clicks in map, clicks in interface, time zoomed in, time
   zoomed out, control groups formed, control groups activated);
8. Achievements: Score graph (graphs scores with historical age on the
   Y axis and game time on the X axis);
9. Achievements: Military graph (graphs scores with historical age on
   the Y axis and game time on the X axis);
10. Achievements: Territory graph (graphs scores with historical age on
    the Y axis and game time on the X axis);
11. Achievements: Resource graph (graphs scores with historical age on
    the Y axis and game time on the X axis);
12. Achievements: Technology graph (graphs scores with historical age on
    the Y axis and game time on the X axis); and
13. Achievements: Time line (each age correlated with game time when it
    was achieved by a straight line graph).

Janie uses these charts and graphs – they are part of the game play, part of the fun of the game – to understand where things went right and where they went wrong, where things can be improved and where no change is needed. She is now prepared to do even better next time. She can even look at the charts and graphs and conclude, not that there were weaknesses in her performance, but that she won by a certain style and would like now to try another one. This is formative or developmental assessment at its best.

Yet what if we wanted to evaluate Janie – to grade her, not just develop her? This is, of course, the classic summative assessment question. This sort of assessment would still be the best record of what she has done and can do (if we set certain conditions for her play). We have to be careful here, though. You will note that in charts 1 and 2, the player gets a "total score." However, this total score (which reflects different things as different victory conditions are set) is a composite of all of the other features dealt with in the charts and graphs. By itself it is pretty meaningless, because one needs to know which of many features is made for the high score in different cases, and these will be different for different players, play sessions, styles of play, and conditions of victory. If this total score floated away from all of these other features, it would be almost totally meaningless (e.g., someone you thought was really good because he or she had a high score could lose to someone you thought less highly of because the "lesser" player engaged in a strategy that focused only on where the "better" player was weak; that is, the "lesser" player would have understood the game as a set of complex features, not one "score").

What if we wanted to help high-level policy makers set standards for real-time strategy game play, just like school superintendents and state and federal educational officials try to do for reading, math, or science? Even these "high-level" folks need to see the total score as one take on a multidimensional feature space. In fact, just as Janie needed these charts and graphs to model her game play so she could theorize it, these officials would need not a score for each Janie, but a model to help them theorize the complex system that constitutes the game *Rise of Nations* and real-time strategy games as a category (itself a complex system – a system of systems made up of different specific games). It is hard to believe that the situation is any simpler for reading, science, or math, unless, of course, one radically simplifies what one means by reading, science, or math – and it is to this issue that I now turn.

IMPLICATIONS

Both the perspective on learning developed here (a situated one) and the examples of game-like learning within well-designed learning activity systems have a number of further implications for testing and assessment, as well as for any deep notion of OTL (Gee 2003b, 2004). If an assessment is testing conceptual knowledge and the ability for students to apply (situate) their learning, then it clearly seems to be the case that students exposed to the kinds of game-like learning we have discussed here have an advantage. They are able to form understandings based on activity and experience, understandings customizable to specific contexts of use. From this basis they can eventually generalize their knowledge without losing the grounding of that knowledge in specific applications.

Even if students exposed to such learning never achieve the full range and generality of an expert (after all, experts have had years of experience), they will know why specific kinds of technical knowledge are important, how they really work, and they will have sensed their own real capacity to fully understand and use that knowledge. Thus, if deep conceptual learning is our goal, it may be that such game-like learning as we have discussed here will become one of the resources we will demand for all students if assessments of their learning are to be fair and based on true OTL at a conceptual level and in a situated way.

Of course, "fair" may not be the right word here, as Pullin has pointed out to me (personal communication). As she points out, "things can be fair; that is, equitably distributed, but offered at a very low level." She prefers the term "meaningful opportunity to learn" rather than "fair opportunity to learn." I agree but want also to point out that, in another sense of the word, it is not "fair" even when we have a low-level test, but some children, and not others, have had the opportunity to learn the material at a deeper level – in my view, they will, in many cases, not only do better on higher-level tests but on such lower-level ones as well.

What about tests and assessments based on verbal information and facts, which dominate our schools and even our legal conceptions of testing and fairness in testing? One hypothesis that a number of people have entertained is that when students engage in situated learning of the sort discussed here, facts and information eventually "come free" (e.g., Gee 2003a; Shaffer 2007). Information and facts that are hard to retain when they are drilled out of any meaningful context come to be learned much more effortlessly when learners are acquiring them as part of their own activity-based purposes and goals – when they are part of "playing the game" the learner wants to play.

If this is true, then such learners have an advantage over other learners even on more traditional information and fact-centered tests. Their situated understandings allow them to perform better on conceptual tests but to still have a better understanding of the words and verbal formulations on traditional tests, because these kinds of words have been integral to the game they have played and the activities they have accomplished. These words have situated, contextually sensitive meanings for these learners. In this case, students exposed only to a verbal information and fact-based curriculum – much less only to skill-and-drill – have not had the same opportunity to learn and to pass even the traditional tests as have more privileged learners.

This problem becomes all the more acute when we realize that many children from privileged homes attain more and more activity- and experience-based situated learning at home, while poorer children do not get it at home or at school. To the extent that digital technologies come to enhance such learning, they may create a yet greater equity divide in terms of higher-order forms of understanding and even in the distribution of traditional test scores, especially in the content areas.

References

Barab, S., S. Zuiker, S. Warren, D. Hickey, A. Ingram-Goble, E. J. Kwon, I. Kouper, and S. C. Herring. In press. Embodied curriculum: Relating formalisms to contexts. *Science Education.*

Barab, S. A., M. Thomas, T. Dodge, R. Carteaux, and H. Tuzun. 2005. Making learning fun: Quest Atlantis, a game without guns. *Educational Technology Research and Development* 5.1: 86–108.

Barsalou, L. W. 1999a. Language comprehension: Archival memory or preparation for situated action. *Discourse Processes* 28: 61–80.

Barsalou, L. W. 1999b. Perceptual symbol systems. *Behavioral and Brain Sciences* 22: 577–660.

Beckett, K. L. and D. W. Shaffer. 2004. Augmented by reality: The pedagogical praxis of urban planning as a pathway to ecological thinking. Ms., University of Wisconsin-Madison. http://www.academiccolab.org/initiatives/gapps.html.

Bereiter, C. and M. Scardamalia. 1993. *Surpassing ourselves: An inquiry into the nature and implications of expertise.* Chicago: Open Court.

Brown, A. L. 1994. The advancement of learning. *Educational Researcher* 23: 4–12.

Brown, J. S., A. Collins, A., and P. Dugid. 1989. Situated cognition and the culture of learning. *Educational Researcher* 18: 32–42.

Buchanan, L. 2004. *Full Spectrum Warrior.* Roseville, Calif: Prima Games.

Chi, M. T. H., P. J. Feltovich, and R. Glaser. 1981. Categorization and representation of physics problems by experts and novices. *Cognitive Science* 13: 145–82.

Clark, A. 1989. *Microcognition: Philosophy, Cognitive Science, and Parallel Distributed Processing.* Cambridge: MIT Press.

Clark, A. 1993. *Associative Engines: Connectionism, Concepts, and Representational Change.* Cambridge: Cambridge University Press.

Clark, A. 1997. *Being There: Putting Brain, Body, and World Together Again.* Cambridge: MIT Press.

Consalvo, M. 2007. *Cheating: Gaining Advantage in Videogames.* Cambridge: MIT Press.

diSessa, A. A. 2000. *Changing Minds: Computers, Learning, and Literacy*. Cambridge: MIT Press.

Environmental System Research Institute. 2003. ArcMap. [Computer Software]. Redlands, Calif.: ESRI.

Games-to-Teach Team. 2003. Design principles of next-generation digital gaming for education. *Educational Technology* 43: 17–33.

Gardner, H. 1991. *The Unschooled Mind: How Children Think and How Schools Should Teach*. New York: Basic Books.

Gee, J. P. 1992. *The Social Mind: Language, Ideology, and Social Practice*. New York: Bergin and Garvey.

Gee, J. P. 2001. Progressivism, critique, and socially situated minds. In *The fate of Progressive Language Policies and Practices*, edited by C. Dudley-Marling and C. Edelsky, 31–58. Urbana, Ill.: NCTE.

Gee, J. P. 2003a. *What Video Games Have to Teach Us About Learning and Literacy*. New York: Palgrave/Macmillan.

Gee, J. P. 2003b. Opportunity to learn: A language-based perspective on assessment. *Assessment in Education* 10: 25–44.

Gee, J. P. 2004. *Situated Language and Learning: A Critique of Traditional Schooling*. London: Routledge.

Gee, J. P. 2005. *Why Video Games Are Good for Your Soul: Pleasure and Learning*. Melbourne: Common Ground.

Gee, J. P. 2006. Oral discourse in a world of literacy. *Research in the Teaching of English* 41: 153–64.

Glenberg, A. M. 1997. What is memory for? *Behavioral and Brain Sciences* 20: 1–55.

Glenberg, A. M. and D. A. Robertson. 1999. Indexical understanding of instructions. *Discourse Processes* 28: 1–26.

Jenkins, H. and K. Squire. 2004. Harnessing the power of games in education. *Insight* 3: 5–33.

Jenkins, H., K. Squire, and P. Tan. 2003. You can't bring that game to school: Designing *Supercharged! Design research*, edited by Laurel, B., 244–52. Cambridge: MIT Press.

Kirschner, P. A., K. Sweller, and R. E. Clark. 2006. Why minimal guidance during instruction does not work: an analysis of the failure of constructivist, discovery, problem-based, experiential, and inquiry-based teaching. *Educational Psychologist* 41: 75–86.

Lave, J. 1996. Teaching, as learning, in practice. *Mind, Culture, and Activity* 3: 149–64.

Lave, J. and E. Wenger. 1991. *Situated Learning: Legitimate Peripheral participation*. New York: Cambridge University Press.

Lehrer, R. and L. Schauble. 2005. Developing modeling and argument in elementary grades. In *Understanding mathematics and science matters*, edited by T. A. Romberg, T. P. Carpenter, and F. Dremock, 29–53. Mahwah, N.J.: Lawrence Erlbaum Associates.

Lehrer, R. 2003. Developing understanding of measurement. In *A Research Companion to Principles and Standards for School Mathematics*, edited by J. Kilpatrick, W. G. Martin, and D. E. Schifter, 179–92. Reston, Va: National Council of Teachers of Mathematics.

McFarlane, A., A. Sparrowhawk, and Y. Heald. 2002. *Report on the Educational Use of Games: An Exploration by TEEM of the Contribution Which Games Can Make to the Education Process*. Cambridge: TEEM.

Martin, J. R. 1990. Literacy in science: Learning to handle text as technology. In *Literacy for a Changing World*, edited by F. Christe, 79–117. Melbourne: Australian Council for Educational Research.

Ochs, E., P. Gonzales, and S. Jacoby. 1996. When I come down I'm in the domain state. In *Interaction and Grammar*, edited by E. Ochs, E. Schegloff, and S. A. Thompson, 328–69. Cambridge: Cambridge University Press.

Rogoff, B. 1990. *Apprenticeship in Thinking: Cognitive Development in Social Context.* New York: Oxford University Press.

Shaffer, D. W. 2004. Pedagogical praxis: The professions as models for post-industrial education. *Teachers College Record* 10: 1401–21.

Shaffer, D. W. 2007. *How Computer Games Help Children Learn.* New York: Palgrave/ Macmillan.

Shaffer, D. W., K. Squire, R. Halverson, and N. P. Gee. 2004. Video games and the future of learning. Madison: University of Wisconsin-Madison. http://www.academiccolab. org/initiatives/gapps.html.

Squire, K. 2003. Video games in education. *International Journal of Intelligent Games and Simulation* 2. http://www.scit.wlv.ac.uk/~cm1822/ijkurt.pdf.

Squire, K. D. 2005. Changing the Game: What Happens When Video Games Enter the Classroom? *Innovate* 1. http://www.innovateonline.info/index.php?view= articleandid=82.

Squire, K. 2006. From content to context: Videogames as designed experience. *Educational Researcher* 35.8: 19–29.

Squire, K., M. Barnett, J. M. Grant, and T. Higginbotham. 2004. Electromagnetism Supercharged! Learning physics with digital simulation games. In *Proceedings of the Sixth International Conference of the Learning Sciences*, edited by Y. B. Kafai et al., 513–20. Mahwah, N.J.: Lawrence Erlbaum.

Steinkuehler, C. A. 2004. Learning in massively multiplayer online games. In *Proceedings of the Sixth International Conference of the Learning Sciences*, edited by Y. B. Kafai, et al., 521–8. Mawah, N.J.: Erlbaum.

Steinkuehler, C. A. 2006. Massively multiplayer online videogaming as participation in a discourse. *Mind, Culture, and Activity* 13: 38–52.

9 Sociocultural Implications for Assessment I

Classroom Assessment

Pamela A. Moss[1]

In this chapter, I develop the implications of the earlier chapters – on socio-cultural and situative perspectives – for the practice of classroom assessment. In chapter 11, Moss, Girard, and Greeno further develop the implications of these perspectives for assessment that crosses the boundaries – from the classroom to the school and from the school to the district, external organization, or beyond – to serve purposes of professional learning, evaluation, and accountability.

Perhaps the central message of the previous chapters on sociocultural and situative (SC/S)[2] perspectives is that if we want to foster learning and opportunity to learn (OTL), we need to understand the dynamic *"relationship between learners and their learning environment"* (Gee, this volume, chapter 4). This includes the relationship between learners and the physical and conceptual tools in their environment; it also includes the relationship between learners and the other people in their environment. In fact, from an SC/S perspective, learning is routinely conceptualized in terms of changes in these relationships. Learners participate more proficiently in the community's activities, disciplinary concepts take on new meanings as they are put to work in solving problems, and so on. Even if one views learning as change in mental representations, the mental representation can only be acquired and demonstrated through interactions between learners and the tools and/or other people in their environment. There is no unmediated access to learning (Gee, this volume, chapter 4). As the word "dynamic" implies, these relationships are always evolving, and it is the individual and group trajectories that are of central importance. This understanding has implications for (1) how assessment is conceptualized – for which elements of the (inter)action within a classroom count as "assessment"; (2) the kinds of questions that might be asked and evidence considered about learning and OTL and for the sorts of interpretations, decisions, and actions that might be taken as a result; and (3) the kinds of criteria that might be used to evaluate the quality of learning and OTL – the individual and community learning trajectories (Greeno and Gresalfi, this volume) – within a classroom.

In the pages that follow, I address each of these implications, albeit somewhat recursively. The chapter is divided into two major sections, one that provides theoretical tools for conceptualizing, enacting, and studying assessment from an SC/S perspective and one that illustrates the (power of the) theory with an extended example of assessment practice.

The first major section, on SC/S assessment theory, is divided into three subsections. It begins with an initial proposal for how assessment might be productively conceptualized when informed by SC/S perspectives. I suggest that assessment be conceptualized around the particular questions or problems that evidence is needed to address (Moss, Girard, and Haniford 2006) rather than around a particular instrument or activity and the circumscribed evidence it provides. Then, drawing on a characterization of assessment by anthropologists Jordan and Putz (2004), I suggest expanding the conventional instrument-based understandings of assessments to incorporate all of the evidence-based evaluations and judgments that occur in interaction in (classroom) learning environments. This includes formal assessments that we recognize as "an assessment" as well as informal assessments, both tacit and explicit, that routinely occur in classroom interaction. The second subsection provides theoretical tools for analyzing a dynamic learning environment, community of practice, or activity system. As such, it suggests both (1) the kinds of evidence that one might want to consider in addressing a question about learning or OTL; and (2) perspectives from which one can illuminate how assessment functions within an activity system to monitor and support learning. I draw heavily on Engeström's (1987, 1993, 1999, 2001) discussions of activity systems and learning to show the organization of activity systems – not just as contexts for assessments, but rather as fundamental and integral to analyses of assessment practices. The third subsection draws on the earlier chapters to suggest a set of criteria – particular kinds of valued learning trajectories – that might be used to evaluate the quality of learning and OTL (for individuals and groups) in an activity system. This entails reference to the kinds of questions that might be addressed, evidence considered, and interpretations, decisions, and actions supported in the practice of assessment.

In the second major section, I illustrate these theoretical perspectives with an extended example of classroom practice. The example is based on

Lampert's (2001) yearlong analysis of teaching and learning in her fifth grade mathematics classroom. Although Lampert's text is not focused on assessment per se, it can nevertheless be read with the question of how she uses evidence to address questions or "problems" about students' learning and her own teaching practice. Three vignettes focus on how she uses evidence (1) to prepare a lesson; (2) while teaching a lesson; and (3) to assess students' accomplishments at the end of a unit. They illustrate how she considers the impact of these (assessment) practices on students' learning and OTL.

The chapter's concluding comments summarize sociocultural implications for the practice of assessment and prefigure the issues that will be addressed in chapter 11 about assessment that crosses classroom boundaries to support professional learning, evaluation, and accountability.

Our work in this chapter contributes to a small but growing body of literature on sociocultural approaches to assessment (Delandshere 2002; Gipps 1999, 2002; Hickey and Zuiker 2003; Shepard 2006) and those based in interpretive social science more generally (Erickson 2007; Johnston 1992; Moss 2004; Moss, Girard, and Haniford 2006). Gipps (1999) suggests that "the requirement is to assess process as well as product; the conception must be dynamic rather than static; and attention must be paid to the social and cultural context of both learning and assessment" (p. 375). Erickson (2007) focuses on "proximal formative assessment," which entails "the continual 'taking stock' that teachers do by paying firsthand observational attention to students during the ongoing course of instruction," focusing on "specific aspects of a student's developing understanding" (p. 187) to help in deciding what pedagogical move to make next. Shepard draws on cognitivist and sociocultural theories to conceptualize formative assessment – "assessment for learning" – to incorporate assessment activities that are both "formal, where students know that they are being assessed, or informal where the gathering of assessment data is done entirely within the context of ongoing instruction" (p. 32). She considers as well the ways in which summative assessment – assessment for the purpose of giving a grade or certifying proficiency – might be shaped so as not to undermine important learning goals supported by formative assessment. Delandshere goes a step further and wonders whether educational assessment might be better conceptualized as inquiry.[3] From these perspectives, assessment becomes not so much a discrete set of activities but rather a way of looking at the evidence available from the ongoing interactions in the learning environment. This conception of assessment as inquiry is, perhaps, closest to the theory of assessment described next.

A THEORY OF ASSESSMENT INFORMED BY
SOCIOCULTURAL PERSPECTIVES

What Is Assessment?

In educational measurement, we tend to conceptualize assessment in terms of an instrument and/or structured activity (e.g., a test) and the circumscribed evidence it provides about student learning. The questions that can be addressed and the interpretations, decisions, and actions that can be supported by the evidence provided are similarly circumscribed.[4] Yet the problems, issues, and questions that teachers (and other education professionals) face and the types of evidence they need to address them are not similarly circumscribed. In describing the problems of teaching, Lampert (2001) uses the productive metaphor of a camera lens shifting focus and zooming in and out. This allows her to address "the problems of practice that a teacher needs to work on in a particular moment ... [along with] the problems of practice that are addressed in teaching a lesson or a unit or a year" (pp. 2–3). Many of the problems are of the "what do I/we do next?" variety, albeit at quite different levels of scale. In the extended example, we will see how Lampert (2001) uses evidence to address different sorts of problems on different time scales: to make decisions about what to do next in her interactions with students, to plan lessons, to develop routines that support them in becoming the kinds of students inclined to collaborate and reason about mathematical ideas, and to take stock of and inform students and their parents about their accomplishments. Certainly good stand-alone assessments provide evidence relevant to important questions like these, but as Lampert's questions suggest, few if any questions or problems educators face can be addressed with a single source of evidence. Different questions/problems require different kinds and configurations of evidence.

An analysis of assessment practice by anthropologists Jordan and Putz (2004) allows us to illuminate and label a variety of ways in which evidence is used in interaction to support and monitor learning and OTL. Based on a series of studies in different workplace and other learning contexts, they developed a three-part framework for characterizing assessment practice that incorporates "the totality of informal and formal judgments, evaluations, measurements, tests, surveys, and metrics that play a role in productive interaction" (p. 346).[5] Briefly, they identify "*inherent* assessments as happening informally and nonverbally in all social situations [when actors choose what to do next]; *discursive* assessments as occurring when members of a social group talk about what they are doing in an evaluative way; and *documentary* assessments as coming about when activities are evaluated according to a scheme that produces numbers and symbols" (p. 346 italics mine). Although it is documentary assessment that we typically think about when we use the term "assessment," I argue (with Jordan and Putz) that inherent and discursive assessments are at least equally significant in monitoring and supporting (or constraining) learning and OTL.

Inherent assessments are "a natural part of all socially situated activities... [They] occur all around us, whenever human begins get together to accomplish any sort of activity in a collaborative cooperative way" (p. 348). For instance, "a listener 'looks puzzled' – the speaker rephrases what she just said. Both individuals have made an assessment" (p. 349). Inherent assessments, they argue, "constitute one of the fundamental mechanisms by which learning occurs, including the kinds of incidental learning we simply think of as normal parts of human development. Even a baby or toddler continuously assesses approval or disapproval of its actions by family members" (p. 359). These assessments are typically tacit or implicit – "they rely on individual nonverbal monitoring, resulting in individual behavioral adjustment" (p. 350) – but they are "absolutely crucial for smooth interpersonal interaction" (p. 359).

In *discursive* assessment, the assessment is explicit: It means to "talk about" the ongoing activity in an evaluative way. Discursive assessments "make issues public, propose common standards, suggest and enforce divisions of labor, and monitor group behavior such that the work will get done (p. 350). "Routine work is filled with a huge number" of these assessments, and they are often crucial for the smooth flow of activities (p. 350).

Parents may talk to their children about what they are already able to accomplish and what they will be able to do soon. A work group may begin to talk about how it is doing, how much more remains to be done, that a particular worker is lagging and why, the impact of defective parts on the speed of an assembly line, or the effect of a plane delay on activities in an airport. (p. 350)

Unlike inherent assessments, discursive assessments become social objects: "[T]hey can be referred to, doubted, agreed with, or revised by people who are part of the group" (p. 350). Again, Jordan and Putz argue that discursive assessments are central to learning. They create:

a shared understanding of individual roles and responsibilities and thereby work out a division of labor. At the same time, these informal assessments create a public verbal representation of the capabilities, resources, and issues for a group that enable them to consider implications of the current state, as they understand it, for behaving more effectively. (p. 350)

Engaging in discursive assessment is also a means through which group members can "demonstrate their proficiency and gain acceptance" (p. 350).

Documentary assessment involves "stable symbolic representation of evaluations in the form of tests, surveys, checklists, plans, targets, and similar instruments" (p. 351). It "occurs when an enduring record of some kind is produced, a set of marks on a piece of paper (or on a computer), that is reflective and evaluative of some activity" (p. 351). Jordan and Putz reserve the term "documentary" for externally mandated assessments that are intended to "evaluate the extent to which pre-established performance targets have been achieved and to establish cross-group comparability" (p. 351). I will use the term a bit more broadly to characterize written assessments that are developed for use within a classroom (e.g., Lampert's [2001] end-of-unit quiz) as well as those that are externally mandated. Thus, documentary assessments, as I use the term, can be externally imposed ("exogenous") or locally developed ("endogenous").[6] Moss, Girard, and Greeno will have more to say about such assessments in chapter 11, when we focus on assessments that cross the boundaries of activity systems. Externally imposed assessments, however, are also interpreted in and shape the ongoing interaction of the local activity systems in which the evidence is provided and used.

Thus, I argue that assessment can be productively conceptualized in terms of *questions or problems* that are being addressed and the kinds of evidence needed/used to address them. I argue further that the use of evidence to address questions or problems – to support interpretations, decisions, and actions – is an ongoing aspect of interaction (whether formally designated as assessment or not). What does this say about the focus of assessment in terms of our understanding of learning and OTL? Although questions can be raised that foreground one or the other, neither is likely to be productively answered without evidence of both. Indeed, from a sociocultural perspective, learning is perceived and understood in terms of evolving relationships among learners and the other elements of their learning environments (Lave and Wenger 1991, 51). Furthermore, questions about OTL require evidence about what is being learned in large part because opportunities to learn must be evaluated in terms of the affordances they actually provide for different learners. As Gee argues (drawing on Gibson 1977, 1979), "an affordance doesn't exist for an individual who can't perceive its presence"; "effectivities" are "capacities ... which the individual has for transforming affordances into action"; and "focusing on affordance-effectivity pairs places the focus not on the individual or the environment but on a pairing of the two, a relationship between them." (Gee, this volume, chapter 4, 81). Although different theoretical perspectives within the SC/S family would use different language, the importance for both learning and OTL of understanding the relationship appears central to all.

How Does Assessment Function within an Activity System?[7]

Although entailing somewhat different emphases, the SC/S perspectives described in this volume all point to the importance of understanding learning, OTL, and assessment as part of an evolving activity system, community of practice, or learning environment consisting of interacting people (with minds and bodies, pasts and futures), the roles and routines they enact, the conceptual and physical tools they use, and the social and institutional structures within which they work (see Gee, chapter 4, for an overview of the different SC/S emphases). This includes classroom and school environments, but it also includes home, peer, and the many other affinitiy groups in which learners participate and the larger social structures in which they are embedded. In this section, I draw on and extend one set of theoretical perspectives referenced in earlier chapters to suggest the ways in which an activity system might be analyzed so as to illuminate the learning trajectories of individuals and the group and the ways in which assessment shapes and is shaped by them (Gee, chapter 4; Greeno and Gresalfi, chapter 7; Lee, chapter 6). More specifically, the goals are to suggest (1) the range of sources of evidence that might be considered in addressing questions about learning and OTL of individuals or groups; (2) analytical perspectives through which particular questions about how assessment functions – shapes and is shaped by the classroom learning environment – might be addressed; and, more broadly, (3) how the larger activity system, including its assessment practices, might be analyzed (designed and evaluated) to illuminate the vision of learning enacted and to foster valued learning trajectories.

From an SC/S perspective, any question about learning, OTL, or how assessment functions to support them requires a shift in our conventional understanding of the *unit of analysis* from an individual learner at least to a learner-operating-with-mediational-means and, in a more complex way, to the larger activity system, community of practice, or learning environment. Focusing on the relationship between learners and tools, Wertsch suggests that we need to take "mediated action (or "individual-operating-with-mediational-means" [p. 26]) as a unit of analysis" (Wertsch 1998, 17). Mediational means are both physical (e.g., texts, calculators, measuring instruments) and symbolic (e.g., concepts, language systems, representational schemes). Mediated action "provides a kind of natural link between

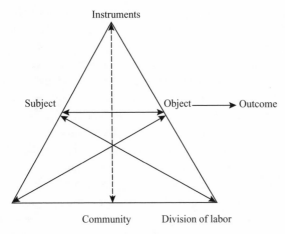

Figure 9.1. Engeström's structure of human activity (adapted from Engeström, 1993, 68).[8]

action,[9] including mental action, and the cultural, institutional, and historical contexts in which such action occurs" (Wertsch 1998, 24). Others foreground the entire community of practice (Lave and Wenger 1991) or activity system (Engeström 1987, 1993, 2001), including conceptual and physical tools and other people, as the unit of analysis. For Lave and Wenger, "a community of practice is a set of relations among persons, activity, and world, over time and in relation with other tangential and overlapping communities of practice (p. 98). With Wertsch, they noted that tools or "artifacts – physical, linguistic, and symbolic" (p. 57) are particularly important because they carry a community's heritage. Artifacts and social structures "leave an historical trace . . . which constitutes and reconstitutes the practice over time" (pp. 57–58). Similarly, for Engeström, an activity system builds on the concept of mediated activity (or individual acting with mediational means) to "explicate the societal and collaborative nature" of actions (1999, 30).[10]

Engeström depicted the components of an activity system as represented in Figure 9.1. Following the model, "the *subject* refers to the individual or subgroup whose agency is chosen as the point of view in the analysis" (p. 67). In a classroom, this would include the perspectives of different students as well as the perspectives of the teacher and any others (e.g., principal, parents) who routinely participate in the classroom activity. "The *object* refers to the 'raw material' or 'problem space' at which the activity is directed" – for our purposes, students' learning – "which is molded or transformed into *outcomes*" – or manifestations of learning – "with the help of physical and symbolic, external and internal *tools* (mediating instruments and signs)" (p. 67). "The *community* comprises multiple individuals and/or subgroups who share the same general object" (p. 67). "The *division of labor* refers to both the horizontal division of tasks between the members of the community" (p. 67) – who does or gets to do what – and "to the vertical division of power and status" (p. 67) – with what authority, accountability, and agency (to use Greeno's [2002] terms). Finally, the *rules* refer to "the explicit and implicit regulations, norms, and conventions that constrain actions and interactions within the activity system," which we would see enacted in the multiple routines in any classroom, including the routines of assessment (Engeström 1993, 67; see also Engeström 1987 for a fuller explication).

As Engeström notes, activity systems are neither static nor closed. They involve ongoing relationships among people and their world, where the elements are continually reproduced and/or transformed. Thus, it is important to understand how an activity system has evolved over time, both in terms of its local history and the "global" history of the concepts, procedures, and tools it inherits (Engeström 1999, 137) – its learning trajectory. It is also important to understand the learning trajectories of individual learners, who bring their own experience, knowledge, and culture to the classroom. As Greeno and Gresalfi note (chapter 7):

Learning by an individual in a community is conceptualized as a trajectory of that person's participation in the community – a path with a past and present, shaping possibilities for future participation. Learning by a group or community is also conceptualized as a trajectory – a path that corresponds to change in the community's practices. (p. 170)

Transformations (or system-level learning) often happen when systems encounter contradictions, when new elements are introduced, or when alternative perspectives and practices are encountered.

A crucial element for our analysis is the understanding that *learning* is a central component of any activity system, whether explicitly intended to foster learning or not (and in chapter 11, we argue that questions about what is being learned are equally relevant to activity systems where educational professionals work with one another as they are to classrooms). As Lave (1993) states, "Learning is an integral aspect of activity in and with the world at all times" (p. 8). It entails a dialectical relationship between experience and understanding. From this perspective, learning does not just happen as a response to teaching (when, they note, what is learned may be quite different from what is intended to be taught); rather, learning happens everywhere, all the time, as we participate in social (inter)action. A learning curriculum unfolds in opportunities for engagement in practice (Lave and Wenger 1991, 57). Further, learning always involves the "construction of identities":

In this view, learning only partly – and often incidentally – implies becoming able to be involved in new activities, to perform new tasks and functions, to master new understandings. Activities, tasks, functions, and understanding do not exist in isolation; they are part of broader systems of relations in which they have meaning.... Learning thus implies becoming a different person with respect to the possibilities enabled by these systems of relations (Lave and Wenger 1991, 53).

With respect to evidence use inside and outside the classroom, this suggests that we need to illuminate and analyze the "learning curriculum" – the opportunities for engagement in practice and the sorts of knowledgeable identities that different approaches to assessment afford teachers, administrators, policy makers, and other professionals as well as students.

To help in organizing these concepts to support the analysis of a learning environment – and the practices of assessment it entails – I draw on four questions initially suggested by Engeström (2001) that would be answered by looking across the elements of an activity system: "(1) Who are the subjects of learning, how are they defined and located? (2) Why do they learn, what makes them make the effort? (3) What do they learn, what are the contents and outcomes of learning? and (4) How do they learn, what are the key actions or processes of learning?" (p. 133).

The first question, about the subjects of learning, focuses our analysis on the perspectives of particular of learners and acknowledges the multivoicedness of learning environments. Learning environments can be productively analyzed from the perspective of different learners, and, as authors of earlier chapters have noted, individual students bring different knowledge, experience, and culture to the classroom that shape the ways in which they interact with the learning opportunities provided. Furthermore, although a primary focus may be on students within classrooms, the "learners" from whose perspective we focus might also be the teacher, or with activity systems outside the classroom, teachers and other education professionals. Finally, learning happens in interactions with other members of the community, and the subjects of learning might equally well be considered the community or the organization in which learning is occurring. Questions about what, why, and how these different learners are learning – and how assessment functions to document and shape learning – are crucial in developing a productive learning environment.

For the second question, "Why do they learn?" I draw on Engström (2001) and Lave and Wenger (1991) to make two crucial distinctions. First, Lave and Wenger (1991) draw a distinction between the *use versus exchange* value of the outcomes of learning. In the communities of practice characterized by Lave and Wenger, increasing participation – engaging in practice useful to the community – was a primary motivation for learning.[11] As Engeström (2001) puts it, "motivation to learn stems from participation in culturally valued collaborative practices in which something useful is produced" (p. 141). Lave and Wenger contrast the use value of learning (learning to know or to participate) with the exchange value (learning to display knowledge, which they see as exemplified by typical testing practices in schools).[12]

Engeström (2001) draws a further useful distinction between simply learning to participate where a stable learning curriculum exists and "expansive learning," when we "must learn new forms of activity which are not yet there" (p. 138).

Standard theories of learning are focused on processes in which a subject (traditionally an individual, more recently possibly also an organization) acquires some identifiable knowledge or skills in such a way that a corresponding, relatively lasting change in the behavior of the subject may be observed. It is a self-evident presupposition that the knowledge or skill to be acquired is itself stable and reasonably well defined. There is a competent "teacher" who knows what is to be learned.

The problem is that much of the most intriguing kinds of learning in work organizations violates this presupposition. People and organizations are all the time learning something that is not stable and not even defined or understood ahead of time. In important transformations of our personal lives and organizational practices, we must learn new forms of activity that are not yet there. (Engeström 2001, 137–38)

In expansive learning, learning might be motivated because learners encounter problems or contradictions within their activity systems, because a new tool or structure was introduced ("a change capsule"), or because they encounter voices that bring alternative practices or alternative ways of viewing the world. Understanding the potential of assessment for provoking, supporting, or impeding expansive learning is also crucial to sound practice from a sociocultural perspective.

Regarding the third question, "What do they learn?" Engeström argues that implicit or explicit in any activity system is an understanding of what counts as more or less advanced: "Our judgments are inevitably based on an implicit or explicit theory of development" (1993, 68).

The answer to this question cannot be addressed by simply examining the expressed intent of a curriculum but must be inferred from the actual practices through which learning occurs and all the resources that structure it. In studies of formal learning environments, Lave and Wenger (1991) argue for the importance of "decentering teaching" in studies of learning (see also Lave 1996):

Dissociating learning from pedagogical intentions opens the possibility of mismatch or conflict among practitioners' viewpoints in situations where learning is ongoing. These differences often must become constitutive of the content of learning. (Lave and Wenger 1991, 114)

This implies that we need to rethink where we look to study learning: "Rather than a teacher/learner dyad, this points to a richly diverse field of essential actors and, with it, other forms of relationships of participation.... The practice of the community creates the potential 'curriculum' in the broadest sense.... A learning curriculum unfolds in opportunities for engagement in practice" (Lave and Wenger 1991, 57). As Lave suggests, "that learning occurs is not problematic," but "what is learned is always complexly problematic" (Lave 1993, 8). They worry, for instance, that:

When directive teaching in the form of prescriptions about proper practice generates one circumscribed form of participation (in school), preempting participation in ongoing practice as the legitimate source of learning opportunities, the goal of complying with the requirements specified by teaching engenders a practice different from that intended. (Lave and Wenger 1991, 97)

To understand what students are learning, we need to study their opportunities for engagement in practice.

Furthermore, "What do they learn?" is not just a question of knowledge (content and skills or changing mental representations) but of the relationship between learners and knowledge, which entails questions of identity and agency as they participate in practice where the knowledge has meaning. We must ask about learners' evolving relation to the discipline and to other people with whom they interact (Greeno 2002; Greeno and Gresalfi, this volume). Greeno (2002) articulates an important distinction between conceptual and interpersonal relations and the different positions afforded to individuals. Interpersonal relations "involve attention to the ways individuals are entitled, expected, and obligated to act toward each other" (p. 3). Conceptual relations involve "attention to the ways that individuals, the class, and groups within the class are entitled, expected, and obligated to act in and toward the subject-matter content of the class" (Greeno 2002, 3–4). Again, this suggests that evidence of learning entails evidence of the interaction between learners and their environment. This highlights the importance of asking questions, not just about what is being learned and how, but about who learners (students or professionals) are becoming in the process. "What do we take competence to be?" (Greeno 2002). With what authority, accountability, and agency are learners positioned vis-à-vis the subject matter and one another? (Greeno 2002)

Engeström's fourth question, "How are they learning?" is a question that must be asked in terms of the on-going actions and interactions that are occurring, dynamically, among actors and their tools in a learning environment. This brings the analysis of the dynamic activity system, described above, into play. It acknowledges that actors bring with them meanings and experiences from their membership in other activity systems that shape how they are learning.

In analyzing an activity system, Engeström (1999) suggests that "it is fruitful to move from the analysis of individual actions to the analysis of their broader activity context and back again" (p. 32). Thus, although these questions appear to be targeted at the learning trajectories of the activity system, they may equally well be asked of any activity within the system, including formal and informal assessment activities. Engeström's approach to the analysis of an activity system reminds us that assessment activities, like all activities, are social situations that entail multiple aspects of an activity system, including physical and conceptual tools, routines through which assessment is enacted (developed, administered, interpreted, and used), roles and responsibilities for different actors in the system, and an implied trajectory of what counts as "progress." Assessment practices interact with other activities in the system to shape the learning trajectory of the group and its individual members. Engeström's approach also reminds us that evidence relevant to any particular question about a learner or group of learners, an activity or multiple activities, is best interpreted in light of the interacting elements of the activity system, the opportunities for learning it provides, and the ways in which learners take up these opportunities. Finally, this approach reminds us that individuals always have at least partially unique learning trajectories, and questions about their learning and OTL need to take into account the perspectives and experiences they bring to a classroom that shape their opportunities to learn.

These elements of an activity system are general analytic concepts that suggest questions to be asked about any group of people interacting, with conceptual and physical tools, around an object. They do not directly address questions about the vision of learning that is guiding or enacted in the learning environment. That is the focus of the next section.

CRITERIA FOR ASSESSING THE QUALITY OF LEARNING AND OTL

The authors in our volume not only suggest that questions about the relationship between learners and their learning environment be addressed; equally importantly, they describe and illustrate particular kinds of powerful learning trajectories to which they believe learners are entitled and the kinds of environments (interacting concepts, activities/tasks, resources, social structures, norms, cultures, capable people, etc.) likely to support them. They also suggest and illustrate kinds of evidence that might be relevant to documenting and supporting these kinds of learning trajectories.

As Gee illustrates (this volume, chapter 4), there are a number of different research discourses that fall under the umbrella of SC/S. Each research discourse foregrounds a somewhat different set of issues: embodiment, meaning, culture, language, participation, and identity. Although there are some disagreements and disjunctions among them that this chapter glosses over (e.g., about the nature and role of mental representations), there are important themes that can be located under the labels "sociocultural" and "situative" to provide criteria for evaluating the quality of learning and OTL. I have summarized them in Figure 9.2 , organized in terms of Engeström's four questions (albeit slightly reordered). These criteria suggest questions that should be asked and evidence gathered, at various levels of scale, to support productive learning trajectories for individuals and groups.

Again, the first question, about the subjects of learning, reminds us of the importance of considering the perspectives and trajectories of different learners, including different students, who may respond differently to the environment's affordances, and teachers and other professionals who are learning to support them. Criteria under the second question, "What do they learn?," include generative topics, complex and domain specific forms of reasoning, multiple perspectives, and identities that support learning in school and beyond. Criteria under the third question, about how they learn, are divided into two sets: on academic learning in the classroom and on social supports in the school. Within the classroom, criteria include tasks with high cognitive demand that build on prior academic and home knowledge and invite conceptual agency; explicit instruction and in-time feedback, tailored to students' individual needs; access to disciplinary concepts and representations; opportunities for participation in meaningful activities and embodied experiences that help learners construct situated meanings. At the school level, criteria encompass various social scaffolds, including academically oriented friendships, connections with colleges and workplaces, capable teachers and

---

Our Criteria for Evaluating the Quality of Learning and Opportunity to Learn[13]
(organized in terms of Engeström's (2001) Questions for a Theory of Learning)

Who are the subjects of learning?

[The criteria in this figure focus on students as learners in classrooms and schools. Analogies may be productively drawn to criteria for teachers, school and district leaders, policy makers, and other education professionals who are learning to support students' learning. Professional learning is considered in Chapter 11.]

What do they learn?

Engagement with
- generative topics and knowledge useful in the world
- questions worth asking
- multiple, juxtaposed values and world views
- complex and domain specific forms of reasoning
- authentic problems within and across disciplines
- disciplinary language and forms of representation

Promoting identities as learners who
- participate, collaborate, and contribute meaningfully to the group's work
- act with authority, accountability, and agency
- value and strive for professional expertise (using knowledge gained through effort and experience, that is valued by others, and that supports innovation as needed)
- view learning as important to growth and development
- acquire habits of mind that sustain learning (questioning, using evidence, seeking alternative explanations, evaluating conclusions)

In preparation for
- effective participation in a democratic way of life
- critical reflection on multiple values and world views
- future productivity
- engagement with significant societal problems and issues

How do they learn (within the classroom)?

Well designed curricula with coherent learning trajectories

Instructional tasks and activities that
- build on prior academic knowledge and experiences as well as home-based cultural knowledge and experiences
- entail high cognitive demand (in relation to what students already know)
- afford conceptual agency – choices in formulating questions, choosing methods, explaining solutions – as well as application of procedures or techniques
- elicit use of evidence and exploration of alternatives

Explicit instruction characterized by
- meta-cognitive instructional conversations (about how students came to know what they think they know, what evidence they use to support claims, and whether there are competing explanations)
- models of disciplinary expertise and problem solving including use of disciplinary language, reasoning, and representation
- explicit connections between academic and every day language
- public and specific reasoning
- just in time instruction and feedback

Individualized instruction, effectively implemented

Figure 9.2. Criteria for evaluating the quality of learning and opportunity to learn.

Participation in
- embodied learning experiences with which students can build useful simulations and situated meanings
- patterns of interaction that help students develop identities that support learning, including collaborative and critical reflection on practice
- activities that permit meaningful contribution to the group's work and that foster interest in and motivation for learning
- communities of practice with common endeavors and shared practices, where differences are leveraged for the benefit of the group

Inherent and discursive forms of assessment that provide evidence of and support learning and OTL

How do they learn (within the school)?

Social scaffolds to support learning through
- academically oriented friendships
- positive and mutually reinforcing relationships among school, home, and community
- connections among school, business, and college to help students develop social capital (acquaintances on whom they can draw)
- explicit socialization

Learning environments rich in physical and technical resources

Strong teachers and leaders who
- are capable of teaching in the ways described above
- hold beliefs that all students can learn
- seek reasons for failure to learn within the activity system rather than within the individual student
- possess deep knowledge of their discipline(s), of disciplinary pedagogies, and of students' socialization and development, language acquisition, and home cultures
- maintain a lifelong engagement with their own learning
- work collaboratively to support students' learning

Documentary assessment that provides evidence of and supports learning and OTL

Why do they learn?

These criteria support a theory of learning in which students learn because they experience learning as meaningful and useful: it enables them to participate in the activities of the community (within and beyond the classroom), to formulate and address problems, to question and evaluate conclusions in light of evidence and alternative perspectives, and to develop "new forms of activity which are not yet there" (Engeström 2001, 138).

Figure 9.2. *(cont.)*

leaders engaged in their own professional learning, and external assessments that support (or at least don't undermine) valued learning trajectories (an issue Moss, Girard, and Greeno address more explicitly in chapter 11). Finally, "Why do they learn?" suggests criteria that prepare learners for lifelong learning and participation in valued activities in which the "curriculum" may or may not be explicit, and expansive learning – collaborative learning from what is not yet there – is what many situations require.

These broad questions and criteria can be focused at various levels of scale, from a particular action or interaction to a particular activity or kind of activity to the set of activities that shape learners' experiences over time. Looking across the chapters, we can see many different kinds of evidence brought to bear on questions of various grain sizes and scale, with and without more formal documentation, from analyses of moment-to-moment action and interaction; of tasks students are given; of students' written work in a variety of contexts (notebooks, projects, quizzes, externally imposed assessments); of conversations that probe students' meanings; of surveys, interviews, and other forms of self-report; and of summaries of actions and accomplishments that digital environments allow. Furthermore, these analyses don't focus just on questions of knowledge and skill but on embodied experience, meaning, language, culture, participation, positioning, and identities enacted. Readers might productively review the chapters in this volume with questions about how evidence is used in mind.

In terms of Jordan and Putz's (2004) discussion of types of assessment, the information obtained in documentary assessments is a tiny part of the information that is generated in classrooms about what students are learning. As multiple examples in this volume illustrate, teachers conduct deliberate "discursive" assessments, asking students questions to probe (and encouraging them to elaborate on) their meanings and to ascertain whether students are learning the terms and procedures they are teaching. Implicit information is rampant in teachers' interactions with students – as, Jordan and Putz argue, it is in all human interactions – as teachers attend to students' facial expressions and directions of attention as they address the class and to the interactional cues that students provide when teachers interact with them individually or in small groups. Of course, the quality of these assessments, in the terms of this volume, depends on the extent to which they support the kinds of learning trajectories implied in the criteria of Figure 9.2.

Sociocultural theories, including activity theory, emphasize the importance of learning – or not learning – the prevailing practices of learning activities in the classroom, which include assessment activities. These include the ways in which students are afforded participatory identities and are positioned in discourse, their being entitled and expected, or not, to ask questions of different kinds, to offer their opinions and ideas about meanings and methods of problem solving and reasoning, and to introduce information about their experiences outside of school in the class discussion. Some aspects of these issues of practice may be discussed and assessed deliberately, often by having rules for interaction that are declared and, to some extent, enforced. Many aspects of the prevailing interactional practices, however, are tacit and are communicated and assessed only implicitly by encouraging students to contribute to class discussions and crediting particular kinds of contributions as appropriate and productive.[14] A robust understanding of the quality of classroom assessment needs to take all of these features into account.

In short, the theory in this section implies that assessments should provide information to understand the interactive processes – among learners, tools, and other people – through which learning evolves over time. It also implies that we need to understand the ways in which assessments are themselves mediational means that shape and are shaped by human (inter)action. Performance in any situation, including an assessment, can be evaluated only in relation to the resources and constraints of the situation that support or impede that performance. Furthermore, we need to question whether performance in any particular assessment situation generalizes to other kinds of interactions in which students' knowledge is put to work (Gee, this volume, chapter 4; Mislevy, Gee, and Moss, in press). We need to acknowledge and study the way in which assessment offers learners identities and positions and presupposes aspects of their identities in the situations where they are assessed. From a sociocultural perspective, the differences in these affordances would be expected to influence opportunities for learners to develop positional identities, possibly learning to act with the kinds of agency they are afforded when they are assessed.

EXAMINING THE PRACTICE OF ASSESSMENT IN A CLASSROOM ACTIVITY SYSTEM: THE CASE OF MAGDALENE LAMPERT'S FIFTH-GRADE MATHEMATICS CLASSROOM

To illustrate the complexities that this relational understanding of learning, OTL, and assessment illuminates, I turn to the case of Magdalene Lampert's teaching practice. I draw on Lampert's (2001) book, *Teaching Problems and the Problems of Teaching*, in which she analyzes her practice across one year of teaching mathematics to a diverse group of fifth-graders. Given the goals of this chapter, I read Lampert's work with the question of how she uses evidence of students' learning to inform her practice and how these evidence-based reflections provide compelling evidence of students' (and Lampert's) opportunities to learn in this classroom.

In describing Lampert's practice, I first use her language and then map this description into the analytical concepts presented in the previous section to summarize what we've learned about the practice of assessment in Lampert's classroom. This should (1) illustrate the usefulness of this set of analytic concepts for illuminating evidence of learning and how it can work to support OTL and (2) highlight ways in which assessment can work in a classroom activity system that, evidence suggests, is largely consistent with the criteria for OTL highlighted in the previous chapters.

Lampert's Conception of Learning and Teaching Mathematics

Lampert's (2001) conception of learning mathematics involves a particular understanding of the content – what it means to *do* mathematics – and of the identities and positions that this entails. Lampert's curriculum was organized around mathematical problems, both practical ones – "like figuring out prices and schedules" and intellectual ones, "like identifying the conditions that make it necessary to conclude that all of the numbers that are divisible by twenty-one are also divisible by seven" (p. 6). "In the course of working on problems," Lampert reports, "[students] investigated different solution strategies," "represented relationships graphically and symbolically," and "disagreed and defended their approaches and clarified their assumptions" (p. 5). A typical day in Lampert's classroom began with one or more problems on the board that students copied into their notebooks, worked on alone or in small groups, and then presented and discussed their work as a whole class. "Learning in my class," she states, "was a matter of becoming convinced that your strategy and your answer are mathematically legitimate" (p. 6).

As Lampert notes, this conception of learning entails the development of an academic identity, of becoming someone "more inclined to study, to initiate the investigation of ideas, and to be identified as someone who will and can do what needs to be to done to learn in school" (p. 268). Her teaching thus involves "influencing students to be the kinds of persons who are academic resources for themselves and for one another" (p. 266). "What students are willing to do with one another and with their teacher in the public space of the classrooms constrains their capacities to study and to learn" (p. 266). She notes how being able "to make a mistake (in front of one's peers), admit one has made it, and correct it" (p. 266) is an essential part of an academic character. She highlights three intellectual virtues appropriated from Georg Polya's (cited in Lampert) *Induction and Analogy in Mathematics* (1954): "*intellectual courage*" or being "ready to revise any one of our beliefs," "*intellectual honesty*," or changing "a belief when there is good reason to change it," and "*wise restraint*," or not changing "a belief wantonly, without some good reason, without some serious examination" (p. 268).

Just like her curriculum, Lampert's representation of her teaching – and the evidence it entails – is similarly organized around problems. As noted in the introduction, she uses the metaphor of a camera lens shifting focus and zooming in and out to represent "the problems of practice that a teacher needs to work on in a particular moment... [along with] the problems of practice that are addressed in teaching a lesson or a unit or a year" (pp. 2–3).

Also, she notes that multiple problems – sometimes with conflicting solutions – need to be solved at once:

> When I am teaching fifth grade mathematics, for example, I teach a mathematical idea or procedure to a student while also teaching that student to be civil to classmates and to me, to complete the tasks assigned, and to think of herself or himself and everyone else in the class as capable of learning. . . . As I work to get students to learn something like "improper fractions," I know I will also need to be teaching them the meaning of division, how division relates to other operations, and the nature of our number system. While I take action to get some particular content to be studied by a particular student in a particular moment, I simultaneously have to do the work of engaging all of the students in my class in the lesson as a whole, even as I am paying different kinds of attention to groups of students with diverse characteristics. And I need to act in a way that preserves my potential to keep acting productively, day after day, throughout the year. (p. 2)

To represent teaching, "We need a representation of the multiple levels of teaching action as they occur in different social relationships over time to accomplish multiple goals simultaneously" (p. 28). Throughout her text, we see how she uses evidence to address different sorts of problems: to get to know her students at the beginning of the year, to plan lessons, to make decisions about what to do next in her interactions with students, and to take stock of their accomplishments. We also see how the way she (and her students) use evidence shapes the nature of learning in that classroom.

Lampert's Methodology

Lampert's (2001) methodology should be considered at two different levels: what she does as part of her routine teaching practice and what she did specially to represent that practice in this text. As part of her everyday teaching practice, she maintains the following records: a daily teacher's journal where she records her plans, her observations of students' work and interactions, and her reflections on what happened; students' notebooks where they record their mathematical work each day; students' responses to quizzes; and narrative reports to parents. Each of these contains evidence of students' learning. The journal allows her to record and revisit evidence of significant oral interactions that would otherwise be available only in memory. As part of the research project that led to this book, she also collected video- and audiotapes of all lessons across the year which were transcribed, structured fieldnotes taken by a classroom observer, seating charts for all lessons, and copies of what was on the chalkboard (p. 40). These specially collected records and her reflections about them allow us to see how she used evidence as part of their routine interactions. Although there are instructive instances of practice with documentary assessment, in the terms of Jordan and Putz, most of the evidence she and her students use is inherent and discursive and in the service of learning.

I have selected three quite different activities in order to represent the way Lampert and her students construct evidence of learning and how they use that evidence to support and assess learning: (1) how she uses evidence to plan a lesson; (2) how she uses evidence collected in the moment and accumulated over time to decide what to do next in an interaction; and (3) how she uses evidence from a more formal assessment to plan lessons, give individual feedback, and teach the nature of accomplishment.

Using Evidence to Prepare a Lesson

Lampert describes her questions about students' capacity while preparing for a series of lessons in late September on how and when to use multiplication and division in solving problems.

It would help to know whether any of my students could already multiply large numbers using the conventional procedure. It would help to know if anyone understood that multiplication is about groups of groups of groups, no matter how big the numbers. It would help to know if anyone would be disposed to work independently in ways that were reasonable and if anyone would be likely to focus more on simply producing answers. (p. 108)

She highlights the evidence she considered from her work with two students – Enoyat and Tyrone – to illustrate a practice she enacts similarly with all students in her class. Here I will focus on the evidence she considers about Enoyat, which includes attention to both the intellectual and social aspects of his learning. Her journaled observations of her students began the first day they entered her classroom. She noted that Enoyat, who was born in Sudan, had "introduced himself in fluent English" and had responded "no" when asked if there was anything in particular he hoped to study. In her journal, she recorded, for the entire class, the names of students who were very active, active, or somewhat active in class discussion that day, listing Enoyat in the "somewhat active" column. She also described what she learned from a review of the standardized test responses of these students from the previous year. Here, her observations are based not on overall scores but on the ways in which students worked on the problems. She noted, for instance, that Enoyat, like some other students in the class, "had not yet made the transition from being able to multiply by a one-digit number to being able to multiply by a two-digit number." She noted that "a few students produced correct answers to all multiplications by using the conventional procedures, but it was hard to tell from these calculations what they understood about the meaning of the numbers or the procedure" (p. 116). The mixture of addition and multiplication in the work of these students suggested that the idea of multiplication as "groups of groups" was not guiding their work. Journal entries on subsequent days listed Enoyat as one of the students who did not participate in class discussion, but who was "working away in a seriously strategic manner." She explains to her readers that "seriously strategic" on that day meant using patterns and relationship to figure out solutions to the problem, which suggested to her that "they had some disposition to think that mathematics was supposed to make sense and that they were competent to figure things out they had not been told how to do" (p. 112). A later journal entry listed Enoyat as one of the students who "was not making abstract deduction from the evidence, but who had arranged the information to show a pattern." These observations are based on what students wrote in their notebooks and on what she had observed from her conversations with them and her observations of their conversations with one another. She noted that when Tyrone first joined the class later in September and was seated next to Enoyat, the two were working productively together, and she recorded later in her journal that Tyrone had picked up the connection between addition and multiplication from Enoyat but had not taken into account the constraints of the numbers (recording $15 \times 4 = 60$ but, when asked to show what 'adding it up' would look like, listed 13s to try to come up with 60). Thus, we see her attend to students' strategies in solving problems – from the previous year's standardized test, from their notebooks, and from their talk with her and each other as recorded in her journal; we see her attend to how students interacted with her, with the material, and with one another; and we see her use her daily journal to record observations sometimes by grouping students according to how they approached a problem or interacted with her and the class and sometimes by recording a particularly relevant point about a particular child. This sort of information – along with what she knew from coursework, reading, her own work with the problems, and previous experience with fifth graders – helped her make decisions about which problems to select ("where to set students down in the mathematical space" [p. 118]) and how to support students' dispositions to reason and collaborate.

Using Evidence While Teaching a Lesson about Rate

Here, we examine how Lampert uses evidence while teaching a lesson that focuses on the mathematics of multiplication as grouping. The lesson (9/28) began, as do most of her lessons, with a problem on the board, which students copied into their notebooks:

a. □ groups of 12 = 10 groups of 6
b. 30 groups of 2 = □ groups of 4
c. □ groups of 7 = □ groups of 21

(Lampert 2001, 143)

Consistent with the established routine, students worked on the problem for about a half hour while Lampert walked around the room, "watching what they are doing, listening to what they are saying, sometimes talking with them" (p. 11). During this time, Lampert noted the major variations in students' solutions and the diagrams they drew, including those students who had no diagram at all. The class then spent the next half hour sharing and discussing their solutions. Lampert describes the problems of teaching she needed to address during this segment:

> In addition to the problems of teaching the mathematical content, I was trying to teach everyone about mathematical discourse, about how to participate in conversations with twenty-six other people, and about themselves as capable doers of the task and thinkers about the ideas in it. (p. 144)

The evidence she gathered during the first half hour, along with what she knew from the sort of ongoing work described above, helped her in deciding where to start the lesson and who she might encourage to share so that the class could consider, and agree or disagree with, a range of instructive solutions. She also considered what she knew about students' capacity to participate comfortably in the public discourse and to allow their solutions to be criticized.

She began the discussion by asking "who has something to say about [part] a?" to signal that she was interested in a broad range of responses, not just right or wrong answers. Her earlier observations had allowed her to "exercise the option of calling on someone...to get a particular piece of mathematics on the table." She called on Richard, even though (as she tells her readers) he was not one of the students who raised his hand[15] and even though she knew, from her observations of their notebooks, that other students would consider his answer wrong. She recorded Richard's conjecture of "22" on the board ("$\boxed{22}$ groups of 12 = 10 groups of 6") and asked him to explain his reasoning. Richard responded, "Because, I timesed twelve and ten. Twelve times ten equals twenty-two." She noted silently that he seemed to confuse multiplication and addition and that he had transposed 10 and 12. She chose to ignore the other hands that were raised to continue her discussion with Richard, both to signal her assumption that there should be "reasoning behind any assertion that would explain why it would make sense" (p. 148) and to pursue the mathematical lessons that Richard's conjecture allowed. She explains to her readers:

> To respond to Richard's assertion, I initiate activities that will make it possible for all of the students to study the connection between the action of grouping and the arithmetic operation of multiplication. Based on my observations of their notebook work in the first part of class, I choose representations for communicating both what I am trying to say and what I think students are trying to say. (p. 149)

She recorded Richard's response in conventional format on the board

$$\begin{array}{r} 10 \\ \times 12 \\ \hline \end{array}$$

and asked him if that is how he did it. She also recorded

$$\begin{array}{r} 12 \\ \times 10 \\ \hline \end{array}$$

and indicated to the class that the first representation means twelve groups of ten and the second means ten groups of twelve. She tells her readers she wanted both to teach students both how to read and write a multiplication conventionally and give them a shared language to use in talking about the problem. She then illustrated how the class might draw a picture to represent Richard's solution by starting to draw groups of twelve under the problem but deliberately leaving it unfinished:

$\boxed{22}$ groups of 12 = 10 groups of 6

$\overset{.}{(12)}\overset{.}{(12)}\overset{.}{(12)}\overset{.}{(12)}$

She offered additional representations of 10 × 12 for the class to consider. She concluded by suggesting that "twenty-two groups of twelve seems like it would be quite a lot of stuff. She tells us that she is giving Richard and the class "tools for reasoning themselves about the appropriateness of their answers" and is establishing a pattern of what "we do to learn math" (p. 151). She took some time as well to explore another mathematical idea: how patterns – in this case, arranging the circles of tens and twelves into even rows so that each row doesn't need to be counted – create mathematical shorts cuts, which she related to times tables. She told us that by doing this, she had been giving Richard a way to make sense of his assertion "$\boxed{22}$ groups of 12 = 10 groups of 6." She returned to Richard and asked him what he thought about "this twenty-two groups of twelve thing." Following several seconds of silence, she asked "What if I had just ten groups of twelve? How many would that be?" He responded, "I don't know." She told us she was not yet sure whether to interpret this as evidence that Richard had learned something – perhaps he knew twenty-two didn't make sense but didn't yet know what did make sense. She returned to the earlier drawing, where she had begun drawing groups of twelve, and asked the class to complete ten groups of twelve in their imagination. She then drew ten groups of twelve on the board in two equal rows so that the board looked like this:

$\boxed{22}$ groups of 12 = 10 groups of 6

⑫ ⑫ ⑫ ⑫ ⑫   ⑥ ⑥ ⑥ ⑥ ⑥
⑫ ⑫ ⑫ ⑫ ⑫   ⑥ ⑥ ⑥ ⑥ ⑥

She started adding the top row out loud to arrive at sixty and asked Richard to consider that if the top row was sixty, how many there would be altogether? He responded "one twenty." She then asked Richard to consider that if ten groups of twelve is 120, what did he think of his idea about twenty-two groups of twelve? "It's wrong," he said. "Is it too big or too small?" she asked. "Too big," said Richard. She pointed to the ten groups of twelve on the board and asked Richard whether the answer could be ten, modeling, she noted, a "guess and check" strategy. Richard said, "no." She then opened the discussion up to other members of the class as they continued to analyze the problem of what to put in the box. While her description continued through to "closure" on each part of the problem, for our purposes, I'll stop here.

Each move she made was based on her in-time evaluation of the new evidence on the table: "Each move is designed and enacted in a particular moment to bring a particular piece of mathematics to students and particular students to mathematics" (p. 176).

After the lesson, she wrote in her journal about where the discussion had gone in ways that she had not anticipated, why she thought this had occurred, and what she did in response. She also noted that although several students had made contributions, she was concerned about the level of participation and about the students who had volunteered but not been called on. She also noted some of the mathematics that students had been working on in small groups that had not been addressed in whole class discussion. She tells her readers:

Evident in the patterns of talk on September 28 is the diversity of students' capacities for doing mathematics in a thoughtful, productive way.... As I was getting to know the students, I was becoming aware of the range of their mathematical diversity and the differences in their dispositions to reflect and make sense of what we were working on. I had tried a few strategies to be responsive to the diversity in this lesson, and I would need to monitor future lessons to see what effect these had on students. Would Richard be reluctant to offer another assertion in a whole-class discussion...? Would [others]..."tune out" because they were frustrated by the level of the discussion? (p. 177)

She noted that her concerns reflected "teaching problems that need to be addressed across time as well as in particular events" (p. 177). Doing so requires "continuously maintaining, monitoring, and modifying the structures that are in place to accommodate what is learned about students and mathematics along the way" (p. 177). The evidence to which Lampert is attending is evidence of the *interaction* among her and her students, and her journaled notes – both questions and documentation of observations – allow her to consider what to do in the next lessons.

Using Evidence to (Teach and) Assess the Nature of Accomplishment

In this section, we see how Lampert evaluates, provides feedback on, and uses the evidence from a quiz. Instructively, the quiz forms the centerpiece of a chapter about "teaching the nature of accomplishment": "A formal assessment like a quiz could be thought of as a one-way communication from students to teacher about what they know and are able to do, working alone and in silence. It can also be thought of the other way around, as a way for the teacher to communicate to students about what kind of performances demonstrate competence" (p. 344).

She describes for her readers the problems she encounters in conceptualizing how to measure progress and teach accomplishment. First, she notes, in order to demonstrate progress, "a student must be able to communicate appropriately about what he or she knows in terms that are understood in that [academic] setting" in which they are learning.

In my classroom, a student would need to be able to represent ideas and strategies in words, drawings, or manipulations in such a way as to convince others that these ideas are being used in ways that make sense. (p. 330)

This implies that she has to *teach* students how to represent their progress. Second, she notes that mathematical accomplishment is "complex and multidimensional" and that students can make progress in different ways:

Sometimes the capacity to make drawings of an idea precedes being able to use that idea in making a correct computation. A student may be able to solve a problem but not to talk about why the strategy used to solve it is appropriate. Being able to use an idea in one context might not carry over to other contexts. (p. 320)

Third, she notes that students come to her classroom at different starting points on all the dimensions of knowing in her classroom. "Communication and representation of progress within the class needs to somehow take account of these variations, both among students and within each student on different measures of accomplishment" (p. 330).

Finally, she notes that in the complex social world of the classroom, progress is largely open to public scrutiny. Students learn about how they are doing in relation to other students; what they learn about their progress "cycles back either to motivate or to suppress their interest in attempting to make further progress" (p. 329). Again, representation of progress must be made in a way that "did not become a restraint on students' interest in making further progress" (p. 329).

The quiz she gave on "fractions" contained six problems of the sort she gives as problems of the day, although, unlike with the daily problems, students were expected to work alone and in silence for the whole class period. The quiz provided space and encouragement for students to experiment and explain their thinking. Students were asked to order fractions with different denominators, translate partially shaded number bars into fractions, determine which fractions with different denominators were equivalent, add fractions, and prove that the given sum of two fractions with different denominators was correct.

She describes the multiple ways in which she used students' responses to the quiz both to help monitor their learning and teach the nature of accomplishment. She first looked over the quiz to identify common mistakes. For instance, a few students had concluded that $1/2 + 1/6 = 2/8$, demonstrating that they did not know how to add fractions. In fact, Ivan had "confidently" concluded that the request to prove $1/2 + 1/4 = 9/12$ was wrong; rather, he showed how he concluded that $1/2 + 1/4 = 2/6$. He explained how he had added the numerators and the denominators. This presented a dilemma for her: How could she nurture "the positive development represented by a mathematical self that has the confidence to make a counterassertion and the recognition that what students like Ivan had done represented a fundamental misunderstanding" (p. 335)?

Before returning her evaluations to students, she decided to bring the problem to the class the next day. She wrote on the board:

> Some people conjectured on the quiz that
>
> $1/2 + 1/6 = 2/8$
>
> Do you agree or disagree?
>
> Write your reasoning.
>
> Try to convince your group of what you think.   (p. 337)

As usual, she walked around the room looking in students' notebooks and listening to their reasons as they talked to one another, noting the variations in the arguments. Some reasoned that 1/2 was larger than 2/8, some used a conventional procedure for adding fractions (although Lampert noted one student's display did not indicate the meaning of the numbers), some drew number bars on graph paper to illustrate why 2/8 was not the correct answer. She noted that some students, including Ivan, used a different way of thinking about the problem in their notebooks than they did on the quiz. Ivan, for instance, had begun to draw number bars; he noted that 1/2 = 4/8, suggesting he could have perceived that 2/8 was too small. Much like in the previous section, she decided whom to call on based on this evidence, and the class worked together to reason about the problem. She tells us that those who had not reasoned correctly on the quiz could listen to the arguments without necessarily choosing to associate themselves with the error. "Instead of identifying those students who made the error as a group that does not have something that the rest of the class does have, I teach by making the common error into an opportunity for all students to study the mathematical reasoning as well as fractions" (p. 358).

In evaluating the quiz to give students individual feedback, she wanted to develop a grading system that addressed her "dual concerns about developing content knowledge and self-image" (p. 336). She wanted to demonstrate the complexity of their progress and support them in seeing themselves and one another as capable of learning. She did not give or record an overall score or grade. Rather, she gave students credit (C), partial credit (PC), no credit (NC), or extra credit (EC) for each question. "With credit, I intended to communicate that work at this level was good enough to indicate that students were doing well in fifth grade mathematics" (p. 351). Extra credit was for those responses "in which students demonstrated that they could use multiple means of representing their understanding... and those that demonstrated that students had made progress toward a more complex kind of understanding from a starting point of being able to competently follow a rule" (pp. 347–48). She noted in her journal that she did not use "EC" consistently across the papers but rather "gave some kids extra credit for the same work that other kids just got credit for if I thought it represented a special accomplishment for that student – this kind of an assessment means that what I see on the quiz is evaluated interactively with what I see in the class, which is harder to document, but necessary to take account of" (p. 344). On each quiz, next to each problem, she wrote one of these symbols and a brief comment (on responses that received EC, PC, or NC). The comment typically suggested what had been done well (e.g., "excellent use of drawings," "good use of different ways of thinking about fractions," "excellent explanation"), or pointed to an error and suggested a new way to evaluate it ("draw this and see if it makes sense," "but you can also add if the bottom number is *not* the same"; to a student who put 5/6 to the right of 4/4 on a number line, "you need to think about what the numbers mean . . . 4/4 is one whole; 5/6 is *less* than one whole". She explained her grading scheme to the class: "If you did something that made sense, I gave you credit. If you did something that did not make sense, it says NC." She went on to explain that they got PC "if part of what you did made sense" and EC "if you did an excellent job of explaining your reasoning." When pressed by Donata, she indicated that credit for every question "would be like getting an A." Grades, however, were not required by the school, and her reports cards involved prose descriptions of students' progress (again reflecting the complexity in assessing mathematical learning).[16] She indicated that she returned the quiz to students in a way that kept her evaluations of their work private to the greatest possible extent.

She argues that the quiz, and the way she evaluated it, "is a resource for teaching that can be used to convey a system of meaning around what is valued and how performance can be differentiated to indicate progress or not. . . . It gives [students] an opportunity to consider a different, more complex way of thinking about their accomplishments and about what they still need to learn" (p. 356).

How Evidence Functions in the Activity System of Lampert's Classroom

The characterization of Lampert's practice serves two purposes for us in this chapter. First, it illustrates the way that assessment (inherent, discursive, and documentary) can function productively within an activity system that, evidence suggests, is largely consistent with the conceptions of OTL reflected in the earlier chapters. Second, it is an example of documentary assessment practice that provides compelling evidence of the opportunities to learn in this classroom. Although the comprehensiveness of the case Lampert has made for her own practice far exceeds anything that would be possible for routine documentation, there is much to learn here about the sort of evidence that warrants the quality of students' OTL. We will return to this in chapter 11.

Routine use of evidence within Lampert's classroom. Much of the evidence Lampert uses is a naturally occurring part of the (written and oral) discourse of the classroom. Some of it (quizzes, students' notebooks) involves naturally occurring written records of students' work; much of it is simply present in the ongoing classroom dialogue. To learn about her students' learning from examples of their work, she examines their solutions and the strategies they used to reach them, problem by problem; she considers the variations in students' performance, the kinds of errors they have made, keeps informal records of these in her journal, and designs her lessons accordingly. Lampert's journal – a routine part of her teaching practice, not specially constructed for this study – serves as an important space for jotting down evidence of interaction that she wants to remember and for analyzing the evidence she has available. We see as well the ways in which discursive assessment – by Lampert and her students – is a routine part of classroom interaction. Everyone participates in discursive assessment of the solutions proposed to problems.

It's important to note that Lampert routinely attends to evidence with a particular problem or question in mind about *what to do next*. Thus, evidence is always considered in light of the question or issue it is addressing: what problems to use in tomorrow's lesson, which mathematical concepts to illustrate with a given problem, what students' likely approaches to a problem will be, which student to call on, how to respond to students' misunderstandings, how to support students' willingness to "study" and question their own solutions, how to support students in being a resource for other students, how to communicate progress to students and their parents, and so on. Although these questions seem to differentially emphasize the social and intellectual aspects of Lampert's classroom, it is important to note (as does she) that teaching always entails both sorts of problems. She records and uses evidence about students' evolving participation and identities alongside evidence of how they solve problems. It's also important to note that her attention to evidence in solving a teaching "problem" was routinely *situated* in the ongoing interaction of which it was a part, *cumulative* in the sense of drawing on other available evidence (fitting this piece of evidence into her evolving understanding of students' learning), and *anticipatory* in the sense of considering how her next move was likely to affect students' learning. Even the more formal quiz was evaluated in light of how it fit with other evidence of students' progress, how the social situation and other affordances/constraints of the quiz were different from the routine classroom interaction, and, equally important, how her response was likely to affect students' sense of themselves as learners, their understanding of accomplishment, and their progress in her class. As her work with the quiz illustrates, her use of evidence always involved consideration of *how her practice, including her assessment practice, shaped students' learning.* We see two instances where documentary assessment was used. At the beginning of the year, we see the way in which she attends to students' performance on last year's standardized test. Instructively, she does not report (or seem to consider) their scores. Rather, she examines their work in solving the problems and considers, as she does with their notebooks, the approaches they took, the sorts of errors they made, and what these indicate about the meaning they make of mathematics. We see, as well, one example of how Lampert reports to parents about their children's progress – prose descriptions of what they have accomplished and what they have to work on – which is intended to represent the complexity of their mathematical performance in ways that grades cannot. Both of these practices ultimately serve endogenous purposes for Lampert in documenting and supporting students' learning.

Lampert's text as documentary evidence of the students' learning/ opportunities to learn in her classroom. Before moving on to a more extended discussion of documentary assessment in chapter 11 – assessment that crosses the boundaries of activity systems – it is useful to consider what we can learn about documentary evidence of learning/OTL from Lampert's documentation of her practice. First, consider the kind of evidence contained in Lampert's text. We see examples of instructional materials (like the problems presented to students), of students' written work, of Lampert's feedback, of classroom interaction in various participation structures, and of the records Lampert keeps. We see this evidence at different points in time so we can trace its evolution. We see Lampert's rationale for the choices she makes in planning and implementing her teaching and her reflection on what happened during her lessons in an evolving dialectical relationship. We see as well the evidence organized always in terms of the questions it addresses for Lampert. We come away with a good sense of the answers to Engeström's questions about what, how, and why students are learning and the extent to which they are afforded the OTL characterized in this volume. The answers to these questions can be confidently constructed because we have multiple types of evidence about this activity system: We see not only the people involved, but also the material artifacts and concepts that are used and produced; we see the norms and conventions reflected in the routine patterns of interaction. From these we can draw well-warranted inferences about the division of labor (including the positions and identities afforded students) and the object and outcomes of learning. The concrete evidence presented provides both illustration and corroboration for what Lampert tells us about her practice. With respect to our criteria of learning/OTL, we see, for instance, that the tasks students undertake support conceptual agency and mathematical reasoning; we see Lampert's continuously updated use of prior knowledge, the connections she makes between students' language and the language of mathematics, and the models of mathematical reasoning they experience; we see patterns of interaction that afford students opportunities to make meaningful contributions to the learning of the group and to evaluate the conclusions they draw in light of evidence and alternatives; we see students progressing along a coherent learning trajectory; and so on. Lampert's text, then, provides an instructive touchstone for the kind of documentary evidence "we" – education professionals in various activity systems – would, ideally, like to have about learning/OTL in a given classroom. The question becomes what kind of documentary evidence is feasible, useful, persuasive... *and* conducive to learning/OTL of students and the education professionals responsible to them. In chapter 11, we turn to these issues.

CONCLUDING COMMENTS

The conceptual framework elaborated here, based in sociocultural perspectives and illustrated via Lampert's (2001) practice, shows how evidence of learning is used to address different kinds of questions at different levels of scale; how many of these questions are fundamentally about what does and does not work to support learning and thus require evidence of the interaction between learners and their environment (including its assessment practices); how assessment practices range from discrete activities designated as assessment to ongoing ways of looking at the evidence available in the environment; how assessment practices always entail multiple interacting elements and function in complex systems that shape and are shaped by them.

In sum, what do SC/S perspectives imply for the sound practice of assessment in classrooms?[17] What is needed is a flexible approach to assessment that begins with the questions that are being asked; that can develop, analyze, and integrate multiple types of evidence at different levels of scale; that is dynamic in the sense that questions, available evidence, and interpretations can evolve dialectically as inquirers learn from their inquiry, *and* that allows attention to the antecedents and anticipated and actual consequents of their interpretations, decisions, and actions.

We also need to recognize that not all assessments should or can be subjected to an explicit documentation – in fact, most assessments are of this variety. Much that might be called assessment is simply a routine part of social interaction in a learning environment. Given this, we need a set of conceptual tools and routines that can be applied, explicitly when needed, but that can also provide actors with adequate information and rules of thumb to shape their daily practice. Thus, we need to consider the meta-issue of how learning environments are resourced – with knowledgeable people, material and conceptual tools, norms and routines, and evolving information about learning – to support sound, evidence-based interpretations, decisions, and actions when explicit inquiry is not possible. We also need to consider the issues of how assessment is supporting the professionals' learning to support students' learning and one another's learning (Moss, Girard, and Greeno, this volume).

Finally, we need to recognize that assessment practices do far more than provide information; they shape people's understanding about what is important to learn, what learning is, and who learners are (Engeström 2001; Lave 1993). Thus, any assessment theory needs to take into account the way in which assessment functions as part of – shaping and shaped by – the local learning environment and its learners. A discussion that addresses the validity of this sort of assessment practice can be found in Moss, Girard, and Haniford (2006).

I close with two important points that this theory highlights and that lay the groundwork for chapter 11 (Moss, Girard, and Greeno). Classroom activity systems are embedded in institutional structures with their own sets of activity systems and are further influenced by other activity systems (at home, in professional organizations) that shape (enable and constrain) and are shaped by local practice. Externally imposed (documentary) assessments, with their associated routines and divisions of labor, are among the most prominent means through which these different activity systems interact. A robust understanding of OTL requires an understanding of these relationships between the classroom and the other activity systems in which it and its actors participate. Second, the practices described above clearly depend on the capacities of teachers and other education professionals to use evidence to support student learning and the extent to which the institutions and organizations in which they work provide them with the resources they need to do so. Thus, we must consider the OTL afforded to teachers and other education professionals. That is the topic to which we turn in chapter 11.

Notes

1. This chapter (by Moss) and chapter 11 (by Moss, Girard, and Greeno) were originally drafted as a single chapter by Moss and Greeno and cited as such in earlier publications. When we divided the chapters, we revised the authorships to reflect the written contributions of the authors. That said, this chapter has been influenced in multiple ways by my conversations with Jim Greeno and his feedback on the text, with Jim Gee and Bob Mislevy (Mislevy, Gee, and Moss, in press), and with Brian Girard and Laura Haniford (Moss, Girard, and Haniford 2006) as well as the other members of the Idea of Testing Project. I am grateful to Jim Gee and Ed Haertel for their thoughtful comments on an earlier draft of the chapter.

2. While some authors in this volume draw distinctions between the terms sociocultural and situative, and indeed acknowledge and name a number of different research discourses that can be subsumed by these terms, looking across the chapters, readers will also find some of the same theorists and perspectives cited under both terms. Consequently, I will use the label SC/S, or sometimes just sociocultural (SC), to signal that I am highlighting a set of themes that have broad relevance to the multiple discourses that can be located under these labels.

3. "We are moving here from an educational practice of assessment where we have defined a priori what we are looking for, to an educational practice where we are participating in activities in which we formulate representations to better understand and transform the world around us. If our purpose is to understand and support learning and knowing and to make inferences about these phenomena, then is seems that the idea of inquiry – open, critical, and dialogic – rather than of assessment (as currently understood) would be more helpful" (Delandshere 2002, 1475).

4. Of course, we have standards that suggest people interpret scores in light of other information about the learner (AERA, APA, NCME 1999), but our conventional theories and practices within the field weren't developed to support the validity of these situated interpretations.

5. The contexts on which their characterization of assessment practice is based include those of airline operations personnel, telephone repair people, midwife apprentices, farm workers, teachers, and mothers and children.

6. In chapter 11, Moss, Girard, and Greeno will also represent what might be called exogenous forms of discursive assessment, where outsiders visit schools, observe classrooms, and talk informally with teachers about their practice.

7. This section draws heavily on Moss, Girard, and Haniford (2006).

8. Figure taken from Gee, this volume, chapter 4.

9. Action, for Wertsch, "may be external as well as internal, and it may be carried out by groups, both large and small, or by individuals" (Wertsch 1998, 23).

10. Communities of practice (Lave and Wenger, 1991) and activity systems (Engestrom, 1987) represent two of a number of different theories of social spaces or "interactive affiliations" (Gee, personal communication, 5/28/07). Critiques and alternatives can be found, for instance, in an edited volume by Barton and Tusting (2006).

11. "An apprentice's contribution to ongoing activity gains value in practice – a value which increases as the apprentice becomes more adept. As opportunities for understanding how well or poorly one's efforts contribute are evident in practice, legitimate participation of a peripheral kind provides an immediate ground for self evaluation. . . . Moving toward full participation in practice involves not just great commitment of time, intensified effort, more and broader responsibilities within the community, and more difficult and risky tasks, but, more significantly, an increasing sense of identity as a master practitioner" (Lave and Wenger 1991, 111).

12. "The commoditization of learning engenders a fundamental contradiction between the use and exchange values of the outcome of learning, which manifests itself in conflicts between learning to know and learning to display knowledge for evaluation. Testing in schools and trade schools (unnecessary in situations of apprenticeship learning) is perhaps the most pervasive and salient example of a way of establishing the exchange value of knowledge. Test taking then becomes a new parasitic practice, the goal of which is to increase the exchange value of learning independently of its use value" (Lave and Wenger 1991, 112).

13. This characterization draws on chapters in this volume by Gee, Greeno and Gresalfi, Lee, Mehan, and Pullin as well as the current chapter. For simplicity, I have appropriated and adapted my colleagues' words from earlier chapters without explicit attribution.

14. This and the preceding paragraph were first drafted by Jim Greeno.

15. Lampert comments that students were likely to question why she did not call on someone who had raised their hand and she notes that students "would continue to conduct experiments to learn more about how to get called on or not" – an instance of students engaging in their own inherent assessment.

16. Here is an example of a report card from 11/4: "Richard's engagement in mathematics has improved tremendously since the beginning of the school year. He is doing a much better job of paying attention, both to the teacher-directed large group lessons and to small group activities, although he still needs to be occasionally reminded not to let himself be distracted. The substance of Richard's work has improved as well. He began the year with a lot of guessing, saying numbers and doing things with them without thinking about what he was doing. Now he is paying attention to patterns and using them to solve problems and thinking about what the numbers in a problem represent. He needs to work more on using drawings and diagrams to represent the information that is given in a problem, and his learning to do this is one of my major goals for him this year.

Richard has some trouble bringing the concept of place value (hundreds, tens, and ones) in numbers together with computational procedures and at this stage that means he has trouble with borrowing in subtraction. He has a good sense of the concept of multiplication, however, and he is able to take large numbers apart, work on parts of them, and then put them back together in a mathematically appropriate way. Another goal that I have for Richard for this year is that he learn to transfer these good mathematical intuitions to performing more formal, abstract procedures correctly. (Lampert 2001, 281)

17. Adapted from Moss, Haniford, and Girard (2006).

References

American Education Research Association, American Psychological Association & National Council on Measurement in Education. 1999. *Standards for educational and psychological testing*. Washington DC: American Educational Research Association.

Barton, D. and K. Tusting. 2006. *Beyond communities of practice*. Cambridge: Cambridge University Press.

Delandshere, G. 2002. Assessment as inquiry. *Teachers College Record* 104: 1461–84.

Engeström, Y. 1993. Developmental studies of work as a testbench of activity theory: The case of primary care medical practice. In *Understanding practice: Perspectives on activity and context, edited by* S. Chaiklin and J. Lave, 64–103. Cambridge: Cambridge University Press.

Engeström, Y. 1987. *Learning by expanding: An activity theoretical approach to developmental research*. Helsinki: Orienta-Konsultit.

Engeström, Y. 1999. Activity theory and individual and social transformation. In *Perspectives on Activity Theory*, edited by Y. Engeström, R. Miettinen, and R. Punämaki, 19–38. Cambridge: Cambridge University Press.

Engeström, Y. 2001. Expansive learning at work: toward an activity theoretical reconceptualization. *Journal of Education and Work* 14: 134–56.

Erickson, F. 2007. Some thoughts on "proximal" formative assessment of student learning. In *Evidence and decision making (Yearbook of the National Society for the Study of Education)*, issue 1, edited by P. A. Moss. Malden, Mass.: Blackwell Publishing.

Gibson, J. J. 1977. The theory of affordances. In *Perceiving, Acting, and Knowing: Toward an Ecological Psychology*, edited by Shaw, R., and Bransford, J., 67–82. Hillsdale, N.J.: Lawrence Erlbaum.

Gibson, J. J. 1979. *The ecological approach to visual preception*. Boston: Houghton Mifflin.

Gipps, C. V. 1999. Socio-cultural aspects of assessment. In *Review of Research in Education*, edited by A. Iran-Nejad and P. D. Pearson, 355–92. Washington, D.C.: American Educational Research Association.

Gipps, C. V. 2002. Sociocultural perspectives on assessment. In *Learning for Life in the 21st Century*, edited by G. Wells and G. Claxton, 73–83. Malden, Mass.: Blackwell Publishing.

Greeno, J. G. 2002. *Students with competence, authority and accountability: Affording intellective identities in the classroom*. The College Board.

Hickey, D. T. and S. J. Zuiker 2003. A new perspective for evaluating innovative science programs. *Science Education* 87: 539–63.

Johnston, P. H. 1992. *Constructive evaluation of literate activity*. New York: Longman.

Jordan, B. and P. Putz. 2004. Assessment as practice: Notes on measures, tests, and targets. *Human Organization* 63: 346–58.

Lampert, M. 2001. *Teaching problems and the problems of teaching*. New Haven: Yale University Press.

Lave, J. 1993. The practice of learning. In *Understanding practice: Perspectives on activity and context*, edited by S. Chaiklin and J. Lave, 3–32. Cambridge: Cambridge University Press.

Lave, J. 1996. Teaching, as learning, in practice. *Mind, Culture, and Activity* 3: 149–64.

Lave, J. and E. Wenger. 1991. *Situated learning: Legitimate peripheral participation.* New York: Cambridge University Press.

Mislevy, R J., J. P. Gee, and P. A. Moss. In press. On qualitative and quantitative reasoning about assessment validity. In *generalizing from educational research: Beyond the quantitative-qualitative opposition*, edited by K. Ercikan and W. -M. Roth. Mahwah, N.J.: Erlbaum.

Moss, P. A. 2004. The meaning and consequences of reliability. *Journal of Educational and Behavioral Statistics* 29: 241–5.

Moss, P. A., B. J. Girard, and L. C. Haniford. 2006. Validity in educational assessment. *Review of Research in Education* 30: 109–62.

Shepard, L. A. 2006. Classroom assessment. In *Educational Measurement*, 4th ed, edited by R. L. Brennan, 623–46. Westport, Conn.: American Council on Education/Praeger Publishers.

Wertsch, J. V. 1998. *Mind as Action.* Oxford: Oxford University Press.

10   Issues of Structure and Issues of Scale in Assessment
      from a Situative/Sociocultural Perspective

Robert J. Mislevy

INTRODUCTION

A situative/sociocultural (S/SC) perspective "views knowledge as distributed among people and their environments, including the objects, artifacts, tools, books, and communities of which they are a part. Analyses of activity in this perspective focus on processes of interaction of individuals with other people and with physical and technological systems" (Greeno, Collins, and Resnick 1997). Accordingly, "a situated view of assessment emphasizes questions about the quality of student participation in activities of inquiry and sense making, and considers assessment practices as integral components of the general systems of activity in which they occur" (p. 37). Research on school learning from the SC perspective "incorporates explanatory concepts that have proved useful in fields such as ethnography and sociocultural psychology to study collaborative work, . . . mutual understanding in conversation, and other characteristics of interaction that are relevant to the functional success of the participants' activities" (p. 7). In such analyses, attention focuses on patterns of interactions that occur in detailed and particular situations, yields "thick" descriptions of the activities, and often produces voluminous data. Studies at this level of detail are essential for understanding the conditions and interactions through which students learn; that is, "opportunities to learn" that particular circumstances afford particular students in light of their particular personal and educational histories of experience.

   Yet no practical assessment at the level of the classroom, let alone a school or a program, can demand scores of hours of video per student, all analyzed by a team of graduate students, each producing a multipage ideographic report. Methodologies for microlevel SC analyses and large-scale assessment must differ, to be sure, but what about explanatory concepts? Is an SC perspective irreconcilable with the very idea of large-scale assessment? Or are

259

there methods and concepts at another level of explanation that can be used, different from but compatible with SC explanations, in the sense that Boyle's Law is compatible with the motions of individual molecules of a gas?

An understanding of assessment that is based solely on experience with large-scale standardized testing might suggest that the answer is no. One sees decontextualized tasks, dissociation from classroom activities, and statistical models originally conceived to answer questions cast in trait and behaviorist psychology. Yet although these testing practices are familiar and widespread, recent advances in technologies, methodologies, and practical needs have given rise to forms of large-scale assessment practices with two key characteristics: They are compatible with an SC perspective in the "levels of explanation" sense of the previous paragraph, and to accomplish this they draw on methods and concepts that have arisen from a psychometric tradition but have been extended or reconceived as necessary to support SC interpretations.

The following presentation argues this case. It uses the "evidence centered" assessment design (ECD) approach described in Mislevy, Steinberg, and Almond (2003) to illuminate the structure of assessment arguments and assessment-design frameworks. The ECD structures have been used for analyzing and designing assessments cast in terms of trait, behavioral, and information-processing psychological perspectives (e.g., Mislevy et al. 2003). It is posited that the same structures hold value for analyzing and designing assessments cast in terms of an SC perspective as well, with the meanings of the elements of the ECD structures appropriately construed.

To this end, we begin by briefly reviewing Toulmin's (1958) structure of arguments, then specializing it to assessment arguments. The central role of the psychological perspective is emphasized. It grounds the interpretation of every element in the argument – the nature of claims one wishes to make about students' learning, interpretations of the things they say, do, or make, and the observational situations in which they act and interact. Although the focus is on assessment arguments from an SC perspective, similarities and contrasts with assessment under trait, behavioral, and information-processing perspectives prove useful. We will see that knowledge about the interrelationship among students, their histories, and assessment contexts plays a larger role in SC assessment and accordingly presents greater inferential challenges for persons further from the assessment context in detail, time, and distance.

High-level representations of models for the formal assessment structures typically used in large-scale assessment settings are then presented. After recalling their uses and meanings in familiar testing practices, we examine

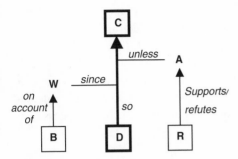

Figure 10.1. Toulmin's (1958) structure for arguments. Reasoning flows from *data* (D) to *claim* (C) by justification of a *warrant* (W), which in turn is supported by *backing* (B). The inference may need to be qualified by *alternative explanations* (A), which may have *rebuttal evidence* (R) that tend to support or refute them.

reconceptualizations that, in a compatible assessment system, would support interpretations consistent with a SC perspective on learning. The assessment argument and design structures help bring out the ways that the situativity of knowledge and the contextualization of interpretation is dealt with in large-scale assessment systems.

These ideas have been put into practice in several places, and a number of them are noted here. The two that play the largest role in the discussion are the Advanced Placement studio art portfolio art assessment (Mitchell 1992) and Hydrive (Gitomer, Steinberg, and Mislevy 1995), an intelligent tutoring system to help Air Force trainees learn to troubleshoot the hydraulics system of the F-15 aircraft. AP Studio Art blends situated classroom practice and large-scale, high-stakes assessment: Work judged centrally at the end of the school year is produced in each of hundreds of participating schools throughout the year, as students and teachers create, discuss, share, and critique pieces. Hydrive is based on information-processing principles, but it functions as a learning tool in ways that are consistent with sociocultural principles and can be used to support decisions cast in trait and behaviorist terms.

ASSESSMENT AS ARGUMENT

Philosopher Stephen Toulmin (1958) proposed a schema for how we use substantive theories and accumulated experience to reason from particular data to particular claims. Figure 10.1 outlines the structure of a simple argument. The *claim* (C) is a proposition we wish to support with *data* (D). The arrow represents inference, which is justified by a *warrant* (W), a generalization that justifies the inference from the particular data to the particular claim. Theory and experience – both personal and formal, such as empirical studies and prior research findings – provide *backing* (B) for the warrant. In any particular case we reason back through the warrant, so we may need to qualify our conclusions because there may be *alternative explanations* (A) for the data. Alternative explanations will themselves be supported or undercut by *rebuttal data* (R). This section extends Toulmin's structure to assessment arguments.

The Relevance of a Perspective on Knowledge and Learning

The foundation of an educational assessment argument is a conception of the nature of proficiency. A psychological perspective shapes the nature of all the elements in the argument structure, and the rationale orchestrates them as a coherent argument. What kinds of things might one wish to say about persons (claims)? What kinds of things does one need to see a person say or do in what kinds of situations (data)? How are they related (warrants)? What is observable is a person's action – actually a constellation of actions, indeed interactions, with elements of the environment and sometimes other people, in some social context. Yet there are countless aspects of persons, situations, and persons' actions within situations to which we might attend, and countless ways we might characterize them. A conception of proficiency shapes what among these we will perceive, and which will constitute data in a given assessment argument.

Discussion is facilitated by using terms from four stereotypical psychological perspectives for thinking about knowledge and learning (adapted from Greeno, Collins, and Resnick 1997; Greeno, Pearson, and Schoenfeld 1997). They differ as to which of the aspects of human learning, thinking, acting, and interacting they bring to the foreground, and consequently in terms of the nature and instantiation of assessment arguments cast in their light.

- *A behaviorist perspective.* The behaviorist psychological perspective focuses on targeted behavior in a domain of relevant situations. Details of both the behavior and the situation, as construed by the observer, are in the foreground; internal mechanisms and representations are moved to the background, even rejected as unscientific in the strictest versions of the perspective. Knowledge is viewed as the organized accumulation of stimulus-response associations, developed and strengthened through reinforcement from the environment, that serve as components of more broadly defined skills.

- *A trait or differential perspective.* Messick (1989, 15) defines a trait as "a relatively stable characteristic of a person – an attribute, enduring process, or disposition – which is consistently manifested to some degree when relevant, despite considerable variation in the range of settings and circumstances." People learn many different things and act in many different situations, not just from one person to the next, but from one time and situation to another for the same person. Variables intended to hold meaning across people over time may be proposed to characterize consistencies within individuals, evidenced as systematic differences among individuals. From the trait perspective, test scores hold value to the extent that behaviors observed in the assessment context are manifest in some context of use, despite differences between the contexts' demands for knowledge of particular content, tools, and social situations. Also in the background for the trait perspective are mechanisms that produce behavior and the conditions of learning that precede it.
- *An information-processing perspective.* Epitomized in Newell and Simon's (1972) *Human Problem Solving*, the information-processing perspective examines the procedures by which people acquire, store, and use knowledge to solve problems. The focus is on "what's happening within people's heads" – not just what a person does in a situation as seen from the outside, as per the behavioral perspective, but in terms of the patterns (meanings) through which a person perceives, construes, and interacts with a situation. Parallels with computation as symbol manipulation play an important role in the information-processing perspective, in the use of rules, production systems, task decompositions, and means–ends analyses.
- *An S/SC perspective.* Much learning is motivated and shaped by the knowledge, goals, constraints, and physical presence of other people. Social organizations, such as families, classrooms, and professions, influence the processes of acquiring, storing, representing, understanding, and creating knowledge. These influences are channeled by particular ways of communicating: genres, conventions, knowledge representations, and so on. "Sociocultural" highlights the activities through which knowledge is created, conditioned, constrained, and brought to bear in the contexts of the technologies, information resources, representational forms, and social systems that constitute the situations in which people act. "Situative" highlights how people construct tailored and specific meanings to each new situation around patterns from past experience, in each instance modifying and extending the repertoire of patterns and experiences they can bring to bear in the next situation.

Of course, neither learning nor assessment can be partitioned neatly into discrete bins with these labels. Yet the methods by which assessments are designed can signal associations with one or more perspectives in ways that dominate the implicit argument. Assessments designed to assess the mastery of standards defined strictly in terms of behaviors in specified situations signify a behaviorist perspective. A trait perspective is indicated when, for example, it is recognized that different people bring different motivations, experiences, and proficiencies to bear in different situations to read different materials, but reading ability is measured by standard materials for all students under the same decontextualized conditions.

Assessment-design considerations under information processing and S/SC perspectives have been shaped by research into the nature and acquisition of expertise. Influential studies carried out on the information-processing perspective expanded rapidly in the 1960s and underscored the importance of the ways experts organize knowledge and use it to solve problems (e.g., Chi, Glaser, and Farr 1988). In the same time period, observational research from a sociocultural perspective revealed the contextualized nature of competence and the importance of culturally determined tools and patterns of interpersonal interactions (e.g., Lave 1988). Contemporary expertise research acknowledges an indispensable interplay between the two (Ericsson 1996). This joint perspective underscores recurring themes in developing proficiency, around which assessment arguments can be framed and assessments can be built. They include the following:

- Language, tools, representation, processes, and strategies. Experts' individual thinking in semantically rich domains is organized around fundamental principles. It surpasses cognitive-processing limitations by employing effective external representations, symbol systems, tools, and approaches to problems. The sociocultural perspective notes that these notions, so important in individual thinking, are developed and acquired in social, cumulative, and interactive processes. To design assessment for a targeted domain, we need to identify the cultural resources – conceptual, physical, and social – people must acquire facility with, not because they need it to apply their knowledge, but because it is their knowledge.
- Situated understandings in terms of general structures. The principles, models, processes, and strategies mentioned above are abstract structures, useful only because they can be used to understand the particulars of countless unique situations (Greeno 1983). Proficiency does not lie simply in being able to recognize or re-create the abstractions. It requires, in every instance, constructing meanings in real-world situations that integrate the

key aspects of those situation and the patterns of the abstract structures – tuned to the purposes, the constraints, and the histories of those situations. To design assessment, we need to identify the ways that people use the tools of the domain.

• Interacting with evolving situations. The construction of meaning is almost always interactive, an interplay between domain patterns and the particulars of an evolving real-world situation. Research highlights the importance of interactivity and iteration in problem solving – continually constructing and reconstructing correspondences between unique real-world situations and general structures, using the structures to make sense of the situations provisionally for further perception and action (e.g., Stewart and Hafner 1994). To design assessment, we need to identify the kinds of situations that call on people to interact with, to react to, to purposefully shape material and social situations.

We can see the interplay of ideas across perspectives in newly emerging assessments. For example, the problems, interfaces, and feedback in Hydrive are all built around the information-processing notions of defining an active path in a problem space, carrying out test procedures, and applying strategies such as space-splitting and serial elimination. Yet the ways Hydrive is used also reflects a sociocultural perspective. This includes problem solving in pairs or small groups to promote communication in terms of this language of troubleshooting, and scaffolding for trainees that decreases as they become more proficient – "cognitive apprenticeship" in the manner of Collins, Brown, and Newman (1989). With feedback turned off, the same simulator can be used to estimate the proportion of problems in the domain a trainee can solve, to support a behaviorally cast decision of whether he or she is ready to go to the flight line or should continue training. Here we see an assessment purpose and assessment procedure cast in behavioral terms, in concert nevertheless with the information-processing and sociocultural grounding of the training system in which it is embedded.

The Structure of Assessment Arguments

Figure 10.2 is an extension of Toulmin's structure to assessment arguments. Although still quite simplified, it incorporates features that help one understand similarities and differences among assessment arguments cast in different psychological perspectives. It is not difficult to relate this structure to formal and familiar assessments, because their visible parts and processes are set up explicitly before the assessment occasion, and they map fairly directly

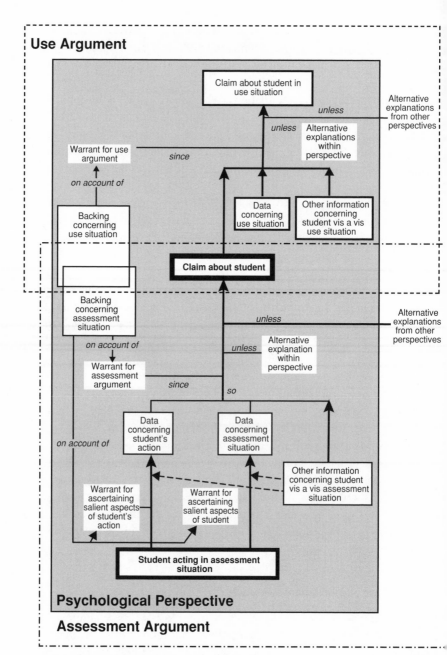

Figure 10.2. Elaborated structure for assessment arguments. Lower rectangle shows assessment argument proper; upper rectangle shows assessment use argument. They share psychological perspective, backing, and claims about student based on assessment.

to elements of the argument. This is the topic of the "Scaling Up" section. The same structure could be used to analyze a conversation between a student and a teacher as they work through, say, making sense of a poem – in this case, with the arguments implicit, constructed on the fly, reconstructed iteratively, moment by moment, as new actions are observed and new meanings are made by all involved.

Figure 10.2 actually distinguishes two main arguments: the assessment argument in the lower dashed rectangle (Mislevy 2003) and an assessment-use argument in the upper rectangle (Bachman 2005). Our attention will focus on the assessment argument, but assessment cannot be understood apart from purpose and use. Even while recognizing the flow from assessment data to assessment use, it is useful nevertheless to distinguish the mediating structure of claims about students in order to understand the role of psychological perspective.

The assessment claims are shown in the center of the figure as output of the assessment argument and data for the use argument. They are the terms in which we organize, summarize, and understand observations made in the assessment setting for subsequent reasoning in the use setting. They connect our thinking about what is observed in assessment settings with our thinking about assessment purposes such as guiding, evaluating, and affording students' learning; evaluating, improving, and monitoring instructional systems; and selecting, placing, and assigning individuals to opportunities. The meaning of the mediating claim is thus integral to both perception of student's actions in the assessment situations and subsequent action in the use situation, all consistent under the guiding perspective. Nearly all of the elements of both arguments are circumscribed in the box labeled "psychological perspective" to emphasize how each is construed through that perspective. Alternative explanations are an exception. Some alternative explanations that we need to ameliorate or take into account rise within the psychological perspective that guides the assessment design project. Yet others can arise from other perspectives, cast in terms of entities, relationships, or explanations that lie outside the narrative space of the guiding perspective.

What Are Data?

With regard to the role of psychological perspective in assessment, a particularly interesting part of the argument structure in the lower box concerns the data that ground the claim about the student. The nature of data, and the actions and situations from which they arise, is driven by the nature of the claims, which are cast in terms of psychological perspectives. Highlighted at the bottom left of Figure 10.2 is a student's actions in a situation, the unit of analysis in assessment: The student says, does, or makes something, possibly extending over time, possibly interacting with others. Interpretations of the actions rather than the actions themselves constitute data in an assessment argument. Note that warrants are required for these interpretations, cast in terms of the psychological perspective and the substantive grounding of the argument. These paths of argumentation from situated actions to data will be expanded in the subsection "Structuring the Use of Information in Interpreting Situations and Actions," as they can exhibit multiple steps and be carried out by different actors with different responsibilities, points of view, or bodies of information. At this first pass, though, we see that an assessment argument generally encompasses three kinds of data:

- aspects of the situation in which the person is acting;
- aspects of the person's actions in the situation; and
- other information about the person's history or relationship to the observational situation. This information may be further required to interpret the action in the situation, interpret the situation as it applies to the particular person, or through which to interpret the aforementioned kinds of data as they pertain to the claim.

Aspects of the Situation and the Action in the Situation

The first two of these are characterizations of aspects of a person acting within a situation that might hold value beyond the single, unique event. More fully, they are understandings of aspects of actions, in particular assessment situations that could help one understand other events that have happened or to anticipate events that might happen with regard to the same person acting in a different situation – past, future, or hypothetical – or, with regard to the situation, what might happen if other persons, similar or different in defined ways, were to interact with situations that are similar in defined ways. Such inferences are needed for educative planning, for a student in the first instance, for designing instruction in the second.

The most common understanding of "assessment data" is characterizations of students' actions in an assessment setting; famously, right or wrong answers, but more broadly, characterizations of qualities in open-ended performances, use of models or strategies, contributions to and interactions in group projects, and so on. Aspects of situations are left in the background, having been thought about by test developers but not seen as part of the data proper. Yet inference from assessment settings to use settings depends critically on a theory (perhaps implicit) of situations. One must make the case that features of the assessment settings reflect features of the targeted-use situations that elicit the relevant knowledge, skill, or propensities, however conceived. Principled design of assessment tasks – features with settings that are relevant and critical, realism at the expense of introducing demands for irrelevant knowledge, for example – thus requires an understanding of features of situations, in light of a conception of the proficiencies that are of interest in those situations (Messick 1994).

These issues have received particular attention in language testing, where the targeted language use often involves complex uses of language in complex situations (Bachman and Palmer 1996; Douglas 2000). How one can simplify and standardize situations to meet practical constraints yet still obtain evidence about inherently social and interactive capabilities is ever a challenge. To this end, background research for proposed revisions of the Test of English as a Foreign Language (e.g., Enright et al. 2000) included insights into the pragmatic and social situations in which people use language (sociolinguistics) as well as into results on the nature and acquisition of language (psycholinguistics). Figure 10.2 explicitly indicates that this backing grounds both the assessment argument and the use argument. The same backing grounds the warrants for interpreting aspects of students' actions and the situations. It may be that the theory on which these evaluations are based requires more than simply observing the action in the situation. Additional knowledge may also be required to condition these judgments as they are used to create assessment settings and evaluate actions within them.

The Role of Other Information

"Other information" data are essential to assessment arguments, even though they are often tacit, embedded in forms and practices. What we know about a particular student acting in a particular situation can influence how we interpret the aspects of the interaction that will constitute data about the person and the situation. In Figure 10.2, this possibility is indicated by the dashed lines from the "other information" box to the lines rising from student's action to "data concerning the student's actions" and "data concerning the situation."

The kinds of additional information that may be required, and the implications for inference that result if they are missing, vary across assessments framed under different psychological perspectives. As a simple illustration, the American Council on the Training of Foreign Language's reading guidelines (ACTFL 1989) contrast Intermediate readers' competence with texts "about which the reader has personal interest or knowledge" with Advanced readers' comprehension of "texts which treat unfamiliar topics and situations" – a distinction fundamental to their underlying conception of developing language proficiency. If we wish to assess students' proficiency in a foreign language, we must decide how we want to think of proficiency. Suppose, on one hand, the target of inference is cast in behavioral terms, as overall proficiency with respect to a domain of tasks. We can predefine successful behavior on each task in the same way for all students regardless of their familiarity, administer a sample of tasks to a student, and thereby obtain direct evidence about expected behavior in the domain. Suppose, on the other hand, the target of inference is level of proficiency through the lens of the ACTFL guidelines. If we know that the context of a given situation is familiar to one student but unfamiliar to a second, the same observed behavior from the two students holds radically different evidential import about their ACTFL levels. Additional information thus conditions the evidentiary value of students' performances. Which of these two conceptualizations of language proficiency is the correct one? This question makes no sense without an assessment purpose in mind. For determining comparative levels of language proficiency and familiarity with a specified knowledge base, successful performance on random samples from the corpus is appropriate. For determining individual students' proficiencies or for the purpose of planning instruction, using texts known to be familiar or unfamiliar to each and characterizing their proficiency from the ACTFL perspective is more useful.

Arguments cast in the behavioral perspective move to the background the role of additional information in characterizing both the student's action and the situation. Ideally, any observer would be able to follow the respective evaluation procedures and come up with the same interpreted data, both with regard to characterizing features of the stimulus situation and features of the action. Bormuth's (1970) linguistic transformation rules for generating a universe of comprehension tasks for a reading passage is an example, with the advertised advantage that any researcher would be led to identical universes of test items based on a given text.

In trait-based arguments, background information comes to the fore for investigating alternative explanations of performance; first, in looking for interactions between performance on tasks and background variables in the form of test and item bias, and second, in circumscribing the range of background characteristics across which inferences can be made without conditioning interpretations of performance on their values. Procedures that have evolved to examine these questions include differential item functioning analyses (DIF; Holland and Wainer 1993) and generalizability analysis (Cronbach et al. 1972).

In information-processing arguments, students' prior experience or famil-iarity with goals, procedures, and representational forms is essential for designing complex performance tasks and then interpreting actions in the resulting situations (Mislevy et al. 2003). Simulation-based task perfor-mances, for example, require interpretations across multiple, continuous sequences of actions and interactions to ground claims about use of strate-gies, familiarity with affordances, and so on. In Hydrive, it is not the particular troubleshooting actions that a student carries out that constitute data, but rather the troubleshooting strategy the action best accords with in light of the actions the student has taken thus far, the evolving information it has provided, and the changes he or she has caused in the situation up to that point.

Arguments cast in SC terms generally require the greatest use of additional information in both interpreting students' actions and characterizing the features of assessment situations. Some relevant aspects of situations such as contexts and materials can be characterized across students, but other elements of situations that are necessary to understand a student's actions require the knowledge of how the student perceives them. Similarly, some aspects of students' actions, such as the meter and word choices, can be characterized from work products alone, but others, such as whether a style or a phrase extends a structure from a student's family experiences, cannot be recognized without knowing that connection.

Section B of an AP Studio Art is the student's "concentration," up to twenty slides, a film, or a videotape illustrating a student-selected theme. An excerpt from Gasser's (1955) classic text gives a feel for how the concentration taps into a fundamental aspect of what it means to "be an artist." Gasser discusses the experience of running into a difficulty in drawing or painting a particular subject and suggests isolating a particular problem and exploring it from a variety of angles:

This is a procedure that insures progress, and it is one that many professional artists follow. They will work a long time on a single theme – anything from a still life containing a textural problem to nocturnes. It can be subject matter of a religious nature, a scene in a foreign country, or the lighting effect on a particular surface. Whatever the subject, the professional artist makes exhaustive studies of it. When he feels that he has interpreted the subject to the extent of his capabilities, he may have a one-man exhibition whose theme is the solution of the problem. It is surprising how few people who view the paintings realize this; most regard it simply as subject matter that has appealed to the artist. This can be partly true, but only the artist knows to what extent he has met the challenge of solving his particular problem. (p. 85)

The work in a concentration is produced over the course of the school year, as students and teachers in each of hundreds of participating schools create, discuss, share, and critique pieces. These interactions are situated with respect to individual students' interests, experiences, and capabilities and with respect to materials, pieces of work, episodes of creation, and discussion. Both the informal assessments represented in ongoing feedback and discussion and the more "official" grades for the work or the course draw on the teachers' in-depth knowledge of local circumstances. Yet these discussions and grades are also shaped by the common requirements by which all portfolios are rated centrally at the end of the year. The generally stated standards are the foundation of the Section B warrants. With every student's unique concentration they must be interpreted anew – by the student and the local teacher interacting in the class and later by the central raters. The determination of a student's topic, the approach he or she takes, the details of individual pieces, and the evaluation of the work are a matter of negotiation between the teacher and the student throughout the year. This experience is at once necessary for assessment and central to the learning experience that AP Studio Art is meant to provide. How these local assessment/learning interactions are aligned with the common, more limited end-of-the-year evaluations is discussed in the subsection "Structuring the Use of Information in Interpreting Situations and Actions."

SCALING UP

The argument structure of the previous section is quite flexible with respect not only to psychological perspectives but also to whether it is constructed before or after observations, to whether an argument is crafted for each new case or the same framework is used for multiple episodes or students, and to how much judgment and additional information may be required for intermediate inferences.

Practical work is not so accommodating. Each assessment has purposes to serve and constraints to meet. Just who needs what information, for what use, at what scale, with what costs, and with what implications for learning at the system level? We may distinguish between small-scale assessments, used in context to guide learning that exploits local additional information and supports local uses, from assessments in which certain key users are distant from the learning context in terms of time, space, and information. These properties characterize large-scale uses, which have the additional property of needing to make assessment arguments for many students.

How can assessment arguments be scaled up and made portable? What trade-offs to the qualities of evidence and the validity of inferences result?

Do the tradeoffs differentially affect arguments from different psychological perspectives? Four courses of action for designing assessments at large scales and conveying information outside the immediate situation are:

- using the same argument structure for many students;
- making the machinery – that is, the processes and artifacts by which the assessment argument is affected – formal and explicit;
- structuring the use of information in interpreting assessment situations and students' actions, and in particular constraining the use of additional information; and
- using probability-based reasoning to synthesize bodies of evidence and characterize the strength of information they provide for claims.

Using the Same Argument Structure for Many Students

The assessment argument structure can be applied to classroom quizzes and standardized achievement tests, to coached practice systems and computerized tutoring programs, and to the informal conversations students have with teachers. In the last of these examples, decisions about kinds of observations, tentative hypotheses, and reasoning from one to the next are unconstrained and assembled on the fly. In the rest, a framework has been predetermined for the kinds of data that will be gathered, the kinds of claims that will be made, and the rationales that support the inference.

If we foresee that similar data can be gathered for similar purposes on many occasions, we can achieve efficiencies by developing standard procedures both for gathering the data and reasoning from it (Schum 1994, 137). A narrative space is predefined – a general story line, the kinds of claims that can be proposed, and the range of data that will support them. The tradeoff is that on one hand, a well-designed protocol for gathering data addresses important issues in its interpretation, such as thinking through the kinds and amounts of evidence that are required to support claims and to head off certain likely or pernicious alternative explanations. The warrant and the backing for many individual arguments can be communicated to the remote user. On the other hand, only those stories that can be framed in the predetermined narrative space can be told.

The term "standardization" associated with testing is best understood in terms of argument structures that are to some degree determined in advance. Standardization concerns the structure of the argument and selected aspects concerning settings, standards, rubrics, representations, instructions, or contexts – and possibly, but not necessarily, the form of the data. We mean to avoid the colloquial identification of standardization with multiple-choice items, independent work, and time limits. There are hundreds of aspects of any assessment that could be standardized or not, to varying degrees, in myriad configurations. They can concern different parts of the assessment argument. Standardization is a strategy for heading off certain alternative explanations for good or poor performance, such as varying amounts of time or support, that could affect students' performance for reasons unrelated to our purposes and thereby weaken claims.

Concerning the situations in which students will act, the idea is to foresee which features of the prospective action-within-situation need to be satisfied by the person in the situation in order to satisfy the requirements of the warrant through which inference will be made. That is, at least some of the conditions of the situation are arranged so that the data concerning the situation needed in the assessment argument will be applicable. The nature of the features depends in part on the psychological perspective in which the warrant is framed. One can predetermine objective features of the situation as seen from the assessor's point of view (e.g., circumstances, directives, materials, and affordances provided in the assessment situation), or more generally stated characteristics of the situation that may be determined by the assessor with additional knowledge of the student, chosen by the student under given constraints, or negotiated by the student and the assessor in ways that satisfy generally stated features of the assessment setting. In behaviorist arguments, objective features are all that count. Objective features may usefully be specified in trait, information-processing, and S/SC arguments as well, but generally stated characteristics are increasingly important, to be determined by specific instantiations that satisfy the generally stated characteristics as they apply to particular individuals and their circumstances. Recall the example of language assessment texts that the assessor knows to be familiar or unfamiliar to a particular student. A student's topic for her AP Studio Art concentration is an example of a negotiated determination of specifics. Two examples of concentrations are as follows (Myford and Mislevy 1996):

My concentration project grew out of a desire to explore angularity in a medium (clay "wheel work") which doesn't easily permit a graceful, lyrical expression of that term. I was initially intrigued by random geometric shapes depicted on rounded surfaces – often repeated on appendages of the main work – sometimes incised or emphasized by a glazing technique. Recently, I have begun to investigate those same geometric planes literally piercing one another as I have initiated an exploration of metal and wood. Reflective qualities and light(ing) have frequently been a concern as well.

The subject of my concentration is minimalist oriental landscapes particularly reminiscent of Chinese and Japanese landscapes. My fascination with landscapes and intense color use inspired me to emulate ancient oriental styles along with minimalist simplification of forms and clutter. I utilized their techniques of depicting the serenity of nature through simple yet bold brushstrokes and colors. My materials comprised watercolors and airbrush. My series began with uncomplicated scenery and gradually building on to bolder use of form and color.

The actions of a student within the assessment situation preconstruction again look ahead to what kinds of features of actions-within-situations are needed in the argument and guides or constrains students' actions so that what they say, do, or make can exhibit the relevant qualities. That is, at least some of the conditions of the assessment are arranged so that the data concerning the student's actions needed in the assessment argument will be applicable. Of all the activity in the assessment setting, certain expectations are made clear to the student regarding the form of the performance that is expected, the qualities it should exhibit, and the (possibly overlapping) qualities in terms of which it will be evaluated. Specific work products may be defined as the agreed-upon trace of action that will constitute the body of evidence to be evaluated – anything from vectors of multiple-choice responses, to keystroke level traces of actions in Hydrive, to videotapes of teaching classroom lessons in teacher certification examinations. Again, the nature of the features depends in part on the psychological perspective in which the warrant is framed. Also, one can again predetermine objective features of the performance as seen from the assessor's point of view (e.g., selection of alternatives, successful repair of a fault in the hydraulics system, completion of the required number and form of pieces in a AP Studio Art concentration) or more generally stated characteristics of the performance that may be determined by the assessor with additional knowledge of the student, chosen by the student under given constraints, or negotiated by the student and the assessor in ways that satisfy generally stated features of the targeted performance. In behaviorist arguments, objective features are all that count. Objective features may usefully be specified in trait, information-processing, and S/SC arguments as well, but generally stated characteristics are increasingly important, to be evaluated in specific performances in accordance with the generally stated characteristics as they apply to particular individuals and their circumstances.

Procedures for evaluating students' performances are again predetermined in specifics or in general terms to be later specified, as may be required to suit the warrant that justifies inference in the assessment argument. Procedures for evaluating students' work products are typical in large-scale assessments. The specified procedures could be automated or require human judgment. The more complex the performances, however, the more important it becomes that students understand the qualities and criteria the evaluation procedures embody. Again, the move away from behavioral arguments is a critical link in not only the assessment argument but in the learning. In Hydrive, understanding that space-splitting in a problem space is a positive feature in evaluation is a facet of understanding what space-splitting is and recognizing when to do it. In assessments such as AP Studio Art and teacher certification examinations, coming to understand the evaluation procedures is integral to learning goals: "[Q]uestions of what is of value, rather than simple correctness ... an episode in which students and teachers might learn, through reflection and debate, about the standards of good work and the rules of evidence" (Wolf et al. 1991, 51).

Few large-scale assessments are less standardized in the traditional sense than the AP Studio Art portfolio assessment. Students have an almost unfettered choice of media, themes, and styles. Yet the AP program provides considerable information about the qualities students need to display in their work, what they need to assemble as work products, and how raters will evaluate them. This allows for a common argument and heads off alternative explanations concerning unclear evaluation standards.

Predetermining all or some links in an assessment argument and then preconstructing assessment elements and prearranging procedures to effect those links offers efficiencies, but it admits the possibility of cases that do not accord with the common argument. The assessor thus acquires two responsibilities: to establish the credentials of the evidence in the common argument and to detect individuals for whom the common argument does not hold. Inevitably, the theories, generalizations, and empirical grounding for the common argument will not hold for some students. These instances call for additional data or different arguments, often on a case-by-case basis.

Predefining the narrative space does not specify the psychological perspective underlying that space, but the implications of this constraint are felt more sorely from an information-processing perspective than from a behavioral or trait perspective, and even more from a S/SC perspective. One loses, it would seem, tailored arguments, thick descriptions, and "emic" (as opposed to "etic") claims. At the level of the distant user of large-scale assessment results, this is generally true. The final AP Studio Art portfolio scores that colleges use to award credit or waive prerequisites are simply numbers on a 0 to 5 scale. As discussed in the subsection "Structuring the Use of Information in Interpreting Situations and Actions," however, the rating process first entails multiple emic (if brief) evaluations of each portfolio; raters then map from their constructed understandings of a body of work to numeric summaries

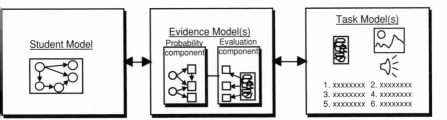

Figure 10.3. High-level view of central models of evidence-centered assessment design.

of the performance in terms of a common framework of evaluation (Myford and Mislevy 1996). To ensure coherence with the S/SC perspective on learning, it is necessary that these private evaluations be cast in the same public framework of meaning that underlies the dispersed-classroom interactions. The probability-based models used in AP Studio Art evaluations, and discussed in the subsection "Using Probability-Based Reasoning," contribute to this end.

Making the Machinery Formal and Explicit

External forms of knowledge representation support distributed cognition, or people working together on tasks that are large, complex, extend over time and space, and use specialized information from multiple sources. These adjectives apply to large-scale assessment. Good knowledge representations embody key entities and relationships in a domain and help people plan and conduct their work in concert with the fundamental principles of the domain. The student, evidence, and task models in the evidence-centered approach to assessment design (ECD) proposed by Mislevy, Steinberg, and Almond (2003) are meant to serve this purpose (Figure 10.3 gives a high-level view of the central models, omitting internal structure and details). These models provide schemas for processes, protocols, and artifacts in educational assessments in order to plan assessments that embody an assessment argument, as described in the section "Assessment as Argument."

In brief, the student model specifies the variables in terms of which we wish to characterize students. It is most closely related to the claims in a Toulmin argument structure. Task models are schemas for ways to get data that provide evidence about students. Task models specify circumstances of observation and students' work products, both of which are involved as forms of data in the Toulmin structure. Evidence models consist of two components that are links in the chain of reasoning from students' performances to their knowledge and skill: The scoring component contains procedures for extracting the salient features of student's performances in individual task situations – that is, ascertaining the values of observable variables – and the probability component contains machinery for updating beliefs about student-model variables in light of this information. The scoring component concerns the reasoning from students' actions to the salient aspects thereof. The probability model concerns synthesizing these data, possibly across multiple tasks, in terms of belief about students, as caricatured in terms of "student-model variables." (As discussed in the subsection "Using Probability-Based Reasoning," student-model variables are better thought of as vehicles for summarizing a reasoner's observations than as properties of students per se.) In informal assessments, this component corresponds with inferences about a student in some terms that rise above the particulars of the performance. In formal assessments, the variables in the student model are the observable variables related through probability models (also discussed in "Using Probability-Based Reasoning").

A more fully detailed representation that can be used for operational work expresses these structures in terms of an object model and a corresponding equivalent XML specification (Riconscente, Mislevy, and Hamel 2005). Filling in the schema as appropriate to an assessment argument explicates the elements needed to make the assessment operational. The goal of standards and protocols is to have structures that maximize sharing while minimizing constraints on the content and meaning of what is shared, much as routers can move packets of information from one computer to another over the Internet without regard to the content of the message as the user sees it, be it text, numbers, music, images, or political tracts with diametrically opposed positions. In structures for assessment elements, just how those elements are fleshed out and what meanings they will acquire in use depends on the assessment argument, which may be cast in any of the psychological perspectives discussed previously. For assessments cast according to different perspectives, the models and variables can have similar formal structures but very different situated meanings. They are alike in some ways, such as the roles they play in argument structures and connections they have with other elements of the assessment, but differ as to the meanings derived from the nature of the data and the claims they are meant to support – much in the way that words acquire situated meaning in contexts ("The coffee spilled, get the mop" versus "The coffee spilled, get a broom" versus "The coffee spilled, stack it again"; Gee, this volume, chapter 8).

Insights from Hydrive and AP Studio Art suggest two ways that explicit structures can facilitate designing larger-scale assessments that are consonant with S/SC considerations. First, the "mechanical" elements can be shared more efficiently. Second, the articulation between assessment arguments and the elements of operational assessment reveals how activities and contexts impart meaning to the elements, and those meanings are (at least, should be) driven by purposes and perspectives rather than by processes and forms.

A student model variable according to a behaviorist assessment might stand for the probability that a student will produce the targeted response to a randomly selected stimulus condition in a behavioral domain. The data that constitute evidence are observers' evaluations of actions, made as objectively as possible, in situations structured as objectively as possible to meet the requirements of the stimulus situation description in the behaviorist warrant. An example is successful repairs of hydraulics system faults in Hydrive to determine whether a trainee is ready for the flight line. Note that a behaviorist assessment argument serves a useful purpose here and is concordant with a learning environment cast in information-processing and sociocultural terms.

Yet the claim space and supporting-data space are not sufficient for the purpose of helping a trainee who is not doing well to improve. Assessment cast according to information-processing perspective is needed (Steinberg and Gitomer 1996), with finer-grained student model variables keyed to practice modules that address facets of declarative, procedural, and strategic knowledge. S/SC considerations remain in the background, because the assessment is embedded within the particular technological and social training environment. The meaning of the student model variables is situated in this context by construction. Are students' values on these variables, reflecting as they do actions within the context, useful for trait-style inferences for other purposes and contexts, such as predicting performance on the flight line or proficiency with different aircrafts? The information-processing research upon which they are based provides some backing to suggest that they may be, in terms of similarities in the reasoning structures that are required across contexts; similarities in affordances and social situations of use offer backing from an SC perspective. Empirical validity studies for the trait-based predictions would be required, though, to provide more fully satisfactory backing for trait-based inferences of this sort.

AP Studio Art portfolio final scores are obtained through the use of psychometric models that were developed for behavioral and trait-based assessment. Yet their situated meanings emerge from the system of learning, producing work, and rating performances. The challenge students and teachers face during the course of the year, and the challenge the central raters face at the end of the year, is to create situated meanings for common standards for quite different behaviors in different contexts – yet in a way that is generally agreed on as valid and fair. As noted earlier, one student's concentration focused on "angularity in ceramics," while another's dealt with an "application of techniques from traditional oriental landscapes to contemporary themes." It would be easier to compare students' performances if everyone were required to work with angularity in ceramics or oriental landscape, or a prespecified sample of topics. Yet these ways of determining the assessment context provide no opportunity to obtain evidence about conceptualizing and realizing one's own artistic challenges. How well the ceramics student might have fared with oriental landscapes is not directly relevant to the claim of interest. What does matter, and what AP Studio Art must examine the fidelity of, is inference about the more abstractly defined qualities that should be evinced in any student's chosen concentration. The emergent meanings of final numeric ratings in AP Studio Art, then, are neither as estimates of proficiency in a domain of behaviors (a behaviorist perspective) nor as measures of qualities inherent in students (a trait perspective). They are, rather, summary evaluations of particular achievements in contexts crafted to help students learn both techniques and ways of thinking in art (an S/SC perspective).

Structuring the Use of Information in Interpreting Situations and Actions

The preceding section discussed how prestructuring spaces of claims and data is one way to scale up, at the cost of flexibility in interpretation. This section considers approaches to prestructure data interpretation that allow some degree of contextualization that is particularly important in arguments cast in SC terms.

Figure 10.4 accommodates the situation of an observer of a student acting in an assessment situation and noticing, in real time and interactively, salient aspects of action and situations as they unfold; constructing claims; re-examining action and situation anew; noticing new aspects; revising claims; and so on. This is how teachers informally assess their students as they interact in small groups, for example, to see how each student is developing ways to communicate mathematical ideas as they solve problems. Figure 10.4 enlarges the assessment argument portion of Figure 10.2 and includes an oval that represents the purview of this "local reasoner." Everything the teacher knows about students, their histories, and their relationships to the situation and to each other is available for fashioning claims and interpreting actions and situations as they unfold. It may be the case that claims and data interpretations are developed jointly with students, as in the daily interactions in AP Studio

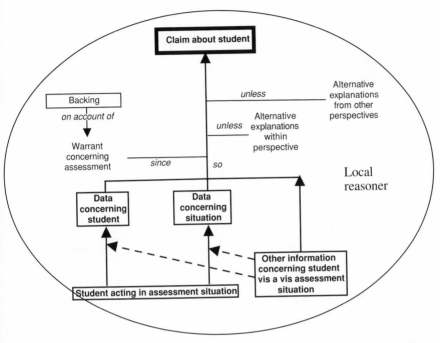

Figure 10.4. Toulmin diagram for an assessment argument, showing the purview of a local reasoner in a fully connected environment with all argument elements in play.

Art classrooms. In this fully connected environment, one can construct and instantiate assessment arguments from any psychological perspective – in particular, those from an SC perspective that demand individualized interpretations of actions in situations.

Of course, just because someone is carrying out assessment in a fully connected environment does not guarantee that the inferences are good. In most domains, novices differ from experts by not always knowing what to look for, how to interpret what they see, and what to do next (Salthouse 1991). Teaching is no exception. Student assessment is one of the standards for accomplished practice that the National Board for Professional Teaching Standards (NBPTS) addresses in its portfolio assessment for NBPTS certification. The preparation material for preparing a portfolio of one's practice in Career and Technical Education, for example, asks candidates if their portfolios will be able to "present evidence of how you use assessment of student work to support learning goals, to facilitate students' growth as career and technical education students, and to inform and shape your teaching practice."[1] Inexperienced teachers can have difficulties because they don't have a good understanding of how students learn, sufficient familiarity with the learning

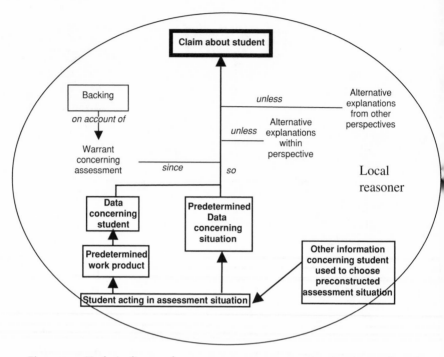

Figure 10.5. Toulmin diagram for an assessment argument, showing the purview of a local reasoner with predetermined work products and assessment situation and no links with contextual information in interpretation.

domain itself, know how to interpret students' actions, or shape situations that will provide clues about students' understanding.

By contrast with an unconstrained assessment in a fully connected environment, a teacher can give a test with well-defined tasks and features predetermined to evoke evidence about some targeted capabilities, to be completed individually and evaluated on the basis of features of prespecified work products alone. Figure 10.5 illustrates this situation. Everything is still under the purview of the local reasoner (i.e., the teacher), but the contextual information does not play a role in determining the data about the student's performance; their evaluations follow predetermined procedures, anything from key matching to human judgment into a common framework. Each of these links could be more fully detailed as Toulmin diagrams in their own right, with warrants, outcomes as claims, and alternative explanations. Generally, contextual information does play a role in determining the data about the situation; however, although the tasks are predefined, the choice of these tasks at this time is motivated by a knowledge of where the students are in their course of learning and options for further learning that can be

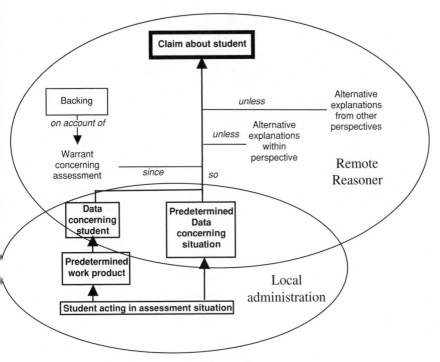

Figure 10.6. Toulmin diagram for an assessment argument for a remote reasoner, show-ing locally gathered data with work products and assessment situation preconstructed and no links with contextual information in interpretation.

informed by the evidence the tasks will evoke. The teacher's inferences are also conditioned by this information.

Consider the reasoner who is distant from the assessment episode or who must deal with hundreds or thousands of assessment episodes. It is not pos-sible to carry out tailored argument construction and observation in a fully connected environment (Figure 10.4). Even with prestructuring, this rea-soner must limit the information he or she works with, or reason with data that summarize more contextualized evaluations from local reasoners. The quality of the local evaluations becomes an issue to the remote reasoner: How can one gauge quality without knowing what information was used or the reasoning process that led to the summary?

To outward appearances, the most common way of scaling assessment up looks very much like the procedures described above for the contextualized use of prestructured situations and interpretations in the classroom. The data interpretation phases of large-scale "drop in from the sky" tests are shown in Figure 10.6. The targeted space of claims is predetermined, as are features of tasks that are meant to elicit evidence to support the claims, specifications of student work products, and evaluation procedures. The features of tasks are known to the remote reasoner (perhaps they were crafted to evince, for example, national science standards). What is missing is the contextualization of the tasks with respect to students' instructional and personal histories. Even if the same evaluations of work products are derived from the same performances, their meanings for the remote reasoner differ from those of the local reasoner. The space of claims that can be supported, and the space of interpretations of the situated actions available to support claims, are both more constrained. Less information is used, but less information is needed to accompany the data for a distant user to know the conditions and procedures that led directly to the data in hand. For arguments cast in behavioral terms, the constrained claim and data space may be fully sufficient. As one moves to trait, information processing, and then to sociocultural arguments, the same data provide less satisfactory evidence to ground the claims of interest; too many alternative explanations accord with the observations.

Figures 10.7 and 10.8 represent two configurations midway between the fully connected local environment for reasoning (Figure 10.4) and the configuration for "drop in from the sky" assessment (Figure 10.6).

Figure 10.7 is the approach taken by AP Studio Art. A work product (e.g., the pieces in the "concentration" section of a portfolio) is provided to the distant reasoner, the myriad details of its genesis and execution stripped away. Yet the evaluation of the work and the aspects of the situation in which the work was conceived and carried out are summarized in written explanations that accompany the portfolio. The student submits not only the pieces but also paragraphs describing the concentration, relating it to the standards and discussing his or her goals, intentions, influences, and other factors that help explain the series of works. This material helps the raters figure out just what it was the student had in mind when producing the series of works in his or her concentration. This is effectively an opportunity for the student to negotiate how the necessarily general principles expressed in the rubrics should be applied to his or her particular work. In the subsection "Making the Machinery Formal and Explicit," we stressed how it was important that the student situate the meaning of the standards in his or her own work, to serve the goals of learning cast in SC terms. Here we stress how it is important that the rationale for this situated meaning be communicated to the distant reasoner (the central raters) to insure coherence between local understanding with systemwide understanding.

Figure 10.8 is an alternative approach for using contextual information locally in large-scale assessment systems. Here the data evaluations are

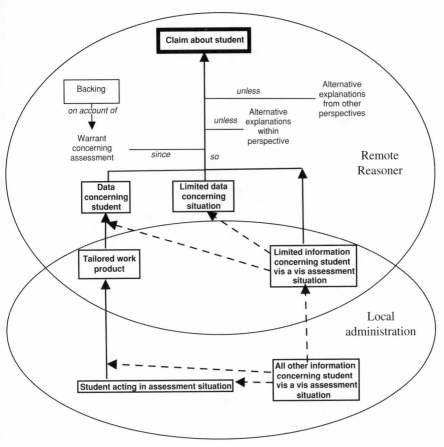

Figure 10.7. Toulmin diagram for an assessment argument, showing a remote reasoner with locally tailored work products and assessment and some limited contextual information for remote interpretation. This is the case of AP Studio Art portfolio concentration sections.

done locally, possibly using additional contextual information, by the local reasoner. The distant reasoner obtains summary evaluations but not the additional information about the situation and the relationship between the student and the situation, which may be integral to the local evaluation. How can the distant observer gauge the value of the local evaluations? Social networks, shared examples, and workshops, as employed in AP Studio Art, all help. More formal strategies include audits (Resnick 1997), shared benchmark performances and interpretations, and semicontextualized evaluations across localities, by which local applications of standards can be adjusted to comport better with systemwide evaluations of comparable work. The "social

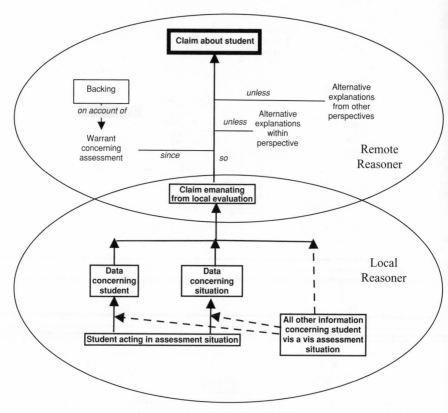

Figure 10.8. Toulmin diagram for an assessment argument, showing a remote reasoner obtaining summary local evaluations of students' actions within assessment situations.

moderation" schemes for adjusting state assessments in Australia reflect the last of these strategies (Linn 1993).

Using Probability-Based Reasoning

Toulmin offers no recipe for characterizing the degree of belief we should assign to claims in a data-based argument or for combining evidence across multiple, possibly overlapping or conflicting pieces of data. Probability-based reasoning supports coherent reasoning from data to claims, specifically through Bayes' theorem. We may construct a probability model that approximates the key features of the situation in terms of variables and their interrelationships. Although probability-based models can be constructed for unique situations (Kadane and Schum [1996] do so for the 395 pieces of evidence in the Sacco-Venzetti trial), it is more common in assessment to preconstruct probability models.

There is an important difference between the variables in a probability model and the corresponding entities, claims, and data in a Toulmin diagram. A claim in a Toulmin diagram is a particular proposition that one seeks to support; a datum is a particular proposition about an aspect of an observation. A variable addresses not only the particular claim or observation, but also other claims or observations that could be entertained. If you know the value of a variable, you also know what it is not. Shafer (1976) defines a "frame of discernment" as all of the possible subsets of combinations of values that the variables in an inferential problem at a given point in time might take. The term "frame" emphasizes how a frame of discernment circumscribes the universe in which inference will take place. The term "discernment" emphasizes how a frame of discernment reflects purposive choices about what is important to recognize in the inferential situation, how to categorize observations, and from what perspective and at what level of detail variables should be defined.

The two main kinds of variables in probability models for assessment are often called student model variables and observable variables (Mislevy, Steinberg, and Almond 2003). Both terms are a bit misleading. Observable variables are associated with aspects of students' situated actions, but they are not actually observed as such. Rather, they are evaluations of things students say, do, or make in situations, through some perspective, and, as has been noted above, possibly conditioned on contextual knowledge about the interrelationship between the student and the situation. AP Studio Art ratings exhibit this character: A rater maps from an emic interpretation of a body of work and a student's explanations into an etic expression in a common framework of evaluation, a value on an observable variable (also see Schutz and Moss 2004). Observable variables are the boundary of the probability model, and the probability model itself places no constraints on the ways, perspectives, or procedures by which values are obtained.

Similarly, student-model variables (SMVs) should not be thought of as literal counterparts of mental capabilities or representations inside students' heads; that is, they should not be reified. Rather, they represent possible ways in which students might be characterized, from the perspective in which an assessment is cast and of a nature grain size that suits the assessment's purpose. As formal entities, SMVs may correspond with conceptions of proficiency cast in trait, behavioral, information processing, developmental, sociocultural, or any psychological perspective. The same perspective will drive the nature of observations and the relationships between them

(Mislevy 2003) – that is, the view of proficiency and its manifestation, in the space of narratives a given probability model is constructed to support.

In a particular assessment with a preconstructed narrative space, we consider a set of aspects of skill and knowledge or propensities or exhibitions toward actions in various situations. These are the variables in a space of student models, particular configurations of values that approximate the multifarious knowledge or propensity configurations of actual students. Depending on the purpose, one might distinguish from one to hundreds of aspects of competence in a student model space. They might be expressed in terms of categories, qualitative descriptors, numbers, or some mixture of these; they might be conceived as persisting over long periods of time or apt to change at the next problem-step. They may concern tendencies in behavior, conceptions of phenomena, available strategies, or levels or aspects of developing expertise. The particular form of the student-model space in a given application is driven by a conception of the nature and acquisition of competence in the context of interest, and the goals and philosophy of the instructional component of the system.

The basic idea is this (see Mislevy 1994, 2003; and Mislevy and Gitomer, 1996, for fuller discussions): In the narrative space, there are different ways we might want to describe a student. Different things we might want to say correspond with different values of SMVs. Hypothetical students with different values of these variables would be likely to act differently in given situations, such as making predictions in line with impetus theory, compared with Newton's laws, if they have certain misconceptions about force, or requiring more support to set up an investigation of an ecological problem. A model is fit from initial observations, which approximates probabilities of observable variables (i.e., salient aspects of situated actions) by hypothetical students at various possible configurations of values of SMVs. Then, in the operational-assessment setting, a real student carries out actions. They are evaluated. Probabilities can be calculated to express how likely those particular actions would be from a student at any given values of SMVs. Extensions to this basic scenario include (1) being able to condition these calculations on contextual variables, student background variables, and aspects of student–situation interrelationships; (2) additional layers in models that correspond with similarities and influences of grouping variables such as schools or classrooms; and (3) effects for raters, so that variation in judgments at the level of mapping situated actions into values of observable variables can be studied. The last of these, which we see next, plays an important role in AP Studio Art.

Figure 10.9 is the student model in Hydrive. It shows a set of evidence models, or clusters of related observable variables that characterize aspects

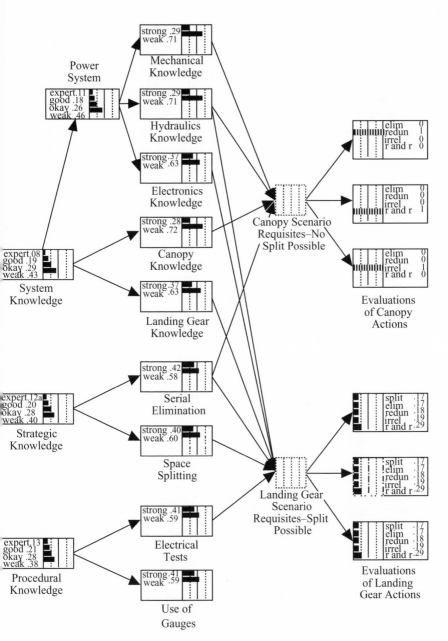

Figure 10.9. Hydrive student model and evidence model.

of students' actions as they work through a problem. Observable variables are defined not in terms of objective aspects of students' actions. Rather, their values take situated meaning as interpretations of sequences of actions in light of a theory of problem solving and a history of the student's actions in the system: A student works him- or herself into a situation; the simulator is able to define an active path of components; the simulator also computes what is knowable about the state of the system given the actions the student has taken thus far. It is then possible to characterize an action sequence as consistent with space-splitting or serial elimination, remove and replace strategies, or determine if it is redundant or irrelevant.

The situated meaning of the SMVs arises from three sources:

- semantic interpretations motivated by an information-processing perspective, according to which troubleshooting actions results from a conjunction of declarative, procedural, and strategic knowledge required in local contexts;
- operational interpretations arising from the way patterns of effective and ineffective troubleshooting actions are synthesized in terms of modeled belief about higher or lower values of the student models that have been involved; and
- action-oriented interpretations in that belief shifting to low values of particular SMVs suggests a lack of skill or understanding or a type and at a grain size that a corresponding practice or tutorial module is likely to help.

In Hydrive, the SMVs are not meant to be measures of traits or simulacra of structures inside trainees' heads. They are effectively pattern recognizers that scan fairly unconstrained sequences of actions in the problem space and note incidents where practice modules are likely to improve proficiency. An information-processing perspective guided the construction of the simulator, the interface, and instructional strategy, and the context and practices of Hydrive's use grounds the situated meaning of the student-model and observable variables.

In AP Studio Art, probability-based models are used to analyze and summarize patterns in ratings across portfolios, students, sections, and raters. An AP portfolio rating session produces more than 100,000 ratings. A probability model is used to analyze information at the emic level, in the form of judges' ratings, although those evaluations summarize individualized emic evaluations that incorporated summaries of contextual information from the students themselves – all this in what is meant to be a common framework of evaluation, insinuated in the general rubric and fleshed out by many examples. The rater-effect statistical models that are employed originated in trait psychology but have evolved to study patterns of variation and consistency across ratings far too numerous to examine individually in depth: Patterns such as amounts of variation expected among informed raters, signals for anomalous scores that merit further attention, and indications of the accuracy of scores obtained in a given rating design as judged against the distribution of ratings that might have occurred had all raters evaluated all work. In this way, those responsible for fairness and validity can identify atypical instances of ratings, works, or ratings or can become aware of new styles or media that need to be accommodated into the evaluation system. In this way, tools from psychometrics are employed not to "measure traits" but to make workable a vast and geographically distributed assessment system that is grounded in the principles of situated learning.

CONCLUSION

An S/SC psychological perspective provides insights into the nature of learning and knowledge that can and should inform instruction and assessment. These insights were gained by applying detailed methods adapted from fields such as ethnography and discourse analysis. These methods are not practical to apply in their full detail for assessment on larger scales, including some within the classroom and especially those meant to extend beyond classrooms, to people and places distant in time and location, and for which resources are severely limited.

It is sometimes possible to design assessment practices for given purposes and contexts that are at a more apt grain size, but which are coherent with an SC point of view at a finer grain size. Insights and methods gained by working through the years at this grain size in psychometrics and educational measurement can be gainfully employed in this project. One sees the variables at the coarser grain size as emergent phenomena from the finer grain size. The variables may even sometimes use exactly the same measurement-model machinery used by behaviorist- or trait-based assessment to synthesize evidence, but the situated meaning of the variables can be quite different. In a suitable large-scale system, such as AP Studio Art portfolio assessment, one can understand values of reported variables as traces of patterns of action in situations that are locally harmonious with learning goals cast in a S/SC perspective.

ACKNOWLEDGMENTS

This work was supported by the Spencer Foundation's "Idea of Testing" project and the Educational Research and Development Centers Program,

PR/Award Number R305B960002–01, as administered by the Office of Educational Research and Improvement, U.S. Department of Education. The findings and opinions expressed in this report do not reflect the positions or policies of the National Institute on Student Achievement, Curriculum, and Assessment, the Office of Educational Research and Improvement, or the U.S. Department of Education. I am grateful to my Idea of Testing colleagues for stimulating discussions on the issues addressed herein, to Lyle Bachman for discussions on test use arguments, and to Drew Gitomer and Lyle Bachman for comments on an earlier draft.

Note

1. Downloaded from the National Board for Professional Teaching Standards Web site on April 2, 2005: http://www.nbpts.org/candidates/guide/whichcert/08EarlyYoungAdult2004.html.

References

American Council on the Training of Foreign Languages. 1989. *ACTFL Proficiency Guidelines*. Yonkers: Author.

Bachman, L. F. 2005. Building and supporting a case for test use. *Language Assessment Quarterly* 2: 1–34.

Bachman, L. F. and A. S. Palmer. 1996. *Language testing in practice*. Oxford: Oxford University Press.

Bormuth, J. R. 1970. *On the theory of achievement test items*. Chicago: University of Chicago Press.

Chi, M. T. H., R. Glaser, and M. Farr, eds. 1988. *The nature of expertise*. Mahwah, N.J.: Erlbaum.

Collins, A., J. S. Brown, and S. E. Newman. 1989. Cognitive apprenticeship: Teaching the crafts of reading, writing, and mathematics. In *Knowing, learning, and instruction: Essays in honor of Robert Glaser*, edited by L. B. Resnick, 453–94. Hillsdale, N.J.: Lawrence Erlbaum Associates.

Cronbach, L. J., G. C. Gleser, H. Nanda, and N. Rajaratnam. 1972. *The dependability of behavioral measurements: Theory of generalizability for scores and profiles*. New York: Wiley.

Douglas, D. 2000. *Assessing language for specific purposes*. Cambridge: Cambridge University Press.

Enright, M. K., W. Grabe, K. Koda, P. Mosenthal, P. Mulcahy, and M. Schedl. 2000. *TOEFL 2000 reading framework: A working paper* (TOEFL Monograph Series MS-17). Princeton: Educational Testing Service.

Ericsson, K. A. 1996. The acquisition of expert performance: An introduction to some of the issues. In *The road to excellence: The acquisition of expert performances, sports, and games*, edited by K. A. Ericsson. Mahwah, N.J.: Lawrence Erlbaum Associates.

Gasser, H. 1955. *How to draw and paint*. New York: Dell.

Gitomer, D. H., L. S. Steinberg, and R. J. Mislevy. 1995. Diagnostic assessment of trouble-shooting skill in an intelligent tutoring system. In *Cognitively diagnostic assessment*, edited by P. Nichols, S. Chipman, and R. Brennan, 73–101. Hillsdale, N.J.: Erlbaum.

Greeno, J. G. 1983. Conceptual entities. In *Mental models*, edited by D. Gentner and A. L. Stevens. Hillsdale, N.J.: Lawrence Erlbaum Associates.

Greeno, J. G., A. M. Collins, and L. B. Resnick. 1997. Cognition and learning. In *Handbook of educational psychology*, edited by D. Berliner and R. Calfee, 15–47. New York: Simon and Schuster Macmillan.

Greeno, J. G., P. D. Pearson, and A. H. Schoenfeld. 1997. Implications for the National Assessment of Educational Progress of research on learning and cognition. In *Assessment in transition: Monitoring the nation's educational progress, background studies*, edited by R. Linn, R. Glaser, and G. Bohrnstedt, 151–215. Stanford: The National Academy of Education.

Holland, P. W. and H. Wainer. 1993. *Differential item functioning*. Hillsdale, N.J.: Erlbaum.

Kadane, J. B. and D. A. Schum. 1996. *A probabilistic analysis of the Sacco and Vanzetti evidence*. New York: Wiley.

Lave, J. 1988. *Cognition in practice*. New York: Cambridge University Press.

Linn, R. L. 1993. Linking results of distinct assessments. *Applied Measurement in Education* 6: 83–102.

Messick, S. 1989. Validity. In *Educational measurement*, 3rd ed., edited by R. L. Linn, 13–103. New York: American Council on Education/Macmillan.

Messick, S. 1994. The interplay of evidence and consequences in the validation of performance assessments. *Educational Researcher* 23: 13–23.

Mislevy, R. J. 1994. Evidence and inference in educational assessment. *Psychometrika* 59: 439–83.

Mislevy, R. J. 2003. Substance and structure in assessment arguments. *Law, Probability, and Risk* 2: 237–58.

Mislevy, R. J. and D. H. Gitomer. 1996. The role of probability-based inference in an intelligent tutoring system. *User-Modeling and User-Adapted Interaction* 5: 253–82.

Mislevy, R. J., L. Steinberg, and R. Almond. 2003. On the structure of educational assessment. *Measurement: Interdisciplinary Research and Perspectives* 1: 3–62.

Mitchell, R. 1992. *Testing for learning: How new approaches to evaluation can improve American schools*. New York: The Free Press.

Myford, C. M. and R. J. Mislevy. 1996. *Monitoring and improving a portfolio assessment system*. CSE Technical Report 402. Los Angeles: National Center for Research on Evaluation, Standards, and Student Testing (CRESST).

Newell, A. and H. A. Simon. 1972. *Human problem solving*. Englewood Cliffs, N.J.: Prentice-Hall.

Resnick, L. B. 1997. Student performance portfolios. In *Psychology and educational practice*, edited by H. J. Walberg and G. D. Haertel, 158–75. Berkeley: McCutchan.

Riconscente, M., R. J. Mislevy, and L. Hamel. 2005. An introduction to PADI task templates. *PADI Technical Report #3*. Menlo Park, Calif.: SRI International.

Salthouse, T. A. 1991. Expertise as the circumvention of human processing limitations. In *Toward a general theory of expertise*, edited by K. A. Ericcson and J. Smith, 286–300. Cambridge: Cambridge University Press.

Schum, D. A. 1994. *The evidential foundations of probabilistic reasoning.* New York: Wiley.

Schutz, A. and P. A. Moss. 2004. Reasonable decisions in portfolio assessment: Evaluating complex evidence of teaching. *Education Policy Analysis Archives* 12. http://epaa.asu.edu/epaa/v12n33/.

Shafer, G. 1976. *A mathematical theory of evidence.* Princeton: Princeton University Press.

Steinberg, L. S. and D. G. Gitomer. 1996. Intelligent tutoring and assessment built on an understanding of a technical problem-solving task. *Instructional Science* 24: 223–58.

Stewart, J. and R. Hafner. 1994. Research on problem solving: Genetics. In *Handbook of research on science teaching and learning,* edited by D. Gabel, 284–300. New York: Macmillan.

Toulmin, S. E. 1958. *The uses of argument.* Cambridge: Cambridge University Press.

Wolf, D., J. Bixby, J. Glenn, and Gardner. 1991. To use their minds well: Investigating new forms of student assessment. In *Review of educational research,* vol. 17, edited by G. Grant, 31–74. Washington, D.C.: American Educational Research Association.

11 Sociocultural Implications for Assessment II

Professional Learning, Evaluation, and Accountability

Pamela A. Moss, Brian J. Girard, and James G. Greeno

This chapter takes up issues of opportunity to learn (OTL) and assessment at the level of schools, considered as organizations. An effort directed toward improving OTL for students in a school is an effort to bring about learning by the organization that is that school. The question we address is part of the general question of OTL for an organization: What kinds of resources, programs, and commitments may be needed or helpful in an effort to improve the learning effectiveness of a school? In keeping with the focus of this volume, we concentrate on issues of obtaining and using information to evaluate and support an organization's progress in changing its practices and achieving stronger OTL.

In Chapter 9, Moss focuses on the practice of assessment, broadly conceived, within a single (classroom) activity system. Here, we enlarge that focus. Assessments and evaluations used to inform changes in practice across a school are practices that cross the boundaries of activity systems to support professional learning, decision making, and accountability. Here, we consider aspects of such practices, especially ways in which teachers and other participants are positioned in the processes.

We begin with the premise that assessment is (or should be) at least, in part, about professionals learning to support students' learning and, in turn, to support one another's learning. Another way of saying this is that it should be about OTL for the professionals in the educational system as well as for students.[1] Professionals interpret and use evidence in a variety of different contexts at different levels of the educational system: in classrooms; in subject-matter departments; in schools; in district, state, and federal education offices; on school boards, commissions, and legislatures; and so on. They have different decisions to make, different sources of evidence, different resources for interpreting the available evidence, and different administrative constraints on their practice. If we want to understand and improve the practice of assessment for learning, OTL, and accountability, we need to understand how professionals working in these different contexts use evidence. This leads to one important set of questions: What evidence do the professionals working in these very different communities of practice need to know that students are increasingly experiencing the sorts of OTL described in the previous chapters? What evidence do they need to know that the professionals to/for whom they are responsible have the OTL and the resources necessary to support students' learning?

A second premise is that artifacts, like assessments and the routines that surround them, do far more than provide information; they shape people's understanding about what is important to learn, what learning is, and who learners are (appropriated from Lave 1993, 10). This suggests a second important set of questions: How are the understandings and actions of educational professionals shaped (enabled and constrained) by the assessment practices in which they engage? How might assessment systems be designed that support educational professionals in the kinds of learning opportunities described in the previous chapters? Thus, we argue, the same types of questions that the earlier chapters suggest should be asked regarding students' learning opportunities should also be asked regarding the learning opportunities for the professionals, in different activity systems or communities of practice, who support them and one another.

In chapter 9, Moss draws on Engström (2001) to argue that assessments are best conceptualized in terms of interactions embedded in activity systems. Engeström's analysis of an activity system calls attention to people who take on different identities and positions (with respect to one another and their tools); the conceptual and physical tools they inherit, adapt, or produce and use; the norms and routines in which they engage; the objects that focus and motivate their actions; and the other communities of practice or activity systems with which they interact. Moss draws on Jordan and Putz (2004) to characterize assessment practices as endogenous or exogenous (externally focused or imposed) and as inherent (tacit), discursive, and documentary.

In this chapter, we focus primarily on what Jordan and Putz (2004) called "documentary assessment." As Moss describes, Jordan and Putz use the term "documentary assessment" to characterize assessments that produce an enduring record, serve primarily the purposes of external authorities, and "occur primarily to evaluate the extent to which pre-established performance targets have been achieved" (p. 351). Clearly, the assessments (tests and other indicators) states are currently using as part of their standards-based accountability systems are examples of documentary assessments, as are the large-scale assessments described by Mislevy (this volume). As Jordan and

Putz point out, teachers' report-card grades are another form of documentary assessment, as are Lampert's narrative assessments of students' progress. Also, as Moss suggests, Lampert's (2001) book might be considered (a touchstone for) a form of documentary assessment of the OTL in her classroom, one where a teacher has made a case (Greeno and Gresalfi, this volume) for her own practice.[2] In this chapter, we analyze four examples that range along a continuum from one where the information by which a school or classroom is evaluated is primarily externally defined to those that make increasingly more room for evidence that represents local practice in its own terms. We conceptualize these boundary-crossing assessment practices as sources of mediational means (Wertsch 1998; Wertsch, Del Rio, and Alverez 1995) that shape local practice in different ways. We draw as well on Star's conceptions of boundary objects, multiway translations, and ecological studies that trace the use of objects across intersecting social worlds to raise important analytical questions that do "not presuppose an epistemological primacy for one viewpoint" (Star and Griesemer 1989, 389). Using the frameworks presented by Moss, which we will develop further, we raise questions intended to illuminate the affordances and constraints of these different types of assessment systems in terms of both documenting and enhancing OTL as conceptualized by the authors of this volume.

We focus on quite different cases of exogenous – discursive and documentary – assessments that cross boundaries between classroom and school and between school and district or consortium (volunteering schools or districts). While all involve an external mandate or expectation to account for practice, they differ in (Jordan and Putz's) terms of how they negotiate the trade-off between the need for comparable information and the (always partially unique) needs of teachers and students in schools. First, we focus on the common case of large-scale, standards-based assessment. Here, we draw primarily on research that illuminates the impact of standardized assessments at the local level (Distributed Leadership Study at Northwestern) and consider evidence-based recommendations for improving this practice of documentary assessment (Data Wise Project at Harvard). Second, we consider a case where a consortium requires a structured, documented self-study at the school level, followed by the consortium's review of the evidence presented, a school visit, and dialogue between school and consortium personnel (Turning Points Model from the Center for Collaborative Education). Finally, we consider a case that strikes an instructive balance between these different sorts of documentary assessment practices (Institute for Learning at University of Pittsburgh), where the system supports and encourages local variation and allows comparison on relevant dimensions across local contexts. Our goal in this chapter is to raise analytical questions that illuminate the focus of the documentary assessments (what they make visible) and the potential impact of different models on local systems so that responsible parties can make better-informed decisions about how to proceed.

ANALYZING ASSESSMENTS THAT CROSS BOUNDARIES OF ACTIVITY SYSTEMS[3]

Framed from within a sociocultural perspective, a documentary assessment is a cultural tool, or better yet, a set of cultural tools – including artifacts, concepts, and routines – that mediates understanding and (inter)action. In the case of large-scale standardized assessments, for instance, the set of cultural tools includes artifacts like stated goals of the assessment, test forms, standards or domain descriptions, guidelines for evaluating performances, score reports, technical manuals, regulations for users, and so on; it includes concepts that represent what is important to learn and what counts as evidence of that learning; it includes expected practices (rules and norms) like standardized administration formats, independent work, and so on; and it entails an implied division of labor (different roles for test developers, teachers, students, parents, administrators, policy makers, and others) in the construction and use of the information. In Greeno's terms (2002; see Greeno and Gresalfi, this volume), it positions the different actors with differential authority, accountability, and agency for making decisions about how their practice is represented and how those representations should be interpreted and used. In short, it provides a partial vision of an activity system through which the assessment is enacted. As Jordan and Putz (2004) suggest:

The very structure of the instruments and the manner of their administration can be seen as indicative of an applied theory about how a particular organization sees itself working. In this sense, documentary assessments are manifestations of a management rationale, providing a complex set of vocabularies and meanings that are linked to educational, political, and economic concepts the organization is devoted to. (p. 351)

That said, it is important to remember that documentary assessments are always interpreted and used in particular local contexts that shape and are shaped by them. Depending on how they are implemented by the central authority – what practices are required/expected to accompany them – and how they are taken up in the local context, they may involve more or less incentive to conform to their particular vision of learning. As Wertsch and colleagues (1995) note, although cultural tools shape action, they do not determine it (p. 22); "they can have their impact only when individuals *use* them" (p. 22). Furthermore, when individuals use the tools in particular settings, both the tools and the setting (or activity system) are transformed (p. 26). Thus, "mediation is best thought of as a process involving the *potential* of cultural tools to shape action, on the one hand, and the unique use of these tools, on the other" (p. 22; italics ours). As we will see, the same tools can be taken up in quite different ways in different environments, to different effects.

Jordan and Putz (2004) describe some important features of externally used documentary assessment that distinguish it from inherent and discursive forms of assessment. First, they note that when written records are produced and taken out of the context in which they were created, there is a loss of information: "We are no longer operating in the lived world of experience but within a symbol system. . . . This translation always involves loss of contextual information" (p. 351). Second, the written record fixes the content of the assessment and allows it to become mobile (externally available) within a larger system. Third, the translation from lived experience to symbol system allows only certain features of the local context to become visible: "The choice of questions to be asked and variables to be measured by these assessment instruments makes certain aspects of an organization's activities visible [to outsiders] and important and hides others" (p. 351). Thus, fourth, they note, documentary assessment makes comparisons across local contexts possible.

Stripping away the context, the why's and how's of a situation, and the confusion of different circumstances, is precisely what is necessary to make cross-unit comparison possible. In some managerial decision-making situations this is desirable. In others, the price may be too high. (p. 354)

Fifth, although expertise, as judged by endogenous assessment, is based on shared and evolving experience, with exogenous documentary assessment, judgments of expertise are based on externally relevant standards (p. 351). To the extent that such documentary assessments are used across hundreds of local contexts, they can have a powerful and widespread impact, for better or worse (Bowker and Star 1999).

Jordan and Putz (2004) suggest that "[d]ocumentary assessments are fruitfully and appropriately used when the objective is comparison of large organizations, units or subpopulations" (p. 354). However, they caution that overreliance on documentary assessment can, and often does, encourage local participants to focus on established indicators while ignoring other features of their practice. This can lead to what they call "work arounds" – such as

manipulating the numbers, changing work practice, and modifying the organizations' structure, climate, and culture (p. 352) that improve appearance
on the indicators without necessarily engaging in real learning or improving
the underlying practice. Thus, "the question that remains to be answered
is, how can we negotiate the trade-off between the requirements of institutions that need comparable numbers and objective measurements for their
purposes and the learners and teachers in schools and workplaces who need
endogenous assessment derived from the activity to be mastered?" (p. 356).

What is critical for managers is to find out how documentary assessments actually influence local work processes and accounting practices – every time a new
measurement procedure gets designed and then applied. Awareness of com-
plementary assessment methods and their specific affordances, drawbacks, and
unintended consequences could be a step toward collaborative codesign of new
organizational structures within which endogenous as well as exogenous, informal as well as formal, evaluation criteria can flourish. (p. 356)

Drawing on their own research in multiple institutional contexts, they argue
for the importance of research that illuminates (1) how documentary assessment actually functions in both the local context where the information is
produced and the external contexts where it is used; and, equally importantly,
(2) how endogenous forms of (inherent and discursive) assessment function
in the local context and how the design of the environment might further
enhance their use. They see these questions as crucial for leaders in local
contexts to address. Also, we note, although district and state educational
systems cannot have access to such evidence for every school and classroom,
it is equally important for those who develop documentary assessment to
have access to cases that illustrate a range of different responses.

   The concept of a "boundary object" or "boundary infrastructure," developed by Star and colleagues (Bowker and Star 1999; Star and Griesemer 1989)
provides additional theoretical resources for the analysis of documentary
assessments. A boundary object is an object that inhabits multiple heterogeneous social worlds [or activity systems] and enables communication and
cooperation across these worlds. "Boundary infrastructures" involve "objects
that cross larger levels of scale than boundary objects" (Bowker and Star
1999, 287), as is typical with centrally mandated documentary assessments.
As they note, participants from different social worlds each "answers to a
different set of audiences and pursues a different set of tasks" (p. 388), and
"because . . . objects and methods mean different things in different worlds,
actors are faced with the task of reconciling these meanings if they wish to
cooperate" (p. 388). Furthermore, "[u]nless they use coercion, each translator

must maintain the integrity of the interests of the other audiences in order to retain them as allies" (Star and Griesemer 1989, 389).

Thus, a boundary object is a particular kind of cultural tool that not only crosses boundaries of activity systems – like documentary assessments – but is also plastic enough to adapt to local needs while maintaining a common identity across sites (Star and Griesemer 1989, 393). It enables translation and therefore cooperation, but without coercion: "They have different meanings in different social worlds, but their structure is common enough to more than one world to make them recognizable, a means of translation. The creation and management of boundary objects is a key process in developing and maintaining coherence across intersecting social worlds" (Star and Griesemer 1989, 393). In Star and Griesemer's terms, a documentary assessment would function as a boundary object when actors in the local context are able to cooperate in providing necessary information to outsiders while maintaining a productive level of authority and agency over their own practice. Star and Griesemer note that the function of boundary objects cannot be understood from a single perspective. Rather, it requires an ecological analysis that examines both local (situated) and shared meanings, that traces the function of the boundary object across worlds and does not, therefore, privilege a single point of view. To what extent, we will ask, do documentary assessments function as boundary objects?

Thus, with documentary assessments, ideally and eventually, one would want to analyze (examples of) all the activity systems in which the assessment functions (how it shapes and is shaped by the local practice). This would include the activity systems through which the assessment was conceptualized, developed, mandated, and implemented; the school and classroom activity systems in which it is responded to, interpreted, and used; the activity systems involving administrators and policy makers at the district, state, and national levels; the activity systems of students' families and peer groups; the activity systems of professional organizations and teacher education institutions that attend to such information; and the "virtual" activity systems of members of the public who attend to evidence about how their educational systems are functioning.

Each of these activity systems, essentially, represents a learning environment (a stance consistent with Lave and Wenger's [1991] argument that learning occurs everywhere, all the time). In classrooms, the primary learners are students; in schools and districts, the primary learners are teachers and leaders.

Entailed in any documentary assessment is also a theory of learning or progress. The crucial questions regarding the implementation of documentary assessment become (1) what is the theory of learning (implicit or explicit) in the assessment itself; (2) how and to what extent does the documentary assessment shape (and become shaped by) the local activity system; and (3) to what extent does the documentary assessment enhance or detract from the local opportunities to learn? Of course, the answer to this last question must be addressed within a particular set of criteria about what constitutes OTL, and we will use the criteria shared by the authors of this volume (and summarized by Moss, this volume, Figure 9.2).

As Moss notes in chapter 9, Engeström (2001, 133) suggests that "any theory of learning must answer at least four questions: (1) Who are the subjects of learning, how are they defined and located? (2) Why do they learn, what makes them make the effort? (3) What do they learn, what are the contents and outcomes of learning? (4) How do they learn, what are the key actions or processes of learning? The relevance of these questions about learning to these different activity systems becomes even clearer when one considers Engeström's characterization of "expansive learning," in which actors "must learn new forms of activity which are not yet there" (Engeström, 2001, 138). Some aspects of these questions are taken up in Moss's discussion of Lampert's teaching in which she is concerned with her students' developing positive learning identities. The issues they raise come up in another way in our examples involving school leadership, professional development, and externally imposed assessments of school performance. In these examples, the focus of assessment is on supporting learning by teachers and other education professionals to strengthen students' opportunities to learn. Our discussions of examples – taken from the Distributed Leadership study at Northwestern University (Spillane 2006), the Data Wise Project at Harvard University (Boudett, City, and Murnane 2005), the Institute for Learning at the University of Pittsburgh (IFL 2003, 2004), and Turning Points 2000 at the Center for Collaborative Education (Jackson and Davis 2000; NPTC 2001, 2002a, 2002b) – consider programmatic efforts to improve classroom practices in schools.

The theoretical resources we draw on, in this chapter and in chapter 9, suggest a set of questions that might be productively asked of each documentary assessment practice and its potential impact on the activity systems in which it is used (see Table 11.1). These include questions about the stated intent of the assessment, about the potential implications of the assessment, and about the actual function of the assessment in local contexts. Answers to the first set of questions can usually be read relatively straightforwardly from the artifacts produced by the assessment developers. Answers to the second set of questions involve critical analysis of the theory of learning implicit in the artifacts. With these questions in mind, it then becomes important

Table 11.1. Analyzing a Documentary Assessment Practice.

Questions about the Stated Intent of the Documentary Assessment

- What is the stated purpose or intended outcome of the assessment?
- Who or what is assessed?
- What is the focus of the assessment? About what does it provide evidence? What are the intended interpretations (or constructs)?
- How is the evidence to be produced?
- Who requires and/or uses the evidence?
- How is the evidence to be used?
- What artifacts are provided or produced?
- What rules or routines does the documentary assessment entail (and what is left open for local adaptation or participation)?
- With what criteria is the quality of the evidence evaluated?

Questions about the Potential Implications of the Assessment

- What does the assessment make visible about local practice (and what does it leave in the background)?
- What is the developmental trajectory implied in the assessment? What is the conception of learning or progress? Are there contradictions among elements of the system?
- What is the implied division of labor within and across activity systems or communities of practice? How is the power to adapt the design distributed? Who does what, with what authority, agency, and accountability?
- What is the incentive for learning or progress? Why do people learn or progress?

Questions about the Actual Function of the Documentary Assessment in the Local Contexts Where the Evidence is Produced and/or Used

(*These questions focus on the implementation of the documentary assessment in local contexts [classrooms, schools, district offices, etc., some of which produce evidence, some of which use the evidence, and some of which do both]. Ideally, one would begin with a description of the local activity system and its implied theory of learning.*)

- Who actually provides the evidence and how? What are the actions/interactions through which the evidence is produced?
- Who uses the evidence and how? What are the actions/interactions through which the evidence is interpreted and used? How is the evidence interpreted? What additional evidence (inherent, discursive, or documentary) is considered? What decisions are made or actions taken?
- How does the local activity system shape the documentary assessment? To what extent are the answers to these questions consistent with developers' intentions? To what extent are there workarounds?
- How does the documentary assessment shape the local activity system? To what extent does it create contradictions (e.g., in conception of learning, in roles for different actors)? How are those contradictions resolved?
- Given a particular theory of learning or progress (like the conception of OTL espoused by the authors in this volume), how and to what extent does the documentary assessment make things better or worse?

to study the local learning environment as the documentary assessment is implemented, to trace the processes through which the evidence is actually produced and used, to illuminate coherences and contradictions between the local activity system and the activity system implied in the assessment, and to consider the extent to which any evolution in the learning environment enhances (or detracts from) the opportunities to learn for students and for the professionals who support them. Thus, answers to the third set of questions require empirical study of the assessment in use.

In the examples that follow, we present information relevant to the questions about the design of the documentary assessment practice, and we highlight evidence that illustrates the way the assessment can be taken up in local contexts. In our concluding comments, we raise questions based on a more critical analysis of the learning theory implicit in these practices.

Example 1: Responding to Test-Based Evidence[4]

The standards-based reform movement, with its emphasis on performance-based accountability, has focused attention on a particular source of evidence about student learning – standardized tests of student achievement – and a theory about how this information would function within the system. As framed by Elmore and Rothman (1999), following the 1994 reauthorization of Title I of the Elementary and Secondary Education Act (ESEA):

> Generally, the idea of standards-based reform states that, if states set high standards for student performance, develop assessments that measure student performance against the standards, give schools the flexibility they need to change curriculum, instruction, and school organization to enable their students to meet the standards, and hold schools strictly accountable for meeting performance standards, then student achievement will rise. (Elmore and Rothman 1999, 15)

The reauthorization of Title I of the ESEA, the No Child Left Behind Act of 2001 (NCLB), signed into law in 2002, greatly expanded the reach and impact of standards-based assessment, tying federal funds to a particular instantiation of this practice that involves sanctions for schools that fail to make adequate yearly progress on the test-based indicators. Since that time, many volumes and reports have been published with studies of the implementation and effects of these practices and recommendations for how to revise the underlying theory to address the problems that have been observed with standards- and test-based approaches to accountability and reform (e.g., Carnoy, Elmore, and Siskin 2003; Commission on No Child Left Behind 2007; Forum on Educational Accountability 2007; Fuhrman and Elmore 2004;

Herman and Haertel 2005; Peterson and West 2003; Skrla and Scheurich 2004). In Examples 1 and 2, we focus on two programs of research and development that examine ways in which leaders and teachers (might) interpret and use the test-based information.

To illustrate how tests and other sorts of evidence of learning and teaching have been incorporated into activity systems at the school level and how these practices might be analyzed with the sorts of resources described, we draw on examples from the work of Spillane and colleagues at the Distributed Leadership Study (DLS).[5] Although Spillane's focus was on "leadership practice," we can nevertheless read his work for how assessment and other evidence of teaching and learning function.

DLS researchers examine how the relationship between leadership activities and teachers' classroom work is shaped by various institutional/social structures in which they are embedded and by conceptual and material tools that mediate those relationships. *Material* resources or tools include artifacts like students' tests and test scores, curriculum guides, textbooks, other printed materials, Internet and other technology resources, observation protocols, state and district standards, forms, and meeting agendas. These tools "mediate" (shape, enable, and constrain) leaders' actions; the sense leaders make of them in turn mediates the impact of the tool. Similarly, leadership practice is shaped by *conceptual* or *cultural* tools that leaders use to "make sense" of the ideas they encounter. These conceptual resources include "language, theories of action, and interpretive schema" that enable "intelligent social activity" (Spillane, Halverson, and Diamond 2001, 23): "[E]ven when a particular cognitive task is undertaken by an individual apparently *in solo*, the individual relies on a variety of sociocultural artifacts such as computational methods and language that are social in origin" (Spillane, Halverson, and Diamond 2001, 23; citing Wertsch 1991).

Leadership activities take place within *institutional and social structures* that also shape them. These include structures (formal and informal relationships and routines) that have been developed within the school, like subject matter or grade-level departments, faculty meetings or classroom observations, and time and space set aside for teachers to plan together or the lack of such opportunities. They also include the many external structures in which schools and their leaders are embedded, like district and state education agencies, professional organizations, legislative requirements, school–community activities, and so on. These are all contexts and routines that bring people together in various configurations for various reasons. They shape the way leadership is practiced and conceptual and material resources, like tests and test scores, are used.

In one line of work, Diamond and Spillane (2004; see also Diamond and Cooper 2007) contrast the use of test-based evidence in four Chicago schools, two that have been placed on probation and are at risk of being restructured and two that are relatively high performing on the district-mandated tests. They note that leadership practices in all four schools showed evidence of attention to test scores, including prioritizing the subject areas and content covered and providing some form of explicit test preparation activities for students. However, they observe important differences in the ways leaders from the different schools interpreted test-based information and used it to inform instruction.

Both of the high-performing schools used test results to identify macro-trends across the school and focus attention on areas of specific needs. In both schools, the "item analysis" was a diagnostic tool that helped them identify where they should focus their attention. (p. 1164)

At the probation schools, the interpretation and use of the data was less focused on its instructional implications. School leaders discussed the need to improve reading and mathematics and did speak in specific terms about subdimensions of these subject areas but did not speak about specific instructional approaches and strategies, as they did in the high-performing schools. In addition, the data [were] used at these schools in pretty much the form in which [they] came from the district. There was less repackaging of the information and limited analysis of specific trends (with the exception of the identification of specific students who were close to "passing" the exam). (p. 1165)

One way that the instructional focus manifested at these schools is in an effort to increase the number of students at or above cutoff points at benchmark grades. In these approaches, school leaders target certain students or certain grade levels for extra assistance in an attempt to reach minimum acceptable performance levels. (p. 1155)

Diamond and Spillane note that in the higher-performing schools, "the resources to enable data interpretation are higher" (p. 1165), that staff work together to analyze the information provided to define specific instructional needs that provide a basis for instructional decisions, and that they are, therefore, more likely to benefit from the information.

DLS researchers describe a number of new organizational structures implemented at one school where test scores showed notable improvement. The principal, concerned that teachers did not have adequate opportunity for interaction with one another or with outside resources, instituted monthly "breakfast club" meetings where teachers talked together about relevant research articles. These meetings subsequently evolved to include opportunities for brainstorming, experimentation, and design of curricular activities

(Halverson 2003; Spillane 2006). In addition, the school leadership instituted a "five week assessment" practice – locally designed school-wide assessments intended to give teachers more current information on student progress relevant to the skills on the yearly district test. The leadership also took regular advantage of the district's yearly requirement for a "school improvement plan" to promote collaborative planning practices among faculty. These and related practices at this school illuminate how external tests function differently in different learning environments.

Example 2: A Model for Using Test-Based Evidence More Relationally[6]

The Data Wise inquiry model (Boudett, City, and Murnane 2005), developed by researchers and graduate students at Harvard in conjunction with teachers and administrators in the Boston Public School system, provides a rich example of how externally mandated tests can be used as part of a local inquiry process. It illustrates, in our judgment, the potential for external tests to serve as boundary objects. The model consists of three basic phases: Prepare, Inquire, and Act (which are developed in detail in their monograph).

The "Prepare" phase consists of building a foundation for data-driven inquiry in a school community by creating a community of adult learners. The Data Wise team notes that school improvement efforts are likely to be more effective if responsibility for data interpretation is shared among members of a school community. They also suggest that the members must have "assessment literacy" – an understanding of how to read and interpret standardized test score reports. Although this can be initially supported by outsiders, such knowledge and capacity needs to become part of the larger community's repertoire.

As part of the initial phase, the Data Wise team suggests that schools create a "data inventory" of the kinds of data that are present in their system. Examples of common data sources available in schools include standardized test results (including both state and district level tests), developmental reading assessments, observation surveys, running records, writing samples, unit assessments, other student background information (e.g., ethnicity and language proficiency), and attendance records.

During the "Inquire" phase, schools study the data that they have at their disposal already to begin to focus their inquiry and consider other data that may be needed to address their questions. Other types of data that might be developed include, for example, artifacts from classroom practice (such as classwork and homework), student interviews, and teacher peer observations. Data Wise makes explicit the potential and value of data, like student work, to challenge teachers' assumptions:

Examining student work helps to surface and challenge many assumptions –
assumptions about what students can and cannot do, about which students can
do what, and about why students are or are not able to do something. (p. 88)

Examining instruction and attending to the particulars of the classroom is
an important source of evidence for such inquiry.

The Data Wise process then proceeds to action and assessment. In parallel
with the development of an action plan is an emphasis on assessing the
action, which creates a new corpus of data with which to start the inquiry
cycle over again. Furthermore, the criteria for success of the action plan may
include both standardized assessments as well as "home grown" measures
determined by the inquiry team.

Thus, in the vignettes of test use across the DLS and Data Wise projects,
we see examples of how formal and informal evidence of teaching and learning are used by teachers and administrators in different social arrangements.
We see different types of evidence, different resources for interpreting them,
different divisions of labor and positioning of adult learners, and different
understandings of the appropriate outcome. Again, the vignettes make evident the importance of understanding the way assessment functions as part
of a complex activity system.

Example 3: Accountability and Assessment in a School Reform Model[7]

The Turning Points comprehensive school reform model provides an example of a system of assessment of OTL and accountability that takes a variety
of types of evidence into account and allows the individual school to "make
a case" for itself to an external authority. In this particular instance, the
accountability is to a reform model organizer, not a public system such as
a district or state education office, but the Turning Points model (and others like it) give us a sense of the possible in creating new accountability
policies.

The Turning Points school reform model is based on the recommendations
and learning that emerged from both the initial Turning Points report of the
Carnegie Council on Adolescent Development (Task Force on Education of
Young Adolescents 1989) on school reform for adolescents and the subsequent
knowledge developed after a decade of implementing the report's recommendations, which are outlined in *Turning Points 2000* (Jackson and Davis 2000).
Although the major aim of these efforts was to change the way adolescents are
taught, they include administrative changes as well. Eventually, this model
was transformed into a New American Schools comprehensive school reform
model. The National Turning Points Center is administered by the Center

for Collaborative Education, which also coordinates regional centers for the Coalition of Essential Schools and the Boston Pilot School Network.

The Turning Points reform model concentrates on middle schools, which they view as a key transition point in adolescent development. The model centers on seven principles to guide its organization and structure:

(1) Teach a curriculum grounded in rigorous, public academic standards for what students should know and be able to do, relevant to the concerns of adolescents and based on how students learn best;

(2) Use instructional methods designed to prepare all students to achieve high standards and become lifelong learners;

(3) Staff middle grade schools with teachers who are expert at teaching young adolescents, and engage teachers in ongoing, targeted professional development opportunities;

(4) Organize relationships for learning to create a climate of intellectual development and a caring community of shared educational purpose;

(5) Govern democratically through direct or representative participation by all school staff members, the adults who know students best;

(6) Provide a safe and healthy school environment as part of improving academic performance and developing caring and ethical citizens; and

(7) Involve parents and communities in supporting student learning and healthy development. (Jackson and Davis 2000, 23–24)

What is of particular interest for this chapter is how these principles come into play in the day-to-day functioning of a Turning Points school, and more specifically their use in a range of assessment and accountability processes that provide a model in which school personnel collectively account for their own practice in meeting the Turning Points benchmarks.

Overview of Accountability and Assessment

Three Turning Points routines demonstrate how learning, OTL, assessment, and accountability are intertwined deeply in implementation. First, Turning Points emphasizes ongoing use of "data-based inquiry and decision making." The general process is described as follows:

When a school uses data-based inquiry in decision making, it engages in an ongoing process of setting its vision, collecting and analyzing data from a variety of sources in order to identify strengths and challenge areas, creating and implementing action plans to address priorities within the challenge areas, and assessing progress before beginning the cycle of inquiry again. (NTPC 2001, 13–14)

As described, this is an ongoing process in which new goals, plans, and data must be reformulated in response to the particular conditions of the students, teachers, and administrators in each school. Turning Points schools draw from a variety of data sources. All Turning Points schools, for example, administer a "Self-Study Survey" to gather data from students, teachers, and administrators. This survey was developed by the Center for Prevention Research and Development at the University of Illinois and collects information on a spectrum of areas, including "learning, teaching, assessment, teaming, leadership, school climate, and student behavior and adjustment" (NTPC 2001, 14). The results of this survey, which include information disaggregated by race, gender and income, are given to the school to explore and study and to help the teachers and administrators make plans for improvement. Other sources of data used in school and team meetings include state test achievement data, peer classroom observations, and student work. Turning Points provides a protocol for teachers to study student work and do peer observation.

Second, every Turning Points school undertakes an Annual Assessment. This self-assessment is centered around a set of benchmarks, which in turn are based on the Turning Points' six areas of practice, described below. This self-assessment is an *internal* process; it allows the schools to see how they are doing in fully implementing the Turning Points model. The Turning Points benchmark guide describes the process as follows:

The leadership team conducts the initial assessment, and in subsequent years the whole faculty engages in the assessment. The process should take no more than 2–3 hours a day. It does not involve actually collecting evidence, but rather citing evidence collected during the course of the year. This process should include setting specific, measurable annual goals for improving learning, teaching, and assessment. The streamlined benchmarks will be used in this process. (NPTC 2002a, 6)

Third – and the focus of the rest of this section – is the School Quality Review (SQR), a learning and assessment practice involving external participants. The stated goal of both the SQR and the Annual Assessment is "to assess how well a school has implemented the Turning Points design and improved learning and teaching" (NTPC 2002b, 2). This is done using a set of benchmarks, to which we will now turn.

The Benchmarks. The Turning Points benchmarks,[8] which are central to both the Annual Assessment and the SQR, are arranged around Turning Points' six areas of practice:

(1) improving learning, teaching and assessment for all students;
(2) building leadership capacity and a professional collaborative culture;

(3) data-based inquiry and decision making;
(4) creating a school culture to support high achievement and personal development;
(5) networking with like-minded schools; and
(6) developing district capacity to support school change (NTPC 2002a, ix).

These areas of practice are general domains that implement the Turning Points principles. The benchmarks provide more detail, specifying several focus areas for each practice. For each focus area, the benchmarks describe four phases of developmental progression for the school "on its way to becoming a Turning Points school" (NTPC 2002a, 3). Table 11.2 presents a sample benchmark for a focus area ("Assessment") within one practice ("Improving Learning, Teaching, and Assessment for All Students"). Other focus areas under "Practice 1" include elements important to assessing OTL: "High Standards for All Students," "High Achievement for All Students," "Intensive Approaches to Literacy and Numeracy," "Varied Instructional and Learning Strategies," and "Strategies to Address Student Diversity." These benchmarks are used in all three of the routines described here (SQR, Annual Assessment, and Data-based Inquiry and Decision-Making), albeit in different ways. They provide a vision and goals in all three instances. Streamlined versions are used in the Annual Assessment process, and the full benchmarks are used as a framework for both the internal data collection and external review that compose the SQR.

The School Quality Review: A Closer Look
Unlike the Annual Assessment, which happens every year and is an internal process for each Turning Points school, the SQR occurs once every four years and involves *external* accountability. The SQR consists of three major steps. First, the school undertakes a self-assessment process, during which the faculty and administration develop a portfolio of evidence showing progress toward the six benchmark goals for Turning Points schools. Second, the school participates in an external evaluation from a visiting team that uses both the portfolio and its own observations in making its assessment. The team then produces a report for the school, detailing strengths and areas in need of improvement to meet the "systematic implementation" phase of the benchmarks. Finally, the school has a chance to read the report and provide a response, detailing plans for improvement and making corrections, which is then sent to the Turning Points regional and national centers. We now turn to each of these steps in more detail.

Table 11.2. Example of Full Benchmark (adapted from NTPC, *Benchmarks to Becoming a Turning Points School*, 2002, 15).

Focus Area: Assessment	Practice 1: Improving Learning, Teaching, and Assessment for All Students			
	Phase 1: Beginning Implementation	Phase 2: Partial Implementation	Phase 3: Demonstrating Implementation	Phase 4: Systematic Implementation
Authentic and Reliable Assessment (Demonstration of Learning)	Student learning is regularly assessed, but a limited number of assessment strategies are used.	Student learning is regularly assessed. Some authentic assessment strategies (including portfolios, exhibitions, and demonstrations) are being used in some grades and disciplines. Some teachers require students to display mastery of academic and social skills in school and real-life situations.	A number of authentic strategies (including portfolios, exhibitions, and demonstrations) are being used in most grades and disciplines. A majority of teachers require students to display mastery of academic and social skills in school and real-life situations.	Continuous assessments, linked to clearly identified standards, are conducted using multiple assessment authentic strategies (such as portfolios, exhibitions, and demonstrations) in all disciplines and grades. Almost all teachers require students to display mastery of academic and social skills in school and real-life situations.

Internal Process: Portfolio Development. Creating the school portfolio is viewed as an important learning process and time for reflection for the school. One of the elements of the SQR that is of particular interest is that developing the portfolio is both locally determined and guided by external guidelines. On the one hand, the process is "standardized" in the sense that every Turning Points school develops a portfolio to show evidence of fulfilling the goals of the benchmarks, and all schools share the same set of benchmarks against which they are to be evaluated. On the other hand, the process for developing the portfolio and which evidence to include is determined by the individual school. For example, the group tasked with coordinating the portfolio needs to determine for itself answers to questions like "How will the team decide which pieces are included in the portfolio? How will disagreements be resolved? At what point should we obtain feedback from, or bring decisions to, the full faculty?" (NTPC 2002b, 13). Furthermore, the selection of evidence as locally determined allows the school to highlight particular successes and unique local solutions to meeting the benchmark goals.

The process of creating the portfolio extends over several months and is coordinated by a central committee of school personnel. Because of routines and practices like the Annual Assessment and Data-Driven Inquiry, much of the data collection needed to complete the portfolio will already have begun. The portfolio itself contains a wide array of types of evidence for school performance and OTL (although they do not use that term).

What sorts of information enter the portfolio? Examples provided in the SQR guide include meeting minutes, observations, presentations, standardized test results, mission statements, attendance records, samples of teacher and student work, and teacher journals. Of course, the different areas of practice require different types of evidence to fulfill the benchmarks. Table 11.3 illustrates the wide range of evidence that might be included in a portfolio to document its practice on each of the benchmarks.

Given this large range of material that could be included, one can imagine an overwhelming amount of information. Turning Points cautions schools that "the portfolio does not include all possible evidence, but rather a thoughtful selection of evidence" (NTPC 2002b, 14).

The portfolio serves purposes beyond the SQR and functions as a boundary object for more constituencies than just the Turning Points' regional and national centers. The portfolio can also be a way to show community members important information about the school for purposes like recruiting students and fundraising (NTPC 2002b, 15).

External Process: The Visit. Once the school's portfolio has been completed (a process that takes several months), an external team reviews the

Table 11.3. Examples of Evidence for Different Practices (adapted from *Turning Points: Benchmarks to Becoming a Turning Points School*, NTPC, 2002).

The Six Turning Points Practices	Examples of Evidence Collected to Assess: *What are some of the concrete things you would see if this practice was being fully implemented?*
PRACTICE 1: IMPROVING LEARNING, TEACHING, AND ASSESSMENT FOR ALL STUDENTS	• Samples of student work from every content area and grade level from the fall and the spring demonstrate consistency of standards, evidence of curriculum and instruction designed to meet them, and student progress in meeting standards. • Notes and videotapes of classroom observations document a wide range of effective instructional approaches. • Course and curriculum descriptions demonstrate both depth and coverage in meeting standards. • Culminating projects and tasks are integrated into all courses. • Teacher- and class-generated rubrics are used for important skill areas such as writing. • Student work demonstrates revision using rubrics and other forms of explicit criteria. • A "walk through" of the school reveals students actively engaged in individual and group projects. • A wide range of reading material is visible in classrooms and is in use by students. • Improvement in standardized test scores is evident.
PRACTICE 2: BUILDING LEADERSHIP CAPACITY AND A PROFESSIONAL COLLABORATIVE CULTURE	• Notes and observations of teacher common planning time meetings demonstrate a focus on teaching and learning and effective use of time. • Interviews and/or surveys of teachers reveal that they feel planning time and professional development activities support their professional growth. • Notices of study-group meetings, leadership team minutes, and topics for faculty-wide discussions are all indicators of professional collaboration, adult learning, and participation in governance. • Leadership team meeting minutes indicate regular opportunities for all faculty to provide input on school-wide issues and decisions.

The Six Turning Points Practices	Examples of Evidence Collected to Assess: *What are some of the concrete things you would see if this practice was being fully implemented?*
	• All established teams have a defined purpose, measurable performance goals, and norms by which all members operate.
	• A structure and protocol are in place for regular peer observation among faculty. Coaches' logs reflect a wide variety of professional development activities.
	• A schedule of in-school and out-of-school professional development activities is posted.
PRACTICE 3: DATA-BASED INQUIRY AND DECISION MAKING	• A comprehensive school plan incorporates references to data from multiple sources: achievement data, self-study charts, focus groups, attendance, drop-out, and discipline records, etc.
	• Opportunities are scheduled for all faculty groups to look at and analyze data.
	• A school portfolio that demonstrates student achievement and progress through a wide range of measures and evidence of learning.
	• Comprehensive, accurate data are easily and readily accessible to all school and community stakeholders.
	• Faculty committee meeting minutes indicate frequent reference to the school's data.
	• Proposals for change are brought before the Leadership Team and the whole faculty by study groups organized around challenge areas.
	• Clear and measurable performance goals are well publicized and known by teachers, students, parents, and the broader community.
	• Faculty engage individually, in teams, and school-wide in action research that informs planning, curriculum development, learning and teaching.
PRACTICE 4: CREATING A SCHOOL CULTURE TO SUPPORT HIGH ACHIEVEMENT AND PERSONAL DEVELOPMENT	• Every student and teacher is fully dedicated to a small learning community.
	• Higher attendance, fewer discipline referrals, and lower drop-out rates are reported.
	• Schedules include longer blocks of learning and regular teacher common planning time.

(continued)

Table 11.3. (*cont.*)

The Six Turning Points Practices	Examples of Evidence Collected to Assess: *What are some of the concrete things you would see if this practice was being fully implemented?*
	• Heterogeneous groups are the norm and no tracking exists.
	• Interviews and/or surveys of students reveal that they feel known and cared for by a significant number of adults in the school, and that they have a significant role in the school.
	• Structures for academic support and health and social services, such as conference logs and schedules, are in place and are used by many students.
	• Records of student involvement and active participation in classroom and school activities and governance.
PRACTICE 5: NETWORKING WITH LIKE-MINDED SCHOOLS	• Teaching and learning strategies are adopted by one school after observing and documenting them in another school.
	• Written feedback from critical friends' visits is reflected in the goals and plans of the host school.
	• Faculty from different schools meet on a more frequent and informal basis.
	• There is regular attendance at network-organized professional development activities.
	• Individuals and teams attending institutes and other professional development activities of the network present reports and other forms of feedback to the faculty.
PRACTICE 6: DEVELOPING DISTRICT CAPACITY TO SUPPORT SCHOOL CHANGE	• A middle school vision that guides policy and program development for the middle grades is adopted by the district.
	• District staff roles provide direct coaching support to Turning Points schools.
	• School budgets reflect that all resources are being redirected to support Turning Points practices.
	• District policies allow lump-sum budgeting and hiring flexibility.
	• Lump-sum budgeting is in use in all Turning Points schools in the district.
	• The district budget reflects Turning Points priorities.

portfolio and conducts a three-day SQR visit. Each of the three days focuses on a different constituent perspective: the first day focuses on students, and team members shadow students through their day and conduct interviews; the second day focuses on the teachers and staff; and finally, the third day focuses on the school as an organization and as part of the larger community.

Just as Turning Points provides clear guidelines for the school regarding what kinds of evidence to include, they likewise provide guidance to the review team. The team may only rely on the portfolio, their observations during the visit, and district data. The kinds of data obtained from the visit include classroom and school observations, interviews, student work, and other data including tests scores and demographic information (NTPC 2002b, 23).

Based on the evidence gathered through the visit and reviewed in the portfolio, the visiting team then scores the school on the full benchmarks and writes a report. Although the school receives scores for the individual six "practices" and the focus areas that they constitute, no overall score is given because "it is inappropriate to capture the complex picture of the school's development with a single statistic" (NTPC 2002b, 26).

Consequences. The SQR team, on the basis of these scores and their narrative, "will make a recommendation to the Turning Points regional and national centers about the continuing membership of the school in the Turning Points network. In general, a school will be reaffirmed as a member school if it receives ratings of mostly 2 and 3 across the benchmark areas. If the school receives ratings of mostly 3 and 4, it will be affirmed as a Turning Points Demonstration School and will be asked to play a larger leadership role in the national network. Finally, in rare instances, if a school receives ratings of mostly 1, it will be asked to withdraw from the network if the areas of concern are not addressed within an agreed upon timeframe" (NTPC 2002b, 26).

More Boundary Crossing: The School Replies. The final step in the SQR process comes when the school responds to the visiting team's evaluation. "To ensure that the SQR team's report becomes a useful part of the school's ongoing inquiry process, the Portfolio Development Team facilitates a school-wide discussion of the findings. This community discussion, which may take place across several different forums including whole faculty, teacher team, student, and parent meetings, should result in the creation of goals, priorities, and action plans" (NTPC 2002b, 27). Once again, this step is seen as a learning opportunity for the school community and a chance to take action to further improve the school's practices.

What Is the Evidence in Support of the Model?
According to their documentation, the Turning Points model is based on
principles and strategies that are grounded in research on best practices and
cover a wide range of school concerns from democratic governance structures
to high academic press. Several studies have examined the effectiveness of
the overall model when highly implemented.

For example, a study of thirty-one schools in Illinois implementing the
Turning Points recommendations investigated the impact of this reform on
a variety of outcomes using cross-sectional comparison based on the level
of implementation. These schools range in location (e.g., urban, suburban,
rural), size, and student demographics for ethnicity and social class. On academic measures such as the state achievement tests, the study reported that
"across subject areas, adolescents in highly implemented schools achieved at
much higher levels than those in nonimplemented schools and substantially
better than those in partially implemented schools" (Felner et al. 1997, 544). In
addition to these academic outcomes, the study also found that "in the most
fully implemented schools, teachers report far lower levels of student behavior problems than do teachers in less implemented and nonimplemented
schools" (Felner et al. 1997, 544).

More recently, Mertens and Flowers (2004) conducted an analysis of the
effectiveness of Turning Points schools in Boston by comparing them with
a matched control set of schools. Looking at Massachusetts Comprehensive Assessment System data, they found that in 2000, the Turning Points
schools were comparable with their matched peers in the percentage of students testing at "Proficient" and "Advanced" levels in reading and math.
However, within these same categories, "Turning Points schools had higher
percentages of LEP [limited Englsh proficient] students at the *Advanced* or
Proficient (24%) [in reading] compared to the control group (16%), the district (22%), and the state (18%) ... [and in math] had higher percentages of
LEP students at the *Advanced* or *Proficient* (12%) compared to the control
group (6%), the district (9%), and the state (8%)" (Mertens and Flowers
2004, 23).

Furthermore, in their analayses of change within these same Turning
Points and control group schools, Mertens and Flowers (2004) found that
the Turning Points schools "had a 10% gain in the percentage of regular education students at the *Advanced* or *Proficient* level in English language arts.
The control group had only a 0.6% gain, 7% for the district, and 5% gain
for the state" (pp. 24–25). Similar gains were not present in mathematics or
history scores.

Mertens and Flowers (2004) also looked at self-study surveys from the Boston Turning Points schools and compared them with the surveys from 40 middle schools in Arkansas, Illinois, Louisiana, Michigan, and Mississippi with similar demographics and location (i.e., urban middle schools with a high percentage of free- and reduced-lunch populations and similar sizes). This comparison allowed investigation into nonachievement-related variables. For example, the survey also allowed comparison on a range of responses from students, including self-esteem, academic efficacy, depression, and behavior problems. The Boston Turning Points schools had similar results to the 40-school urban sample. Both Boston Turning Points and the larger self-study sample compare favorably with national data on the survey from non-Turning Points schools; Turning Points students "have higher levels of self-esteem and efficacy and lower levels of depression" (Mertens and Flowers 2004, 19)

Example 4: Evaluation in a Program Focused on Professional Development[9]

Our fourth example discusses the Institute for Learning (IFL), which works with urban school district partners, providing materials and assistance, including Institute learning sessions, for their professional development work. In its words, "Since its inception in 1995, the Institute for Learning has served as a liaison between its parent institution, the Learning Research and Development Center of the University of Pittsburgh, and working educators in school systems nationwide. It brings to educators the best current knowledge and research about learning processes and principles of instruction. Its mission is to provide educators with the resources and training they need to enhance learning opportunities for all students. The Institute serves as a think tank, a design center for innovative professional development systems in the schools, and an educator of core groups of school professionals" (IFL 2003).

Design Principles
IFL's strategy was set out in a paper by Resnick and Glennan (2002). Most generally, they believe that a program of educational improvement will be most effective if it is focused on teaching and learning, the instructional core, rather than "tinkering with bureaucratic arrangements and oversight systems while leaving details of instruction to teachers" (p. 4). The IFL program is designed with major attention to results of research that support

assumptions about learning that have significant implications for classroom practices. Resnick and Glennan articulated five design principles that refer to characteristics of districts working toward reform:

(1) a commitment to an effort-based concept of intelligence and education;
(2) a focus on classroom instruction throughout the district;
(3) a culture emphasizing continuous learning and two-way accountability – the core elements of nested learning communities – throughout the system;
(4) continuing professional development for all staff, based in schools and linked to the instructional program for students; and
(5) coherence in standards, curriculum, assessment, and professional development. (2002, 12–13)

The first of these is an interesting transformation of a major research finding, primarily by Dweck (e.g., Dweck 2000; Dweck and Bempechat 1983). Dweck has shown that students who tend to be attracted to and engaged in challenging academic activities also tend to attribute their successes to stable personal characteristics (e.g., being smart) and their failures to transitory personal or situational factors (e.g., being tired or an unfair test), and they answer questions about what it means to be smart in ways that are consistent with an incremental theory of intelligence, in which being smart is assumed to result from experience in activities that adds to one's intellective capabilities. These students have what Dweck called a learning orientation, which contrasts with a performance orientation, shown by students who avoid challenging academic activities, attribute their failures to stable personal characteristics (e.g., not being smart) and their successes to transitory personal or situational factors (e.g., being lucky that day), and answer questions about what it means to be smart in ways consistent with an entity theory of intelligence, in which being smart is assumed to be a fixed, inherent (often, inherited) trait.

IFL's design principle – educators should be committed to an effort-based theory of intelligence and education – is more than a simple application of Dweck's empirical and theoretical advance. IFL's principle advocates a belief about intelligence on the part of professional educators, especially teachers. It assumes, then, that if teachers and other professionals in a district or school hold an incremental theory of intelligence, this will have a positive effect on students' learning. Dweck's research showed that there can be a link between *students'* beliefs about intelligence and their own learning. IFL's principle requires a significant extension of Dweck's conclusion. An argument for this extension was presented by Resnick and Nelson-LeGall (1997).

IFL's third design principle is also an extension of a proposition supported by research. Research on educational reform has shown that having a supportive environment for teachers' continuous learning can be an important factor in the success of reform efforts (e.g., McLaughlin and Talbert 2001). IFL's principle argues for a culture of learning that includes all of the professionals in the system. Its concept of nested learning communities recognizes that learning by members of the community with different responsibilities makes a difference; for example, teachers need to learn in ways that have an impact on their interactions with students and principals, and principals need to learn in ways that have impact on their interactions with teachers and members of the central administration. Yet all members of the community are expected to participate with two-way accountability. The learner is accountable to her or his supervisor(s) for making the effort required for learning to succeed, and the supervisor(s) are accountable for providing resources and support that are needed for the learning effort to be successful.

Principles of Learning

IFL presents itself as "bringing to educators the best current knowledge and research about learning processes and principles of instruction." A significant project has been formulating principles that are based on conclusions of research in terms that make them directly applicable in educational practice. This effort is consistent with an argument presented by A. L. Brown (1994) and J. S. Brown (1991) concerning an essential factor in bringing about significant change in a practice. They argued that the conduct of a practice depends on underlying *first principles* (A. L. Brown) or *tacit assumptions* (J. S. Brown), which organize the practice and that practitioners appeal to in making sense of and justifying their actions. If the practice people want to institute would rest on different assumptions from the ones that are in place, then a change in the practice requires changing the underlying assumptions held by the practitioners. It is possible to change superficial aspects of the practice without changing the underlying assumptions, but that is likely to be ineffective, resulting in a practice that does not achieve its intended goals or is brittle in situations that require flexible understanding.

The Principles of Learning that IFL presents are:

- organizing for effort, which includes:
  - clear expectations;
  - fair and credible evaluations;

- ◦ recognition of accomplishment; and
- ◦ curriculum geared to standards;
- academic rigor in a thinking curriculum;
- accountable talk;
- socializing intelligence;
- self-management of learning; and
- learning as apprenticeship.

As an example, socializing intelligence is the principle that mainly derives from Dweck's research on attributions and beliefs about intelligence. The principle, however, is a set of beliefs and commitments that IFL advocates for the adult members of the school community as well. A slightly expanded statement of this principle is:

Socializing intelligence

- Beliefs
  - ◦ I have the right and obligation to understand and make things work.
  - ◦ Problems can be analyzed and I am capable of that analysis.
- Skills
  - ◦ A tool kit of problem-analysis skills (meta-cognitive strategies) and good intuition about when to use them
  - ◦ Knowing how to ask questions, seek help, and get enough information to solve problems
- Dispositions
  - ◦ Habits of mind
  - ◦ Tendency to try actively to analyze problems, ask questions, get information (IFL 2003)

This statement is more than a translation of Dweck's research findings and conclusions. For one thing, they are *oughts*, not *ises*. They are not in the form of hypotheses that can figure into scientific explanations of activities that we can observe.

They are, however, in a form that can figure into another kind of explanation. This is the kind of explanation that members of a practice can construct for each other so they understand the reasons for their actions, either already taken or planned. They can function as premises in arguments that occur in a discourse of practice. They provide illustrations of articulations of first principles or tacit assumptions. IFL's statement of its principle of socializing intelligence articulates assumptions of a practice that imply reasonable ways of acting if Dweck's conclusions about intelligence are an accurate account of the nature of intelligence. Indeed, Dweck's research and IFL's formulation of this principle provides an example of a way in which the explanatory principles of a scientific account and a set of articulated principles of a practice can be related. They clearly share a great deal of substance, but they are far from being identical.

IFL activities focus on bringing about conceptual change on the part of district personnel to reach understanding of and commitment to the Principles of Learning. In a recent study of three IFL districts, district personnel report that their participation in IFL has advanced their understanding and provided them with language with which to develop plans and a vision for their practices. However, IFL has recognized increasingly that district personnel are likely to need support in developing practices that are consistent with the principles. IFL, therefore, is directing much of its effort toward the development of tools that can facilitate this transition. For example, in mathematics, tools include a mathematical task analysis guide based on Stein et al.'s (1996) classification of cognitive demands and some unit-planning tools.

Assessments to Serve Organizational Learning: Learning Walks

A tool involving a learning activity that is used widely in IFL districts is called Learning Walks (IFL 2004). Walkers, who may be principals, the superintendent, teachers, parents, students, or other interested persons, walk through the school, stopping for brief observations in classrooms, and discussing what they observe with each other in the hallways and in a debriefing conversation, and provide constructive feedback. This activity needs to be preceded by professional development so that the participants understand that its purpose is to increase mutual understanding of the Principles of Learning and ways in which teaching can achieve them.

The Learning Walks activity provides another example of distributed leadership, in Spillane's (2006) sense. Indeed, the distribution of authority and accountability among members of a school and district community is spread even more widely than in the case of Example 1. Depending on who participates in a learning walk, the activity may bring into the process other teachers, even parents, in addition to the administrative leaders of the school or district.

The breadth of participation that IFL encourages in Learning Walks is consistent with the design principles of fostering a culture that emphasizes continuous learning and two-way accountability in nested learning communities and continuing professional development for all staff. Learning Walks are designed to provide useful feedback for the teachers whose classes are observed, of course, but they are also designed to contribute to learning and

understanding on the part of the walkers, affording administrators opportunities to learn about conditions in classrooms in which efforts to improve
instruction have to take place, affording other teachers opportunities to learn
how their colleagues are addressing issues of teaching practice, and affording
parents and others from the larger community opportunities to understand
and appreciate their school's efforts to improve student learning.

Assessing OTL in Schools: Instructional Quality Assessment

IFL addresses the need for assessing opportunities to learn that are afforded
in the classrooms of its partner districts in a program called Instructional
Quality Assessment (IQA). The goals of the IQA effort are "to develop assessment of the quality of instruction at the individual teacher level that serves
[three] purposes, that is, is of a high technical quality, feasible to use on a
large scale, and provides information that could be useful for professional
training" (Matsumura et al. 2006, 7).

An IQA assessment includes classroom observation and examination of
student work. Evaluations based on these data are focused on three the-
matic constructs that correspond to three of IFL's principles of learning:
academic rigor, accountable talk, and clear expectations. In IQA protocols,
these correspond to evaluating the level of cognitive demand of tasks and
activities, aspects of classroom talk, and expectations that the teacher com-
municates to students regarding the quality of their work. The classroom
observation records activities, with ratings of the presence or absence of
specific kinds of evidence and field notes, according to specific observation
protocols. The rubrics focus on observable aspects of classroom activity, not
on teachers' assumptions about learning. Their rubrics for reading instruction include a focus on academic quality of texts that the classes discuss.
They also drew on characterizations by Snow (2002) of thought processes for
inferring meaning from a text, identifying levels of (1) recognition and recall
of specific content; (2) comprehension, reflected in summarizing, paraphras-
ing, explaining, or translating text; and (3) application, analysis, synthesis,
and evaluation of text components. For mathematics rubrics, they drew on a
framework of characterizing cognitive demands of mathematical tasks (Stein
et al. 1996). Their four-level characterization includes (1) reciting something
from memory; (2) performing a procedure without connection to general
mathematical concepts; (3) considering general mathematical concepts in
relation to a procedure; and (4) doing mathematics, which involves consideration of meanings of mathematical concepts, principles, and representations.

A recent study of IQA involving thirty-four seventh-grade and
eighth-grade classes (Matsumura et al. 2006) provided promising results.

Independent raters agreed on more than 80% of their specific ratings on a four-point scale of the dimensions they judged in classroom observations and on more than 70% of their specific ratings of dimensions of classroom assignments. Students' scores on reading comprehension scales of the SAT-10 achievement test were significantly correlated with IQA scores of instruction in their classes. Scores on mathematics scales of SAT-10 were not correlated significantly with IQA scores. Matsumura et al. (2006) conjectured that the quite highly structured curriculum used in the schools of the study may have prevented effects on learning that could be associated with the dimensions of instruction measured by IQA. Another possibility that occurs to us is that the mathematics scales of SAT-10 might not be sensitive to aspects of learning for which IQA measures opportunities.

CONCLUSIONS

In closing, we return to the questions we raised in Table 11.1 that, we suggested, might be productively asked about (the design of) any documentary assessment system that crosses boundaries from a focal learning environment like a school or classroom to and from another (learning) environment, like a consortium or a district or state education agency, to support decision making, accountability, and professional learning. In our representation of examples, we intended to sketch brief answers to questions about the "stated intent" of each documentary assessment. Our goal across the examples was to illustrate a range of documentary assessment practices and use the comparisons to highlight issues that those responsible for designing or otherwise participating in such systems might want to consider. Here we focus on the second set of questions about the potential implications of such systems: (1) what they make visible; (2) what the trajectory of learning or progress is for students, professionals, and the organizations in which they work; (3) what authority, agency, and accountability students and professionals are positioned with; and (4) what the incentive is for progress. As the third set of questions in Table 11.1 implies, we recognize that the answers to these questions can't be addressed simply by looking at what the assessment system provides; they must also be answered by looking at what happens in (different) local contexts when the system is put to work: how local actors attend to it (or not), understand and interpret it, and act and interact in light of those understandings (Spillane and Miele 2007); in short, how the system mediates and is mediated by local practice. With the exception of Spillane's work, the case-based evidence we have provided barely touched on this third, and crucial, set of questions.

Conventional practice in performance-based accountability, as instantiated in NCLB, for instance, makes only a limited set of information available about the local environment for use: student test scores in reading, math, and now science (disaggregated by various subgroups to address equity concerns), participation rates, high school completion rates, and percentage of teachers meeting the definition of highly qualified. As Diamond and Spillane (2004) make clear, these indicators are taken up in different ways in different contexts with different effects. The work of the Distributed Leadership Study and Data Wise point to the importance of attending to other indicators of student learning and to the capacity of professionals in the local context to interpret and use the information well. In the Data Wise project, in which the intent was to intervene in local practice, we saw the value of using test scores to generate hypotheses for additional study as part of a local inquiry process that also attends to instructional practice. The trajectory of learning that the assessment design makes available is specified in terms of state standards for student learning that are instantiated (always more narrowly) in particular standardized achievement tests. NCLB's program of assessment, with its required sanctions for schools that fail to meet adequate yearly progress on its indicators, removes certain decisions from local educators' hands and increases the salience of improving performance on these particular indicators, especially in low-performing schools. The quality of the achievement tests – in providing (or limiting) student access to powerful learning opportunities – becomes a crucial issue. Equally important, questions about the generalizability of evaluations of students' knowledge, based on their participation in the social situation of the test, to participation in the many other social situations in which knowledge is used, remains an open question that the system does not provide resources to answer (Gee, 2007; Mislevy, Gee, and Moss, in press). Similarly, questions about how and why students' performance on the test improves (or fails to improve) are not addressable with the resources the system provides. Large-scale assessments of the sort Mislevy (this volume) describes would provide a substantially different target of instruction from the paper-and-pencil tests currently used in many states and, as envisioned, would begin to explicitly take some questions of context into account. Better standardized assessments, however – even great ones – still require knowledgeable local interpreters, "on the ground," to situate the information within the particular learning trajectories of their students and always entail crucial questions about generalization to other social situations where the knowledge is put to work (Mislevy, Gee, and Moss, in press).

The Turning Points and IFL projects explicitly shift (or expand) the focus of attention in these directions: to incorporate indicators of resources, instructional practices, and school culture and a broad range of locally relevant evidence of student learning in what the system requires be made visible. Thus, they point to evidence of the various elements of an activity system that shape student learning and are central to understanding OTL. Here, the trajectory of learning, and the indicators through which progress is evaluated, focus on professional and organizational learning as well as on student learning. Participation in these programs entails certain routines – the Learning Walks, the annual taking stock, and the semiregular school quality review – that provide opportunity for evidence-based collaborative learning. It is important to note that both of these involve long-term collaborations between schools and districts or external organizations.

The principles and criteria that guide these programs leave substantial room for local tailoring. The idea of encouraging evidence to be tailored locally to promote productive internal monitoring has much merit. It provides one of the horns of a dilemma, however. The other horn is the value of having information about OTL that is comparable across different settings. IFL has developed the IQA to begin to address this concern; however, even there, they leave substantial room for locally relevant evidence. A goal of IQA is to provide information that can be compared across settings as well as to facilitate local learning.

The evaluation of OTL that IQA provides is intricately tied to IFL's theory of learning. Even so, IQA's principal architect takes the view that the role of direct assessments of instructional quality, such as the IQA, is not to measure teachers' beliefs (although that can be valuable as a related activity) but rather to be concerned with what teachers do with their students – how they talk with them, what tasks they give them, and how they assess student work, because these are what matter for student learning (Matsumura, personal communication, 3/12/07). We are wary of this view, for reasons discussed by A. L. Brown (1994) and J. S. Brown (1991). If a desired practice rests on different assumptions[10] from those held by practitioners, and they do not change their assumptions, their conduct of that new practice is likely to be assimilated into their persisting assumptions in ways that undermine the goals and values that are intended in the new practice. Of course, whether the Brown–Brown conjecture is valid and applies to the relation between teachers' assumptions about learning and the learning outcomes that result from the teaching behavior assessed by IQA are empirical questions requiring research. Indeed, the IQA group has such research in progress (Matsumura, personal communication).

There are also questions about homogeneity and, therefore, commensurability between different classrooms. Is there more than one way to achieve qualities such as academic rigor, clear expectations, self-management of learning, or accountable talk? One might think so. And if there is, does a rubric necessarily filter observations to count one version and discount another?[11] There also are important questions about ways in which classroom events provide different OTL for different students in the same classroom. For example, Gresalfi (2004) documented ways in which different students characteristically took up affordances for participation in two mathematics classrooms.

IFL, Turning Points, and Data Wise (although proposing somewhat differ-ent professional learner trajectories) address the challenge of students' OTL with a message: Learning is not just for students; it is the main imperative for everyone in a school district. Furthermore, everyone in the district shares the responsibility for successful learning by others as well as by themselves. Outside groups, like those involved in these reform projects, can be called on for assistance, at least in organizing the program of ubiquitous learning in the district or school and supplying resources and ideas for carrying it out. Yet learning throughout the school and district is the main joint enterprise of the community.

This is a radical departure from the prevailing view of learning by school professionals, which has been assumed to consist of participation in work-shops and courses that are organized by people outside of the school. It is aligned with an idea developed by Cochran-Smith and Lytle (1999) that they called knowledge *of* teaching, distinguished from knowledge *for* teach-ing and knowledge *in* teaching. Knowledge for teaching is public, generated outside educational practice, usually by the academy. Knowledge in teaching is private, generated in the personal experience of a professional, and mainly not sharable with other professionals. Knowledge of teaching is public and local, generated within a community of professional practice, drawing on both outside resources and experiences of the participating professionals. The community of learners that projects like IFL and Turning Points envi-sion, advocate, and endeavor to support creates versions of knowledge that are understood to be generated through collaboration of the members of the community; hence, is knowledge of practice.

As the sociocultural principles in which our writing is grounded remind us, all activity systems are learning environments. We need to consider what, why, and how the professionals as well as the students in the system are learning. The design of an assessment system provides opportunities for participation in a social practice and positions educators and their students with differential authority, accountability, and agency. If we want educators and students to engage in what Engström calls expansive learning – learning new forms of activity which aren't yet there – we need to develop assessment systems that are coherent with that goal.

Notes

1. This is a point Carol Lee has made as well.
2. We are, perhaps, pushing the bounds of Jordan and Putz's definition, slightly, to include assessments where there is more deference paid to locally developed representations of progress, but maintain their characterization of documentary assessment as entailing an enduring record and an externally mandated requirement to account for performance.
3. Some of the text in this section and in Examples 1 and 2 overlaps with text in Moss, Girard, and Haniford (2006) and Moss and Piety (2007).
4. This case description was prepared by Pamela Moss.
5. Unlike our other three examples, DLS is not a reform effort. It is a study of leadership practice in schools, which includes attention to how standardized assessments function in school organizations. As such, it provides a useful window into practice with externally mandated standardized assessments.
6. The discussion of the Data Wise example was prepared by Brian Girard.
7. The discussion of the Turning Points example was prepared by Brian Girard.
8. Turning Points' use of "benchmark" is different from more common usages of the term. The benchmarks are rubrics, and they "are standards of success that tell us about a school's performance in relation to desired outcomes. As a tool for self-assessment, benchmarks provide schools with targets to move toward as they engage in school reform. Benchmarks help answer the question: *How far has the school progressed in implementing the principles and practices of the Turning Points design?*" (NTPC 2002a, 1–2).
9. Prepared by James Greeno. We are grateful for conversations with Lauren Resnick and Nancy Israel, and for conversations and comments on an earlier version by Lindsay Clare Matsumura.
10. A. L. Brown called these first principles. J. S. Brown called them tacit assumptions that underlie a practice.
11. One possibility is that culturally sensitive instruction, such as Lee's (this volume), includes the features of practice that IQA assesses, in common with more standard versions of good teaching. On this view, the aspects of instruction that make it culturally sensitive are in addition to these features, and rubrics could be added to those already formulated to reflect cultural sensitivity. But this issue also requires further research and analysis.

References

Boudett, K. P., E. A. City, and R. J. Murnane, eds. 2005. *Data wise: A step-by-step guide to using assessment results to improve teaching and learning.* Cambridge: Harvard University Press.

Bowker, G. C. and S. L. Star. 1999. *Sorting things out: Classification and its consequences.* Cambridge: MIT Press.

Brown, A. L. 1994. The advancement of learning. *Educational Researcher* 23(8): 4–12.

Brown, J. S. (1991, January-February). Research that reinvents the corporation. *Harvard Business Review*, pp. 102–111.

Carnoy, M., R. Elmore, and L. L. Sisken. 2003. *The new accountability: High schools and high stakes testing.* New York: Routledge Falmer.

Cochran-Smith, M. and J. Lytle. 1999. Relationships of knowledge and practice: Teacher learning in communities. *Review of Research in Education* 24: 249–305.

Commission on No Child Left Behind. 2007. *Beyond NCLB: Fulfilling the promise to our nation's children.* Washington, D.C.: The Aspen Institute.

Diamond, J. B. and J. P. Spillane. 2004. High-stakes accountability in urban elementary schools: Challenging or reproducing inequality? *Teachers College Record* 106: 1145–76.

Diamond, J. B. and C. Cooper. 2007. The uses of testing data in early elementary schools: Some lessons from Chicago. In *Evidence and decision making (Yearbook of the National Society for the Study of Education)*, issue 1, edited by P. A. Moss. Malden, Mass.: Blackwell Publishing.

Dweck, C. and J. Bempechat. 1983. Children's theories of intelligence: Consequences for teaching. In *Learning and motivation in the classroom*, edited by S. Paris, G. Olson, and H. Stevenson, 239–56. Hillsdale, N.J.: Lawrence Erlbaum Associates, Inc.

Dweck, C. S. 2000. *Self-theories: Their role in motivation, personality, and development.* Philadelphia: Taylor & French/Psychology Press.

Elmore, R. F. 1996. Getting to scale with good educational practice. *Harvard Educational Review* 66(1): 1–26.

Elmore, R. F. and R. Rothman. 1999. *Testing, teaching, and learning: A guide for states and districts.* Washington, D.C.: National Academy Press.

Engeström, Y. 2001. Expansive learning at work: Toward an activity theoretical reconceptualization. *Journal of Education and work* 14(1): 134–156.

Felner, R. D., Jackson, A. W., Kasak, D., Mulhall, P., Brand, S., & Flowers, N. 1997. The impact of school reform for the middle years: Longitudinal study of a network engaged in Turning Points–based comprehensive school transformation. *Phi Delta Kappan* 78: 528–32, 541–50.

Forum on Educational Accountability. 2007. *Redefining accountability: Improving student learning by building capacity.* Author.

Fuhrman, S. H., and R. F. Elmore. 2004. *Redesigning accountability systems for education.* New York: Teachers College Press.

Gee, J. P. 2007. Reflections on assessment from a sociocultural/situated perspective. In *Evidence and decision making (Yearbook of the National Society for the Study of Education)*, issue 1, edited by P. A. Moss. Malden, Mass.: Blackwell Publishing.

Greeno, J. G. 2002. *Students with competence, authority and accountability: Affording intellective identities in the classroom.* New York: The College Board.

Gresalfi, M. S. 2004. *Taking up opportunities to learn: Examining the construction of participatory mathematical identities in middle school students.* Palo Alto: Stanford University.

Halverson, R. R. 2003. Systems of practice: How leaders use artifacts to create professional community in schools. *Education Policy Analysis Archives* 11(37).[http://epaa.abu.edu/cpaa/vlln37/]

Herman, J. L. and E. H. Haertel. 2005. *Uses and misuses of data for educational accountability and improvement (Yearbook of the National Society for the Study of Education)*, issue 2. Malden, Mass.: Blackwell Publishing.

Institute for Learning. 2003. Informational packet, Learning Research and Development Center, University of Pittsburgh.

Institute for Learning. 2004. *Learning Walk SM Sourcebook*. Learning Research and Development Center, University of Pittsburgh.

Jackson, A. W. and G. A. Davis. 2000. *Turning Points 2000: Educating adolescents in the 21st century*. New York: Teachers College Press.

Jordan, B. and P. Putz. 2004. Assessment as practice: Notes on measures, tests, and targets. *Human organization* 63: 346–58.

Lampert, M. 2001. *Teaching problems and the problems of teaching*. New Haven: Yale University Press.

Lave, J. 1993. The practice of learning. In *Understanding practice: Perspectives on activity and context*, edited by S. Chaiklin and J. Lave, 3–32. Cambridge. Cambridge University Press.

Lave, J. and E. Wenger. 1991. *Situated learning: Legitimate peripheral participation*. Cambridge: Cambridge University Press.

Matsumura, L. C., S. C. Slater, B. J. Junker, M. Peterson, M. Boston, M. Steel, and L. Resnick. 2006. *Measuring Reading Comprehension and Mathematics Instruction in Urban Middle Schools: A Pilot Study of the Instructional Quality Assessment*. CSE Technical Report 681. University of California, Los Angeles: CRESST.

McLaughlin, M. W. and J. E. Talbert. 2001. *Professional communities and the work of high school teaching*. Chicago: University of Chicago Press.

Mertens, S. B. and N. Flowers. 2004. *Assessing the success of Turning Points in Boston public schools*. Paper presented at the American Educational Research Association Annual Meeting, April 12–16, 2004, San Diego, Calif.

Mislevy, R J., J. P. Gee, and P. A Moss. In press. On qualitative and quantitative reasoning about assessment validity. In *Generalizing from educational research: Beyond the quantitative-qualitative opposition*, edited by K. Ercikan and W.-M. Roth. Mahwah, N.J.: Erlbaum.

Moss, P. A., B. Girard, L. Haniford. 2006. Validity in education assessment, Review of Research in Education, 30, 109–162.

Moss, P. A. and P. J. Piety. 2007. Introduction: Evidence and decision making. In P. A. Moss, (Ed.) Evidence and Decision Making. The 106th Yearbook of the National Society for the Study of Education, Part I. Malden, MA: Blackwell Publishing.

National Turning Points Center. 2001. *Design Overview*. Boston: Author.

National Turning Points Center. 2002. *Benchmarks to Becoming a Turning Points School*. Boston: Author.

National Turning Points Center. 2002. *School Quality Review*. Boston: Author.

Peterson, P. E. and M. R. West. 2003. *No child left behind? The politics and practice of school accountability*. Washington, D.C.: Brookings Press.

Resnick, L. B. and T. K. Glennan, Jr. 2002. Leadership for learning: A theory of action for urban school districts. In *School districts and instructional renewal*, edited by A. M. Hightower et al. New York: Teachers College Press.

Resnick, L. B. and S. Nelson-LeGall. 1997. Socializing intelligence. In *Piaget, Vygotsky and beyond*, edited by L. Smikth, J. Dockrell, and P. Tomlinson, 145–58. London: Routledge.

Skrla, L. and J. J Scheurich. 2004. *Educational equality and accountability: Paradigms, policies, and politics*. London: Routledge Falmer.

Snow, C. E. 2002. *Reading for understanding: Toward a research and development program in reading comprehension.* Santa Monica: RAND Corporation.

Spillane, J. P. 2006. *Distributed leadership.* San Francisco: Jossey-Bass.

Spillane, J. P., R. Halverson, and J. B. Diamond. 2001. Investigating school leadership practice: A distributed perspective. *Educational Researcher* 30(1): 23–28.

Spillane, J. P. and D. B. Miele. 2007. Evidence in practice: A framing of the terrain. In *Evidence and decision making (Yearbook of the National Society for the Study of Education),* issue 1, edited by P. A. Moss. Malden, Mass.: Blackwell Publishing.

Star, S. L. and J. R. Griesemer. 1989. Institutional ecology, "translations" and boundary objects: Amateurs and professionals in Berkeley's Museum of Vertebrate Zoology, 1907–39. *Social Studies of Science* 19: 387–420.

Stein, M. K., B. W. Grover, and M. Henningsen. 1996. Building student capacity for mathematical thinking and reasoning: An analysis of mathematical tasks used in reform classrooms. *American Educational Research Journal* 33: 455–88.

Task Force on Education of Young Adolescents. 1989. *Turning Points: Preparing American Youth for the 21st Century.* Washington, D.C.: Carnegie Council on Adolescent Development.

Wertsch, J. V. 1991. *Voices of the mind: A sociocultural approach to mediated action.* Cambridge: Harvard University Press.

Wertsch, J. V. 1998. *Mind as action.* Oxford: Oxford University Press.

Wertsch, J. V., P. Del Rio, and A. Alverez. 1995. Sociocultural studies: History, action, and mediation. In *Sociocultural studies of mind,* edited by J. V. Wertsch, P. Del Rio, and A. Alverez, 1–36. Cambridge: Cambridge University Press.

12   Assessment, Equity, and Opportunity to Learn

Diana C. Pullin[1]

Although assessment has a long history in American education, at no time in the nation's history has it been so prominent and pervasive as it is today. Due to state initiatives and the No Child Left Behind Act of 2001 (NCLB) (P.L.107–110, 2002), externally mandated testing is currently seen as the primary means of driving education reform, a means through which evidence-based decisions can be made to achieve accountability, allocate resources, inform parents and taxpayers, and credential educators. This is in addition to the longstanding and widespread use of tests to determine placement of individuals in special education or gifted programs, grade-to-grade promotion, certification for graduation, allocation of scholarships and vouchers, special intervention in instructional programs, accreditation of schools, and higher education admissions. Testing, however, is only one type of educational assessment, and in the nation's schools there are a wide range of assessment practices used by teachers and other educators, the primary users of assessment information and the primary providers of learning opportunities to students. The work represented in this volume is intended to challenge our understandings of the roles of assessment in schools and to reform our perspectives on the relationships between assessment, learning, and the provision of meaningful learning opportunities.

The epistemological underpinning of most of the theories and practices of large-scale, standardized testing in American schools have been dominated by one discipline, psychometrics (Moss et al. 2005). In fact, widespread use of standardized testing in classrooms and schools (Shepard 2000) and in public decision making about schools and students (Heubert and Hauser 1999) suggests that "beliefs and practices informed by psychometrics have become so deeply ingrained in the American educational system that it has become difficult to see them as choices arising in particular sociocultural circumstances or to imagine that things could be otherwise" (Moss et al. 2005, 66).

The Spencer Foundation-funded project "The Idea of Testing" that led to this book was conceived in an effort to broaden perspectives beyond the dominant, psychometrically driven paradigm in testing and to foster a new dialogue on the intersections of learning and assessment. The current system of externally mandated, high-stakes achievement testing is in many ways coherent with the underlying view of knowing and knowledge it embodies. The current system, however, falls short in recognizing the broad range of evidence-based perspectives on successful teaching and learning and the use of assessment of, and for, learning.

Our multiyear symposium of a sociologist, a sociolinguist, psychologists, testing experts, sociocultural researchers, policy analysts, and an attorney produced a provocative and challenging series of conversations leading to the chapters you've just read. Even in the face of the challenges and constraints inherent in discussions across our disciplines and in our efforts to understand assessment practices and their relationship to learning, from our earliest discussions, one notion resonated among all of us. The power of this idea was, no doubt for each of us, due to the magnetic pull of this principle in the work each of us had done independently over the course of our professional lives. We quickly agreed that, from any of our perspectives, measuring outcomes is important, but that the *way* achievement is assessed is also important. Equally significant are the implications of assessment for equity and social justice, insuring that *all* students, particularly those most at risk of educational failure, are the beneficiaries of an effective *opportunity to learn* (OTL) meaningful content. For each of the authors represented in this volume, the most important idea of testing is not the metric or the measure, but instead, the constructive role of assessment as a critical component of high-quality teaching and learning.

This leads to a dramatically new perspective on OTL, not in terms of content covered and scores attained, but instead based on a more complex view centered on aspects of learning activities and the role of assessment as part of the learning environment. This view rests on both a particular theory of assessment and a particular theory of learning and also seeks to focus on a new understanding of the interactions between the two. From this sociocultural/situative (SC/S) perspective, learning is the result of activities and interactive experiences between learners and the mediating influences of other people and the tools of their environment (Gee, this volume; Greeno and Gresalfi, this volume). The path to learning varies for each individual based on the environment and affordances an individual is offered and can use.

The outcomes of learning are not simply the acquisition of information and skills, but the creation of self-aware learning identities marked by the capability to invoke useful knowledge in real-world settings based not only on information and skills, but also on the use of such abilities as reasoning, problem solving, and critical reflection (Gee, this volume, chapter 4; Greeno and Gresalfi, this volume; Moss, this volume; Moss, Girard and Greeno, this volume). Educators and policy makers seeking to facilitate learning must take into account that learning only occurs for those who are able to take advantage of learning opportunities. Assessment is an important component of learning activities and constitutes a range of activities from both the formal and informal reflective activities of classroom teachers to the highly formal, standardized, documentary activities associated with the National Assessment of Educational Progress (NAEP) or a state high-stakes testing program. All assessment activities must rest on a theory of learning and recognition of the fundamental importance of the usefulness of assessment in supporting student learning and in shaping our understanding of how learning occurs and what is important to learn (Mislevy, this volume; Moss, this volume; Moss, Girard, and Greeno, this volume).

It is from these theories of learning and assessment, and the relationships between them, that the authors came to expand their view of OTL. From this perspective, the relationship between assessment, learning, and OTL is complex, highly contextual, and continually evolving in any educational setting and for each learner within that setting (Moss, this volume). From this perspective, assessment offers a reflection of learning and the quality of learning, but it also offers a reflection of, and serves as a facilitator for, opportunities to learn (Moss, this volume). It is also a perspective all of our authors would admit is still in need of further conceptualization and refinement in implementation.

Concern for issues of equity arises throughout the work here. Historically, assessment practices have played a significant role in the reproduction of social inequality (Mehan, this volume; Pullin and Haertel, this volume). Reconceptualizing assessment without at the same time reconceptualizing instruction will have little benefit for culturally or otherwise diverse students or for any students for that matter. The goal of instruction is, of course, learning, and meaningful learning is broader and deeper than the type of learning associated with most contemporary testing systems, particularly those created in response to current external accountability mandates. Our new OTL perspective addresses an underlying aim to equalize learning opportunities for all. Learning is meaningful only when it affords each and every individual the opportunity to develop a self-identity as a competent learner, to participate effectively in learning communities, and to acquire a knowledge structure for a sustained trajectory of progress toward continuing acquisition of deep new knowledge and real-world proficiency in the use of that knowledge. Assessment is productive only when it is deeply embedded in learning activity systems to both continuously test deep conceptual understanding and allow all students, no matter their backgrounds or capabilities, to situate their learning in meaningful ways. This perspective also promotes assessment practices that support ongoing professional learning to support student learning, informing decision making for the constant improvement of instructional practice and meaningful accountability for knowledge worth knowing and using.

LEARNING AND LEARNING OPPORTUNITIES

This volume begins with an overview of traditional notions of OTL and its relationship with testing. Assessment can influence the content of curriculum and instruction, enable more effective targeting of instructional resources, and influence the teaching and learning processes. It can provide accountability information to students, parents, educators and policymakers, and the public. Assessment can expand educational opportunity. Assessment can also limit opportunity and reproduce existing inequality (Mehan, this volume; Pullin and Haertel, this volume).

At present, public schools throughout the United States strive to meet the provisions of NCLB that include an explicit statement that the nation's goal is to "ensure that all children have a fair, equal, and significant opportunity to obtain a high-quality education." The law goes on to state that all students should "reach, at a minimum, proficiency on challenging State academic achievement standards and state academic assessments" (20 USC 6301). Assessments, in short, are seen as a way to define the outcome of our endeavors to promote educational opportunity and to implement a commitment to ensure that *all* learners achieve at a high level.

Yet whether the relationship between OTL and testing is implicit or explicit, the consideration of OTL as an issue of social, educational, or even legal policy has been addressed with ambivalence throughout our educational history. Since the mid-twentieth century, a social policy goal of seeking equality of educational opportunity has been frequently articulated. The nation has never completely embraced a clear commitment to ensure that all children receive a fair and effective opportunity to learn important content, knowledge, skills, dispositions, and concepts. There are increasing equity concerns about an achievement gap between advantaged students and those traditionally poorly served by our schools. At the same time, there are mounting suggestions that we fall short in preparing students for a global, technology-driven economy. At the heart of any consideration of learning and learning opportunities is consideration of the content of what should be learned, who should be expected to learn it, and how it should be taught. The authors of this volume share a concern that many current forms of learning, as embedded in tests and enacted in classroom practices, are insufficient to meet our needs as a nation.

The authors of this volume argue that if we want to understand learning and OTL, we must understand the relationship between learners and their learning environment. Learning is a continual and dynamic activity, in school and out, for both students and educators (Lee, this volume; Moss, this volume; Moss, Girard and Greeno, this volume; Pullin, this volume) and each member in any learning community constructs (and reconstructs) an identity as a learner during interactions with others and with the learning environment.

Many sociologists and ethnographers have questioned whether students in fact have equal access to OTL or whether, instead, schools provide greater opportunities to some students than to others (Mehan, this volume). The assertion that schools are competitive, meritocratic institutions organized to facilitate *individual* success rests heavily on several assumptions about the relationships between opportunity and learning. Most important, this perspective assumes that the responsibility of the student is to work harder; failure results because a student (and/or the family) did not try hard enough or did not have the social, economic, or intellectual capital necessary to foster achievement at the highest levels. This seems to be the perspective adopted by many of the current cadre of education reformers. This perspective focuses more heavily upon individual responsibility than the provision of learning opportunities by educational institutions, educators, and policy makers (Mehan, this volume). Indeed, there is growing evidence that individuals can dramatically mediate the opportunities that are afforded them through their implicit and explicit choices about participation in schooling (Greeno and Gresalfi, this volume; Mehan, this volume; Ogbu 2003). Even oppositional responses to schooling can sometimes be explained as a form of resistance to institutional failures to provide meaningful equality of opportunity (Mehan, this volume).

The work represented here argues, however, that the functioning of educational institutions and educators can be more powerful than individual responsibility. Opportunities to learn are not equally distributed across a population of students but are instead unevenly distributed to different races, genders, classes, disabilities, and language groups (Mehan, this volume;

Pullin, this volume). Schools often perpetuate social, cultural, and economic inequalities; some argue that this is the role of schools in our society (Mehan, this volume) or that individuals exploit schools to ensure their own competitive advantages (Labaree 1997). This volume asserts that we know much more about how to make educational institutions far more effective for *all* students than current teaching and testing practices suggest. The sociological and situative research and perspectives described throughout this volume offer a more complex and nuanced understanding of the teaching and learning process than is represented in many current education policies and practices.

Greeno and Gresalfi (this volume) offer a situative perspective on learning that further illustrates the complexity of the OTL problem, addressing considerations beyond what the traditional "content alignment" approach to OTL would suggest (see Pullin and Haertel, this volume). Learning is a trajectory of participation that occurs only through participation in a community of learners engaged in activities in which new capabilities are summoned. Therefore, OTL is determined by the types of activities in which learners have the opportunity to participate and the kinds of participation they are afforded. Learning is also governed both by individual agency in participating in learning activities (Gee, this volume; Greeno and Gresalfi, this volume; Mehan, this volume) and by the ways in which learning systems allow individuals to participate. Opportunities arise from the doing, from affordances available to a student based on the resources and practices to which the student as learner is exposed, the tasks presented, and the intellectual models and rigor required for the tasks presented.

The learning trajectories in which an individual participates within a particular activity system, such as a classroom, a school building, or a district or state constitute the primary institutional sources for the OTL available to a student. Family, community, and after-school or summer jobs also constitute important learning opportunities for students. An increasing panoply of other informal opportunities to learn are embedded in the games, Internet offerings, and other media selections increasingly available to a growing number of learners (Gee, this volume, chapter 8).

In schools, the vital role of educators in organizing schools and classrooms for learning involves constant reflection, thoughtful attention to the relationships among learners and with the teacher, and deep understanding of the nature of effective practice in a particular domain of knowledge (Lee, this volume; Moss, this volume). Educators are, in short, engaged in the ongoing practice of studying how to foster progress on a learning trajectory with the particular students with whom they work (Moss, this volume). When educators are presented with traditional assessment data, its their presumption of a correct interpretation of a test score, and external mandates to improve test scores, educators often perceive obligations to proceed in a manner that may not serve the best interests of all students. Externally mandated assessment practices can define teaching practice, and current assessment practice doesn't necessarily provide good evidence for good teaching practice.

However we wish them to practice, educators are themselves learners shaped by their own opportunities to learn. In addition to the OTL circumstances for an individual student, there must also be consideration of the OTL for educators themselves and for a classroom, a school, or a district. These consist of resources and practices to support learning and affordances for learning in these communities based on who is participating in a learning community, as well as the information, resources, and practices used by individuals and groups within the community (Greeno and Gresalfi, this volume; Lee, this volume; Moss, this volume). OTL can be defined, at least in part, in terms of the resources needed to promote learning, including qualified teachers, appropriate facilities and textbooks, supplies, technology, and other services (Mehan, this volume; Pullin and Haertel, this volume). Teachers, in this vision of schools, play particularly powerful roles as mediators in the construction of social capital for low-status students (Mehan, this volume).

Indeed, teachers and other educators, with their capacity to provide learning opportunities, are perhaps the most critical variables in the system. The OTL for education professionals to enhance their capabilities to support students' learning and support one another's learning is an essential component of OTL and assessment practice (Moss, Girard, and Greeno, this volume). Learning communities of educators (Moss, Girard, and Greeno, this volume) and the distributed responsibility for learning systems (Spillane 2004) are cornerstones in the provision of OTL to students. For these educator-learners, assessment provides evidence and impetus to focus learning activities and interventions in particular ways. Knowledge of teaching (Cochran-Smith and Lytle 1993) is a shared, local, communal, professional practice that arises for a community of learning professionals to construct students' learning opportunities.

These issues raise questions about what OTL means, how it might be productively conceptualized at different levels of the educational system, what constrains and enables it, and how it can be assessed in a way that supports rather than undermines learning. We can derive a series of new principles about OTL from current sociological, sociocultural, and situative perspectives, principles that can serve as a set of standards for meaningful and equitable learning in our contemporary, high-tech global world. We have set out below our collective articulation of those principles, based on our work in this volume.

Just as ideas of testing and assessment are bound up with particular views of learning, any conception of OTL embodies a conception of learning and a set of judgments about what is worth measuring. OTL is often conceived as students' opportunity to learn what is tested, but we argue that, first, we should be certain that tests reflect the kinds of learning we really want. Prior definitions of OTL incorporate quite limited conceptions of match between content and performance requirements at fairly low levels of complexity, curriculum mapping, and time on task (Pullin and Haertel, this volume).

OTL and the relationship between OTL and assessment should be seen as being far more complex. There is a need to frame our understanding of the effect of testing (for better or worse) on OTL. Also important is the need to understand the extent to which students' test performance should be interpreted as an indicator of OTL. Assessment and OTL must embody approaches more explicitly and meaningfully designed to promote equity in access to a high-quality education for all students, particularly those from diverse backgrounds or with atypical learning needs. Learning takes place in complex social systems, and those systems and the activities and interactions among those within them must be understood in order to understand what, how, and why people learn (Gee, this volume; Mehan, this volume; Moss, Girard, and Greeno, this volume; Pullin, this volume).

Standard methods of assessing learning and OTL miss the nexus between individuals and their situations. Evaluating OTL requires an assessment of the relationship between learners and their particular learning environment as well as an understanding of how learning occurs (Moss, this volume). Central to this inquiry are the backgrounds students bring to school, the experiences students and their educators have in school, the externally imposed frameworks in which schooling occurs (including assessments), and the out-of-school occasions that also shape learning (Lee, this volume; Gee, this volume; Mehan, this volume; Pullin, this volume).

Students are expected to learn and to participate in the prevailing practices of learning activities in the classroom. They are called upon to exercise their identities as learners in that classroom (Moss, this volume). Yet students do not all participate fully and effectively in these learning activity systems. Students have all had their own prior experiences with school before they enter into a new learning experience. And students come to school having had, and they will continue to have, widely varying opportunities to have learned outside of school the capabilities that facilitate their acquisition of the practices the schools need to promote. These practices go well beyond the kinds of content and skill that are normally taught explicitly in schools. However, in many cases students may have acquired the precursors of these practices in forms that the schools may not recognize but which the schools could build on if they understood them. Students' academic identities can be developed without loss of their home identities. Students can learn the skills, manners, and norms (cultural capital) presumably inherited by elite students when educators appropriate students' language and cultural resources (Lee, this volume; Mehan, this volume) and provide other supports from students' experience (Gee, this volume, chapter 8). Further, OTL and learning in school are not only a function of the school, educators, and students, but also of the organizations and identities historically and developmentally linked with, and beyond, the school. For example, the workplace of students with out-of-school jobs and as well as after-school activities, both organized and informal, impact OTL, either diminishing chances for meaningful access to schooling or, conversely, providing richer stimuli for personal growth than is afforded in schools. These influences should be taken into account in both designing and integrating assessments of OTL and learning in schools.

Research on the acquisition of expertise consistent with new views of knowing and knowledge support new ways of schooling. There are exciting exemplars demonstrating that these ways of structuring teaching and learning are effective for all students and in particular for those traditionally underserved. As Gee (this volume, chapter 8) illustrates so vividly, some of the most powerful exemplars of good learning and assessment practices exist largely outside of school in such contexts as video games and in much more engaging, and educational, ways than the activities in many classrooms.

The reforms envisioned by this project to promote meaningful OTL will require coordinated changes at all levels of the system. Changing our assessments will not be sufficient but will be a necessary component of true reform.

ASSESSMENTS FOR LEARNING

Taking, or administering, a test is an increasingly frequent activity in our nation's schools. It is also a learning activity. However, the current focus on externally mandated assessment for accountability has drawn attention away from assessment's importance in the local learning environment. Assessment is not only a judgment of the end product of a student's learning activity. Assessment, in all its formal and informal, explicit and intangible ways, is a part of all meaningful learning activities. Assessment – the variety of ways evidence is gathered and used to support and document learning activities – is an inherent and explicit part of learning activities in every local context,

a classroom or a school. Assessments can be documentary, externally mandated and heavily symbolic, such as the state assessments required under
NCLB (Moss, this volume). Assessment can also be an informal, ongoing,
almost invisible part of what every teacher does every day to foster each
student's learning activities. However they are conceptualized, assessments
can play a variety of roles in our educational system. Yet all assessments rest
upon particular judgments of how and why people learn and what should be
learned (Mislevy, this volume; Moss, this volume). Assessment arguments
or theory and the purposes and nature of assessment depend on the values
associated with the nature of proficiency, definitions of what is to be learned,
and the inferences and uses to be made from assessment information (Mislevy, this volume). Given the portrayal of teaching and learning offered in
this book, the vision of assessment based upon the perspectives articulated
here calls for a revision of current assessment approaches and practices.

Most current large-scale, documentary educational assessments address
a very limited range of knowledge and proficiencies and afford very incomplete representations of individual learning and institutional accomplishment. Most do little, if anything, to evaluate OTL for individuals. We are
still only beginning to understand the implications of a broader theory of
learning for assessment practice. Yet clearly many current forms of assessment are inadequate to inform the provision of adequate and meaningful
opportunities to learn deep and important knowledge for all students. Furthermore, most contemporary assessment practices fail to take into account
current knowledge on effective teaching and learning. An increasing amount
of assessment practice is what Greeno has termed "reproductive test taking," which is largely coupled with educational practice focusing on passive
absorption of knowledge, knowledge often defined only by what is efficiently
testable. For some students who are particularly disadvantaged by our educational system, this does represent a form of OTL they may not have previously had, the opportunity to at least learn what is covered on the test in that
instrumental way courts and legislators have often called for in requiring the
provision of OTL (Pullin and Haertel, this volume). Yet this sort of opportunity falls far short of what we know we can, and should, do for students.
Each assessment rests on a presumption about what it is important to make
inferences about, what students should be learning, and how that learning
should be valued.

Formal and informal assessments are at the core of educational practice,
with teachers using a continual flow of evidence of learning to monitor and
support decisions about what to do next (Moss, this volume). Assessment
informs teaching and learning, whether it is the informal evidence of a look

of dismay on a struggling student's face or a state's criterion-referenced standardized test data measuring the adequate yearly progress (AYP) of third graders in a particular school as mandated by NCLB.

Assessments should illuminate the relationships and interactions among resources, learners, and educators (Gee; this volume, chapter 4; Moss, this volume), as well as the contexts of schooling (Mehan, this volume; Pullin, this volume). The sociological, situative, and sociocultural perspectives described in this volume call for assessment evidence that would allow formal and informal assessment activities that are highly integrated within teaching and learning systems and would afford thick descriptions and explanations of what individual students know and can do in particular circumstances. These assessments would dynamically and continuously, through both formal and informal means, assess the process and consequences of teaching and learning, allowing judgments both of the outcomes of a learning activity as well as the opportunities afforded to learn (Moss, this volume). These approaches might more closely resemble the types of performance assessments that began to be described in the literature in the 1990s but were often abandoned in the press for accountability testing at the turn of the century. The "evidence centered" approach articulated by Mislevy (this volume) recognizes the importance of a perspective on knowledge and learning but allows the adaptation of more traditional assessment approaches to encompass a richer set of evidence informed by the perspectives discussed here. This assessment approach would gather more information about the interrelationship among students, their backgrounds and histories, and the contexts of assessment, bringing to the fore the specific activities and contexts through which knowledge is brought to bear. Mislevy's descriptions of the AP Studio Art exam (this volume) and Pullin's descriptions of assessment approaches for students with disabilities (this volume) offer examples of current practice where assessments can support meaningful local decision making about teaching and learning that are in many ways consistent with the theoretical designs contemplated by the authors of this volume.

The purposes and uses of assessments and the information they generate are important. While ethnographers and other researchers revel in thick descriptions of individuals and interactions, the imperatives for many users of assessment information are efficiency and effectiveness. The assumptions on which traditional large-scale assessments rest are that they are efficient, allowing the rapid gathering and dissemination of information about large numbers of students and that they are effective, providing useful evidence of educational achievement. Although there are indubitably efficiencies, particularly efficiencies of scale, associated with current assessment systems, the authors of this volume argue that the information provided by these systems falls far short on the measure of usefulness. Assessment is the acquisition of evidence about learning and OTL, but assessment is also a means through which learning and OTL develop (Mislevy, this volume; Moss, this volume). More meaningful purposes for assessment and wider-ranging uses are attainable when assessment serves not to measure particular student traits or simple attainments but instead to provide a more complex set of indicators grounded in the principles of situated learning and founded on the understanding that assessment is a fundamental component of activity systems within classrooms and schools. This assessment system would rest upon the creation of a set of standardized expectations for collecting information about students and the creation of formal and explicit processes and activities to gather information in context, structuring the use of information in arriving at interpretations of student performance and the use of probability-based reasoning to synthesize and characterize information about students (Mislevy, this volume). At the heart of this approach, the resulting information is seen as having a powerful use at the local level as one important source of assessment evidence informing teaching and learning for individual students. Compilations of this information, accompanied by such techniques as audits, benchmarking, and portfolios (see Mislevy, this volume), can afford policy makers the types of information they need to inform their decision making and give local educators the evidence for hypotheses concerning performance, particularly when they can identify atypical performance or when they identify the need for new content or approaches.

Although psychometrics focuses on validity of presumptive interpretations, interpretations by test users (i.e., what scores mean to them) are never really fixed; they are always situated in social and cultural practices and in individual understandings (or sense making). An assessment system embracing the broader perspectives articulated in this volume could function as a more powerful mechanism for enhancing the quality of education for a broader range of learners. For example, there should be available to educators (classroom teachers, principals, district leadership) and to parents assessments that reveal developmentally where students' understanding – their representations of understanding – rest in a trajectory of the range of paths along which competency is likely to evolve (Greeno and Gresalfi, this volume). Such assessments should provide one source of usable information about what underlies students' reasoning so that clear instructional decisions can be made; they must play a formative role in helping to foster each individual's trajectory for progress in learning to at least the most basic levels of adequacy.

For standardized assessments, especially those that result in consequential decisions (for individuals or organizations), the prerequisites of assessment must be more transparent and fair (Mislevy, this volume; Pullin and Haertel, this volume). They must have clarity and specificity in the nature of the attribute/capability to be assessed (including context). The uses/purposes or intended interpretations based on assessments must be clearly stated before the assessment is implemented. There must be appropriate validity evidence for the interpretations of assessment data. The utility of large-scale assessment at both the individual and group levels for improving opportunities to learn must be made more explicit.

There are innovations not far removed from the mainstream of traditional assessment that can usefully inform new approaches to teaching, learning, and assessment. Assessment problems can be conceived in a manner that respects the situated character of human activity and uses statistical/psychometric tools not to estimate levels of psychological traits but instead to determine whether a complex patterning of evidence is consistent with one or another possible narrative/explanation about teaching and learning. The design of such assessments necessarily relies on deeper understanding (better models) of the performances being assessed and requires highly principled assessment task design (Mislevy, this volume). Researchers should be refining the science of assessment, funders should be supporting these initiatives, and policy makers should be considering these advancements as they design and implement education policy.

There are also innovations far from the mainstream of traditional assessment practice that can usefully inform new approaches to teaching, learning, and assessment. For example, good modern video games instantiate important learning principles supported by recent research in cognitive science and have the potential to help us create better learning systems that address the provision of meaningful opportunity to learn.

PRINCIPLES FOR MEANINGFUL OTL AND ASSESSMENT

The goal of schools is to enable every student to develop the capabilities to effectively participate as a lifelong learner in the practices of modern society. The goal of assessment is to provide useful information to enhance educational opportunity for each and every student, to inform decisions about what will be needed to optimize the learning trajectories for each and every student. The relationship among assessment, learning, and OTL is far more complex than contemporary educational policy, and much of educational practice, currently acknowledge. As a result of the work represented in this volume, the authors have reached a consensus that the following fundamental principles should drive all considerations of assessment, learning, and the provision of meaningful opportunity to learn for *all* students.

1. Every student has the right to a meaningful opportunity to learn and to be assessed fairly and in a way that supports his/her further accomplishments and development.

2. Students must have effective access to appropriate resources, such as well-prepared teachers, well-designed curricula, appropriate class size, sufficient and current laboratory equipment, books, and technology, as well as comfortable and safe facilities.

3. Students should be offered education in schools adhering to high standards and academic rigor with sufficient depth and breadth of coverage of the concepts, content, skills, and understandings in the intended curriculum.

4. Classrooms must offer learners not just the same "content" but must strive to equalize affordances for action, participation, and learning through adaptive approaches to instruction for each learner.

5. Because comprehension requires the ability to simulate relevant experiences in the mind, in order to receive an adequate education, all learners must be offered the range of necessary experiences with which they can build good and useful simulations to tap what is really necessary for deep understanding in the content areas (e.g., science, math, social studies, history).

6. Learning for humans is mediated by "smart tools"; that is, representations, technologies, and other people networked into knowledge systems. Thus, learners must be offered equal access to such smart tools.

7. Learning takes place within activity systems, systems that, in school, should be a form of a community of practice. Thus, we must consider more than the information to which the learner has been exposed. All of the other elements in the system need to count as well, including access to the forms of participations and social interaction that make one an agent and knower in the system.

8. Content learning in school requires learning new forms of language and the identities, values, content, and characteristic activities connected to these forms of language (e.g., the language of literary criticism or of experimental biology). Every learner has the right for these "new cultures" to be introduced in ways that respect and build on the learner's other cultures and indigenous knowledge, including his

or her home-based vernacular culture and peer-based and "popular culture" cultures ("discourses").

9. Students should receive academic and social supports differentiated to address their individual strengths and needs as learners.

10. Students should participate in instruction organized in ways that build on the cultural capital and forms of prior knowledge they construct from their experiences outside of school and across their years of schooling.

11. Students should routinely experience instruction that provides them with opportunities to participate in meaningful activities based on models of expertise, expert problem solving, and in-time feedback on the progress of their learning in ways that are usable and motivating and empower them to construct identities and skills that allow them to participate effectively in school and across a variety of out-of-school settings.

12. Students should have experience, within disciplines and across their years of schooling, with rigorous instruction that focuses on powerful and generative topics, concepts, and problem-solving strategies in ways that help them make sense of how their learning is useful in the world.

13. Parents should have access to timely, useful, and credible information about their children's education, what is required for their children to successfully participate in school, and what parental supports and forms of participation are required for educational success.

14. Schools should act in a deliberate, intensive, and explicit fashion to generate socialization opportunities and access to resources for students whose parents are unable to provide these supports.

15. Educators and policy makers at all levels of the educational system should have access to timely, useful, and credible information about learners' and organizations' trajectories of progress. They should use this evidence to guide effective practice and facilitate learning for their students, for other actors in the educational system, and for themselves.

16. Educators themselves should have meaningful opportunities to learn, empowering them to create learning communities and principles of practice to generate knowledge for teaching, and facilitating opportunities to learn for all students.

17. Schools, other social organizations, and communities should cultivate relationships to enhance the variety and quality of opportunities for learning outside school and to support the transitions between in-school and less formal learning opportunities.

18. Because assessment practices shape people's understanding about what is important to learn, what learning is and how it occurs, and who learners are, educators, policy makers, parents, and the public must more explicitly consider the relationships among assessment, learning, and opportunity to learn in making individual and public policy choices about schools and schooling.

19. Assessment practices must be fully and purposefully integrated as formative activities within well-designed learning activity systems to test conceptual understanding, inform which steps to take next to enhance the progression of learning, and allow students to apply their knowledge in meaningful ways.

20. Assessments should provide information to understand the relationship among resources and learning and the interactive processes (among learners, tools, curricula, and other people) through which learning evolved, or failed to evolve, over time.

21. Assessments should illuminate both the depth of a learner's conceptual understanding and the individual's progress in a meaningful trajectory of learning.

22. All assessment practices, including large-scale documentary assessments, need to be interpreted in light of other relevant evidence about a student or group of students.

23. Education professionals, particularly members of the research community, must play a more successful role in studying these issues and in informing the profession, the policy community, and the public about the appropriate relationships between assessment, learning, and opportunity to learn. The field of education has far to go to truly provide meaningful opportunity to learn to all students.

24. Education policy makers should themselves have opportunities to learn about more meaningful and appropriate uses of assessments, how students learn, and the limitations and misuses of current approaches to assessment. These new forms of assessment should be the policy tools of the future to create the educational structures required to facilitate system-wide change of the sort imagined here.

CONCLUSION: OTL AND THE IDEA OF TESTING

Students, parents, educators, and communities share the obligation of ensuring fair OTL for each learner and every participant in the system. Assessments, equity, and OTL are, and should be, inextricably interrelated. Our present approaches to all three fall far short of reaching the promise of meaningful and pervasive educational improvement contemplated by the authors of this book.

The current education reform movement has brought an unprecedented level of very desirable public attention to issues of schooling in our society. Some civil rights advocates have embraced these approaches as the best solution to the years of educational deprivation suffered by low-income and minority children. At the same time, privatization advocates have asserted that these reform initiatives present the best approach to dismantling what they deem a moribund public educational system.

The current trend for education reform driven by results, primarily relying on large-scale, standardized tests, has driven some shift in the provision of OTL, or at least OTL as measured by test scores. Many low-performing schools have improved test scores (Mehan, this volume). Yet an achievement gap between white and certain minority students and between affluent and less affluent students persists. Increasingly, questions arise about whether what students are learning is what they should be learning – meaningful and deep conceptual understanding and the capacity to apply that learning in important contexts.

None of these policy disputes nor any of these educational initiatives fully takes into account the full range of perspectives presented here. The authors of this volume suggest that we know more and can do more to enhance assessment approaches to improve educational attainment than our current social policies and educational practices often reflect. In the face of a growing body of evidence that the current unacceptable relationship between class and performance in the United States can be mitigated, we need to learn more about how to promote equity while providing meaningful educational outcomes.

In the not-too-distant future, the nation will face an important and challenging moment. Inevitably, the current massive effort to use standardized testing to drive education reform will fail to meet all of the expectations attached to it and will face calls for change. Education reform is, after all, "steady work" (Elmore and McLaughlin 1988). The next wave of reform may be occasioned by concerns about what students are learning, about the ongoing achievement gap, or about the struggle over allocation of resources to support education. It will surely focus attention on the capacity of education professionals and schools to provide education. At that moment, policy makers and professionals will be called upon to reassess our social policy goals and to implement, or privilege, particular educational and assessment approaches. The odds are high, of course, that the policy choices will be based on political expedience and the need for bureaucractic efficiency. The odds are equally high that these policy choices will not fully take into account, or perhaps even consider, the current state of scientific knowledge concerning teaching, learning, and assessment.

The authors of this volume would argue for a thoughtful reconsideration of the policy and educational alternatives. The "idea of testing," however it is conceived, is a powerful one. In the view of our authors, the traditional "idea of testing" has been insufficiently informed by the variety of scientific perspectives that expand and enhance our understanding of learning and knowing, our definition of effective teaching, and our conceptualizations of meaningful assessment. The chapters in this volume call for changes in schooling as well as changes in assessment. They present a different perspective on the role of schools in our society as well as views on teaching and learning and the organization and operation of schools that differ markedly from many, if not most, of the education-reform initiatives currently being implemented in our nation. An alternative view of what should be valorized as learning outcomes is also suggested here. According to this perspective, learning embodies the acquisition of important basic skills and knowledge but also fosters the construction of deep understanding of meaningful knowledge within a learning community and develops transferable, and transformative, reflective and critical thinking skills in a truly democratic context. Finally, the conceptualization of education and learning offered here by necessity calls for a different approach to assessment than current education reform initiatives embrace. The nation's current heavy reliance on a rise in test scores gives us neither the outcomes we need or the education our children deserve.

Note

1. This chapter synthesizes the work of all the participants of the Spencer Foundation's Idea of Testing Project. The author takes responsibility for any shortcomings in this presentation of the work of the group, but has made an effort to reflect the accomplishments of the group's collaboration and its recommendations for principles for improvement. The author expresses her gratitude to Pamela Moss and Fritz Mosher for their comments on earlier drafts and to Andrew Ho for his assistance during the project in summarizing the conversations of Project members.

References

Cochran-Smith, M. and S. Lytle. 1993. *Inside/outside: Teacher research and knowledge.* New York: Teachers College Press.

Elmore, R. and M. McLaughlin. 1988. *Steady work: Policy, practice, and the reform of American education.* Santa Monica: The Rand Corporation.

Heubert, J. P. and R. M. Hauser, eds. 1999. *High stakes: Testing for tracking, promotion, and graduation.* Washington, D.C.: National Academy Press.

Labaree, D. 1997. *How to succeed in school without really trying: The credentials race in American education.* New Haven: Yale University Press.

Moss, P. A., D. Pullin, J. P. Gee, and E. H. Haertel. 2005. The idea of testing: Psychometric and sociocultural perspectives. *Measurement: Interdisciplinary Research and Perspectives* 3: 63–83.

Ogbu, J. with A. Davis. 2003. *Black American students in an affluent suburb: A study of academic disengagement.* Mahwah, N.J.: Lawrence Erlbaum.

Shepard, L. A. 2000. The role of assessment in a learning culture. *Educational Researches* 29(7), 4–14.

Spillane, J. 2004. *Standards deviation: How schools misunderstand educational policy.* Cambridge, Mass.: Harvard University Press.

Index